Pro iOS Table Views and Collection Views

Using Swift 2

Tim Duckett

Apress®

Pro iOS Table Views and Collection Views: Using Swift 2

ISBN-13 (pbk): 978-1-4842-1243-1

ISBN-13 (electronic): 978-1-4842-1242-4

Managing Director: Welmoed Spahr
Lead Editor: Michelle Lowman
Development Editor: James Markham
Technical Reviewers: Tiago Duarte and Michael Thomas
Editorial Board: Steve Anglin, Pramila Balan, Louise Corrigan, Jonathan Gennick, Robert Hutchinson, Celestin Suresh John, Michelle Lowman, James Markham, Susan McDermott, Matthew Moodie, Jeffrey Pepper, Douglas Pundick, Ben Renow-Clarke, Gwenan Spearing
Coordinating Editor: Mark Powers
Copy Editor: Mary Behr
Compositor: SPi Global
Indexer: SPi Global
Artist: SPi Global

Distributed to the book trade worldwide by Springer Science+Business Media New York, 233 Spring Street, 6th Floor, New York, NY 10013. Phone 1-800-SPRINGER, fax (201) 348-4505, e-mail orders-ny@springer-sbm.com, or visit www.springeronline.com. Apress Media, LLC is a California LLC and the sole member (owner) is Springer Science + Business Media Finance Inc (SSBM Finance Inc). SSBM Finance Inc is a Delaware corporation.

For information on translations, please e-mail rights@apress.com, or visit www.apress.com.

Apress and friends of ED books may be purchased in bulk for academic, corporate, or promotional use. eBook versions and licenses are also available for most titles. For more information, reference our Special Bulk Sales–eBook Licensing web page at www.apress.com/bulk-sales.

Any source code or other supplementary material referenced by the author in this text is available to readers at www.apress.com/9781484212431. For detailed information about how to locate your book's source code, go to www.apress.com/source-code/. Readers can also access source code at SpringerLink in the Supplementary Material section for each chapter.

For Lucy, Kath, and Isaac

Contents at a Glance

Contents

About the Author

Tim Duckett designs and builds software for mobile platforms with iOS and Android, and for back-end systems with languages like Go and Ruby.

Having started out in the business in the last century, he's worked with all kinds of clients in all kinds of sectors.

Along the way he picked up an MBA and is a certified project manager, but asks that you don't hold those against him.

He lives in Berlin in Germany, with his family and two large dogs.

In his spare time, he walks the dogs, tries to improve his schrecklich Deutsch, takes photographs with obsolete equipment, and continues on what will likely be a lifelong quest to find the perfect single malt.

You can find him online at http://adoptioncurve.net, and on places including Twitter and GitHub as timd.

About the Technical Reviewers

Tiago Duarte studied Software Engineering in the Faculty of Engineering of the University of Porto (Portugal). After working for 5 years at multiple companies, he is now embracing his own projects.

Inspired by Apple, he sees in iOS an opportunity to do what he likes best: to create new experiences.

Despite this passion for iOS and mobile devices in general, he believes that people are becoming slaves of technology and that "virtual reality" is driving us away from what really matters. How much time do we spend on social networks scrolling around? What if we used that time to visit our families and friends, instead of scrolling through their lives on a screen?

Living by the words "Mens sana in corpore sano," Tiago likes to take the body and the mind to their limits. Reading and training have been daily routines since a young age.

Michael Thomas has worked in software development for more than 20 years as an individual contributor, team lead, program manager, and vice president of engineering. Michael has more than 10 years of experience working with mobile devices. His current focus is in the medical sector, using mobile devices to accelerate information transfer between patients and health care providers.

Acknowledgments

It's my name on the cover, but there's a whole host of people without whom this book would never have happened.

At Apress, Mark Powers and Michelle Lowman kept me on track from one end of the project plan to the other, and were very gracious about my procrastination and constant content changes. Mary Behr hunted down all the rogue 'u's that I tried to hide in the word "colour". Tiago and Michael were both kind and constructive as the technical reviewers, and if they laughed at my mistakes, they didn't tell me.

There is a group of fantastic current and former colleagues – Martin, Marco, Eduardo, Eli, Johannes and many more - in various locations around Europe who have been sources of inspiration, support, and fanfarres of squirrels during projects both successful and not-so-successful.

Tom Armitage is responsible for taking the only decent picture of me in existence.

Finally, none of this would have happened without the unconditional love and support of my family, who put up with me writing this book while we embarked on a rollercoaster of moving between four houses in three different countries in the space of two years. I don't tell them this nearly often enough, but - I'm very lucky to have them.

Acknowledgments

Introduction

If you're an iOS app developer, chances are you'll be using table and collection views somewhere in your development projects. They're the bread and butter of iOS apps. With them, you can create everything from the simplest of lists to fully tricked-out user interfaces.

Table and collection views are two of the more complex components found in UIKit. Using them for (potentially boring!) standard user interfaces is quite simple, but customizing them can become much more challenging.

This book has a task-oriented focus to assist you when implementing customized table and collection views. Although it delves deeply into the APIs, you can always choose the level of detail you want to dive into. This book aims to be a reference and customization cookbook at the same time, useful for beginners as well as intermediate developers.

What This Book Covers

Chapter 1, "Table Views Quick Start", introduces the table view with some examples of the current state of the art. After showing you something of what's possible, we'll start out with a very simple table view–based app for the iPhone, which will introduce you to the UITableView and its main elements. The app will also act as a starting point for later versions, and it'll be a working prototype that you can use as the basis for your own experiments.

In **Chapter 2, "How The Table Fits Together"**, you'll look at how the parts of the table view work together. You'll see the main types of UITableViews and their anatomy. You'll learn how to create them both with Interface Builder and in code, and how to use the UITableViewController class as a template.

Chapter 3, "Collection View Quick Start", switches focus to UICollectionView to showcase what's possible with this powerful and infinitely flexible control. Like Chapter 1, we'll start with a simple example that can act as a starting point for more advanced topics, and provide a working prototype as the basis for your experiments.

Chapter 4, "How the Collection View Fits Together", looks at how the parts of the collection view work together. You'll see how they are similar – but even more flexible – than UITableViews, and the component parts of their anatomy. You'll learn how to create them both with Interface Builder and in code, and how to use the UICollectionViewController class as a template.

Chapter 5, "Feeding Data To Your Views" is about where tables and collection views get their data and how you get it there. It shows how they keep track of sections and rows, and covers some of the software design patterns that the UITableView and UICollectionView classes exploit.

Chapter 6 "How The Table Cell Fits Together", focuses on the cells that make up tables. You'll see how cells are structured internally, and how they're created and reused. It also covers the standard cells types that come for free with the UITableView classes.

In **Chapter 7, "Improving the Look of Cells"**, you will start to look at the process of going beyond standard cell types to customize the look and feel of your table views. This chapter covers some of the quickest ways to make the cells look the way you need them to.

Chapter 8, "Creating Custom Cells With Subclasses", covers the most powerful and flexible way of customizing every aspect of cells to use in table and collection views. With great power comes great responsibility – but it's worth persevering so that your able to achieve complete mastery of the look, feel and behaviour of your apps.

Chapter 9, "Improving Interaction", steps you though the process of embedding interactive controls in table and collection views; implementing pull-to-refresh; exploiting gesture recognizers, and implementing in-view search.

Chapter 10, "Using Tables for Navigation", covers an almost-ubiquitous feature of the iOS user interface, and shows how tables can be used to navigate through a hierarchy of data in a simple and consistent way.

The constrained size of the iOS user interface presents some challenges when it comes to presenting large amounts of data. **Chapter 11, "Indexing, Grouping, and Sorting"**, presents some ways of arranging the data in tables, to help users find their way.

Chapter 12, "Selecting and Editing Content", shows how you can use tables and collection views to manage data. It covers how to add, delete, and rearrange the information, and some of the interface aspects that this entails.

Chapter 13, "Static Tables", is an introduction to an often-overlooked use of table views to present controls and information in a static way. These can often be used as a short-cut to simplifying otherwise complex layouts.

Chapter 14, "Tables in WatchKit", looks at the challenges of table-based interfaces with Apple's first venture into wearable technologies. The small form factor and low power of the Apple Watch presents some challenges, but effective use of tables can be the key to engaging user interactions.

Chapter 15, "Collection View Flow Layouts", looks at one of the most useful components of the UICollectionView family, which allows you to very rapidly build sophisticated line-oriented layouts with a minimum of complex calculations.

When a line-based layout isn't sufficient to deliver the interface you need, collection views can be completely customized. **Chapter 16, "Collection View Custom Layouts"** looks at taking complete control over every aspect of the collection view's look and feel.

Chapter 17, "Animated And Interactive Collection Views", takes them to the limits of what's possible in interactive interfaces. Combining collection views with gesture recognizers and custom layouts allows you to create interfaces that are limited only by your imagination.

The Style of This Book

I've tried to bridge the gap between two styles of book—the in-depth treatment of every last little detail, and the cookbook of specific point solutions. Both have their place, but sometimes I find that descriptions of very detailed, elegant solutions with lots of features can obscure the detail of the problem I'm trying to solve. Equally, sometimes cookbook solutions are too specific and don't easily lend themselves to adapting to my specific situation.

In the code examples that follow, I've tried to balance the two styles. The visual polish and extraneous functions are kept to a minimum, which hopefully results in examples that illustrate how to build a solution while also acting as a building block for your own code.

About the Second Edition

Nothing in the technology world stays still for long, and Apple frameworks are no exception. The first edition published in 2012 predated the iPad, collection views, a complete overhaul of the iOS design language, and one of the most exciting developments in software development for a long time.

With the introduction of Swift in 2014, Apple have taken all the very best parts of a myriad of programming languages and paradigms available, and combined them with their legendary frameworks and APIs to produce something that completely lives up to the superlatives used to describe it. The open-sourcing of Swift at the end of 2015 will make for some very interesting developments in the months and years to come.

I've spent many happy years working with Objective-C, but with Swift things have taken a giant leap forward. This book uses Swift exclusively, as I suspect I and many other iOS developers will be doing for the foreseeable future.

This book was written using Swift 2.0, WatchKit 2.0 and Xcode 7.1. It's as up-to-date and current as it's possible to be when covering a dynamic and rapidly-changing world – when things change, updates and errata will be available from the Apress site and the book's source code on GitHub.

The Book's Source Code

You can download the source code for each chapter's examples from the Apress site (www.apress.com/9781484212431) or from GitHub at https://github.com/timd/ ProiOSTableCollectionViews.

Although that's the quickest way to get up and running, I encourage you to take the extra time to key in the code yourself as you go along. With Xcode's code completion, it doesn't take that long, and code that has flowed through your eyes and brain, and then out to your fingers, is much more likely to sink in and make sense.

Where to Find Out More

Beyond the pages of this book, there's a wealth of other information available online (not to mention the great range of other Apress titles):

- For a general overview, Apple's "**Table View Programming Guide**" and "**Collection View Programming Guide**" are detailed guides that cover most of the topics in this book. They are both available from the Apple Developer Portal, or in Xcode's documentation.

- Apple's **iOS Developer Library** has full documentation for all Cocoa Touch libraries, as well as the Swift language. It tends not to include examples in the documentation itself, but the Library is the one-stop shop for a detailed reference for each class, protocol, library and language.

- **Online forums** are a fantastic resource. Sites such as Stack Overflow (www.stackoverflow.com) are the place to go for practical advice. Chances are, a number of people will have met and overcome the same problem that you're experiencing, and the answer will be there. Stack Overflow's customs and practices can be a little daunting at first, but it's worth persevering. There are no stupid questions, after all, just questions that haven't been answered yet.

- A general **Google search** will often throw up answers from blogs. There are some extremely talented individuals out there who regularly post about how to do this or that with iOS and Objective-C, and many of them also point to source code on their sites or GitHub and the like.

- Apple also provides some fairly detailed **source code examples**. Your mileage may vary with these. I sometimes find that they can be a bit overcomplicated and can obscure the core technique that I'm trying to grasp. But they shouldn't be overlooked, if only because they've been written by engineers with an intimate understanding of the frameworks.

- **Universities such as Stanford and MIT** place entire semesters' worth of lecture modules online, both on their sites and on iTunes U. Their technical education is some of the best on the planet, and some of the online lectures are taught by current and former Apple engineers. These are definitely worth checking out.

- **Local user groups** meet regularly around the world. It's an iron law of software that there's always someone who knows more than you do about a topic, and problems are always less daunting when discussed with them over a beverage or two.

- **Mailing lists** have had a renaissance in the last couple of years. Some excellent examples (which often cover not just coding topics, but design and business issues as well) are http://iosdevweekly.com, http://natashatherobot.com and http://ios-goodies.com

Finally, if you've battled with—and resolved—some gnarly issue, then *post about it yourself*, whether that's on your own blog or a site like Stack Overflow. Even if the topic has been covered numerous times before, there's always room for another take on a problem. Your unique point of view could be just what someone else needs.

Contacting the Author

Tim Duckett can be found online at http://adoptioncurve.net and on places like Twitter and GitHub as @timd.

Chapter 1

Table Views Quick Start

In this chapter, you'll start your exploration of table views. This chapter begins with an overview of what table views are and some examples of how they're used in practice. Then, in the second section, you'll build a simple "Hello, world"-style table view app to introduce you to the components behind the user interface and help you contextualize the detail that will come in later chapters.

If you're just starting to use table views, it's worth taking some time to build a very simple one from scratch before diving into the gnarly details. However, if you've reached the stage where you feel more confident about how the components of the table view jigsaw fit together and want to get straight into the code, feel free to skip the rest of this chapter completely. I'll cover the elements in detail later, so you won't miss out.

What Are Table Views?

Examples of table views can be found everywhere in iOS apps. You are already familiar with simple tables, implemented as standard controls such as the iPhone's Settings app or the iPad's Mail app, shown in Figure 1-1.

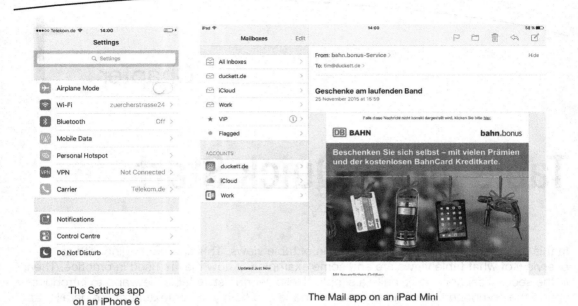

The Settings app
on an iPhone 6

The Mail app on an iPad Mini

Figure 1-1. Some basic table-based applications

At the other end of the scale, the default look, feel, and behavior of the table view and cells can be customized to the point where they are hardly recognizable as table views at all. Figure 1-2 shows some examples.

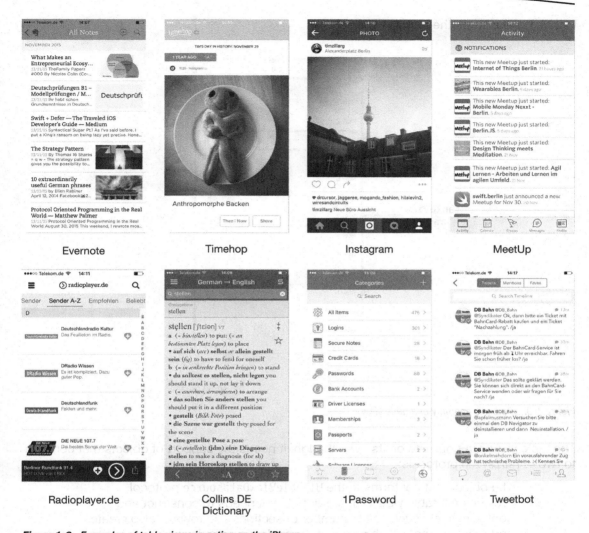

Figure 1-2. *Examples of table views in action on the iPhone*

The Anatomy of a Table View

The table view displays a list of elements, also known as table view cells, that can be scrolled vertically. The table view is composed of two physical parts:

■ The container part—the tableView itself—is a subclass of UIScrollView and contains a vertically scrollable list of table cells.

■ Table cells, which can be instances of one of four standard UITableViewCell types or custom subclasses of UITableViewCell that can be customized as required.

Figure 1-3 illustrates the parts of a table view.

Figure 1-3. The basic anatomy of a table view

The table view can't operate on its own, though; it needs the support of objects that conform to two UITableView protocols:

- The object that conforms to the UITableViewDatasource protocol provides the table view with the data that it needs to construct and configure itself, such as the number of sections and rows. It also creates and provides the cell objects that the table view displays.

- The object that conforms to the UITableViewDelegate protocol is responsible for handling user interaction with the table, such as selection, editing, and ordering.

A very common pattern is for the UIViewController instance that manages the view in which the table lives to also act as the data source and delegate. As you'll see later in Chapter 5, this doesn't always have to be the case; it can help to make the architecture of your app cleaner if those functions are delivered by other classes.

Creating a Simple Table View App

In the rest of this chapter, you'll build a simple "Hello, world" style table view app from scratch. It will show you how the container, cells, data source, and delegate all fit together and give you an app that you can use as the basis for your own experiments.

I'm going to take it deliberately slowly and cover all the steps. If you're a confident Xcode driver, you won't need this hand-holding—just concentrate on the code instead.

Still with me? Okay—you're going to do the following:

- Create a simple, window-based application skeleton.
- Generate some data to feed the table.
- Create a simple table view.
- Wire up the table view's data source and delegate.
- Implement some very simple interactivity.

It's a very straightforward but useful practice. Onward!

Creating the Application Skeleton

For this application, you're going to use a simple structure: a single view managed by a view controller, and a Storyboard file to provide the content for the view. Fire up Xcode and select the Single View Application template, as shown in Figure 1-4.

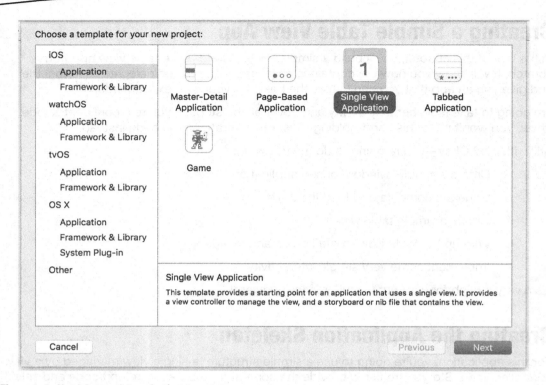

Figure 1-4. Xcode's template selection pane

Note   With each new release of Xcode, Apple frequently (and pointlessly) changes the templates that are included. You may see a set that is different from those shown in Figure 1-5. Check the description of the templates to find the one that provides a single view application.

Call the application **SimpleTable**. You're going to build an iPhone version, but you don't need Core Data or any tests.

Make sure those options are selected as needed, as shown in Figure 1-5.

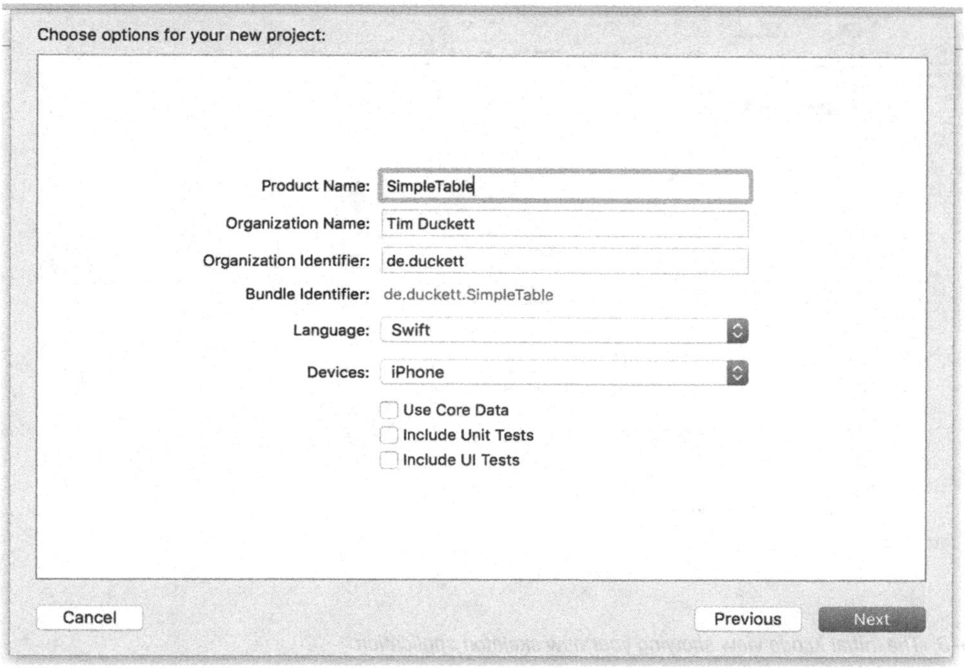

Choose options for your new project:

Product Name:	SimpleTable
Organization Name:	Tim Duckett
Organization Identifier:	de.duckett
Bundle Identifier:	de.duckett.SimpleTable
Language:	Swift
Devices:	iPhone

☐ Use Core Data
☐ Include Unit Tests
☐ Include UI Tests

Cancel   Previous   Next

Figure 1-5. Name the application

Finally, you need to select where you want to save the project. You don't need to worry about creating a local Git repository for this project unless you particularly want to.

When you've reached this point, you'll see the project view of Xcode, with the initial skeleton of your application. It'll look something like Figure 1-6, assuming that you've stuck with the SimpleTable application name.

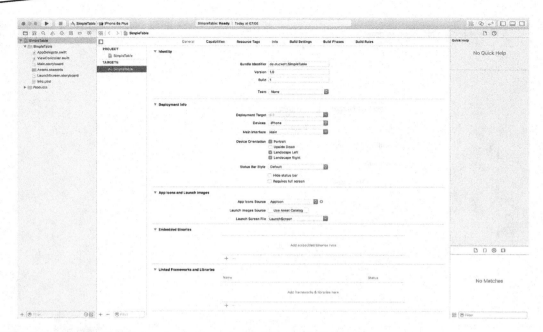

Figure 1-6. The initial Xcode view showing your new skeleton application

You'll see that you have the following:

- An app delegate (`AppDelegate.swift`)
- A view controller (`ViewController.swift`)
- A Storyboard file (`Main.storyboard`)

At the end of this chapter, you'll look again at how these fit together. For the moment, you'll be working with the view controller and the Storyboard file.

At this point, you can run the app to verify that it compiles correctly. Go to **Product ➤ Run** or press Command+R and you'll see the app's launch screen and an empty white view. Now you're ready to start building the table view.

Generating Some Data

Before you start with the table view itself, you need to create some data to feed it. Because this is a simple table example, the data is going to be simple too. You'll create an array of strings that contains some information to go into each cell.

The data array will need to be ready by the time the data source is called by the table view, so where to create it? There are several options, but one obvious place is in the view controller's `viewDidLoad` function. It's safe to create it here.

You're also going to need a way of passing the array of data around the application. This process requires a property that can be accessed by the various functions that will need access to the data.

Let's get started. Open the `ViewController.swift` file shown in Figure 1-7 and begin by creating the property.

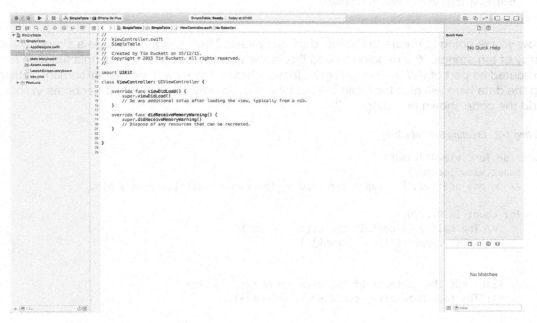

Figure 1-7. Editing the `ViewController.swift` file

> **Note** To save space from now on, I'm not going to show the full Xcode interface—just the code that you need to enter.

Add in a declaration for the property so that the code looks like Listings 1-1.

Listing 1-1. Declaring the Property

```
import UIKit

class ViewController: UIViewController {

    var tableData = [String]()

    override func viewDidLoad() {
        super.viewDidLoad()
        // Do any additional setup after loading the view, typically from a nib.
    }

    override func didReceiveMemoryWarning() {
        super.didReceiveMemoryWarning()
        // Dispose of any resources that can be recreated.
    }

}
```

> **Note**   To save space, in future listings I'll only show the added or amended code with enough
> additional lines to establish the context.

Now you're going to create the actual data array itself. Your data array will be a simple array of ten strings. You're going to add this in the `viewDidLoad` function, as this function is executed as part of `UIViewController`'s lifecycle before the view is visible on-screen. Setting up the data here will give the table the data it needs to draw itself before it becomes visible. Add the code shown in Listings 1-2.

Listing 1-2. Creating the Data Array

```
override func viewDidLoad() {
    super.viewDidLoad()
    // Do any additional setup after loading the view, typically from a nib.

    for count in 0...10 {
        // The cell will contain the string "Item X"
        tableData.append("Item \(count)")
    }

    // Print out the contents of the data array into the log
    print("The tableData array contains \(tableData)")

}
```

Let's run the application to see that data array being created. The user interface isn't doing much yet, but you'll be able to see the data that you're going to feed to the table.

Run the application in the Simulator by pressing Command+R or by choosing **Product ➤ Run**, and then take a look at the logger output

```
The tableData array contains ["Item 0", "Item 1", "Item 2", "Item 3", "Item 4", "Item 5",
"Item 6", "Item 7", "Item 8", "Item 9", "Item 10"]
```

Creating the Table View

As it stands, the user interface for your application is a bit dull. You haven't added the table yet! This needs fixing.

Click the `Main.storyboard` file in the project explorer, and you'll see the Storyboard open in the Interface Builder pane, as shown in Figure 1-8.

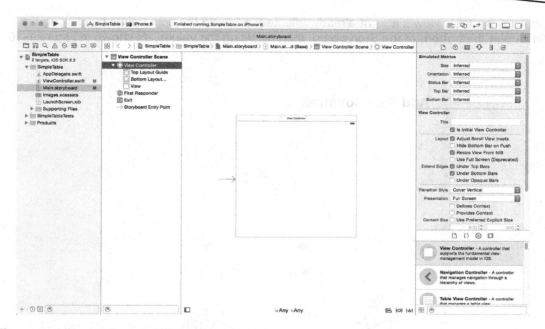

Figure 1-8. Editing the Storyboard file in Interface Builder

In the Objects browser at the bottom right, find the `TableView` item and drag it out onto the view in the center; this will act as the container for the table view. The scene's Document Outline will now look like Figure 1-9.

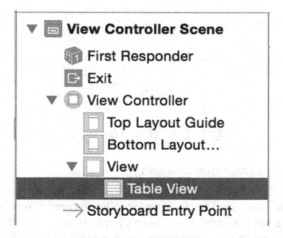

Figure 1-9. The scene's Document Outline after adding the `UITableView`

To make the table display properly in any view size (and if the device is rotated) you need to add some AutoLayout constraints.

Highlight the table view if it's not already selected, and add the constraints by clicking the Pin icon at the bottom of the Storyboard, then updating the values, as shown in Figure 1-10.

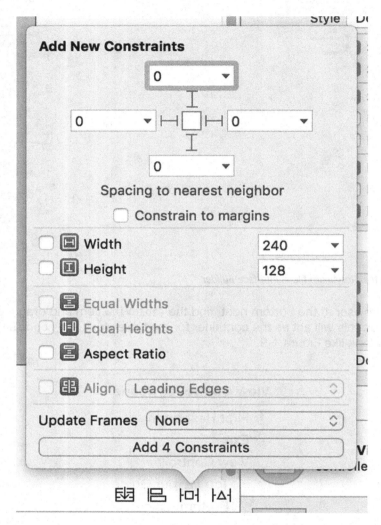

Figure 1-10. Adding the table view's AutoLayout constraints

Believe it or not, that's all you need to do in order to implement the most basic table view. It won't display any data yet because you haven't implemented the `UITableViewDataSource` protocol functions, and it certainly won't have any interactivity—but the app will run.

To prove this, run it again (Command +R), and marvel at your awesome application in the Simulator, as shown in Figure 1-11.

Figure 1-11. A functional, albeit not very impressive, table view application

What's more, you can even rotate the Simulator and the table view will resize itself (shown in Figure 1-12).

Figure 1-12. *The table view rotated*

Okay—maybe this isn't *all* that impressive. Let's complete the wiring up of the table view so that it actually *does* something.

Conforming to the Table View Protocols

The table view that you've just created needs both a data source and a delegate; the data source will provide the table with the information it needs to configure itself plus the cells to display, while the delegate will handle interactions like cell selection.

You need to conform your ViewController class to both the UITableViewDataSource and UITableViewDelegate protocols.

> **Note**   Data sources and delegates are covered in detail in Chapters 3, 4, and 5.

In the class, update the class declaration so it looks like Listing 1-3.

Listing 1-3. Conforming the Swift Class to the UITableDelegate and UITableDataSource Protocols

```
class ViewController: UIViewController, UITableViewDataSource, UITableViewDelegate {
```

This will tell the compiler to expect the required functions to have been implemented. Immediately you'll see Xcode display a warning that the ViewController doesn't yet conform to the protocol (shown in Figure 1-14).

Figure 1-13. The Xcode error

You'll fix this in moment, but first, let's wire up the table to the ViewController class.

Wiring Up the Data Source and Delegate

Your ViewController object will be ready shortly, but the table view itself doesn't yet know that the view controller will act as both a data source and a delegate. You need to connect the two together.

There are two ways of doing this: visually (though Interface Builder) or in code. For this example application, you'll use Interface Builder, so click the Storyboard file to open it again.

Right-click the table view object (either in the main Interface Builder or in the objects tree in the middle pane), and you'll see the Table View property HUD, as shown in Figure 1-14.

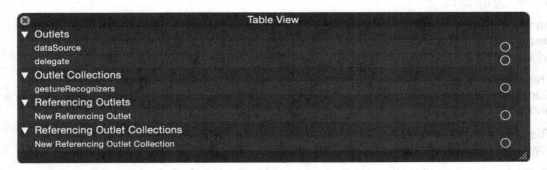

Figure 1-14. The Table View property HUD

It's showing the two Outlet properties that you're interested in: the dataSource and the delegate.

To connect these, mouse-over the circle to the right of the dataSource entry. The circle changes to a plus symbol. Click and drag from this symbol and a blue line extends out.

Mouse-over to the File's Owner item in the object tree, and it becomes highlighted in blue. Release the mouse, and the dataSource is now connected.

Next, repeat the same process for the delegate: drag from the plus symbol to File's Owner, drop, and connect.

The Table View properties HUD will now show that both the dataSource and the delegate are connected to the View Controller, as shown in Figure 1-15.

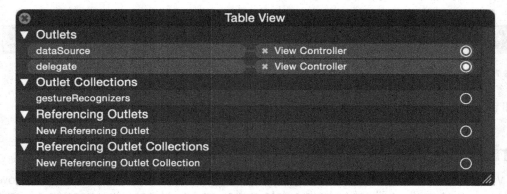

Figure 1-15. The dataSource and delegate are now connected to the View Controller

Displaying the Data

Now that you have the table view wired up to its delegate and dataSource, you're in a position to start making it do something. A logical next step would be to get the table view to display its data.

As the table view draws itself, it asks its dataSource to provide cells that can then be displayed. You'll look at this process in a lot more detail in Chapters 3 and 5, but for now let's get those cells created.

The UITableViewDataSource protocol has two required functions and nine optional ones. Because this is a simple example, you're going to implement only the two required functions and one optional one.

The first required function, tableView(_:numberOfRowsInSection:) returns the number of rows that the section will eventually contain.

The second required function, tableView(_:cellForRowAtIndexPath:), creates and returns the cell itself.

The optional function is numberOfSectionsInTableView(_:). It's optional in your app because you're using a table with a single section, and by default the number of sections in a table is 1.

Later, when you look at more complex sectional tables, this function definitely *will* be required, so I'm including it here even though it's not strictly necessary.

numberOfSectionsInTableView(:)

You have a simple table with one section, so this function is going to be pretty trivial. Switch to ViewController.swift or ViewController.m, where you can create the function, shown in Listing 1-4.

Listing 1-4. The numberOfSectionsInTableView(:) Function

```
//MARK: UITableViewDatasource functions

func numberOfSectionsInTableView(tableView: UITableView) -> Int {
    return 1
}
```

> **Note** The MARK lines are compiler directives. They're not used during compilation, but they demarcate sections of the code during the writing process. If you pull down the breadcrumb menu or press Crtl+6 at the top of the Edit pane, you'll see that these lines break up the list of functions and make the code easier to navigate. Using these directives is not a big deal now, but as your classes grow, they can be a real lifesaver when trying to find a particular function among others.

tableView:numberOfRowsInSection(:)

In order to draw itself successfully, the table view needs to know how many rows are going to appear in the section (your simple table view has only one section).

Earlier, you created an array to hold your data and populated it with this string. The section will have as many rows as there are elements in the array.

The Array class has a useful function for returning the number of elements in an array:

```
tableData.count
```

In the view controller class, add the function as shown in Listing 1-5.

Listing 1-5. The tableView:numberOfRowsInSection: Function

```
func tableView(tableView: UITableView, numberOfRowsInSection section: Int) -> Int {

    return tableData.count

}
```

Pretty straightforward, yes?

Creating Cells

Now that you've connected the table view to the ViewController it's time to start creating cells.

Whenever the table needs a cell, it asks its data source to provide one by calling the cellForRowAtIndexPath: function. The data source will either create a brand new instance of a cell, configure it, and hand it back to the table view, or it will dequeue a previously-created instance from its cache, before configuring and handing this back.

You'll look at the caching and dequeueing mechanisms in more detail in Chapter 5, but for now just bear in mind that the data source uses its cache to vastly improve the performance of the table view.

To begin, add the function in Listing 1-6 to the view controller class, and then I'll step through what it does.

Listing 1-6. The tableView:cellForRowAtIndexPath: *Function*

```
func tableView(tableView: UITableView, cellForRowAtIndexPath ↵
indexPath: NSIndexPath) -> UITableViewCell {

    let cell = tableView.dequeueReusableCellWithIdentifier("CellIdentifier", ↵
    forIndexPath: indexPath)

    cell.textLabel!    .text = tableData[indexPath.row]

    return cell

}
```

Let's start by looking at the function itself:

```
func tableView(tableView: UITableView, cellForRowAtIndexPath ↵
indexPath: NSIndexPath) -> UITableViewCell {
```

This returns an instance of UITableViewCell and takes the following two parameters:

- The tableView that is calling for the cell (because this class might be the data source for numerous tables, it needs to identify which table it's dealing with)

- An indexPath, which has a row property identifying the table row for which the cell is being requested

The first line of the functions attempts to grab a previously-instantiated cell from the tableView's cache with the dequeueReusableCellWithIdentifier: function:

```
let cell = tableView.dequeueReusableCellWithIdentifier("CellIdentifier", forIndexPath: ↵
indexPath)
```

Behind the scenes, the data source will have either dequeued an existing cell instance or it will create a fresh one for you. You don't have to worry about this because the function is guaranteed to return a cell instance that you can work with, so you're ready to configure its contents.

> **Tip** The use of cell identifiers is something you'll explore in much more detail in Chapter 5. For now, you can get by thinking of this as a label that identifies which kind of cell you're using. This table has only one kind of cell, hence the single identifier.

Creating a Prototype Cell

A prototype cell is a "blueprint" that is used by the UITableViewDataSource to create an actual cell when called for. The data source uses the cellIdentifier string that you provided in the cellForRowAtIndexPath function to determine which prototype is the basis of which type of cell.

Switch to the Storyboard, and select the UITableView by clicking on the Table View item in the Document Outline. You'll see that the table view in the canvas shows Prototype Content, and the Attributes Inspector shows Dynamic Protoypes in the Content dropdown.

Create a prototype cell by increasing the number in the Prototype Cells box to 1, as shown in Figure 1-16.

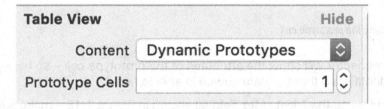

Figure 1-16. Increasing the number of prototype cells

Now you can select the newly-created prototype cell, by selecting in the Document Outline shown in Figure 1-17:

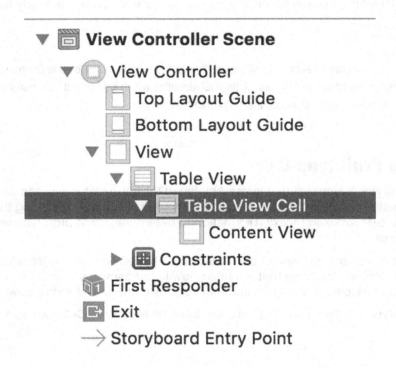

Figure 1-17. *Selecting the prototype cell*

The Attributes Inspector will show the attributes of the prototype cell – so here you can add the cell's cell identifier so that the data source is able to find it.

Add CellIdentifier to the Identifier field as shown in Figure 1-18 – make sure that you match the cell identifier exactly with the string that you used in the ViewController. Then save the Storyboard, and switch back to the ViewController.

Table View Cell

Style	Custom
Identifier	CellIdentifier

Figure 1-18. *Setting the cell identifier*

Configuring the Cell

Once the data source has created or dequeued a cell instance, you can configure its contents before handing it back to the table view.

You'll look at cells in much more detail in Chapter 6, but for now all you need to know is that a UITableViewCell contains a UILabel outlet called textLabel that you can set the text property of, like

```
cell.textLabel!.text = tableData[indexPath.row]
```

The cellForRowAtIndexPath() function is passed an NSIndexPath parameter by the tableView ; this indicates the section and row of the table that the cell is intended for.

You're not interested in the section, because your table only has one, but you can use the row property of the indexPath parameter to retrieve the corresponding String (or NSString) from the tableData array.

Finally, your configured cell is returned to the tableView with

```
return cell
```

Running the App

At this stage, you have some data and a table view, and you have wired up the functions that feed the table view with the data. Run the application, and you'll see your table resplendent with content, as in Figure 1-19.

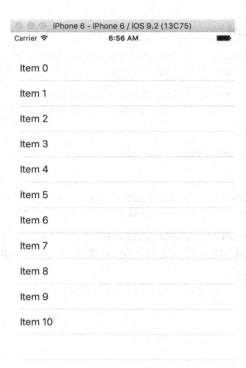

Figure 1-19. The table replete with content

On that triumphant note, it's time to make the table respond to some user input.

Adding Some Interactivity

You can legitimately feel quite pleased with yourself at this point. You have a table view that takes in data, displays it on the screen, and can scroll around (try scrolling the table if you haven't already). You can also select cells by tapping them, and the table view will highlight the selected row.

All of this functionality comes for free with an instance of UITableView, which saves you an awful lot of time getting a table view up and running. But eventually, you're going to want it to do much more. This is where the UITableViewDelegate comes in.

Whenever the table receives some kind of interaction (tapping on a row to select it, for example) it will ask its delegate to handle that for it. Think of the table view as "outsourcing" the details of how to respond to the delegate.

UITableViewDelegate provides a host of functions that allow the table and the cells (among other things) to react to user input. These functions support selecting, editing, reordering, and deleting cells, in addition to configuring how the table view looks. For the moment, you'll take a look at just one of those functions, which enables a row to react to being tapped by the user.

tableView:didSelectRowAtIndexPath:

Your table view already responds in a somewhat limited way to user input. When you tap a cell, it's highlighted in a light grey color. Behind the scenes, the table view makes a call to the delegate indicating two things: that a row has been selected, and which row that was.

If the delegate implements the tableView:didSelectRowAtIndexPath: function, it can use that to fire off some other activity. For example, in the iPhone's Contacts app, a view showing the contact's details will be displayed. In iTunes, the song shown in the row will start playing. And so on.

You're not going to do anything quite so ambitious here. When a row is tapped, you'll log the event into the debugger, and you'll then pop up a modal dialog box showing which row has been tapped.

To begin, enter the function in Listing 1-7 into the ViewController.

Listing 1-7. The tableView:didSelectRowAtIndexPath: Function

```
// MARK:
// MARK: UITableViewDelegate functions

func tableView(tableView: UITableView, didSelectRowAtIndexPath indexPath: NSIndexPath) {

    let messageString = "You tapped row \(indexPath.row)"

    let alertController = UIAlertController(title: "Row tapped", ↵
    message: messageString, preferredStyle: .Alert)

    let okAction = UIAlertAction(title: "OK", style: .Default, ↵
    handler: nil)

    alertController.addAction(okAction)

    self.presentViewController(alertController, animated: true) {
        print("\(messageString)")
    }

}
```

Let's unpack this function. The `tableView(_:didSelectRowAtIndexPath:)` function doesn't return anything and takes the following two parameters:

- The `UITableView` instance that called the function (as with the data source, the delegate could respond to more than one table view and therefore needs to be able to distinguish between them)

- The `indexPath` whose `row` property corresponds to the row that was tapped

First, you create a string that will be displayed in the log and the alert controller:

```
let messageString = "You tapped row \(indexPath.row)"
```

Next, you create the `UIAlertController`:

```
let alertController = UIAlertController(title: "Row tapped", ↵
message: messageString, preferredStyle: UIAlertControllerStyle.Alert)
```

The alert controller needs a `UIAlertAction` button:

```
let okAction = UIAlertAction(title: "OK", style: UIAlertActionStyle.Default, ↵
handler: nil)
alertController.addAction(okAction)
```

Finally, you present the `UIAlertController` and send a message to the debugger as the completion action of the presentation:

```
self.presentViewController(alertController, animated: true) {
    print("\(messageString)")
}
```

> **Tip** Most developers spend as much time looking at the output of the debugger as they do actually writing code. To make the debugger console visible if it isn't already, do one of the following: choose **View ➤ Debug Area ➤ Show Debug Area** from the menu, type Command+Shift+Y, or click the middle of the three View icons at the top left of the Xcode toolbar.

Run the code by pressing Command +R (if the Simulator is still running, select the option to quit). Then tap a row at random. If all goes well, you'll see something like Figure 1-20.

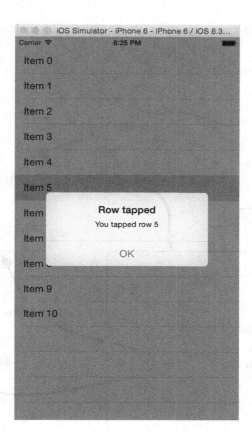

Figure 1-20. *Tapping a row*

Congratulations—that's a fully functional, responsive table you've just built there!

Understanding How the App's Objects Fit Together

Before you leave the SimpleTable app for more adventurous exercises, it's worth looking at how the various objects fit together. The app has three main objects:

- The app delegate
- The view controller
- The view, which has the table view embedded within it

Figure 1-21 shows how the three objects relate, together with their outlets.

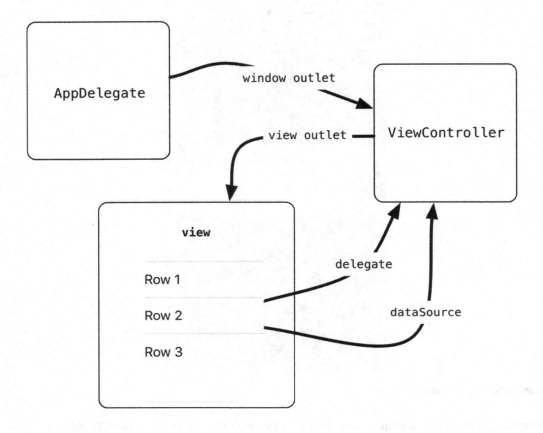

Figure 1-21. The object diagram

The AppDelegate's window has a rootViewController property, which is connected to the ViewController object. This in turn has a view outlet, which is connected to the view object in the Storyboard file. Embedded in the Storyboard is the UITableView instance, which has delegate and dataSource properties. These are linked back to the ViewController.

Obviously, this is a pretty simple application, but as applications get more complex, it's worth spending time to sketch out an object diagram. If a picture's worth a thousand words, as the saying goes, an object diagram is worth at least a thousand lines of comments!

Summary

In this chapter, you created a very basic table view stage by stage:

- To start, you created some data to display in the table.

- Then, using Interface Builder, you created an instance of UITableView in the window.

- The view controller conformed to the UITableViewDataSource and UITableViewDelegate protocols so that it could provide the data for the table and the response to interaction.

- You implemented the code required to create cells for the table.

- Finally, you made the table react to user input.

From here, it's time to look in much more detail at how tables and cells are constructed, together with how they can be customized and made to respond to user interaction.

Chapter 2

How the Table View Fits Together

In this chapter, you're going to take a whistle-stop tour of table views and the elements from which they're built. Although this chapter does not present a lot of code, it will provide a useful foundation for later when you start to customize table views.

Along the way, you'll look at the following:

- The types and styles of table views
- The anatomy and dimensions of table views
- `UITableView`'s relationship to the `UIScrollView` superclass
- Creation of table views in code and with Interface Builder
- Use of the `UITableViewController` class to take advantage of its template methods

Understanding Table Views

At its simplest, a *table view* is a list of items that can (often) be scrolled vertically. Because this is a common interface design pattern, UIKit provides a powerful suite of classes and protocols to make the creation and management of table views as simple and as effective as possible.

Table views can range from a very plain list created by using one of the standard styles provided by the SDK to something so customized that it's barely recognizable as a table at all. Figure 2-1 shows some examples of table views.

Figure 2-1. *Examples of table views—the built-in Settings app, the 1Password password manager and the Collins German Dictionary app*

The Settings app uses grouped static rows, while the 1Password app is a plain table view with a search bar. The Collins German Dictionary app uses cell customization to create custom typography effects. Despite the differences in visual appearance, all three of these apps are based around UITableViews and have identical interaction patterns.

Working with the UITableView Family

At the heart of the table view are the classes, protocols, and view objects that make up the members of the UITableView family:

- The UITableView and UITableViewController classes
- The UITableViewDelegate and UITableViewDataSource protocols
- The UITableView and UITableViewCell view objects

All six work together. The classes provide the core functionality for the table view, the protocols define various data and interaction methods, and the view objects provide the physical user interface.

The UITableView Class Hierarchy

The UITableView class is a subclass of UIScrollView, which in turn inherits from UIView, UIResponder, and ultimately NSObject, as shown in Figure 2-2.

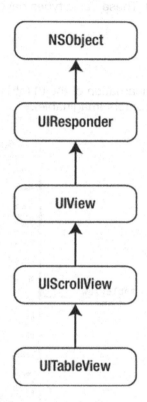

Figure 2-2. *The UITableView inheritance chain*

This means that UITableView benefits from much of the functionality provided by its parent classes. For example, UIScrollView provides the scrolling of the table, while UIResponder allows the table cells to respond to user touches and swipes.

Note   In an attempt to reduce confusion, I'll use UITableView when I'm referring to the *class*, tableView when I'm referring to a *specific instance* of a UITableView, and "table view" when I'm talking about *table views in general*.

Choosing the Type of Table View

Although their visual appearance can be customized to the point where it's almost difficult to recognize them as instances of the UITableView class at all, table views come in one of two basic forms: plain and grouped. These basic types have two variations: indexed and sectioned.

The Plain Table

The *plain table* is the basic vanilla incarnation of the UITableView. Figure 2-3 shows an example (with possibly the dullest content imaginable).

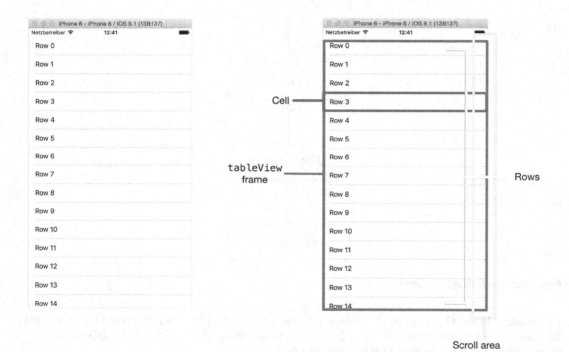

Figure 2-3. A plain table view and its components

The plain table is the version that is created by default when dragging into a view in Interface Builder, although the type can be specified when creating a table view in code:

```
var tableView: UITableView = UITableView(frame: tvFrame, ↵
style:.Plain)
```

If the number of rows in the tableView doesn't fit in the frame, the table can be scrolled to reveal more rows. Scroll indicators appear in the right-hand scroll area when the table is in motion.

The Indexed Table

The *indexed table* builds on the plain table by adding an extra navigation aid in the form of an index that appears on the right-hand side of the table view, adjacent to the scroll area. Figure 2-4 shows an example.

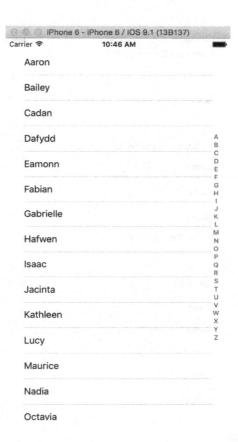

Figure 2-4. An indexed table

Implementing indexes involves UITableViewDataSource protocol methods, and is covered in detail in Chapter 11.

The Sectioned Table

The *sectioned table*, as its name suggests, groups its rows into sections. These sections can have headers. Figure 2-5 shows an example of relatively simple text headers, which could be replaced with complex `UIView` objects if needed.

Figure 2-5. A simple sectioned table

This type of table view utilizes several `UITableViewDataSource` protocol methods to configure the behavior of the sections, and is covered in Chapter 11.

The Grouped Table

The *grouped table* takes things one step further by separating the sections into a style that is distinct from the table view's background. Figure 2-6 shows the difference between sections and groups.

Figure 2-6. *Comparing sections and groups*

Each section has a header and footer. These are `UIViews`, and are returned by two `UITableViewDelegate` methods:

```
func tableView(tableView: UITableView, viewForFooterInSection ↵
section: Int) -> UIView?
```

```
func tableView(_ tableView: UITableView, viewForHeaderInSection ↵
section: Int) -> UIView?
```

Although you can manipulate the view that comprises the entire header and footer, often it's enough just to be able to set the titles. `UITableViewDataSource` has two methods to support this:

```
func tableView(tableView: UITableView, titleForHeaderInSection ↵
section: Int) -> String?
```

```
func tableView(tableView: UITableView, titleForFooterInSection ↵
section: Int) -> String?
```

If for any reason you need to find the dimensions of the headers and footers, the UITableView can return these as CGRect values with the following methods:

```
func rectForHeaderInSection(_ section: Int) -> CGRect
func rectForFooterInSection(_ section: Int) -> CGRect
```

The dimensions of the entire section (header, footer, and content) are available by calling the following:

```
func rectForSection(_ section: Int) -> CGRect
```

Setting TableView Dimensions

One way to visualize a `tableView` is to think of it as a window that provides a view of a conveyor belt of cells. The number of cells that are visible through the window depends on the size of the window—indicated by the `tableView`'s `frame` property—and the height of each cell. The `frame` property is a CGRect with height and width values.

The overall length of the conveyor belt—or more properly, the height of the `tableView` in points—is available through the `contentSize` property, which returns a CGSize. From there you can access the `width` and `height` values.

At the top and bottom of each "belt" of cells, you can add a UIView as a static header and footer. These are set through the `tableHeaderView` and `tableFooterView` properties, respectively. Figure 2-7 illustrates a `tableView`'s dimensions.

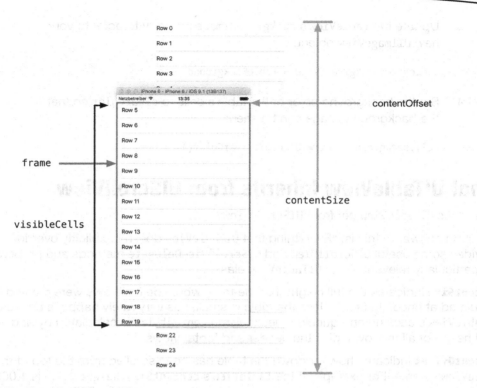

Figure 2-7. The dimensions of a tableView

The cells that are visible at any given moment can be accessed en masse through the tableView's visibleCells property. This is an Array and is updated as the table scrolls up and down.

Controlling the Background of a UITableView

Setting an image as the background of a UITableView is possible, albeit slightly-convoluted. There are four steps.

1. Create an instance of a UIImageView and set its image property to the image that you want to appear behind the table.

    ```
    let tableBackgroundImage = UIImageView(image: UIImage(named:"myImage"))
    ```

2. Set the UIImageView's frame property so that it's the same size as that of the tableView:

    ```
    tableBackgroundImage.frame = tableView.frame
    ```

3. Update the `tableView`'s `backgroundImage` property to point to your new `UIImageView` object:

    ```
    tableView.backgroundView = tableBackgroundImage
    ```

4. Set the background color of the table's cells to `clearColor` so that the background image can be seen:

    ```
    cell.backgroundColor = UIColor.clearColor()
    ```

What UITableView Inherits from UIScrollView

What does `UITableView` get from `UIScrollView`?

The short answer to this is, "Everything that `UITableView` doesn't explicitly override." This provides some useful `UIScrollView` and `UIScrollViewDelegate` methods and properties that are particularly relevant to the `UITableView` class.

contentSize indicates the full height that the table would be if all rows were created and populated at once. (In fact, unless the table is small, this very rarely happens because of `UITableView`'s caching and queuing mechanism.) `contentSize` is calculated by adding the total height of all the rows, plus the header and footer views.

contentOffset indicates how far down the table has been scrolled from the top of the `tableView`'s frame. For example, if the `tableView`'s `contentSize.height` value is 1,000 points, and the table is scrolled halfway down, the `contentOffset` would be 500 points.

Two `UIScrollViewDelegate` methods are particularly useful if you want to know when your user is scrolling the table around.

scrollViewWillBeginDragging `tableView` starts moving, and **scrollViewDidScroll** is called multiple times while the table scrolls.

This is where you could get the new `contentOffset` value and update anything that needed to change as a result.

> **Note**   Although `UITableView` is a subclass of `UIScrollView`, table views can only scroll vertically.

Creating UITableViews

Any discussion of how to go about creating `UITableViews` has to come with a caveat: on their own, `UITableViews` don't really do very much. In order to become populated with data and interact with your user, they need the support of a class that implements the `UITableViewDelegate` and `UITableViewDatasource` protocols.

Having said that, in order to get a `UITableView` onto the screen, you need to be able to draw it. You have two options here: create it visually using Interface Builder in a XIB file or Storyboard or create it programmatically in code.

Creating a UITableView in Interface Builder

Creating a `UITableView` in Interface Builder is a massively challenging process.

1. Open your Storyboard.

2. Drag a `UITableView` from the Objects browser onto your view, as shown in Figure 2-8.

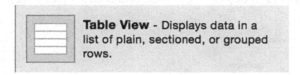

Table View - Displays data in a list of plain, sectioned, or grouped rows.

Figure 2-8. The UITableView item in the Objects browser

Okay, I lied. It's actually pretty straightforward. But there are a couple of details to take care of, so the process is worth stepping through.

Placing a UITableView into Another View

Although you'll often see table views full-screen, you're not restricted to that option. You can make your table views any size you want. This is pretty simple: drag the `UITableView` object onto the view in which it's going to appear, and adjust the AutoLayout constraints as needed (see Figure 2-9).

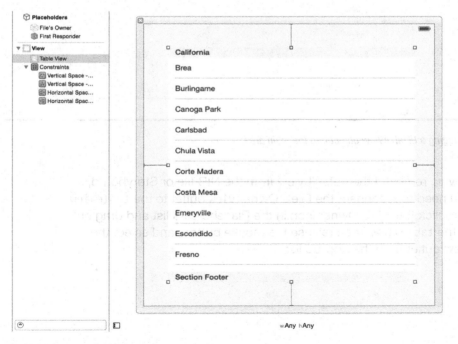

Figure 2-9. Placing a UITableView into another view

Placing a Full-Screen UITableView

If, on the other hand, your tableView will always be shown full screen, there's not really much point in creating it as a child of another view that will never be shown.

The process in this scenario is slightly different.

1. Delete the existing view object from the NIB file or Storyboard.

2. Drag a UITableView object into the central area (Figure 2-10).

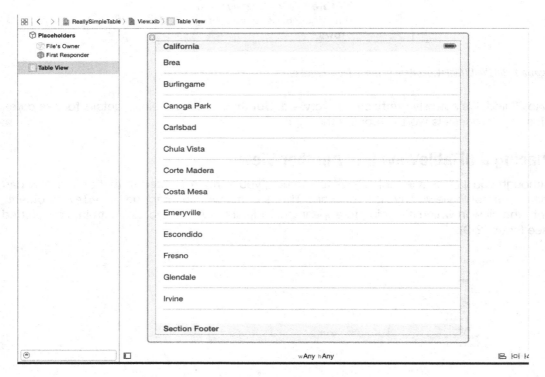

Figure 2-10. Dragging a UITableView object into the main area

3. Having removed the default view from the NIB file or Storyboard, you need to reconnect the File's Owner view outlet to the tableView. Ctrl-click the File's Owner icon in the Placeholders list and drag out to the tableView. Then release the mouse button, and select the View outlet from the pop-up list.

> **Caution**   It's easy to forget to reconnect the view outlet if you've deleted the object it was once connected to. If you don't reconnect, your app will crash with an error something along the lines of
>
> `*** Terminating app due to uncaught exception 'NSInternalInconsistency Exception', reason: '-[UIViewController _loadViewFromNibNamed:bundle:] loaded the "PlainTable" nib but the view outlet was not set.'`

4. After the view outlet is reconnected, hook your new `tableView` up to its `dataSource` and `delegate`.

The chances are that the class that will act as `dataSource` and `delegate` will also be the File's Owner. If that's the case, you can connect these by Ctrl-clicking and dragging from the table to the File's Owner icon and selecting `dataSource` and `delegate` from the pop-up options.

Creating a UITableView Programmatically

In Chapter 1, we built a simple app with a table view using Interface Builder.

Following the maxim of *anything you can do in Interface Builder, you can also do in code*, the alternative way of creating a `UITableView` is to do so in code. It's a four-step process.

1. Create an instance of `UITableView` with a size and a style.

2. Set the new `tableView`'s delegate and dataSource properties.

3. Add the new `tableView` to the `superView`.

4. Call the new `tableView`'s `reloadData` method to make sure it updates.

Listing 2-1 shows an example of how you could do this in a `UIViewController`'s `viewDidLoad` method.

Listing 2-1. Adding a tableView Programmatically

```
override func viewDidLoad() {

    super.viewDidLoad()
    // Do any additional setup after loading the view, typically from a nib.

    tableView = UITableView(frame: self.view.frame, style:.Plain)
    tableView.delegate = self
    tableView.dataSource = self

    self.view.addSubview(tableView)
    tableView.reloadData()

}
```

> **Caution**   Having set the `delegate` and `dataSource` properties of your `tableView`, it will expect (nay, demand!) that the controller adopts the `UITableViewDelegate` and `UITableViewDataSource` protocols—in particular, that the `numberOfSectionsInTableView:`, `tableView:numberOfRowsInSection:` and `tableView:cellForRowAtIndexPath:` methods are implemented.
>
> If those protocols haven't been implemented correctly, the app will crash when the `tableView` is loaded, complaining that the `dataSource` hasn't returned a cell.

Creating a UITableView with UITableViewController

In order for a `tableView` to operate successfully, it needs a number of `UITableViewDelegate` and `UITableViewDataSource` methods to be implemented.

Although Xcode's autocompletion helps with the typing, creating all the methods by hand will probably induce repetitive strain injury. Save your wrists, speed things up, and create a subclass of `UITableViewController` instead!

The process is delightfully simple. Instead of creating an instance of a vanilla `UIViewController`, drop down the subclass list and select `UITableViewController` instead, as shown in Figure 2-11.

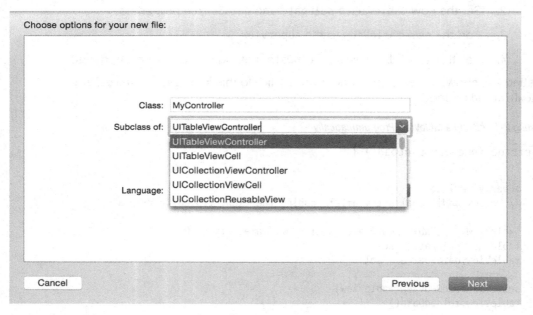

Figure 2-11. Creating an instance of UITableViewController

The new class files will be created as usual, but with some added extras. In addition to the usual `UIViewController` methods, you'll find some stubbed-out `UITableViewDataSource` methods in the file (see Figure 2-12).

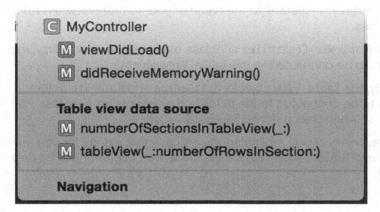

Figure 2-12. The UITableViewDataSource methods

This is the minimal subset of `UITableViewController`, delegate, and dataSource methods that you need to get going, and the class's header file declares it as conforming to the two protocols.

Xcode also provides a slew of other methods that are commented out:

```
override func tableView(tableView: UITableView, canMoveRowAtIndexPath indexPath: ↵
NSIndexPath) -> Bool

override func tableView(tableView: UITableView, moveRowAtIndexPath fromIndexPath: ↵
NSIndexPath, toIndexPath: NSIndexPath)

override func tableView(tableView: UITableView, commitEditingStyle editingStyle: ↵
UITableViewCellEditingStyle, forRowAtIndexPath indexPath: NSIndexPath)

override func tableView(tableView: UITableView, canEditRowAtIndexPath indexPath: ↵
NSIndexPath) -> Bool
```

None of these have to be implemented, but they are there as skeleton methods ready to be uncommented if you need them.

Connecting UITableViewController Outlets

If you selected the *"with XIB for user interface"* option when creating the `UITableViewController` subclass, the XIB file will contain a `UITableView` that comes already connected to its `delegate` and `dataSource`.

If you *didn't* select the option to create the XIB file, you'll need to connect things up manually once you've created the XIB file yourself.

- First, create a new `View` file and then delete the `UIView` object that is added for you, and replace it with a `UITableView` object.

- Next, set the interface's `File's Owner` by selecting the `File's Owner` icon in the `Placeholders` list, then changing the `Custom Class` field in the `Identity Inspector` to the name of your `UITableViewController` subclass.

- The `UITableViewController` subclass exposes a view property; this needs to be connected to the `Table View` object.

- Finally, the `Table View` object's `dataSource` and `delegate` outlets need to be connected to the `UITableViewController` subclass via the `File's Owner` object in the `Placeholders` list.

At this point, you've effectively replicated the process that's done for you automatically when you create a new `UITableViewController` subclass with the *"with XIB for user interface"* option selected.

Summary

This short chapter introduced the anatomy and core components of the `UITableView`.

There are two basic styles of table view:

- Plain
- Grouped

Table views can also be split into sections, and provided with an index.

Although they can look different, the different types of table view have similar component parts and dimensions. They also inherit methods and properties from the `UIScrollView` parent class.

Like many of UIKit's components, it's possible to create `UITableViews` both visually—using Interface Builder—and programmatically. Anything that can be done with Interface Builder can also be done in code.

Implementing the `tableView`'s controller as a subclass of `UITableViewController` allows us to cut down on creating methods manually and use the templates that are provided.

In Chapter 5, you'll learn how your newly created `UITableView` is fed with data, and how it works in conjunction with the `UITableViewDelegate` and `UITableViewDataSource` protocols.

Chapter 3

Collection Views Quick Start

In this chapter, you'll start your exploration of collection views. It begins with an overview of what collection views are and some examples of how they're used in practice. Then in the second section, you'll build a simple "Hello, world"-style collection view app to introduce you to the components behind the user interface and help you to contextualize the detail that's going to come in later chapters.

If you're just starting to use collection views, it's worth taking some time to build a very simple one from scratch before diving into the gnarly details. However, if you've reached the stage where you feel more confident about how the components of the collection view jigsaw fit together and want to get straight into the code, feel free to skip the rest of this chapter completely. I'll cover the elements in detail later, so you won't miss out.

What Are Collection Views?

A collection view provides a way of managing and displaying an ordered set of data items with customizable and interactive layouts.

Collection views consist of data items displayed in cells, together with supplementary views that can display additional information for things like section headers and footers, or additional metadata about the items themselves.

Decoration views are purely visual components that can be used to display interface elements like backgrounds and borders; they don't include any variable data elements.

The collection view builds on the table view control by providing the potential for much more complex layouts. Whereas a table view can display items in a single column, collection views can present items in layouts ranging from linear grids to circles and every conceivable layout in between, as shown in Figure 3-1.

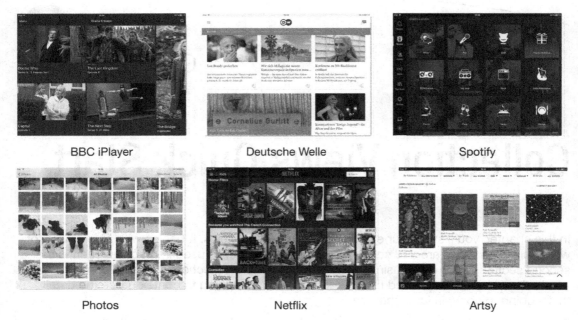

BBC iPlayer   **Deutsche Welle**   **Spotify**

Photos   **Netflix**   **Artsy**

Figure 3-1. *Examples of collection views in action*

The UICollectionView control works with four other objects, shown in Figure 3-2. The collection view itself is managed by a UIViewController. The model contains the data that will be displayed in the collection view; this is supplied to the collection view itself by the UICollectionViewDataSource. Interactions with the collection view are handed by an object acting as the UICollectionViewDelegate.

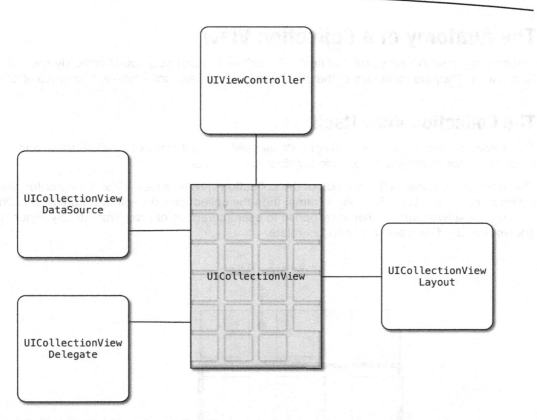

Figure 3-2. The collection view and supporting objects

UICollectionView uses the model-view-controller pattern to organize itself. The data that drives the contents of the items and supplementary views is provided by the model object, while the UICollectionView control itself is the view component. The controller part is normally a UIViewController, but the role of the controller can also be split across different objects that act as delegate and dataSource.

The layout of a collection view is managed by a UICollectionViewLayout object that tells the collection view how each cell, supplementary view, and decoration view should be positioned within the bounds of the collection view itself by configuring the various layout attributes of each item. Changes in layouts can be animated and react to interactions.

As with UITableView, collection views use a dequeuing and recycling approach to creating and managing cells. This allows collection views to manage potentially huge numbers of individual data items while maintaining fast scrolling and animation performance, and all within the stringent memory limitations of an iOS device.

There's a detailed description of how the dequeueing mechanism works with UITableView in Chapter 5; UICollectionView operates in exactly the same way, with the addition of supplementary and decoration views as well as item cells.

The Anatomy of a Collection View

The collection view displays a list of items—or cells—that can be scrolled vertically and horizontally. They are instances of the UICollectionView class and come in two physical parts.

The Collection View Itself

The visible container part, the collectionView itself, is a subclass of UIScrollView, and is responsible for displaying a collection of data items as cells.

These are laid out inside the bounds of the collection view's contentView. If the contentView is larger than the collectionView's frame, then the collection view will take care of scrolling the content view around, either in response to user interaction or programmatically. Figure 3-3 shows how the frame and contentView relate.

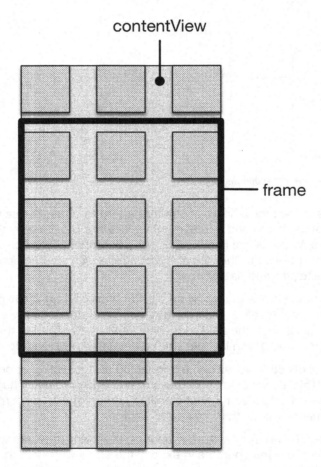

Figure 3-3. The frame and contentView

As the content view scrolls around, the collection view will create and remove items from it as required; this is a balance between ensuring that items are always created and placed in time to be visible as that part of the content view scrolls into the frame, but not creating and maintaining so many items that aren't visible so that the memory consumption of the collection view is excessive.

In exactly the same way as a UITableView, the collection view uses a queue of preexisting items that it can dequeue and recycle as required. Just before an item scrolls into the visible area, the collection view will grab it from the queue and configure it with the correct data. Once the item scrolls out of the visible area, the collection view will dump it back onto the queue ready for eventual reuse.

In this way, a collection view can appear to create and display thousands of items while only needing to create a small fraction of them as actual objects to maintain in memory.

Collection View Cells

Collection view cells are instances of UICollectionReusableView or its subclasses. They have one of three roles:

- **Item cells**, which are created as instances of UICollectionViewCell. These are analogous to the cells of a table view, and are used to display the main data items. In a gallery app, for example, the cells are likely to display thumbnail images of the photos in an album.

- **Supplementary views**, which are instances of UICollectionReusableView. These are entirely optional, and can have a variety of purposes. In grid-type layouts, such as a photo gallery, they're often used to provide metadata about sections by acting as headers and footers. In more complex layouts, they can be used to display additional information about items.

- **Decoration views**, which are also instances of UICollectionReusableView. These are independent of the collection view's model and don't display any data. Typically they're often used to display graphical elements such as backgrounds or section highlights.

Figure 3-4 shows the conceptual parts of a collection view with a grid layout, with the various types of views highlighted.

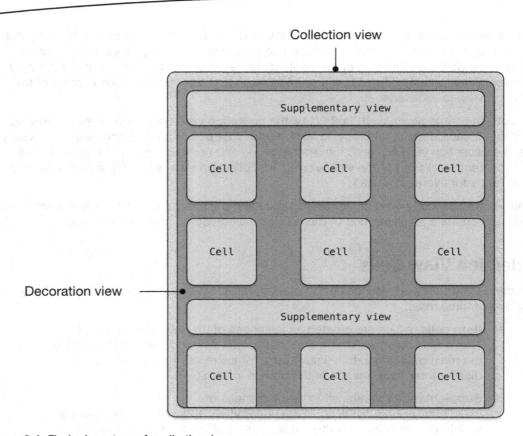

Figure 3-4. *The basic anatomy of a collection view*

Figure 3-5 shows a collection view in action in the iOS iBooks app. It uses cells to show the book covers, supplementary views to contain the download control, and a decoration view to provide the "shelf" effect.

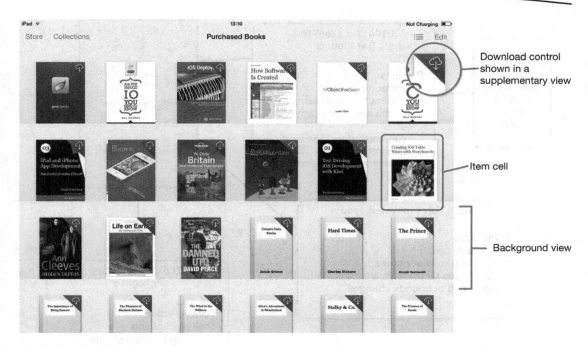

Figure 3-5. The iBooks app

The Supporting Objects

The collection view control itself is pretty dumb; it relies on the support of four other objects in order to display its data:

- **Model**
- **Datasource**
- **Delegate**
- **Layout**

Each object has a specific role to play in supporting the collection view, and their organization is based on the model-view-controller architecture. Figure 3-6 shows how the four objects interrelate.

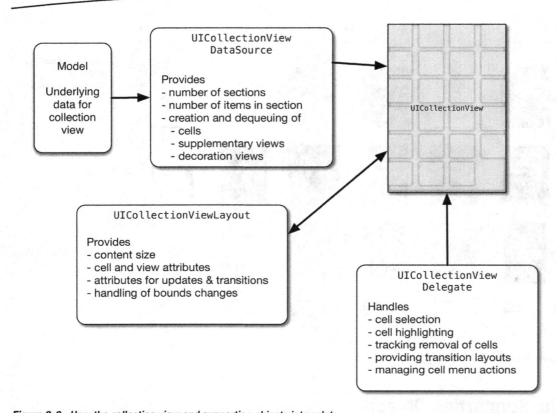

Figure 3-6. How the collection view and supporting objects interrelate

The Collection View's Model

The model contains the data that will be displayed in the collection view through the datasource. As the name suggests, it's part of the model component of the model-view-controller architecture.

Models can take many forms, and will depend on the way that the data in your app needs to be managed. At its simplest, the model may be a one-dimensional array that contains a set of Strings. More complex models may involve two-dimensional arrays to split the data into sections, or could retrieve data from a local Core Data database or an external network source.

Regardless of what form the model takes, it doesn't communicate directly with the collection view. That's the role of the datasource.

The Collection View's Datasource

The responsibility of the datasource object is to supply the collection view with cells, supplementary views, and decoration views when requested so that they can be displayed by the collection view. It forms the other part of the model component of the model-view-controller architecture.

The relationship between the collection view and its datasource is defined by the UICollectionViewDataSource protocol. There are mandatory functions that the collection view's datasource must implement, and some optional ones.

The datasource can be a standalone class that conforms to the UICollectionViewDataSource protocol, or it can be the collection view's view controller. There are no hard and fast rules about which approach is correct, but regardless of how its implemented, it's vitally important that the datasource is able to return data to the collection view as fast as possible in order to maximize performance.

The Collection View's Delegate

Handling user interaction with the collection view is the responsibility of the delegate object, which forms one part of the controller component of the model-view-controller architecture.

The delegate is a class that implements some or all of the functions defined by the UICollectionViewDelegate protocol. It handles selection and highlighting of the collection view's items. There are no mandatory functions in the UICollectionViewDelegate protocol, but the collection view must have a delegate object set.

The Collection View's Layout

Unlike UITableView, a UICollectionView control has no knowledge about how it should lay out items in its content view. It relies on a UICollectionViewLayout object to provide layout attributes for every item.

Each item in the collection view (cell, supplementary view, or decoration view) has a corresponding instance of UICollectionViewLayoutAttributes , shown in Figure 3-7. It manages the layout-related attributes for the item, and is created by the UICollectionViewLayout object when requested by the collection view.

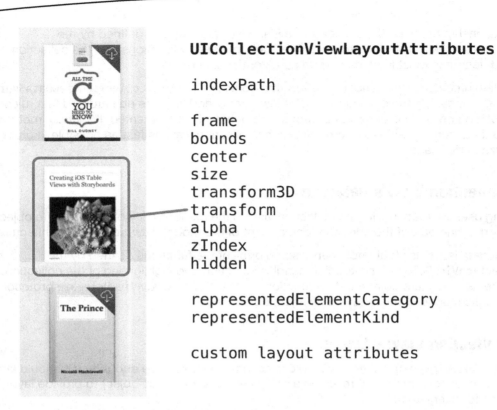

Figure 3-7. UICollectionViewLayoutAttributes

Having requested the attributes for each item, the collection view then uses them to position the item in its content view. The attributes control the size, position, transform, and opacity of each item, but you can also supplement them by subclassing `UICollectionViewLayoutAttributes` and adding your own custom properties.

If your collection view layout is based around a line of items, with or without line breaks, then you can take advantage of the `UICollectionViewFlowLayout` class, which takes care of much of the layout requirements for you. You normally only need to specify item sizes and inter-item and inter-line spacing; then the flow layout will calculate everything else for you.

For more complex layouts, you need to create a custom layout as a subclass of `UICollectionViewLayout`. With this, you're responsible for calculating all the necessary attributes to display the items correctly.

Creating a Simple Collection View App

In the rest of this chapter, you'll build a simple "Hello, world"-style collection view app from scratch. It will show you how the container, datasource, delegate, layout, cells, and views all fit together and give you an app that you can use as the basis for your own experiments. The end result will display a deck of cards in suits, as shown in Figure 3-8.

Figure 3-8. The completed app

I'm going to take it deliberately slowly and cover all the steps. If you're a confident Xcode driver, you won't need this hand-holding—just concentrate on the code instead.

Still with me? Okay, you're going to do the following:

- Create a simple, window-based application skeleton
- Generate some data for feeding the collection view
- Create a simple collection view
- Wire up the collection view's datasource and delegate

- Implement the collection view's layout

- Add some very simple interactivity

It's all very straightforward, but useful practice nevertheless.

Creating the Application Skeleton

For this application, you're going to use a simple structure: a single view managed by a view controller and a Storyboard to provide the content for the view.

To begin with, create a new project in Xcode and select the Single View Application template, as shown in Figure 3-9.

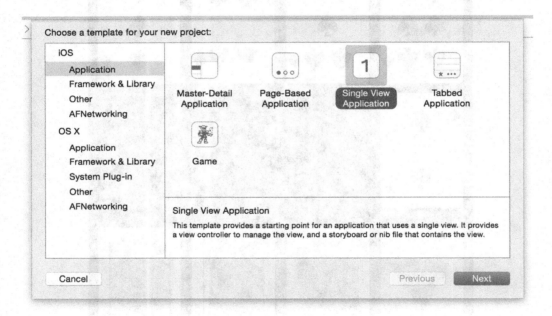

Figure 3-9. Xcode's template selection pane

Call the application **SimpleCV**, as shown in Figure 3-10.

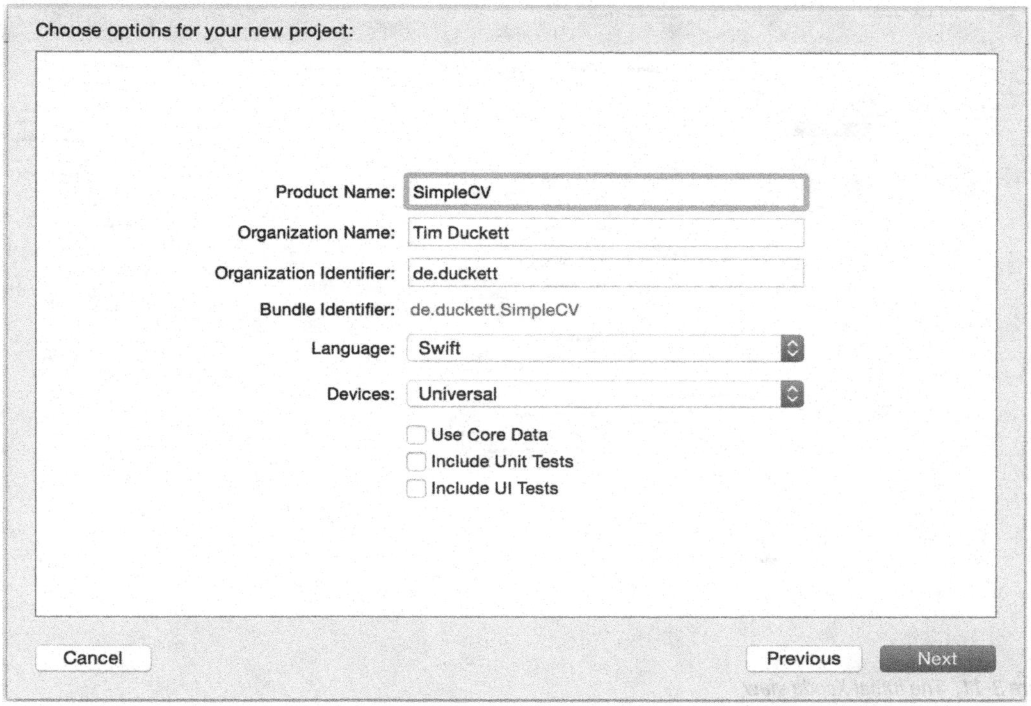

Choose options for your new project:

Product Name: SimpleCV

Organization Name: Tim Duckett

Organization Identifier: de.duckett

Bundle Identifier: de.duckett.SimpleCV

Language: Swift

Devices: Universal

☐ Use Core Data
☐ Include Unit Tests
☐ Include UI Tests

Cancel   Previous   Next

Figure 3-10. Name the application

Save the project somewhere appropriate, and you'll see the project view of Xcode, with the initial skeleton of your application. It'll look something like Figure 3-11, assuming that you've gone with the SimpleCV application name.

Figure 3-11. The initial Xcode view

You'll see that you have the following:

■ An app delegate (`AppDelegate.swift`)

■ A view controller (`ViewController.swift`)

■ A Storyboard (`Main.storyboard`)

■ An asset catalog (`Images.xcassets`)

■ Supporting files and folders for unit tests, frameworks, and products

Creating Some Data

Before you start with the collection view itself, you need to create some data to feed it with. You're going to create the model for the collection view from a directory containing the four card suits.

Adding the Card Images

In the source code for this book, you'll find a `cards` folder than contains five subdirectories. Each subdirectory contains the `png` image for each card. First, drag the cards folder into the project folder, as shown in Figure 3-12.

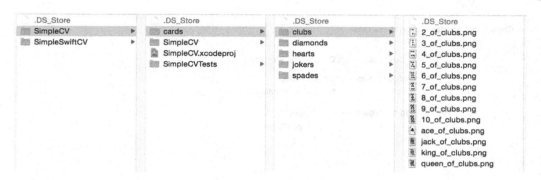

Figure 3-12. The card images

Next, drag the cards folder from the Finder into Xcode, and drop it so that it's inside the SimpleVC folder, as shown in Figure 3-13.

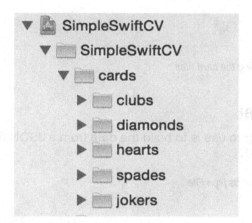

Figure 3-13. Adding the card images to the project

When adding the folder, make sure that you select the options to copy items into the destination folder and to create groups for any added folders, as shown in Figure 3-14.

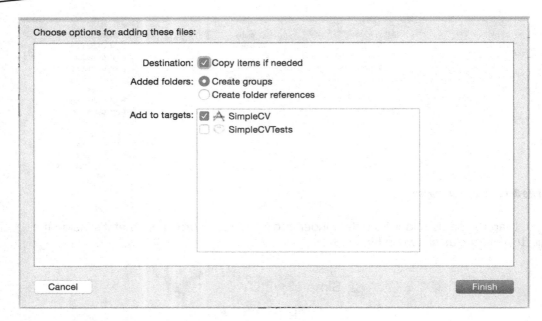

Figure 3-14. The options for adding the card files

Building the Model

The approach you're going to use is to build the data from a JSON file. The structure of the JSON looks like Listing 3-1.

Listing 3-1. An Extract from the cards.json File

```
{
    "suits": [
        {
            "suitName": "Spades",
            "packOrder": 1,
            "cards": [
                {
                    "cardName": "Ace of Spades",
                    "cardImage": "ace_of_spades.png",
                    "suitOrder": 1,
                    "cardValue": 14
                },
                {
                    "cardName": "King of Spades",
                    "cardImage": "king_of_spades.png",
                    "suitOrder": 2,
                    "cardValue": 13
                },
```

```json
        {
            "cardName": "Queen of Spades",
            "cardImage": "queen_of_spades.png",
            "suitOrder": 3,
            "cardValue": 12
        },
        ...
        ]
    },
    {
        "suitName": "Hearts",
        "packOrder": 2,
        "cards": [...]
    },
    {
        "suitName": "Diamonds",
        "packOrder": 3,
        "cards": [...]
    },
    {
        "suitName": "Clubs",
        "packOrder": 4,
        "cards": [...]
    },
    {
        "suitName": "Jokers",
        "packOrder": 5,
        "cards": [
            {
                "cardName": "Black Joker",
                "cardImage": "black_joker.png",
                "suitOrder": 1,
                "cardValue": 1
            },
            {
                "cardName": "Red Joker",
                "cardImage": "red_joker.png",
                "suitOrder": 2,
                "cardValue": 2
            }
        ]
    }
    ]
}
```

To save you having to create the JSON file from scratch, it's available in the downloadable source code.

The model will be stored as an Array of Dictionaries in a property in ViewController. Add this at the top of the class:

```
class ViewController: UIViewController {

        var suitsArray = [Dictionary<String, AnyObject]()
        ...
```

Here, you're declaring that suitsArray will be an array of Dictionaries. Each dictionary will have a String as a key and can store an AnyObject as the corresponding value (this will allow you to store Strings, Ints, and other Arrays, as you'll see in a moment.)

Next, you need a function to load the data from the JSON file. This will read the JSON file from disk and parse it as dictionaries into the suitsArray array.

Although you're only building a simple example application, it's still a good idea to get into good habits around handling errors. Parsing JSON can be hazardous; the source JSON might not exist, and it might prove impossible to parse. In either of those situations, you need to handle the resulting errors.

To do this, first you add an enum to describe the potential error cases. Add this at the top of the class, underneath the suitsArray declaration:

```
enum ParsingError: ErrorType {
    case MissingJson
    case JsonParsingError
}
```

This declares an enum that conforms to the ErrorType protocol. You're creating two possible values for the errors that this enum will describe: MissingJson, to indicate that there was a problem with the source data, and JsonParsingError, to show that something went wrong with the parsing of the JSON into the suitsArray.

Now add a new function at the bottom of the class called setupData(), as shown in Listing 3-2.

Listing 3-2. The setupData() Function

```
// MARK:
// MARK: Data setup

func setupData () throws {

    guard let filePath = NSBundle.mainBundle().pathForResource("cards", ↵
      ofType: "json"), jsonData = NSData(contentsOfFile: filePath) else {
          throw ParsingError.MissingJson
    }

    do {
        let parsedObject = try NSJSONSerialization.JSONObjectWithData(jsonData, ↵
    options: NSJSONReadingOptions.MutableContainers) as! NSDictionary
        suitsArray = parsedObject["suits"] as! Array
```

```
    } catch {
        throw ParsingError.JsonParsingError
    }
}
```

Firstly, the function tries to load the `cards.json` file. It will throw a `MissingJson` error if it can't find it or there's some problem loading it. If everything is OK, then the JSON will be loaded into the `jsonData` object.

Next, the `jsonData` object is parsed into an `NSDictionary`. Since this might fail, it's wrapped in a do-catch block that will throw a `JsonParsingError` if anything fails. You're indicating that things might go wrong by using the `try` keyword in front of the `JSONObjectWithData` function.

You're also force-unwrapping the result of the parsing into an `NSDictionary`. This might also fail, but at least you'll handle the error if either operation goes wrong.

The `suitsArray` property will have the structure shown in Figure 3-15.

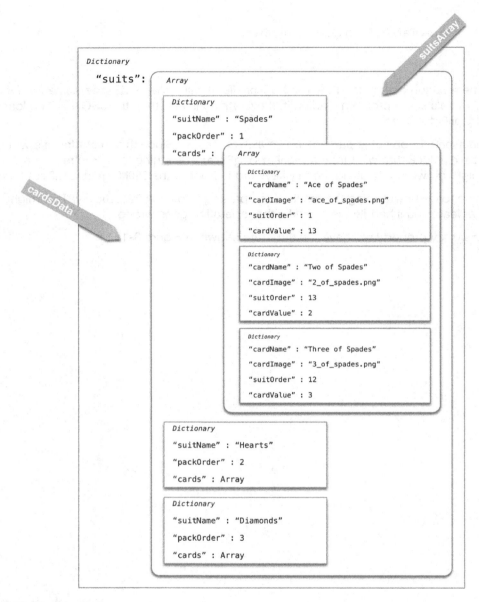

Figure 3-15. *The data structure*

An individual section or item in a UICollectionView is referenced by an NSIndexPath value. Figure 3-16 shows how the indexPath section and row values map onto suits and cards.

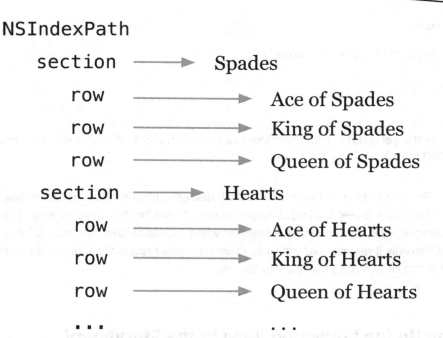

Figure 3-16. Mapping between collection sections and rows

The data model needs to be set up before the collection view starts asking for data, so add a call to the setupData function in the ViewController's viewDidLoad function, as shown in Listing 3-3.

Listing 3-3. The Updated viewDidLoad() Function

```
override func viewDidLoad() {

    super.viewDidLoad()
    // Do any additional setup after loading the view, typically from a nib.

    // Configure data

            do {

        try setupData()

    } catch ParsingError.MissingJson {

        print("Error loading JSON")

    } catch ParsingError.JsonParsingError {

        print("Error parsing JSON")
```

```
    } catch {

        print("Something went wrong")

    }

}
```

This wraps the setupData() function inside a do-catch block. If any errors are thrown, they'll be handled here.

> **Tip**   There's no reason why you couldn't put this data setup code in the viewDidLoad function itself, but I prefer to keep this kind of thing separate in its own function. There are a couple of advantages to this approach. Firstly, it keeps the viewDidLoad function compact and easier to read. Secondly, it will make unit testing your view controllers much easier if you can decouple this sort of data setup process from the view lifecycle.

Setting Up the Collection View in the Storyboard

With the data set up, you can now set about wiring up the interface. This will be very simple, with a single collection view that fills the full screen.

In order to configure the collection view, you need to connect it to the view controller, so create an IBOutlet property in the ViewController implementation file:

```
class ViewController: UIViewController {

    var suitsArray = [Dictionary<String, AnyObject>]()
    @IBOutlet var collectionView: UICollectionView!
    ...
```

Next, switch to the Storyboard and drag a UICollectionView object from the Object Browser into the view, and let it snap to fill the full screen, as shown in Figure 3-17.

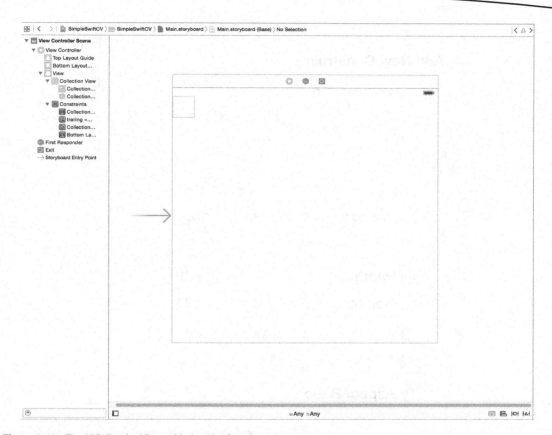

Figure 3-17. The UICollectionView added to the Storyboard

UICollectionViews that are dragged into Storyboards come with a single prototype cell (that's the white outline at the top-left of the collection view). You aren't going to need this. You can leave it there, but Xcode will pop up a warning about requiring reuse identifiers. To keep the project tidy, highlight the Collection View Cell item in the Scene tree, and press the Backspace key to delete it.

With the UICollectionView in place, you now need to connect it to the view controller's outlet (drag down from the File's Owner placeholder to the collection view, and select the collectionView outlet from the HUD).

Next, set the File's Owner placeholder as the delegate and datasource of the collection view (drag from the collection view up to the File's Owner placeholder, and select the datasource and delegate outlets from the HUD).

The final task is to set up the collection view's AutoLayout constraints so that it fills the full width and height of the view regardless of the orientation of the device, but doesn't underlap the status bar.

Highlight the Collection View if it's not already selected, and add Leading, Trailing, Top, and Bottom constraints to it by clicking the Pin button at the bottom of the Storyboard view, as shown in Figure 3-18.

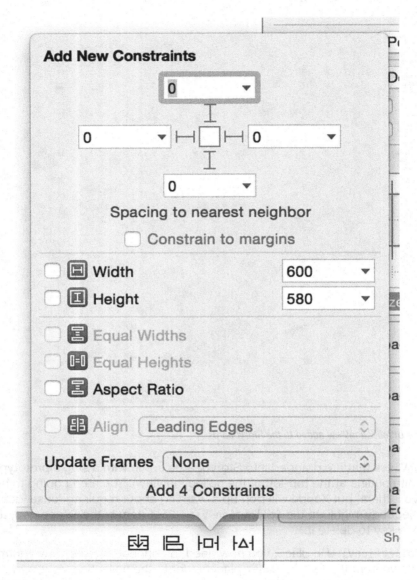

Figure 3-18. Adding new constraints

With those three connections established, you can switch back to the ViewController's implementation file and start configuring the collection view in code.

Setting Up the delegate and dataSource Funtions

As with UITableView, UICollectionView relies on the assistance of a delegate and a dataSource object to provide it with cells, supplementary and decoration views, as well as layout and configuration information at runtime.

This can be any class that conforms to the UICollectionViewDelegate and UICollectionViewDataSource protocols. It's normally regarded as best practice to use a separate class to act as delegate and dataSource, as this means that each class has specific role (in software engineering terms, this is the Single Responsibility Principle).

In the projects in later chapters, you'll take this approach, but to keep this one as simple as possible, you'll use the ViewController.

By connecting the collection view's delegate and dataSource outlets in Interface Builder, you've already told the collection view that the ViewController class will be acting as delegate and dataSource. Now you need to set up the class to do this.

The first step is to conform the class to the three protocols as shown in Listing 3-4.

Listing 3-4. The Updated SCVViewControllerC

```
import UIKit
class ViewController: UIViewController, UICollectionViewDataSource, &#x00C9;
UICollectionViewDelegate, UICollectionViewDelegateFlowLayout {
...
```

The third protocol, UICollectionViewDelegateFlowLayout, extends the UICollectionViewDelegate protocol with some optional functions that assist UICollectionViewFlowLayout with attributes like cell sizes. You'll look at that in a moment, but while you're updating the header file, it's as good a time as any to add this in.

> **Note**   The UICollectionViewDelegateFlowLayout is an additional protocol that defines some flow layout-specific functions for attributes such as cell sizes. You can think of it as "extending" the UICollectionDelegate protocol to define the extra functions, similar to adding additional functions to a Swift class by adding an extension.

The UICollectionViewDataSource protocol is responsible for providing the data and views that the collection needs at runtime. At a minimum, you need to implement two functions:

- collectionView(_:numberOfItemsInSection:)

- collectionView(_:cellForItemAtIndexPath:)

There's also a third, optional function that you can to implement:

- numberOfSectionsInCollectionView(_:)

As the names suggest, the first function returns the number of items in the current section; this will correspond to the number of cards in each suit.

The second is where you create or dequeue a UICollectionViewCell, configure its content, and pass it to the collectionView that can then display it.

The third (optional) function returns the number of suits; in your collection view, each suit will sit inside its own section.

> **Tip**   Unless you tell it otherwise by implementing the
> `numberOfSectionsInCollectionView(_:)` function, the collection view will assume that
> there's only one section.

The numberOfSectionsInCollectionView: Function

The `numberOfSectionsInCollectionView:` function tells the collection view how many sections will be needed to display the data contained in the model. In your example, this is the number of suits in the deck of cards.

Add the code in Listing 3-5 to the bottom of the `ViewController`.

Listing 3-5. The numberOfSectionsInCollectionView: Function in Objective-C

```
func numberOfSectionsInCollectionView(collectionView: UICollectionView) -> Int {
    return suitsArray.count
}
```

> **Tip**   When the collection view calls one of these three datasource functions, it passes in a
> reference to itself as one of the parameters. This means that by checking which one is being
> passed in, you can serve multiple collection views with the same datasource function(s).

The collectionView:numberOfItemsInSection: Function

Now you can implement the function that determines the number of items that will be displayed in each section. With your data model, this will be the number of cards in the suit.

Add the `collectionView:numberOfItemsInSection:` function to the bottom of the `ViewController`, as shown in Listing 3-6.

Listing 3-6. The collectionView:numberOfItemsInSection: Function

```
func collectionView(collectionView: UICollectionView, numberOfItemsInSection ↵
section: Int) -> Int {
    let cardsDictionary = self.suitsArray[section]
    let cardsArray = cardsDictionary["cards"] as! NSArray
    return cardsArray.count
}
```

This function is very straightforward: it gets the dictionary containing the suit from the relevant element of the `suitsArray`, then grabs the array containing the card items and returns their count.

The collectionView:cellForItemForIndexPath: Function

The `collectionView:cellForItemAtIndexPath:` function is where the magic happens.

This is the function that is called repeatedly by the collection view when it needs a new cell to display, and is responsible for either creating or dequeueing a cell, configuring it, and handing that cell over to the collection view on demand.

The question that immediately arises is "where does the cell come from in the first place?" Unlike `UITableView`, `UICollectionView` doesn't have any "standard" cell types. You have to create them yourself from scratch.

You can do this in two ways: by creating a nib file, or creating a custom `UICollectionViewReusableView` or `UICollectionViewCell` subclass. Then when you're configuring the collection view as it's instantiated, you register the nib file or class together with a cell reuse identifier.

This process of registration tells the collection view where the cells are to be sourced from. The reuse identifier acts as a "tag" to tell the different cell types apart. Although your simple example only has a single cell type, you can have many different kinds to display different types of data within the same collection view.

In the spirit of a simple example, you're going to create a very simple Xib file to contain your `UICollectionViewCell` template. Create a new file (File ➤ New ➤ File) and select the View item from the User Interface section, as shown in Figure 3-19.

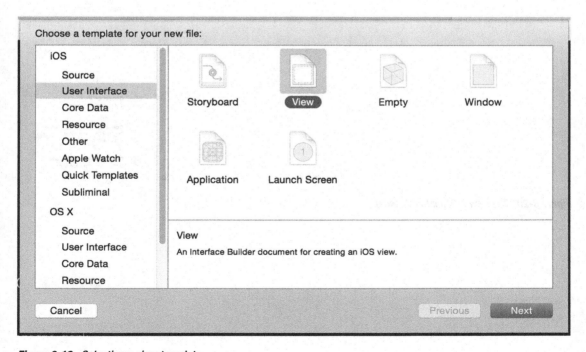

Figure 3-19. Selecting a view template

The device family setting isn't important, so click Next to step through this and then give your new file a name. I'm calling mine `CollectionViewCell`. Click the Create button, and you'll be presented with a new `UIView` in the Interface Builder.

Somewhat counterintuitively, the first thing you need to do with your new file is delete the view that's been provided for you. Select it in the list of Placeholders, and then press the Delete key.

Now find `UICollectionViewCell` in the Object Brower in the Utilities area on the right of the Xcode window, and drag it out into the main area. You should end up with something looking like Figure 3-20.

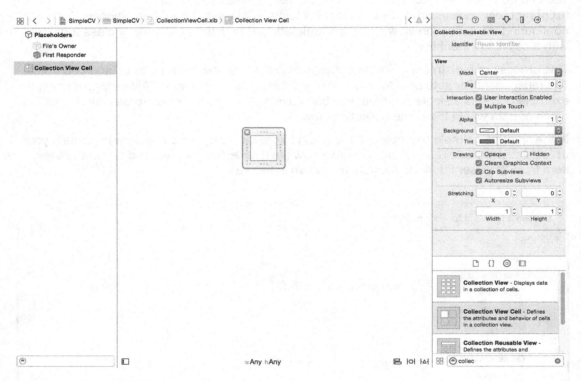

Figure 3-20. The new UICollectionViewCell

Now you need to add a `UIImageView` to the cell to display the card, so drag one from the Object Browser and drop it into the cell, as shown in Figure 3-21.

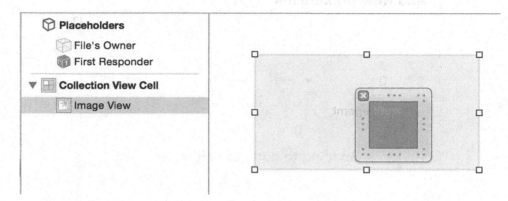

Figure 3-21. The UIImageView inside the cell

Note that the image view is bigger than the cell itself. Use AutoLayout constraints to "glue" the image view to the cell frame, so that when the cell is resized, the image view will grow with it.

Select the image view in the view tree, click the Pin button at the bottom of the Storyboard view, and add four constraints, as shown in Figure 3-22.

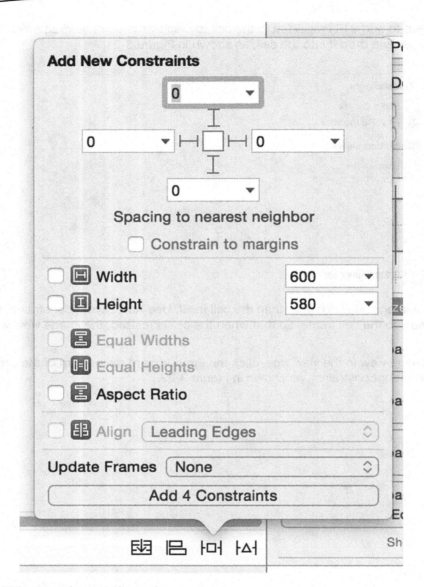

Figure 3-22. Adding constraints to the image view

Finally, select the image view again, open the Attributes Inspector if it isn't visible, and add a tag to the image view, as shown in Figure 3-23.

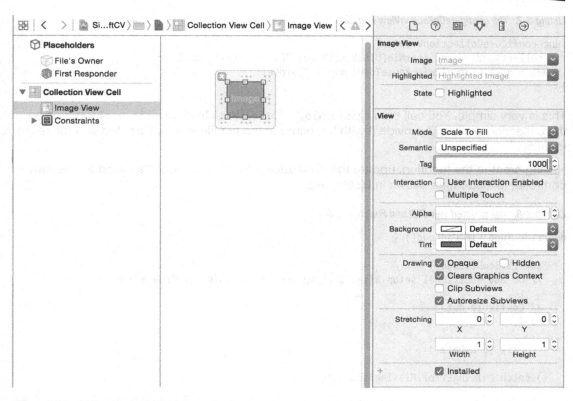

Figure 3-23. Adding the tag to the image view

Caution   Accessing in-cell controls through tags can be a brittle process. It relies on the tag set in the Storyboard matching exactly with the tag used to refer to the control in the code. If you have a cell with more than a single control, it's safer to connect them via outlets in a custom `UICollectionViewCell` subclass.

That's it as far as the user interface is concerned. The rest of the configuration of your `UICollectionViewCell` will take place in code. Switch back to the `ViewController`'s implementation file, and you're ready to continue.

Having created the nib file containing your cell, you need to register it with the collection view. The obvious place to do this is as the view controller loads, so you're going to take the same approach I used to create the data for the collection view, and create a separate function that will be called by the view controller's `viewDidLoad` function.

Create a new function called `configureCollectionView`, as shown in Listing 3-7.

Listing 3-7. The configureCollectionView Function

```swift
func configureCollectionView() {
    collectionView.registerNib(UINib(nibName: "CollectionViewCell",↵
 bundle: nil), forCellWithReuseIdentifier: "CardCell")
}
```

This is very simple. You call the `registerNib(_:forCellWithReuseIdentifier:)` function on the collection view, and provide it with the name of the nib file you just created and the reuse identifier.

Having created the function, update the `viewDidLoad` function so that it's called as the view controller is loaded, as shown in Listing 3-8.

Listing 3-8. The updated viewDidLoad Function in Swift

```swift
override func viewDidLoad() {

    super.viewDidLoad()
    // Do any additional setup after loading the view, typically from a nib.

    // Configure data
    do {

        try setupData()

    } catch ParsingError.MissingJson {

        print("Error loading JSON")

    } catch ParsingError.JsonParsingError {

        print("Error parsing JSON")

    } catch {

        print("Something went wrong")

    }

    // Configure collection view
    configureCollectionView()

}
```

With the cell's nib registered, you're in a position to implement the `collectionView(_:cell ForItemAtIndexPath:)` function, as shown in Listing 3-9.

Listing 3-9. The collectionView:cellForItemAtIndexPath: Function

```
func collectionView(collectionView: UICollectionView, cellForItemAtIndexPath indexPath:
NSIndexPath) -> UICollectionViewCell {

    let cell: UICollectionViewCell = collectionView.dequeueReusableCellWithReuseIdentifier
("CardCell", forIndexPath: indexPath)

    let suitDictionary = suitsArray[indexPath.section]
    let cardsArray = suitDictionary["cards"] as! [Dictionary<String, AnyObject>]
    let cardDictionary = cardsArray[indexPath.row]

    let cardImageName = cardDictionary["cardImage"] as! String
    if let cardImage = UIImage(named: cardImageName) {

        if let imageView = cell.contentView.viewWithTag(1000) as? UIImageView {
            imageView.image = cardImage
        }

    }

    return cell

}
```

Just like UITableViews, UICollectionView maintains a queue of cells that can be recycled when required to remove the need to maintain one cell per item, and to reduce the memory overhead to an absolute minimum.

When the collection view needs a new cell to display, it calls the collectionView(_:cellFor ItemAtIndexPath:) function on its datasource, passing over a reference to itself and the index path for which the cell is required.

The datasource dequeues a cached cell of the appropriate type with the dequeueReusable CellWithReuseIdentifier(_:forIndexPath:) function. If a queued cell is available, it will be returned; otherwise a new one will be created in the background.

Regardless of which happens, the collection view guarantees that it will return an instance of UICollectionViewCell that you can then configure with the relevant data for this item.

It's worth noting that the same datasource can serve several collection views, hence the collection view sending a reference to itself along with the request, so that the datasource can keep track of which collection view it's responding to.

It's also at this point that the rationale for the reuseIdentifier becomes clear. You may have a collection view that displays several types of cells, all of which will have a different identifier. By supplying the identifier when you ask for a cell to be dequeued, you can control the kind of cell that will be returned.

With a UICollectionViewCell returned, you can now configure it. First, you grab the relevant suitDictionary from the suitsArray by getting the object that exists at the index corresponding to the index of the item in the collection view.

The card details are stored as dictionaries in elements of an array. The index of the element you need will correspond to the row value of the indexPath parameter passed into the cellForItemAtIndexPath function.

Having retrieved the `cardDictionary`, you can access the image name through the `String` object identified by the `cardImage` key. The PNG image is loaded into a `UIImage` object.

If there is a valid `UIImage` object, then you attempt to access the `UIImageView` in the cell. This has a tag of `1000`, so can be accessed through the `contentView`'s `viewWithTag()` property.

As this property returns an optional, you need to check that it's unwrapped before setting its image property to the card image that you just created.

Finally, the cell is returned to the collection view that's asking for it.

Go ahead and run the app. You might be surprised at what you see. It's not looking bad, but something isn't quite right yet, as you can see in Figure 3-24.

Figure 3-24. The not-quite-right collection view

Configuring the Layout of the Collection View

The problem you have right now is that the collection view doesn't really know how it should lay out its items. It does its best, but there's room for improvement.

There are two ways of doing this: you could create a UICollectionViewLayout subclass and apply this to the collection view, or you can take the simpler (but ultimately less flexible) approach and configure the collection view directly.

Because this is a simple app, let's take the simple approach. Select the collection view in the Storyboard, then switch to the Size Inspector. Update the Collection View values so they match Figure 3-25.

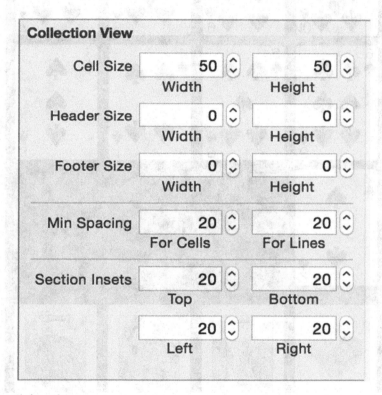

Figure 3-25. Adjusted size values

Now if you run the app again, you'll see that the item, line, and section spacing look much better, as shown in Figure 3-26.

Figure 3-26. *The new spacing values in action*

You may have noticed that you didn't update the values for the cell size. As it turns out, you didn't need to because the collection view is clever enough to fit the cell size to the contents when using a very simple layout like this.

The App in Action

With all these steps complete, you can now run the app! If you try rotating the device or simulator, you'll see that the collection view layout is automatically updated, and the items flow neatly to fill the bounds of the view, as shown in Figure 3-27.

Figure 3-27. The app running in landscape orientation

Summary

In this chapter, you created a very basic collection view stage by stage:

- To start, you created some data to display in the collection view.

- Then, using Interface Builder, you created an instance of `UICollectionView` in the window.

- The view controller conformed to the `UICollectionViewDataSource` and `UICollectionViewDelegate` protocols so that it could provide the data for the collection view and responses to interaction.

- You implemented the code required to create cells for the collection view.

- You tweaked the layout to control how items are laid out within the bounds of the collection view.

This has been an indication of the power of UICollectionView. By setting four attributes, you created a layout that can handle any number of items of any size and any orientation, and do all of this with a tiny memory footprint and smooth scrolling performance thanks to the caching of cells.

The structure of the app that you built here is the basis of all collection view-based apps, so you can use this as a starting point for your own projects. As you delve deeper into UICollectionView, you will reuse many of the same patterns.

Now it's time to look in much more detail at how collection views and cells are constructed, together with how they can be customized and made to respond to user interaction.

Chapter 4

How The Collection View Fits Together

In this chapter, you're going to take a whistle-stop tour of collection views and the elements from which they're built. Although this chapter does not present a lot of code, it will provide a useful foundation for when you start to customize collection views.

Along the way, you'll look at the following:

- The anatomy and dimensions of collection views
- `UICollectionView`'s relationship to the `UIScrollView` superclass
- How to create collection views in code and with Interface Builder
- Use of the `UICollectionViewController` class to take advantage of its template methods

What Are Collection Views?

A collection view provides a way of managing and displaying an ordered set of data items with customizable and interactive layouts.

Collection views consist of data items displayed in cells, together with supplementary views that can display additional information for things like section headers and footers, or for additional metadata about the items themselves.

Decoration views are purely visual components that can be used to display interface elements like backgrounds and borders; they don't include any variable data elements.

The collection view builds on the table view control by providing the potential for much more complex layouts. Whereas a table view can display items in a single column, collection views can present items in layouts ranging from linear grids to circles and every conceivable layout in between. Some examples are shown in Figure 4-1.

BBC iPlayer   Deutsche Welle   Spotify

Photos   Netflix   Artsy

Figure 4-1. Collection view examples

The Architecture of a Collection View

The UICollectionView class is part of the UIKit framework, and is a subclass of
UIScrollView, which in turns inherits from UIView, UIResponder, and ultimately NSObject, as
shown in Figure 4-2.

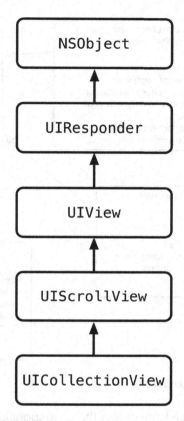

Figure 4-2. The inheritance tree of UICollectionView

The UICollectionView control works with four other objects, shown in Figure 4-3. The collection view itself is managed by a subclass of UIViewController, either directly or as an instance of UICollectionViewController that inherits from UIViewController.

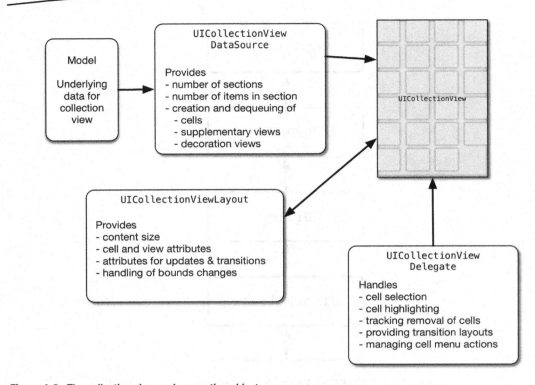

Figure 4-3. The collection view and supporting objects

The UICollectionViewDataSource is an object that is responsible for getting data from the data model. It uses this to inform the collection view of the number and type of items that are to be displayed, and it creates and configures the items before passing them to the collection view itself.

Interactions with the collection view (selections, highlighting, focusing, etc.) are handled by an object acting as the UICollectionViewDelegate.

UICollectionView uses the model-view-controller pattern to organize itself. The data that drives the contents of the items and supplementary views is provided by the model object, while the UICollectionView control itself is the view component.

The controller part is often a UICollectionViewController subclass, but the role of the controller can also be played by another separate class, or even split across different classes that act as delegate and dataSource independently of each other.

> **Tip** The UIViewController subclasses that also act as a UICollectionView datasource and delegates often have a tendency to become rather large. To avoid your project succumbing to "Massive View Controller" syndrome, it's worth considering whether it would be better structured with a separate class to manage the collection view, while the view controller sticks to its normal role.

The layout of a collection view is managed by a UICollectionViewLayout object that tells the collection view how each cell, supplementary view, and decoration view should be positioned within the bounds of the collection view itself by configuring the various layout attributes of each item. Changes in layouts can be animated and react to interactions.

Although collection views and table views are similar in terms of their basic operation (each uses a datasource to provide items to display, and a delegate to handle interaction), the collection view layout provides a much greater degree of flexibility in configuring its appearance.

As with UITableView, collection views use a dequeuing and recycling approach to creating and managing cells. When cells are created, they're tagged with a cell identifier that allows the collection view to keep track of the cell type.

As cells scroll out of the visible area, they're stored in a cache from where they can be dequeued and recycled as "new" cells are needed to display items that are about to scroll into view. By using the cell identifier, the collection view can handle the dequeuing and recycling of multiple types of cells.

Creating cells is an expensive operation, so this approach allows collection views to manage potentially huge numbers of individual data items while maintaining fast scrolling and animation performance, and all within the stringent memory limitations of an iOS device.

There's a detailed description of how the dequeuing mechanism works in Chapter 5.

The Anatomy of a Collection View

Collection views are instances of the UICollectionView class, and display a list of items—or cells—that can be scrolled vertically and horizontally. They're instances of the UICollectionView class and come in three physical parts.

The Collection View Itself

The visible container part, the collectionView itself, is a specialized subclass of UIScrollView, and is responsible for displaying a collection of data items as items.

Just like UIScrollView, the collection view's frame acts as a "window" over the content view, which, depending on the number and size of the items being displayed, may be larger than the frame itself.

The content items are laid out inside the bounds of the collection view. If the contents are larger than the collection view's frame, the collection view will handle scrolling the content around, either in response to user interaction or programmatically. Figure 4-4 shows how the frame and content relate.

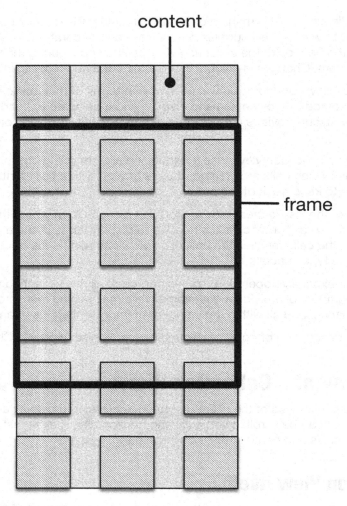

Figure 4-4. The frame and content view

If the number and size of items means that they *can* all fit within the collection view's frame, then the content won't scroll.

The overall size of the content view is calculated by the collection view's layout, and is recalculated every time the number of sections and/or items changes.

Figure 4-4 shows a collection view with a layout that arranges items in rows and columns, but this doesn't have to be the case. With custom layouts you can implement rows, columns, circles, or pretty much any arrangement in between. Regardless of how the items are arranged, however, the collection view will handle scrolling if they don't all fit into the collection view's frame.

As the content view scrolls around, the collection view will create and remove items from it as required. This is a balance between ensuring that items are always created and placed in time to be visible as that part of the content view scrolls into the frame, but not creating and maintaining so many items that aren't visible so that the memory consumption of the collection view is excessive.

In exactly the same way as a `UITableView`, the collection view uses a queue of preexisting items that it can dequeue and recycle as required. Just before an item scrolls into the visible area, the collection view will grab it from the queue and configure it with the correct data. Once the item scrolls out of the visible area, the collection view will dump it back onto the queue ready for eventual reuse.

In this way a collection view can appear to create and display thousands of items while only needing to create a small fraction of that amount as actual objects to maintain in memory.

Collection View Items

Collection view items are instances of `UICollectionReusableView` or its subclasses. They play one of three roles:

- **Item cells**, which are created as instances of `UICollectionViewCell`. These are analogous to the cells of a table view, and are used to display the main data items. In a gallery app, for example, the cells might display thumbnail images of the photos in an album.

- **Supplementary views**, which are instances of `UICollectionReusableView`. These are entirely optional and can have a variety of purposes. In grid-type layouts, such as a photo gallery, they're often used to provide metadata about sections by acting as headers and footers (album names, for example). In more complex layouts, they can be used to display additional information about items, such as image metadata.

- **Decoration views**, which are also instances of `UICollectionReusableView` (and also optional). These are independent of the collection view's model and don't display any data. Typically they are used to display visual elements such as backgrounds.

Figure 4-5 shows the conceptual parts of a collection view with a grid layout, with the various types of view highlighted.

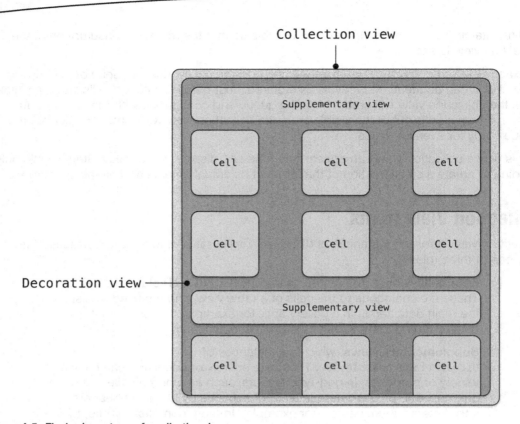

Figure 4-5. *The basic anatomy of a collection view*

Figure 4-6 shows a collection view in action in the iOS iBooks app. It uses cells to show the book covers, supplementary views that contain the download control, and a decoration view to provide the background gradient "shelf" effect.

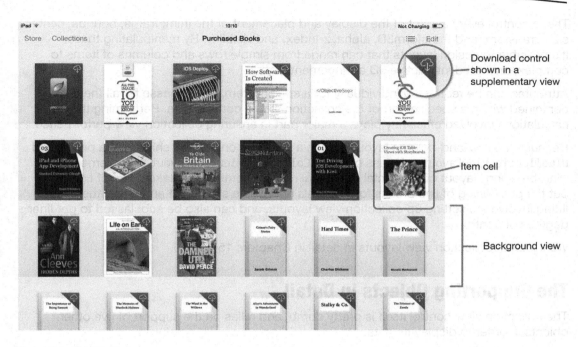

Download control shown in a supplementary view

Item cell

Background view

Figure 4-6. The iBooks app

Unlike UITableViewCell, UICollectionViewCell doesn't have any predefined cell types. Instead you get an empty contentView into which you can place your own controls. For this reason, when you're building collection views you'll always end up creating at least one cell object.

Cells can be created in several ways:

- Visually as prototype cells in a Storyboard
- Visually as a collection view cell in its own .xib file
- In code, by configuring a "standard" instance of UICollectionViewCell
- As a custom UICollectionViewCell subclass

We'll look at all four approaches in later chapters.

Collection View Layouts

Unlike table views, collection views don't know anything about how to lay out the positioning of their items. Instead, they rely on a separate object, a collection view layout, to determine the attributes of each item at any given moment. The collection view then uses those attributes to figure out where each item should appear and how it should look.

The layout of a collection view is a subclass of UICollectionViewLayout and is responsible for calculating the overall content size of the collection view, together with the layout attributes for each individual item whenever the collection view requests it.

These control every aspect of the display and placement of the item: frame, bounds, center, size, transform and transform3D, alpha, z-index, and visibility. By manipulating these, it's possible to design layouts that can range from simple rows and columns of items to complex, animated interactive 3D arrangements.

Attributes can be requested individually for a specific item, or en-masse for all the items contained within a specific part of the collection view's content area. Performing the calculations involved efficiently plays a major part in ensuring collection view performance.

Because the row-and-column layout is such a common one, `UIKit` ships with a predefined `UICollectionViewLayout` subclass called `UICollectionViewFlowLayout`. It implements a "line-breaking" layout of horizontal or vertical rows of items, and it takes care of figuring out the positioning of line breaks for you. This removes a significant amount of the heavy lifting involved in setting up collection view layouts, and can also be subclassed to get finer degrees of control.

We'll look at collection view layouts in detail in Chapters 15 and 16.

The Supporting Objects in Detail

The collection view control itself is pretty dumb, and relies on the support of five other objects in order to display its data:

- **View controller**
- **Model**
- **Datasource**
- **Delegate**
- **Layout**

Each object has a specific role to play supporting the collection view, and their organization is based on the model-view-controller architecture. Figure 4-7 shows how the five objects interrelate.

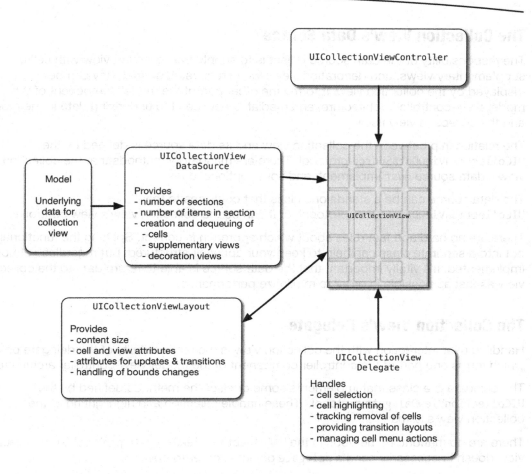

Figure 4-7. How the collection view and supporting objects interrelate

The Collection View's Model

The model contains the data that will be displayed in the collection view through the data source. As the name suggests, it's part of the model component of the model-view-controller architecture.

Models can take many forms; the form will depend on the way that the data in your app needs to be managed. At its simplest, the model may be a one-dimensional array that contains a set of Strings. More complex models may involve two-dimensional arrays to split the data into sections, or could retrieve data from a local persistent database or an external network source.

Regardless of what form the model takes, it doesn't communicate directly with the collection view. That's the role of the data source.

The Collection View's Data Source

The responsibility of the data source object is to supply the collection view with cells, supplementary views, and decoration views when requested so that they can be displayed by the collection view. It forms the other part of the model component of the model-view-controller architecture, and mediates between the underlying data in the model and the collection view itself.

The relationship between the collection view and its data source is defined by the UICollectionViewDataSource protocol. There are mandatory methods that the collection view's data source *must* implement, and some optional ones.

The data source can be a standalone class that conforms to the UICollectionViewDataSource protocol, or it can be the collection view's view controller.

There are no hard and fast rules about which approach is correct. Splitting the functionality out into a separate class can help to keep your app well-structured, but regardless of how its implemented, it's vitally important that the data source is able to return data to the collection view as fast as possible in order to maximize performance.

The Collection View's Delegate

Handling user interaction with the collection view is the responsibility of the delegate object, which forms one part of the controller component of the model-view-controller architecture.

The delegate is a class that implements some or all of the methods defined by the UICollectionViewDelegate protocol. These handle selection and highlighting of the collection view's items.

There are no mandatory methods in the UICollectionViewDelegate protocol, so a collection view doesn't necessarily need a delegate object in order to operate.

Just like the datasource, the delegate is often the UIViewController subclass that manages the view in which the collection view lives. However, there's no reason why that has to be the case. It can help keep classes to a manageable size if you create a standalone class to act as the delegate.

We'll look at both data source and delegates in more detail in Chapter 5.

The Collection View's Layout

Unlike UITableView, a UICollectionView control has no knowledge about how it should lay out items in its content view, and so it relies on a UICollectionViewLayout object to provide layout attributes for every item.

Each item in the collection view (cell, supplementary view, or decoration view) has a corresponding instance of UICollectionViewLayoutAttributes. These define the layout-related attributes for the item, and are created by the UICollectionViewLayout object when requested by the collection view.

Having requested the attributes for each item, the collection view then uses these to position the item in its content view. The attributes control the size, position, transform, and opacity of each item, but you can also supplement to control other properties of the items by subclassing UICollectionViewLayoutAttributes and adding your own custom properties.

If your collection view layout is based around a line of items, with or without line breaks, then you can take advantage of the UICollectionViewFlowLayout class, which takes care of much of the layout requirements for you. You will normally only need to specify item sizes and inter-item and inter-line spacing, after which the flow layout will figure out how to arrange everything else for you.

For more complex layouts, you'll need to create a custom layout as a subclass of UICollectionViewLayout. With this, you're responsible for calculating all the necessary attributes to display the items correctly.

We'll look at flow layouts in more detail in Chapter 15 and custom layouts in Chapter 16.

Creating Collection Views

Because a UICollectionView relies on the support of its delegate and datasource, the process of creating one can be broken down into two stages:

- Setting up the visual elements, either in a Storyboard, an Interface Builder xib file, or in code
- Setting up the supporting classes in code

Although both steps need to be completed before the collection view will function, you can do either one first. We'll go into more detail about creating and configuring the supporting classes in Chapter 15. For the moment, let's look at what is involved in creating the interface.

Creating a UICollectionView with Interface Builder

There are three approaches to creating UICollectionViews with Interface Builder:

- Embedding a UICollectionView object inside an existing view in a Storyboard scene or XIB file
- Creating a UICollectionViewController object as an entire Storyboard scene
- Creating a XIB file containing a UICollectionView as part of the process of adding a UICollectionViewController subclass to the project

Embedding a UICollectionView into an Existing View

Embedding a UICollectionView into an existing view in a Storyboard or XIB is very easy.

1. Open the Storyboard or XIB in Interface Builder.

2. Drag a UICollectionView object from the Object Browser into the main view, as shown in Figure 4-8.

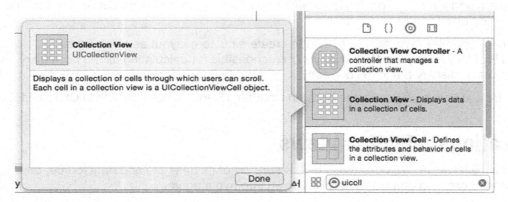

Figure 4-8. A UICollectionView object in the Object Browser

3. Set up the AutoLayout constraints so that the collection view will be sized correctly. Often the collection view will be full-screen, although of course it can be placed in the interface with any size using the appropriate constraints.

It's common for the roles of the collection view's delegate and datasource to be played by the view controller that owns the scene in which the collection view is placed. If this is the case, you can connect these directly in Interface Builder.

1. Select the collection view in Interface Builder, then Ctrl-click and drag up to the view controller object in the object tree.

2. As the mouse cursor hovers over the view controller object, it will be highlighted. Release the mouse button, and a popover showing the delegate and datasource will appear, as shown in Figure 4-9.

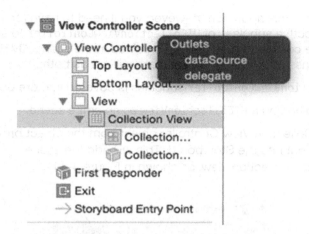

Figure 4-9. Connecting the delegate and datasource

3. Click each in turn to connect the collection view's delegate and datasource to the view controller.

> **Caution**   Just connecting the delegate and datasource outlets doesn't implement any of the functionality in the view controller that the collection view will need to work. You're responsible for making sure that the class implements the required methods from the `UICollectionViewDelegate` and `UICollectionViewDatasource` protocols. This is covered in Chapter 5.

Adding a UICollectionView as a Storyboard Scene

If you have a `UICollectionView` that will be displayed full-screen, then you can add it to the Storyboard as an entire scene. The advantage of taking this approach is that the collection view is the root view of the scene, rather than being a subview of a parent `UIView`. The difference in structure is shown in Figure 4-10.

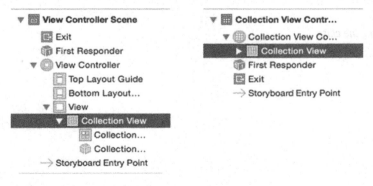

Figure 4-10. Comparing a subview with an entire scene

There's a prerequisite for this approach, however; you'll need to have (or implement before you try to run the project!) a subclass of UICollectionViewController to act as the delegate and datasource for the collection view that is contained in the scene. By default, the collection view scene assumes that its parent class will act as both.

Creating this UICollectionViewController subclass is covered in more detail in Chapter 5.

There are two steps to adding a UICollectionView as an entire scene.

1. Select the Collection View Controller object from the object browser, then drag it out into the Storyboard. This will add the scene containing the collection view, as shown in Figure 4-11.

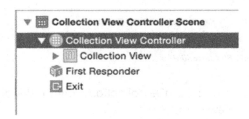

Figure 4-11. Selecting the Collection View Controller

2. Update the scene's Custom Class properties so that it belongs to your UICollectionViewController class. Select the Collection View Controller in the scene's tree, as shown in Figure 4-11, then switch to the Identity Inspector in the Utilities panel and update the Custom Class field as shown in Figure 4-12. In this example, the project contains a UICollectionViewController subclass called MyCollectionViewController.

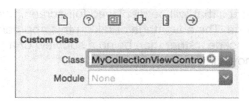

Figure 4-12. Updating the class

Adding a UICollectionViewController Subclass to the Project

To speed up the process of creating UICollectionViewController subclasses, Xcode ships with a preconfigured template. This creates a subclass with stubbed-out UICollectionViewDataSource and UICollectionViewDelegate methods, and optionally, a XIB file containing the collection view itself.

To create a UICollectionViewController subclass using the template, follow these steps.

1. Open the template chooser with File ➤ New ➤ Cocoa Touch Class, and click the Next button (shown in Figure 4-13).

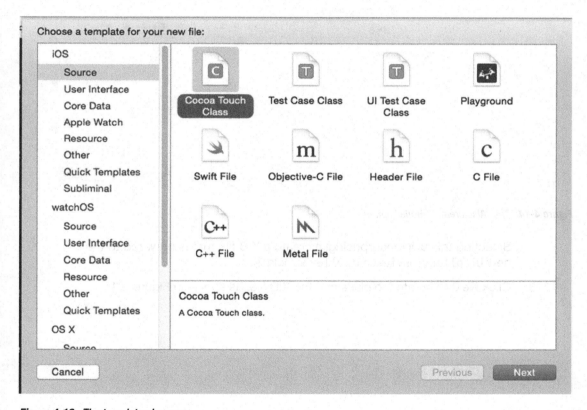

Figure 4-13. The template chooser

2. Give the class a name, and optionally select the "Also create XIB file" option if you want the template to create the Interface Builder file for you (shown in Figure 4-14).

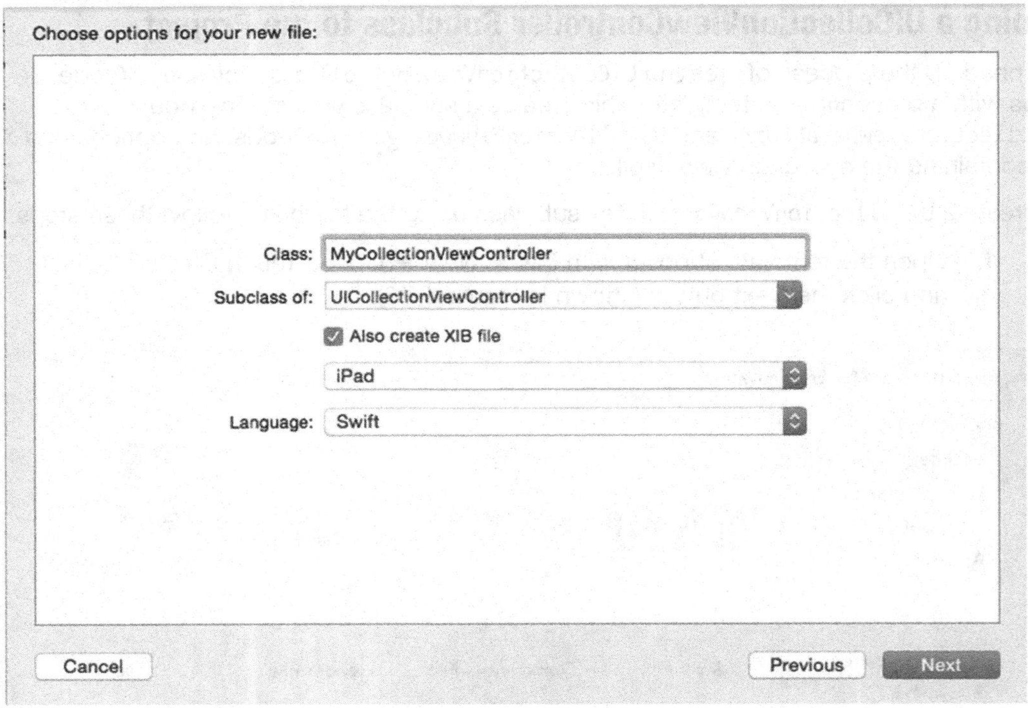

Figure 4-14. *The "Also create XIB file" option*

Selecting this will (unsurprisingly) create a XIB file that is prewired to the new `UICollectionViewController` subclass.

3. Click Next to create the class and the XIB file, as shown in Figure 4-15.

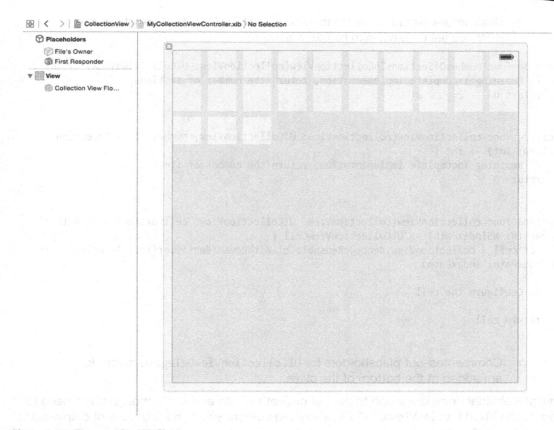

Figure 4-15. The resulting XIB file

The XIB file will be automatically named. Assuming your UICollectionViewController subclass is called MyCollectionViewController.swift, the XIB file will be named MyCollectionViewController.xib.

The XIB is created with the collection view's delegate and datasource properties connected to the parent class and a placeholder UICollectionViewFlowLayout object.

In the UICollectionViewController subclass, you'll see some placeholder code that contains the following:

- A private property for the cell's reuse identifier:

  ```
  private let reuseIdentifier = "Cell"
  ```

- In the viewDidLoad method, the collectionView registers the UICollectionViewCell class using the identifier:

  ```
  self.collectionView!.registerClass(UICollectionViewCell.self, ↵
  forCellWithReuseIdentifier: reuseIdentifier)
  ```

■ Basic implementations of the three required UICollectionViewDataSource methods are created, with helpful warnings:

```
override func numberOfSectionsInCollectionView(collectionView: UICollectionView) -> Int {
    // #warning Incomplete implementation, return the number of sections
    return 0
}

override func collectionView(collectionView: UICollectionView, numberOfItemsInSection
section: Int) -> Int {
    // #warning Incomplete implementation, return the number of items
    return 0
}

override func collectionView(collectionView: UICollectionView, cellForItemAtIndexPath ↵
indexPath: NSIndexPath) -> UICollectionViewCell {
    let cell = collectionView.dequeueReusableCellWithReuseIdentifier(reuseIdentifier, ↵
forIndexPath: indexPath)

    // Configure the cell

    return cell
}
```

■ Commented-out placeholders for UICollectionViewDelegate methods are added at the bottom of the class.

This placeholder code is enough to get the project to build and run, although you'll need to update the UICollectionViewDataSource methods before you'll see any content displayed in the newly-created collection view.

Creating a UICollectionView in Code

Following the mantra that "anything you can do visually, you can do in code," it's entirely possible to create UICollectionViews in code if you prefer this to the visual approach.

Assuming that you already have a UIViewController class that will act as the collection view's delegate and datasource, this process has five steps. Listing 4-1 shows an example, assuming the class has a UICollectionView property called myCollectionView.

Listing 4-1. Creating a UICollectionView in Code

```
override func viewDidLoad() {
    super.viewDidLoad()

    let myFlowLayout = UICollectionViewFlowLayout()
    // Configure flow layout here…

    myCollectionView = UICollectionView(frame: view.frame, collectionViewLayout: myFlowLayout)
```

```
    myCollectionView.dataSource = self
    myCollectionView.delegate = self
    myCollectionView.registerClass(UICollectionViewCell.self, forCellWithReuseIdentifier: ↵
"ReuseIdentifier")

    view.addSubview(myCollectionView)

}
```

Stepping through this,

1. A UICollectionViewFlowLayout is created and configured (collection view layouts are covered in Chapters 15 and 16).

2. Having created a flow layout, the myCollectionView property is then instantiated with a UICollectionView. It uses the flow layout just created, and will fill the full view by setting its frame to the same dimension as the view's frame.

3. The collection view's datasource and delegate are connected to the view controller (having done this, you'll need to ensure that the UIViewController implements the required UICollectionViewDataSource and UICollectionViewDelegate methods).

4. The UICollectionViewCell class is registered with the collection view and given a cell identifier so that cells can be created and dequeued.

5. The collection view is added to the view controller's view.

Summary

In this chapter, you looked at UICollectionView and the elements from which it's built. With this background knowledge, you're ready to start building and customizing collection views in your projects.

This is just the starting point, however. In Chapter 5, you're going to look at the process of feeding data into the collection view so that it can be displayed. In Chapters 15 and 16, you'll look at building collection view layouts to format and customize the data that is presented. Chapter 17 will look at how to customize collection view cells themselves.

Chapter 5

Feeding Data to Your Views

When working with table and collection views, it's important to bear in mind that on their own, they are able to do very little. Just as it takes a small army of ground staff (not to mention the flight crew!) to get an airliner off the tarmac and into the skies, so tableViews and collectionViews need the help and support of other objects in order to function properly.

One of the main parts of building tableViews and collectionViews is getting the objects to play nicely together, so this chapter covers the following:

- Where the views gets their data, and how you get it there
- How the views keep track of cells and sections
- An initial look at how the views handle interaction
- An overview of the architecture patterns that the UITableView and UICollectionView classes exploit

Some of this chapter's content might feel somewhat abstract and theoretical—but sticking with it is worthwhile. Developing your expertise with iOS (and tableViews and collectionViews especially!) often requires dealing with situations where you find yourself thinking, "Where the heck did *that* come from?" Figuring out what *that* is and *where* it came from is generally a case of understanding the design patterns that iOS uses—some of which are covered in this chapter.

UITableView, UICollectionView, and Delegation

On its own, UITableView and UICollectionView are pretty puny creatures. Although they handle the tasks involved in displaying and scrolling of cells themselves, they rely on external support for pretty much everything else.

That's not a weakness, though. By passing off their responsibility for other functions to external objects, you end up with code that's much more modular, robust, and easier to debug. The process of passing off that responsibility is known as *delegation*.

Understanding Delegation

Delegation is an application design pattern in which one object requests–or *delegates*–another object to complete a task on its behalf.

An analogy for this is the delegation that takes place in a restaurant. You *could* place your order yourself by walking to the kitchen and telling the chef what you want, but in most establishments, you *delegate* that task to the wait staff. The process of informing the chef of your order still gets completed; it's just that you've *delegated* it to somebody else.

In a restaurant, you wouldn't normally have a formal definition of how you're going to delegate things to the wait staff. There's an unspoken assumption that they're going to get your order to the kitchen. But in software, that's just not clear enough, so the processes are usually spelled out in protocols.

You can think of protocols as informal contracts that define what tasks one party will do on behalf of another and that outline how the information will be exchanged between them.

By conforming to a protocol, one of the parties (or objects, if we're thinking in software terms) is promising to implement the tasks that the other party will ask for, assuming that they're asked in the correct way.

Figure 5-1 illustrates this pattern, which can occur in a couple of scenarios:

- The first object is notifying the second that some event is about to occur, is occurring, or has occurred.

- The first object is asking the second object for input.

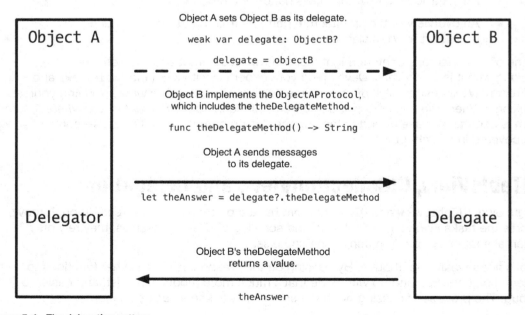

Figure 5-1. The delegation pattern

Those are pretty dry descriptions, so let's look at a couple of examples.

A Delegate Example: collectionView(_:didSelectItemAtIndexPath:)

When an item in a table or collection view is selected, it calls the collectionView(_: ↵
didSelectItemAtIndexPath:) or tableView(_:didSelectRowAtIndexPath:) method of
its delegate with two parameters: a reference to itself (the collectionView or tableView
parameter) and the indexPath of the selected item.

The delegate can then respond to the selection event. It could do something to the calling
view, trigger some external action, or just ignore the message completely.

For example, tapping an item often causes a detail view to be loaded, so the collection ↵
View(_:didSelectItemAtIndexPath:) method might look similar to Listing 5-1.

Listing 5-1. An Example collectionView(_:didSelectItemAtIndexPath:)Method

```
func collectionView(collectionView: UICollectionView, didSelectItemAtIndexPath ↵
indexPath: NSIndexPath) {

    let detailView = DetailViewController(nibName: "DetailViewController", bundle: nil)
    detailView.modalPresentationStyle = UIModalPresentationStyle.FullScreen
    detailView.selectedItem = self.dataModel[indexPath.row]
    self.presentViewController(detailView, animated: true, completion: nil)

}
```

A dataSource Example: tableView:cellForRowAtIndexPath

You've met the tableView(_:cellForRowAtIndexPath:) method several times before. When
the tableView is ready to display a cell, it asks its dataSource to return a UITableViewCell for
the specified indexPath so that the cell can then be displayed inside the table itself.

The dataSource object will implement the tableView(_:cellForRowAtIndexPath:) method,
as shown in Listing 5-2.

Listing 5-2. An Example tableView(_:cellForRowAtIndexPath:) Method

```
func tableView(tableView: UITableView, cellForRowAtIndexPath indexPath: NSIndexPath) ↵
 -> UITableViewCell {

    let cell = tableView.dequeueReusableCellWithIdentifier("cellIdentifier", forIndexPath:↵
indexPath)

    // cell properties will be configured here

    return cell

}
```

The point of all this is that by separating out the functionality, you can split view concerns from model concerns and use a controller to coordinate the two.

> **Tip** UITableViewDatasource and UITableViewDelegate are *both* examples of delegate protocols; it's just that one is explicitly named as a delegate, while the other has a slightly different name.

Setting Delegates

Objects and delegates don't just get together magically. There needs to be an explicit connection. Objects that have delegates have a delegate property, which can be set in code. Alternatively, you can use Interface Builder to do the same thing visually.

In the case of table and collection views, you can also set both delegate and dataSource by using Interface Builder. You Ctrl-Click the view and then drag the connection to the File's Owner icon. Figure 5-2 shows how to do this to a tableView.

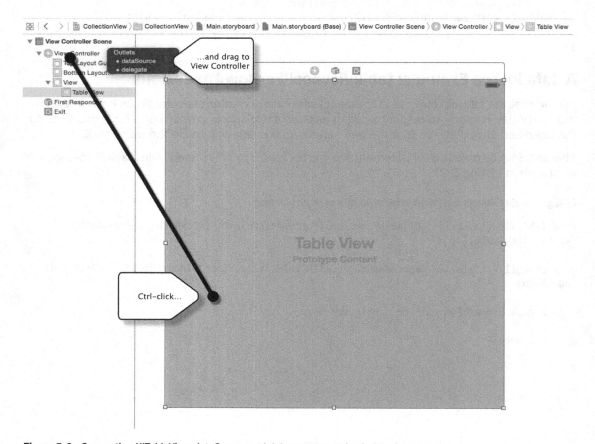

Figure 5-2. Connecting UITableView dataSource and delegate properties in Interface Builder

It's common for a view's controller class to also be the dataSource and the delegate, although there's no reason why that has to be the case. If you have a number of views being supplied by the same datasource, for example, it might make more sense to create a stand-alone object to act as the datasource for some or all of them. The same can also be true of delegates.

Getting an object and its delegate to play nicely together can feel a bit intricate at first, so it's worth taking a quick look at how this is done.

Wiring Up an Object with a Delegate

Think back for a moment to our two example objects, shown in Figure 5-3.

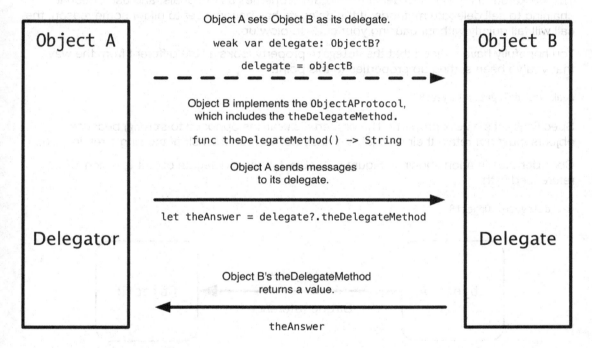

Figure 5-3. The delegate pattern, again

In order for objectB to act as objectA's delegate, you need some way of connecting the two. This requires setting the delegate property of objectA to point to the instance of its delegate class, in this case objectB.

If objectA has a property called delegate, as shown here:

```
weak var delegate: ObjectB?
```

Then objectA can set the instance of objectB as the delegate:

```
delegate = objectB
```

Delegates and Memory Management

There's a subtlety here that's important to be aware of. Although objectA is the object with the delegate property, it's objectB that is the delegate.

This leads to an interesting memory management–related side effect, which you'll need to bear in mind. Although objectB has been set as objectA's delegate, objectA will be unaware if objectB goes out of existence. objectA will continue to send messages to what it *thinks* is its delegate.

As long as that delegate object exists, obviously that's not a problem. However, if the delegate object disappears, objectA will send messages to a nonexistent object, and the program will crash.

The workaround for this is to declare delegate properties as optionals, and use optional chaining to call delegate methods. If the delegate has become set to nil for some reason, the call will fail quietly without causing your code to blow up.

You hopefully have noticed that the delegate property looks a little different from the way that you've been setting up properties to this point:

```
weak var delegate: ObjectB?
```

Specifically, it's a weak property. The property is weak (as opposed to strong) because objects *must not* retain their delegates. If they do, you run the risk of causing a retain loop.

Consider the situation shown in Figure 5-4: object A has a delegate object B, which is referenced with

```
var delegate: ObjectB
```

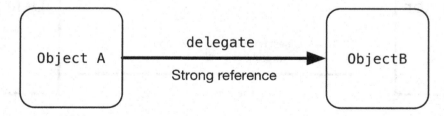

Figure 5-4. *A strong reference*

If object B receives a dealloc message, it won't be deallocated because it is still owned by the strong reference from object A, as shown in Figure 5-5.

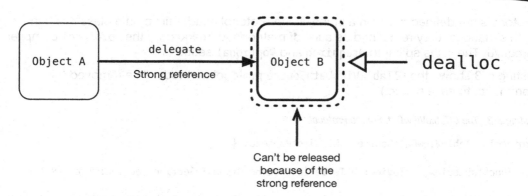

Figure 5-5. *After a dealloc message*

Compare that with the situation in Figure 5-6, where object A has a weak optional reference to object B.

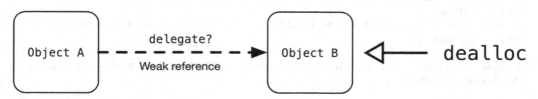

Figure 5-6. *A weak optional reference*

If object B receives a `dealloc` message in this situation, shown in Figure 5-7, the weak reference will allow it to be deallocated, and because object A refers to it as an optional property, it's perfectly legal for it to become `nil` as far as object A is concerned.

Figure 5-7. *A Weak Reference After Deallocation*

Defining Protocols

Methods are defined in protocols so that objects and their delegates know the methods that each is expected to implement and respond to. A *protocol* is simply a list of methods — sometimes required and sometimes optional — that an object promises to implement.

If a protocol method is required, the object adopting the protocol must implement it. Otherwise, the compiler will complain, and the project won't build. Optional methods are, well, optional, so the compiler won't moan if they are missing.

Protocols are defined either in a stand-alone protocol header file or in a class itself. In both situations, they're defined as a list of methods, demarked by the @protocol compiler directive. The list is split into @required and @optional sections.

Listing 5-3 shows the UITableViewDataSource protocol methods. (I've removed the comments to save space.)

Listing 5-3. The UITableViewDataSource Protocol

```
protocol UITableViewDataSource : NSObjectProtocol {

    func tableView(tableView: UITableView, numberOfRowsInSection section: Int) -> Int

    func tableView(tableView: UITableView, cellForRowAtIndexPath indexPath: ↵
    NSIndexPath) -> UITableViewCell

    optional func numberOfSectionsInTableView(tableView: UITableView) -> Int

    optional func tableView(tableView: UITableView, titleForHeaderInSection section: ↵
    Int) -> String?
    optional func tableView(tableView: UITableView, titleForFooterInSection section: ↵
    Int) -> String?

    optional func tableView(tableView: UITableView, canEditRowAtIndexPath indexPath: ↵
    NSIndexPath) -> Bool

    optional func tableView(tableView: UITableView, canMoveRowAtIndexPath indexPath: ↵
    NSIndexPath) -> Bool

    optional func sectionIndexTitlesForTableView(tableView: UITableView) -> [String?]
    optional func tableView(tableView: UITableView, sectionForSectionIndexTitle ↵
    title: String, atIndex index: Int) -> Int

    optional func tableView(tableView: UITableView, commitEditingStyle editingStyle: ↵
    UITableViewCellEditingStyle, forRowAtIndexPath indexPath: NSIndexPath)

    optional func tableView(tableView: UITableView, moveRowAtIndexPath ↵
    sourceIndexPath: NSIndexPath, toIndexPath destinationIndexPath: NSIndexPath)

}
```

This tells us that although the UITableViewDataSourceProtocol defines myriad methods, only two of them have to be implemented in order for the table to function. The rest are optional.

> **Note**   Strictly speaking, in order to work, a tableView needs to know the number of sections it has. You'll notice that the UITableViewDataSource protocol lists numberOfSectionsInTableView as an optional method, which seems a little counterintuitive. A tableView gets around this by assuming that unless the dataSource says otherwise, the table view has just the one section.

ACCESSING PROTOCOL DEFINITIONS IN XCODE

When you implement a protocol method in your classes, that method needs to be implemented exactly as it's defined in the protocol. That can lead to a lot of typing, so it's much easier (and safer) to copy the method name directly from the protocol itself. You'll end up spending a *lot* of time checking protocol documentation, so here's a quick way of accessing it. If you hold down the Option key and hover the mouse cursor over the protocol name in an Xcode window, the cursor changes to a question mark and the name becomes a hyperlink. Clicking that link pops up a summary window.

Clicking any of the highlighted terms opens either the help file in the Xcode Organizer or the relevant code file itself.

Using UITableView's Delegate Methods

Both `UITableView` and `UICollectionView` use the delegate pattern to obtain data from their `dataSource` and to handle user interaction and configuration (see Figures 5-8 and 5-9). Despite the name, their `dataSource` is a form of a delegate, just one with specific responsibilities.

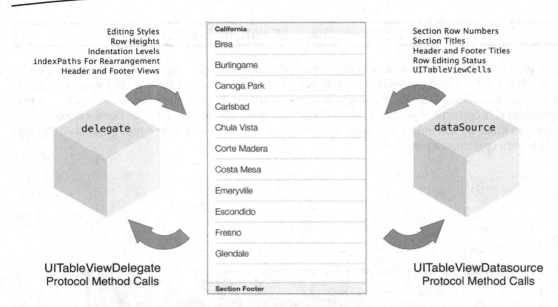

Figure 5-8. *How the tableView interacts with its delegate and dataSource*

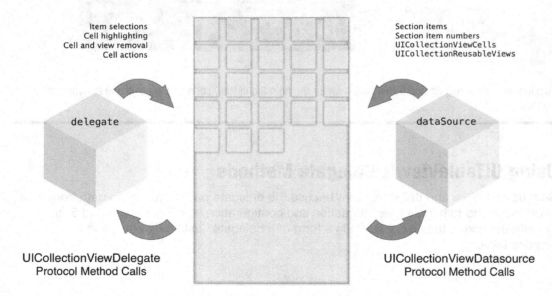

Figure 5-9. *How the collectionView interacts with its delegate and dataSource*

Having seen how the views use the delegation pattern, you can then start to look at the detail of how the dataSource and delegate operates. Although the processes are the same, UITableView and UICollectionView delegate protocols are declared separately, so we'll look at each one in turn.

Using UITableViewDelegate Methods

The UITableViewDelegate handles the following:

- Configuring the tableView's rows

- Configuring the header and footer of sections

- Managing the selection of rows

- Editing rows

- Managing accessory views

- Reordering rows

Table 5-1 shows the methods available in the UITableViewDelegate protocol.

Table 5-1. UITableViewDelegate Protocol Methods

Method	Purpose
Configuring Rows	
tableView(_:heightForRowAtIndex Path:)	Returns the actual calculated height of the row as a CGFloat.
	This overrides any table-wide value set for the row height.
tableView(_:estimatedHeightFor Row AtIndexPath:)	Returns the estimated height of the row as a CGFloat.
	Providing an estimated value can help to speed up the table, which has to calculate the total height of all cells when it first loads.
	Deferring the calculation of cell height until actually required means that time won't be wasted with calculations for cells that aren't yet visible.
tableView(_:indentationLevelFor Row AtIndexPath:)	Returns the indentation level for the current row as an Int.
tableView(_:willDisplayCell:for Row AtIndexPath:)	Called to tell the delegate that the table is just about to display the cell at this row.
	This provides the final opportunity to customize cell settings like selection or background color.
	Does not return anything.

(continued)

Table 5-1. (*continued*)

Method	Purpose
Managing Accessory Views	
tableView(_:editActionsForRow AtIndexPath:)	Returns the UITableViewRowActions that are available for this row.
	If you don't override this method, the cell will display the standard accessory controls.
tableView(_:accessoryButton TappedForRowWithIndexPath:)	Tells the delegate that the accessory button has been tapped for this row.
	You will often see this used to push in a new view as a drill-down detail view for the data model element relating to this row.
	Does not return anything.
Managing Accessory Views	
tableView(_:willSelectRowAt IndexPath:)	Tells the delegate that the row is about to be selected. It's triggered by a touch up inside the cell.
	It returns an NSIndexPath for the row that the table should select (it's possible to select *another* row in response to a selection).
	If the row should *not* be selected, return nil.
tableView(_:didSelectRowAt IndexPath:)	Called after the row is selected.
	You can use this method to deselect the other rows in the table if only one can be selected at a time.
	Does not return anything.
tableView(_:willDeselectRowAt IndexPath:)	Called just before the cell is deselected.
	Returns an NSIndexPath if you want to deselect *another* row.
	If you want to prevent the row being deselected, return nil.
tableView(_:didDeselectRowAt IndexPath:)	Called after the row is deselected.
	You could use this method to remove any selection indicator from the cell at this row.
	Does not return anything.
Managing Section Headers and Footers	
tableView(_:viewForHeader InSection:)	Returns an optional UIView to use as the header for the current section.
tableView(_:viewForFooter InSection:)	Returns an optional UIView to use as the footer for the current section.
tableView(_:heightForHeader InSection:)	Returns the height of the header for the current section as a CGFloat.

(*continued*)

Table 5-1. (*continued*)

Method	Purpose
tableView(_:estimatedHeightFor Header InSection:)	Returns the estimated height of the header for the current section as a CGFloat.
	Providing an estimated height can help to improve the table's performance by speeding up the calculation of the overall content height.
tableView(_:heightForFooter InSection:)	Returns the height of the footer for the current section as a CGFloat
tableView(_:estimatedHeightFor Footer InSection:)	Returns the estimated height of the footer for the current section as a CGFloat.
	Providing an estimated height can help to improve the table's performance by speeding up the calculation of the overall content height
tableView(_:willDisplayHeader View: forSection:)	Tells the delegate that the header view is about to be displayed to allow a last chance for it to be customized before display.
	Does not return anything.
tableView(_:willDisplayFooter View: forSection:)	Tells the delegate that the footer view is about to be displayed to allow a last chance for it to be customized before display.
	Does not return anything.
Managing Editing of Rows	
tableView(_:willBeginEditing Row AtIndexPath:)	Tells the delegate that the table is about to go into editing mode. The table's editing property is set to true, and a Delete button is displayed in this row.
	This method gives you the chance to update the app's view to handle the change in mode.
	Does not return anything.
tableView(_:didEndEditingRow AtIndexPath:)	Called when the table leaves editing mode.
	Does not return anything.
tableView(_:editingStyleForRow AtIndexPath:)	Returns a UITableViewEditingStyle to control what editing control is displayed in the cell.
	If this method isn't implemented, the control defaults to Delete.
tableView(_:titleForDelete ConfirmationButtonForRow AtIndexPath:)	Returns an optional String to use as the title of the Delete confirmation button.
	This title can be localized.
tableView(_:shouldIndentWhile Editing RowAtIndexPath:)	Returns a Bool that tells the table whether it should indent the cell's background while it is in editing mode.

(*continued*)

Table 5-1. (*continued*)

Method	Purpose
Reordering Cells	
tableView(_:targetIndexPath ForMove FromRowAtIndexPath: toProposedIndexPath:)	Returns an NSIndexPath to indicate where a cell should be moved to during reordering.
Tracking View Removal	
tableView(_:didEndDisplayingCell : forRowAtIndexPath:)	Called when a cell has been removed from the table. Does not return anything.
tableView(_:didEndDisplaying HeaderView:forSection:)	Called when a header view has been removed from the table. Does not return anything.
tableView(_:didEndDisplaying FooterView:forSection	Called when a footer view has been removed from the table. Does not return anything.
Copying and Pasting Row Content	
tableView(_:shouldShowMenuForRow AtIndexPath:)	Returns a Bool to indicate to the table view whether an editing control should be displayed for this row. Return false if you want to prevent copying of or pasting over this cell.
tableView(_:canPerformAction: fo rRowAtIndexPath:withSender:)	Returns a Bool to indicate to the table view whether the Copy or Paste command should be available for this row.
tableView(_:performAction:forRow AtIndexPath:withSender:)	This function is called when the user taps Copy or Paste in the cell's editing menu. Does not return anything.
tableView(_:shouldHighlightRow AtIndexPath:)	Returns a Bool to indicate whether a row should be selected or not in response to touch events. If you don't override this method, it will default to true.
tableView(_:didHighlightRowAt IndexPath:)	Called when the row is highlighted. Does not return anything.
tableView(_:didUnhighlightRowAt IndexPath:)	Called when the row highlighting is removed. Does not return anything.

Using UICollectionViewDelegate Methods

The UICollectionViewDelegate handles the following:

- Managing the selection of cells
- Managing the highlighting of cells
- Tracking the insertion and removal of cells and views

- ■ Providing a transition layout
- ■ Managing actions for cells

Table 5-2 shows the methods available in the `UICollectionViewDelegate` protocol.

Table 5-2.

Method	Purpose
Managing Selected Cells	
collectionView(_:shouldSelectItem AtIndexPath:)	Returns a Bool to control whether the item should be selected.
	The default return value is true.
collectionView(_:didSelectItem AtIndexPath:)	Called when an item is selected in the collection view.
	This method isn't called if you select an item programmatically.
	Does not return anything.
collectionView(_:shouldDeselectItem AtIndexPath:)	Returns a Bool to control whether the item should be deselected.
	The default return value is true.
collectionView(_:didDeselectItem AtIndexPath:)	Called when an item is deselected in the collection view.
	This method isn't called if you deselect an item programmatically.
	Does not return anything.
Managing Cell Highlighting	
collectionView(_:shouldHighlightItem AtIndexPath:)	Returns a Bool to control whether an item should be highlighted in response to a touch.
	The default return value is true.
collectionView(_:didHighlightItem AtIndexPath:)	Called when an item is highlighted in response to a user touch (this doesn't get called if the cell is highlighted programmatically).
	Does not return anything.
collectionView(_:didUnhighlightItem AtIndexPath:)	Called when an item is no longer highlighted.
	This doesn't get called if the highlighting is removed programmatically.
	Does not return anything.

(continued)

Table 5-2. (*continued*)

Method	Purpose
Tracking Addition and Removal of Views	
collectionView(_:willDisplayCell: forItemAtIndexPath:)	Called when the cell is about to be displayed.
	This is the preferred way of tracking when a cell is added to the collection view. You shouldn't track from within the cell itself.
	Does not return a value.
collectionView(_:willDisplay SupplementaryView: forElementKind:atIndexPath:)	Called when the view is about to be displayed.
	This is the preferred way of tracking when a view is added to the collection view. You shouldn't track from within the view itself.
	Does not return a value.
collectionView(_:didEndDisplaying Cell:forItemAtIndexPath:)	Called when the cell is removed from the collection view.
	This is the preferred way of tracking when a cell is removed to the collection view. You shouldn't track from within the cell itself.
	Does not return a value.
collectionView(_:didEndDisplaying SupplementaryView:forElementOfKind: atIndexPath:)	Called when the view is removed from the collection view.
	This is the preferred way of tracking when a view is removed to the collection view. You shouldn't track from within the view itself.
	Does not return a value.
Providing a Transition Layout	
collectionView(_:transitionLayout ForOldLayout:newLayout:)	Returns the custom transition layout to use when moving from the supplied old to the new layouts.
	If this method isn't overridden, the collection view will use a standard UICcollectionViewTransitionLayout.
	Returns a UICollectionViewTransitionLayout.
Managing Actions for Cells	
collectionView(_:shouldShowMenu ForItemAtIndexPath:)	Returns a Bool to indicate whether an editing menu should be displayed for the item.
	Returns false by default.
collectionView(_:canPerformAction: forItemAtIndexPath:withSender:)	Returns a Bool to indicate whether the specified action can be performed for the item.
	Returns false by default.
collectionView(_:performAction: forItemAtIndexPath:withSender:)	Performs the specified action on the specified item.

(continued)

Table 5-2. *(continued)*

Method	Purpose
Managing Collection View Focus	
collectionView(_:canFocusItemAt IndexPath:)	Returns a Bool to control whether the item can be focused. The default return value is True.
collectionView(_:shouldUpdateFocus InContext:)	Returns a Bool to control whether the focus update specified by the given context should occur. By default this returns false.
collectionView(_:didUpdateFocusIn Context:withAnimationCoordinator:)	Called when a focus update in the provided context occurred. Does not return a value.
indexPathForPreferredFocusedViewIn CollectionView(_:)	Returns the NSIndexPath for the preferred focused view in the provided collection view.

Datasources

Datasources have a pretty straightforward role in life: they provide data and information about data and they handle manipulation of data. Like delegates, the dataSource protocols for UITableView and UICollectionView are similar but different, so we'll look at each one individually.

The UITableView dataSource

A UITableView needs three key pieces of information in order to successfully draw itself and its cells:

- The number of sections in the table
- The number of rows in the section
- The cells that belong in the rows within the sections

The dataSource exists to provide this information.

Getting the Number of Sections in the Table

A simple table has only one section, so tableviews will assume this is 1 unless the numberOfSectionsInTableView(_:) method is implemented and returns something different.

Although numberOfSectionsInTableView(_:) is an optional method, I tend to always implement it so that it's there. Because this is the first method that gets called, you can also speed things up by returning 0 if the dataset for your table is empty—after which the tableView assumes that it's not going to get any additional data, and stops asking.

Getting the Number of Rows in the Section

Assuming that there's data to display, the tableView(_:numberOfRowsInSection:) method is called. The tableView calling the method supplies the section number as an integer, and the method returns the number of rows (also as an integer).

Getting Cells That Belong in This Row of This Section

Creating cells to be displayed is at the heart of setting up the tableView. This is where your code will need to return an instance of a UITableViewCell for the tableView to display, each time the tableView(_:cellForRowAtIndexPath:) method is called.

The tableView will provide the section and row numbers as an indexPath, and it's up to your tableView(_:cellForRowAtIndexPath:) method to retrieve the data from the model, dequeue the cell, configure it, and return it as quickly as possible.

How the Key Information Is Obtained by the Table

The conversation between the four objects involved–the view controller that contains the tableView, the tableView itself, and the delegate and dataSource objects belonging to the tableView–takes place in a specific order. This is illustrated in Figure 5-10.

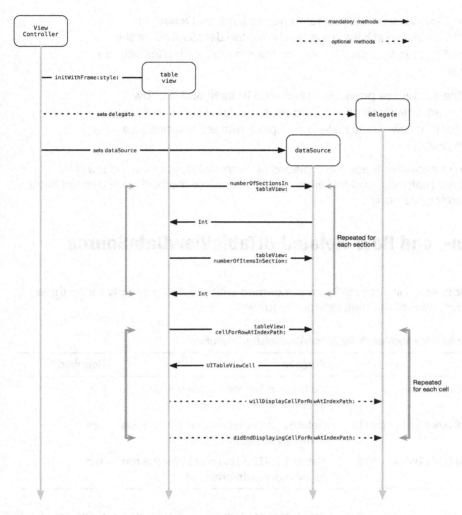

Figure 5-10. *Messaging between view controller, tableView, and datasource*

1. First, the view controller allocates and instantiates the `tableView`, and then sets the `delegate` and `dataSource` properties.

2. Once in existence, the `tableView` asks the `dataSource` for the number of sections for itself, and the `dataSource` replies with an `NSInteger` value.

3. Then the `tableView` provides a reference to itself and a section number in an `indexPath` instance, and asks the `dataSource` for the number of rows in that section. Again, the `dataSource` replies with an `NSInteger`.

4. Finally, the `tableView` provides a reference to itself and the row number in an `indexPath` object, and asks the `dataSource` to supply the cell for that row. The `dataSource` replies with an instance of a `UITableViewCell`.

After your `dataSource` provides these three pieces of information, your `tableView` is in business. These three methods, and the other eight `dataSource` methods, are defined in the `UITableViewDataSource` protocol.

Cell-, Section-, and Row-Related UITableViewDataSource Methods

Three main methods, listed in Table 5-3, are concerned with providing exactly those three pieces of information. Two of the methods are required.

Table 5-3. Cell, Section And Row Methods Of The UITableViewDataSource Protocol

Method	Purpose	Required?
`numberOfSectionsInTableView(_:)`	Returns an Int for the number of sections in the table view	No
`tableView(_:numberOfRowsInSection:)`	Returns an Int for the number of rows in the given section	Yes
`tableView(_:cellForRowAtIndexPath:)`	Returns a UITableViewCell for the row at the index path provided	Yes

Although the `tableView` needs to know the number of sections required, the default value is 1, which is why you'll often see `numberOfSectionsInTableView` omitted from simple tables.

Title- and Index-Related UITableViewDataSource Methods

There are four methods that create and manage the table's titles and indexes. Table 5-4 lists these methods.

Table 5-4. UITableViewDataSource Protocol Title And Section Methods

Method	Purpose
tableView(_:titleForHeaderInSection:)	Returns a String containing the header title for the given section
tableView(_:titleForFooterInSection:)	Returns a String containing the footer title for the given section
sectionIndexTitlesForTableView(:_)	Returns an optional Array of Strings containing titles for the index list that appears down the right side of an indexed table (for example, A, B, C, D, and so on)
tableView(_:sectionForSectionIndex Title:atIndex:)	Returns an Int for the index number of the section with the given title and section title index

Insertion-, Removal-, and Reordering-Related UITableViewDataSource Methods

The remaining UITableViewDataSource protocol methods handle inserting, deleting, and reordering rows within the tableView. Table 5-5 lists these methods.

Table 5-5. Insertion-, Removal-, and Reordering-related UITableViewDataSource Methods

Method	Purpose
tableView(_:canEditRowAt IndexPath:)	Returns a Bool that depends on whether the given row is flagged as being editable.
	If this method isn't implemented, the tableView assumes that *all* rows can be edited.
tableView(_:canMoveRowAt IndexPath:)	Returns a Bool that depends on whether the given row is flagged as being able to move within the table.
	If this method isn't overridden, the default will be false.
tableView(_:moveRowAtIndexPath: toIndexPath:)	Instructs the dataSource to move a row from one location to another.
	This method also needs to update the underlying data model if the change is to persist.
	Doesn't return a value.
tableView(_:commitEditingStyle: forRowAtIndexPath:)	Instructs the dataSource to commit the insertion or deletion of a row by calling the insertRowsAtIndexPath: withRowAnimation or deleteRowsAtIndexPath:withRow Animation tableView methods.
	Doesn't return a value.

The UICollectionView dataSource

A UICollectionView operates in a very similar way to a UITableView when it comes to the key pieces of information needed in order to successfully draw itself and its cells.

Specifically, it needs

- The number of sections in the collection view
- The number of items in each section
- The cell for each item within the sections

The UICollectionView dataSource exists to provide this information.

Getting the Number of Sections in the Table

A simple collection view has only one section, so collection views will assume this is 1 unless the collectionView(_:numberOfSectionsInCollectionView:) method is implemented and returns something different.

Although numberOfSectionsInCollectionView is an optional method, I tend to always implement it so that it's there. Because this is the first method that gets called, you can also speed things up by returning 0 if the dataset for your collection view is empty—after which the collectionView assumes that it's not going to get any additional data, and stops asking.

Getting the Number of Items in the Section

Assuming that there is data to display, the numberOfItemsInSection(:_) method is called. The collectionView calling the method supplies the section number as an integer, and the method returns the number of items (also as an integer).

Getting Cells That Belong To This Item of This Section

Creating cells to be displayed is at the heart of setting up the collectionView. This is where your code will need to return an instance of a UICollectionViewCell for the collectionView to display, each time the collectionView(_:cellForItemAtIndexPath:) method is called.

The collectionView will provide the section and item numbers as an indexPath, and it's up to your cellForItemAtIndexPath method to retrieve the data from the model, create the cell, and return it as quickly as possible.

Getting Supplementary Views That Belong To This Index Path

Although supplementary views are optional, you provide them in much the same way that collection view cells are provided: they are dequeued in response to a request from the collection view.

The collectionView will provide the section and item numbers as an indexPath together with the type of supplementary view required, and the collectionView:(_viewForSupplementaryElementOfKind:atIndexPath:) method is responsible for retrieving data from the model, creating and configuring the supplementary view, and returning it as quickly as possible.

How the Key Information Is Obtained by the Collection View

The conversation between the four objects involved—the view controller that contains the collectionView, the collectionView itself, and the delegate and dataSource objects belonging to the collectionView—takes place in a specific order. This is illustrated in Figure 5-11.

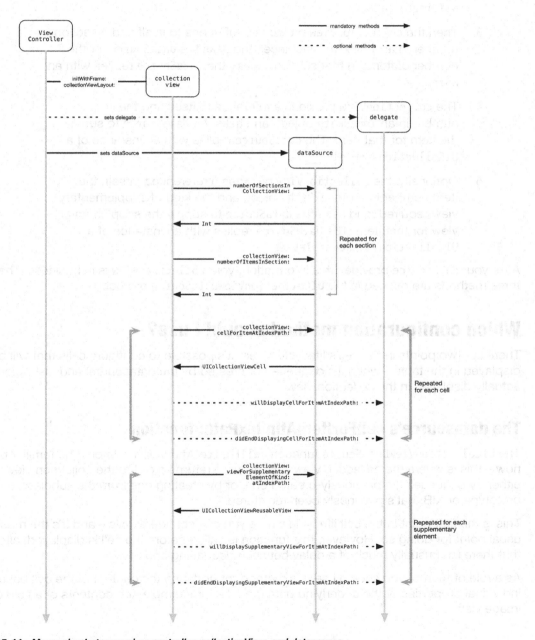

Figure 5-11. Messaging between view controller, collectionView, and datasource

1. First, the view controller allocates and instantiates the collectionView, and it then sets the delegate and dataSource properties.

2. Once in existence, the collectionView asks the dataSource for the number of sections for itself, and the dataSource replies with an NSInteger value.

3. Then the collectionView provides a reference to itself and a section number in an indexPath instance, and asks the dataSource for the number of items in that section. Again, the dataSource replies with an NSInteger.

4. The collectionView provides a reference to itself and the item number in an indexPath object, and asks the dataSource to supply the item for that item. The dataSource replies with an instance of a UICollectionViewCell.

5. Optionally, the collectionView provides a reference to itself, the item number in an indexPath object, and the kind of supplementary view required, and asks the dataSource to supply the supplementary view for that item. The dataSource replies with an instance of a UICollectionViewReusableView.

After your dataSource provides this information, your collectionView is in business. These three methods are defined in the UICollectionViewDataSource protocol.

Which configuration method should I use?

There are two points in the cell's lifecycle where it's possible to configure cells that will be displayed in the table – when it's dequeued or created by the datasource; and just before it's actually displayed in the collection view.

The datasource's cellForItemAtIndexPath: function

The UICollectionViewDataSource function cellForItemAtIndexPath should be familiar by now – this is where the collection view's datasource returns a cell to the collection view either by dequeueing a previously-created one, or by creating one from the subclass, prototype or XIB that's previously been registered.

This is the first point in the cell lifecycle where you *can* configure cells – and it's the most usual point for doing so. However, this function is called before the cell is displayed, albeit that there isn't usually much of a delay between dequeuing and display.

As a rule of thumb, you should use this method for updating the content of the cell based on individual properties of the underlying data model – for example, the contents of a field or an image view.

The delegate's willDisplayCellAtIndexPath: function

The UICollectionViewDelegate function willDisplayCellForItemAtIndexPath: is called by the collectionView just before it displays each cell. This happens immediately before the cell is drawn in the collection view, so it's the last point where you can tweak the cell's contents before display.

It is possible to change the cell's contents here, but there are a couple of reasons why you should restrict the changes to small, specific ones:

- If you use this method to update the cell contents, you're blurring the distinction between the roles of the collection view's dataSource and delegate objects. That can make it harder to refactor in the future, and could lead to messier code.

- This function is called just before the cell is displayed, so if it's slow to complete it will adversely affect the collection view's scrolling performance.

As a rule of thumb, you should restrict the use of this function to updating the contents of the cell based on selections, for example setting or removing checkboxes.

Cell-, Section-, and Item-Related UICollectionViewDataSource Methods

Four main methods, listed in Table 5-6, are concerned with providing that information. Two of the methods are required.

Table 5-6. Cell, Section, And Item Methods Of The UICollectionViewDataSource Protocol

Method	Purpose	Returns	Required?
numberOfSections InCollectionView(_:)	Returns the number of sections in the collection view	NSInteger	No
collectionView(_: numberOfItemsInSection:)	Returns the number of items in the given section	NSInteger	Yes
collectionView(_: cellForItemAtIndexPath:)	Returns a UICollectionViewCell for the item at the index path provided	UICollection ViewCell	Yes
collectionView(_: viewForSupplementary ElementOfKind:atIndexPath:)	Returns a UICollectionReusableView to use as the supplementary view for the item at the index path provided	UICollection ReusableView	No

Supplementary views are optional and only need to be provided if your collection view layout requires them.

Although the collectionView needs to know the number of sections required, the default value is 1, which is why you'll often see numberOfSectionsInCollectionView omitted for simple collection views.

The Thing to Bear in Mind About dataSource Methods

Although table and collection views look simple enough on the surface, there's a lot going on underneath. Key to a good user experience is scrolling that is smooth and instantaneous. One of the main complaints you'll hear about iPad rivals, for instance, is that their scrolling stutters and is jerky.

In order for the views to scroll smoothly, your dataSource must be prepared to provide data *as soon as it's asked for*. Delays in returning data mean delays in drawing the cells and updating the view's layout—and that means jerks and stutters in the user interface.

Making the data available immediately can have various forms, caching data queries being an obvious one. And needless to say, retrieving live tableView or collectionView data from a network source is a *spectacularly* bad idea.

If your data isn't available immediately, it'll probably be necessary to provide placeholder information and go back to update missing values later, when the data becomes available.

UITableView has three sets of methods that can be used for this: reloadData reloads the whole table, while reloadRowsAtIndexPath updates specific rows. reloadSectionIndexTitles and reloadSections:withRowAnimation: update the specified sections.

UICollectionViews handles updates in a very similar fashion: reloadData reloads the whole of the collection view, reloadSections: does the same for a specific section, and reloadItemsAtIndexPaths: reloads a number of specific items.

Implementing the dataSource and delegate Protocols

A common pattern is for the view controller that is responsible for the view in which the table or collection view appears to act as the dataSource and delegate, although read on in this chapter as to why that might not always be a good idea!

> **Note**   Everything in this section applies equally to both UITableView and UICollectionView, so for "table view" read "collection view," and vice versa.

In order for a table view to use a class as its dataSource or delegate, the class has to conform to the UITableViewDataSource and UITableViewDelegate protocols. There are two ways of doing this: the first is to declare the class's conformance and implement the required methods in the body of the class, as shown in Listing 5-4.

Listing 5-4. An Example Class Acting as UITableViewDataSource and UITableViewDelegate

```
class ViewController: UIViewController, UITableViewDataSource, UITableViewDelegate {

    // mark: -
    // mark: UIViewController methods

        // ...
        // UIViewController methods here
        // ...
```

```
// mark: -
// mark: UITableView methods

func numberOfSectionsInTableView(tableView: UITableView) -> Int {
    ...
}

func tableView(tableView: UITableView, numberOfRowsInSection section: Int) -> Int {
    ...
}

func tableView(tableView: UITableView, cellForRowAtIndexPath indexPath: ↵
NSIndexPath) -> UITableViewCell {
    ...
}

}
```

A "Swiftier" way to do this is to add an extension to the UIViewController, as shown in Listing 5-5.

Listing 5-5. Using an Extension for Protocols

```
import UIKit

class ViewController: UIViewController {

    // ...
    // view controller methods here

}

extension ViewController: UITableViewDataSource, UITableViewDelegate {

    func numberOfSectionsInTableView(tableView: UITableView) -> Int {
        ...
    }

    func tableView(tableView: UITableView, numberOfRowsInSection section: Int) -> Int {
        ...
    }

    func tableView(tableView: UITableView, cellForRowAtIndexPath indexPath: ↵
    NSIndexPath) -> UITableViewCell {
        ...
    }

}
```

Laying out your code in this way makes a clearer separation between the UIViewController methods and the dataSource/delegate functions—and makes it easier to refactor these functions out into a separate class if you need to do this later.

All About indexPaths

Table and collection views describe their layouts in terms of instances of the `NSIndexPath` class. Technically, these are representations of paths to nodes within a collection of nested arrays.

However, that's an extremely complicated description of what `NSIndexPath` objects are in the context of views, so I'd stick to thinking of them in much more simple terms.

As far as a `tableView` is concerned, an `indexPath` has two properties: a `section` and a `row`, shown in Figure 5-12. Both of these are instances of `Int`.

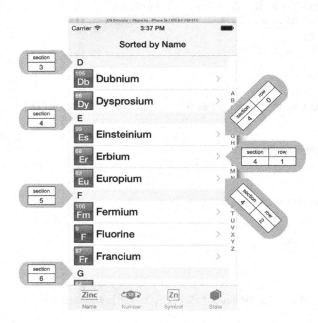

Figure 5-12. indexPath sections and rows

A `collectionView` thinks of an `indexPath` in very similar ways, but instead of `rows`, we refer to `items`. So in the context of a collection view, we refer to `itemAtIndexPath` rather than `cellAtIndexPath`.

As you can see, the table uses `indexPaths` to identify `sections` and `rows`. The iPhone Simulator is running Apple's The Elements sample code, and it's scrolled down to the elements beginning with the letter *D*.

The elements are grouped in sections according to their first letter. Because D is the fourth letter of the alphabet, the elements beginning with D appear in section 3 (remember, `indexPath` numbering, as with `NSArrays` and so on, starts at 0).

There happen to be three elements beginning with the letter *E* (including the fantastically named *einsteinium*—atomic weight 252, discovered in 1952—the app has all the details). These are placed in rows 0, 1, and 2 (again, `indexPath` rows start at 0). This allows each row to be uniquely identified in the table. In the case of einsteinium, it's found in the `indexPath` with `section == 3` and `row == 0`.

Creating indexPaths is somewhat fiddly, so the UITableView class extends NSIndexPath with a category that provides some convenience methods for creating indexPaths with sections and rows. One of these is indexPathForRow:inSection. Listing 5-6 shows a (somewhat contrived) example of the kind of thing you could do to locate a specific cell.

Listing 5-6. Locating a Specific Cell

```
func findEinsteiniumCellContents() {

    let einsteinIndexPath = NSIndexPath(forRow: 1, inSection: 3)

    let einsteinCell = tableView.cellForRowAtIndexPath(einsteinIndexPath)

    let elementName = einsteinCell?.textLabel?.text

    print("The element name is \(elementName)")

}
```

The Model-View-Controller Design Pattern

To the untutored eye, an iOS application opened in Xcode looks like a mess of code. With a bit of familiarity, though, it's possible to discern that different aspects of the application have different functions.

At the front end, the user interface presents information to, and receives input from, the user. We typically think of a "user" as being a human, but the analogy still works if the user is in fact another system, as would be the case if the interface were an API.

Behind the scenes, virtually all applications contain data of some form or another. Sometimes that data is sourced externally, such as the HTML that a web browser displays. Other times, the data is maintained internally to the application. Storing the application state such as high scores is an example.

Sitting between the two, you need some logic—the application logic—to get and present data to the user interface, and to receive and process input from the user. You also need logic to manage the internal state of the application.

That "division of labor" has been formalized into an application architecture pattern called the *model-view-controller* pattern, illustrated in Figure 5-13. It divides the application into three areas:

- *Views*: In iOS terms, these are the views (or interfaces) that are created in Interface Builder or programmatically within the code.

- *Controllers*: Controllers provide the application's internal logic. They tend to be easier to spot in iOS apps because they often have names such as ScoreTableViewController.

- *Models*: Models manage the data within the application. A model can be as simple as an NSArray containing some NSStrings or a full-blown Core Data setup.

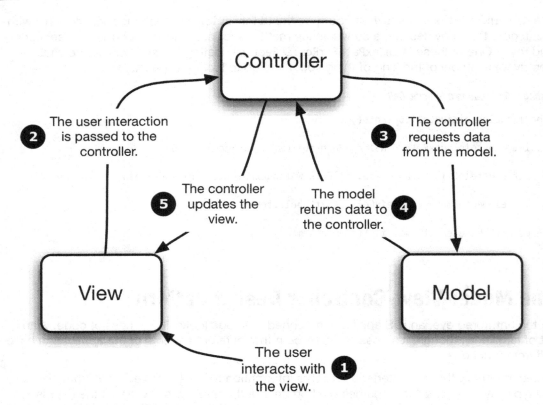

Figure 5-13. The model-view-controller pattern

Crudely speaking, the controllers fetch and process data from the models that gets passed to the views for consumption by the user. The user interacts with the views, and the results of those interactions are handled by the controllers.

Various analogies have been rolled out to illustrate the model-view-controller pattern, but the one that works best for me is the process that goes into making a movie.

Before you can go watch a movie, someone needs to write it. So the process starts with a screenwriter pouring out their soul over a typewriter and creating a script. That's the model: it's the source of the data that will later be used to create the cinematic experience.

In order to bring the script to life, you need actors. (Okay, the analogy breaks down slightly if you're thinking about the latest Pixar blockbuster, but animated characters still need voices, right?) They're the views, responsible for presenting the data of the script to the audience (via the medium of the camera, of course).

The person who sits between the writer and the actors—the controller in our programming analogy—is the director. The director is responsible for interpreting the script and telling the actors how to go about presenting it.

There's room for analogic subtlety here, as well. Good actors will take the director's direction along with the script's dialogue and add their own interpretation that takes the performance from something resembling a tree to one that will win them an Oscar.

That's where the interfaces come in. Consider the graceful gradients and subtle shading of the iOS interface, versus the, well, less-graceful and less-subtle interfaces of certain mobile devices that weren't designed in Cupertino...

Why Use the Model-View-Controller Pattern?

At first, the MVC pattern might seem like an unnecessary complication, especially for small applications. But thinking about—and building—applications in this way brings some benefits:

- *Modularity*: Each functional element of the application manages its own area of concern. The models deal with reading and writing of data, while the views handle presenting the information. This means that changes to one functional element don't necessarily affect others. You could completely change the underlying database engine, for example, and the views would remain the same.

- *Multiple views*: Consider the differences in the user interface between the iPhone and the iPad. If your application's logic were embedded in the views, you'd need to create it twice—once for the smaller screen of the iPhone, and again for the bigger screen of the iPad. By sticking with the MVC pattern, the same set of models and controllers can feed *both* versions of the interface.

- *Efficiencies*: Separating out the layers of the application allows for tricks such as threading and background processing. You can kick off a data-retrieval process while the views are still loading, for example, to take advantage of the iOS device's multitasking capabilities.

- *Testability*: By breaking applications into discrete areas, you can test each one individually. If a `tableView` relies on a `dataSource`, as part of the process of testing the table you can substitute the datasource with a "stand-in"object that returns known values. This means that you can pinpoint the source of any errors much more easily.

- *Reuse*: If your application involves the use of several table or collection views, you can reduce duplication of code and features by creating a single `dataSource` or `delegate` to serve several views. Much of the supporting framework that an individual view needs will be common with others. Less code means fewer sources of bugs, and less to maintain.

MVC and iOS

iOS is a model-view-controller-centric framework, although compared to many SDKs— particularly web frameworks—the MVC nature of iOS is sometimes a bit hidden. This will be especially the case if you've come to iOS from web frameworks such as Rails or Django. These make the separation of each layer very obvious. Each one has a set of files in separate directories called `models`, `views`, and `controllers`.

iOS, on the other hand, is more subtle. You can create views with XIB files, which are clearly views. But you can also create views programmatically with code inside view controllers, and that's where things start to get potentially confusing. Similarly, a `tableView` or `collectionView`'s data comes from a model, but that model could be as "extracted" as a SQLite database managed by Core Data, or as "embedded" as an `Array` created in the `viewDidLoad` method inside a view controller!

The key to staying sane with MVC in the iOS world is to remember that MVC is a conceptual framework, rather than something more absolute, such as a set of directories. If you bear in mind that the table's data comes from a model, and that model is actually the `Array` mentioned, you'll still be thinking (and working) in an MVC way.

MVC, tableViews, and collectionViews

The obvious question is now, "How does MVC fit with table and collection views?"

Fortunately, the answer is relatively straightforward. The table or collection view itself is the view. It presents the user interface and intercepts user interaction such as taps and scrolling flicks.

The data that the table or collection view presents comes from the model. As mentioned, that could be as simple as a single `Array` that you create as you load the view, or something a lot more complex involving Core Data or information retrieved from an external network source.

The controller elements are the object(s) that act as the `tableView` or `collectionView`'s `delegate` and `dataSource`. The `delegate` receives messages from the table or collection view and deals with events such as a user tapping an item or swiping a cell. The `dataSource` "feeds" the table or collection view its data by retrieving it from the model.

Improving the App Structure

If a view controller is also acting as the `datasource` and `delegate` of a table or collection view, it can rapidly grow to the point where you begin to suffer from "Massive View Controller" syndrome. It's not unheard of for view controllers to grow to hundreds of lines long (the record for the largest one I've ever seen is 6,500 lines, and I'd just like to make it really clear that I wasn't responsible for it getting that big!)

Massive View Controllers are a problem for projects for a number of reasons: they violate the "single responsibility principle" of object-orientated design; they're hard to test; they increase the risk of source control conflicts; and if they're too big they can simply cause Xcode to keel over and crash when you try to edit them.

It follows, then, that splitting up your large classes into smaller ones can help prevent some or all of these problems.

How to Split Out Datasources and Delegates

Because you're responsible for connecting table and collection views with their datasources and delegates, you're not restricted to only using the view controller that manages the table or collection view in the view hierarchy.

Assuming that you're beginning with the datasource and delegate methods in the view controller, then there are X steps to separating things out

Step 1: Create a Separate Class

Start by creating a separate class. I usually name mine something along the lines of ContactsTableHelper to make it clear which table it's working with, and that it's acting as both datasource and delegate.

Next, move the datasource and delegate methods into this new class. You'll need to declare that the new class will conform to the dataSource and delegate protocols; and remove this from the view controller:

```
class TableViewHelper : NSObject, UITableViewDataSource, UITableViewDelegate {
}
```

Step 2: Link the Table View to the New Class

With the new class created, you need to connect the table view to it. If you've created the link in code, this needs to be updated by adding a property for the new class:

```
let tableViewHelper = TableViewHelper()
```

Then you can update the dataSource and delegate properties of your tableView from

```
tableView.dataSource = self
tableView.delegate = self
```

to

```
tableView.dataSource = tableViewHelper
tableView.delegate = tableViewHelper
```

If you've made the connections visually, the process is slightly different. First, in your Storyboard you'll need to drag an Object placeholder from the Objects browser to the view hierarchy on the left, as shown in Figure 5-14.

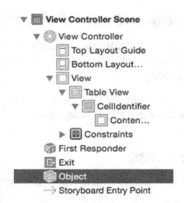

Figure 5-14. Adding an Object Placeholder

With the new Object placeholder selected, switch to the Identity inspector, and update its Class value to TableViewHelper, as shown in Figure 5-15.

Figure 5-15. Updating the Class

Now you can connect the tableView's dataSource and delegate properties by Ctrl-Clicking in the tableView, and dragging over to the TableViewHelper placeholder, as shown in Figure 5-16.

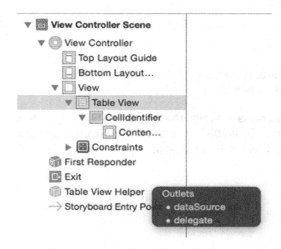

Figure 5-16. Reconnecting the dataSource and Delegates

Once connected, this will lazily instantiate an instance of the `TableViewHelper` class when the table is loaded and use it as the `dataSource` and `delegate` of the table view instead of the view controller.

Summary

This chapter has covered a lot of fairly heavy conceptual stuff, but all of the concepts tie back into table and collection views in some way. The data that is displayed by a `tableView` or `collectionView` is provided by the `dataSource`, while the user's interaction with the view is handled by the `delegate`. Both of these are examples of the delegation design pattern, while the division of labor between the `tableView` or `collectionView`, its controllers, and the underlying data is the model-view-controller architecture pattern in action.

Both the `dataSource` and `delegate` functions are defined by their respective protocols: `UITableViewDataSource`, `UITableViewDelegate`, `UICollectionViewDataSource`, and `UICollectionViewDelegate`. Building `tableViews` and `collectionViews` is a process of implementing (at least) the required methods, and often some of the optional ones as well.

Armed with an understanding of where the data comes from, and how the views handle interactions, you're ready to dive into the details and start the process of customization.

Chapter 6

How the Table Cell Fits Together

In this chapter, you're going to take a detailed look at table cells and how they work. In order to be able to customize them, it's important to understand the anatomy of cells, and how they're created and reused.

You'll see the following:

- The internal structure of a table cell
- The standard cell types that come for free with UITableView
- How to create prototype cells
- The configuration of default cell content
- The use of accessory views
- How the cell creation and recycling process works

This covers everything you need to know in order to create default-styled cells and perform basic configuration of them. Configuring cells is often a case of knowing when to intervene in the creation and reuse process. Later in Chapters 7 and 8, you'll build on this when you create customized cells.

Understanding the Anatomy of a UITableViewCell

The first thing to bear in mind about UITableViewCells is that they are UIView objects. The UITableViewCell class inherits from UIView, which means that the features of UIViews are available to you in UITableViewCells. Figure 6-1 shows the class hierarchy of UITableViewCell.

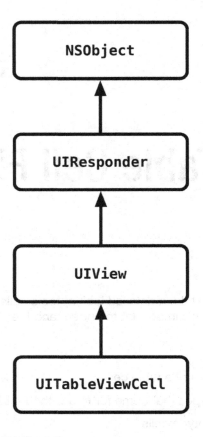

Figure 6-1. *The class hierarchy of UITableViewCell*

Because UIView inherits in turn from UIResponder, this also means that it's possible to interact with cells by using gestures. I'll show you some of the effects that this enables in Chapter 9.

Basic Structure of the Cell

The vanilla cell has five component parts, shown in Figure 6-2.

- A *frame* and *bounds*, which describe the cell's location and size
- The *backgrounds*, which you'll look at in the next section
- The *cell content*
- An optional *accessory view*
- An automatically placed *editing control*, which appears when the cell is in editing mode

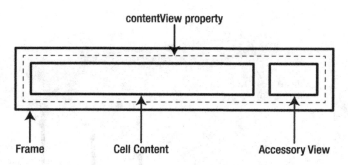

Figure 6-2. *The basic layout of a cell in normal mode*

The content of the cell can be accessed en masse through the contentView property, which is a UIView. You can add and remove subviews, and the contentView will take care of moving things around to allow the editing control to fit.

When switched to editing mode, the cell's contentView is reduced in width by about 40 points, and an editing control is inserted at the left side, as shown in Figure 6-3.

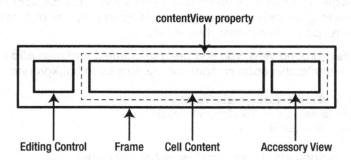

Figure 6-3. *The basic layout of a cell in editing mode*

The editing control can be either a green insertion control or a red deletion control.

Note   When designing custom cells that will be edited, it's important to make sure that the layout of the content view can cope with being automatically resized. Chapter 8 covers this topic.

The Cell's Background Views

The cell has several background views, which are "stacked" along the Z-axis, as shown in Figure 6-4.

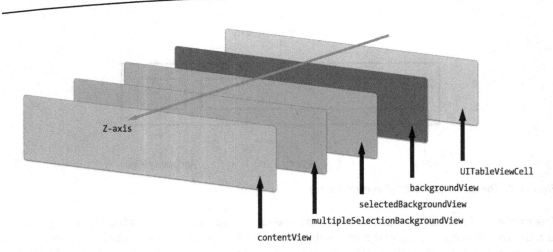

Figure 6-4. *The background views*

Opaque content in upper views will obscure the content of the lower views, and empty views are effectively invisible. The two selection background views, `selectedBackgroundView` and `multipleSelectionBackgroundView`, normally have an alpha property of 0; this is toggled between 0 and 1 in response to cell selection events.

To add a specific background view, you first need to create it and then add it to the relevant cell property. For example, this code snippet will create a cyan background:

```
let backgroundView = UIView(frame: cell.frame)
backgroundView.backgroundColor = UIColor.cyanColor()
cell.backgroundView = backgroundView
```

You can also use this approach to add images as backgrounds:

```
if let selectedIimage = UIImage(named:"selectedBg") {
    cell.selectedBackgroundView = UIImageView(image: selectedImage)
}
```

The image will be toggled on and off as the cell is selected and deselected.

Because the background views are arranged along the Z-axis, it's very important that you only add custom controls to the cell's `contentView`. Adding them to the cell itself will give inconsistent results if they become obscured by one of the background views. There may also be layout problems caused by the cell's `contentView` being resized to show in-cell editing controls when the table goes into editing mode.

> **Caution**   Despite the power of the graphics processor in iOS devices, compositing the various
> layers in cells does come with some overhead. This is especially the case when dealing with layers
> with transparency such as background images. Basically, the more areas of transparency there are
> in layers, the slower the compositing will be.
>
> To make your table views as performant as possible, it's important to keep transparency to a
> minimum wherever you can. This is covered in more detail in Chapter 8.

Content and Accessory Views

Content and accessory views are instances of UIView, which means that they have all the
properties and methods of a "normal" UIView. You'll be exploiting these properties and
methods when you go on to create customized cells.

Designing Prototype Cells

Before cells can be created by the table view's datasource, you need to build prototypes,
which you can think of as being the templates from which new cells are created.

In simple situations, it may be enough to use one or more of the four standard cell types
that UITableView provides for free. As your app interface becomes more sophisticated, the
standard types may not be sufficient, and you'll want to create custom cells. The custom cell
process is covered in detail in Chapter 8.

Even if you're only going to use standard cells, it's still important to understand the options
for creating their prototypes. You have three options:

- Creating cells visually in separate XIB files, one for each cell type
- Laying out cells visually in Storyboards
- In code, by creating instances of standard cell types and updating the
  in-cell controls

Although different, the three approaches all have the same end result, so which you decide
to use is a largely a matter of personal preference. We'll look at each one in turn.

The Code for This Chapter

The sample app for this chapter is set up with a tabbed interface, each tab demonstrating
a table using one of the different techniques for cell creation. Each view controller has a
basic set of data wired up ready, so you can use them as a starting point for your own
customization.

Creating Prototype Cells in XIB Files

This approach relies on creating the prototype cell in a standalone XIB file, then associating the XIB with a cell identifier as part of the table view configuration process.

Note   The table created using prototype cells in XIB files is displayed in the XIB table tab in the sample app. The view controller for this tab is XibTableViewController. All the associated source and XIB files can be found in the Xib-based table cells folder in Xcode.

As the table view is set up, the XIB will be loaded and "inflated" to create prototype instances, which the datasource can then use by accessing the data outlets and setting these with the values from the cell's model.

The process has five steps:

- Creating the XIB file
- Adding the cell object into the XIB
- Laying out the prototype cell
- Registering the XIB with a cell identifier as the table view is configured
- Creating and configuring instances of the cell in the datasource methods

You can create tables with multiple types of cells using this technique, simply by repeating the process for each different kind of cell and giving it a different identifier. Then in the tableView's dataSource you can dequeue and configure the relevant cell type based on the data in your table's model.

Creating the XIB File

Creating a new XIB file isn't complicated: select the File ➤ New ➤ File menu option and then the Empty item from the User Interface section, as shown in Figure 6-5.

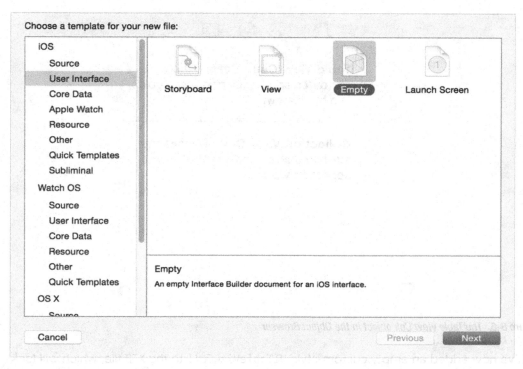

Figure 6-5. *Creating a new XIB file*

Give the file a name (I'm using `XibCell.xib`), and then click the Create button.

Adding the Cell Object to the XIB

With an empty XIB file, you're now ready to add the table view cell. From the `Object Browser`, select the `Table View Cell` object, as shown in Figure 6-6, and drag it out into the canvas.

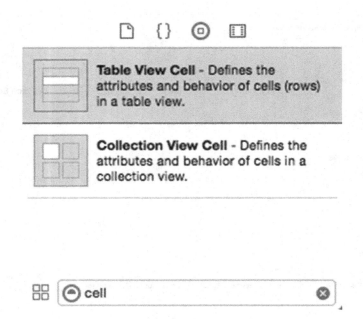

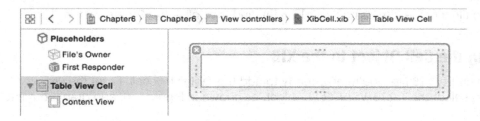

Figure 6-6. The Table View Cell object in the Object Browser

You've now added an empty custom-style `UITableViewCell` to the XIB file, which will look like Figure 6-7.

Figure 6-7. The new cell in the Canvas

Laying Out the Prototype Cell

At this point, you're ready to configure its layout. You'll look at creating customizing cells in detail in Chapter 7. If you only need one of the four standard cell types, you can quickly change this by selecting it from the Style drop-down in the Attributes inspector, as shown in Figure 6-8.

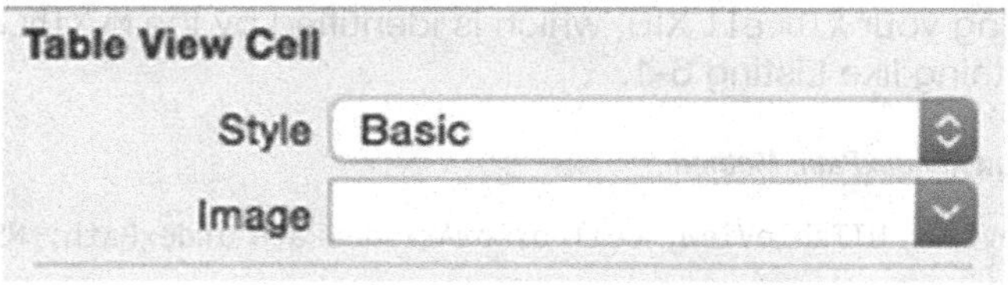

Figure 6-8. Selecting the cell's style

This will convert the cell into one of the four standard types. There are more details about how to access the outlets in each one of the standard styles later in this chapter. For now, select the Basic type so that you get a cell with a built-in Title label.

You'll also need to set the cell's Identifier, which you'll use in a moment to identify the cell to the table. This is an arbitrary String value, but it's important!

Set it to something descriptive because it will be the table view's link between the XIB and the cell object, as you'll see next. In the sample project, I've set it to MyXibCell, and created a property for it:

```
let kCellIdentifier = "MyXibCell"
```

Telling the Table View About the XIB

With the cell created, you need to inform the table view that it's going to load its prototype cells from a XIB file. This has to be done *before* the datasource makes any attempt to dequeue a cell from the table, so a good place to set this up is in the view controller's viewDidLoad method.

Add the following to the XibTableViewController's viewDidLoad: method:

```
tableView.registerNib(UINib(nibName: "XibCell", bundle: nil), forCellReuseIdentifier: ↩
"MyXibCell")
```

Here, you're informing the table view that it should use the contents of the XibCell nib file for cells that are identified with MyXibCell. The table view will expect that the top-level object in the XIB is an instance of UITableViewCell or a UITableViewCell subclass.

If you have several cell types, you can associate them with the table view by repeating this process, remembering to provide the appropriate (and unique) cell identifier each time.

Creating and Configuring Cells

With the cell type(s) registered with the table view, it's time to update the cellForRowAtIndexPath: method to dequeue and configure the cells.

This doesn't differ significantly from the process you've seen in previous chapters: dequeue the cell with the correct identifier, configure it, and return it to the table view.

Assuming you're using your XibCell XIB, which is identified by the MyXibCell identifier, the code will look something like Listing 6-1.

Listing 6-1. The cellForRowAtIndexPath: Method

```
func tableView(tableView: UITableView, cellForRowAtIndexPath indexPath: NSIndexPath) ↵
 -> UITableViewCell {

    let cell = tableView.dequeueReusableCellWithIdentifier("MyCellIdentifier", ↵
  forIndexPath: indexPath)

    // Configure the cell...
    cell.textLabel!.text = tableData[indexPath.row]

    return cell
}
```

If you added a standard cell type to your XIB, then it will be dequeued with all the controls ready for use, and you can configure it as normal in the cellForRowAtIndexPath: method. Configuring custom cells is covered in detail in Chapter 8.

Creating Prototype Cells in Storyboards

Laying out the design of your cells can be easier when it's done visually. In the section above, you looked at the process of doing this in a standalone XIB file, but if you prefer, you can do exactly the same in a Storyboard instead.

When you look at a UITableView in a Storyboard, you'll see that it comes with an empty section for prototype content, as shown in Figure 6-9.

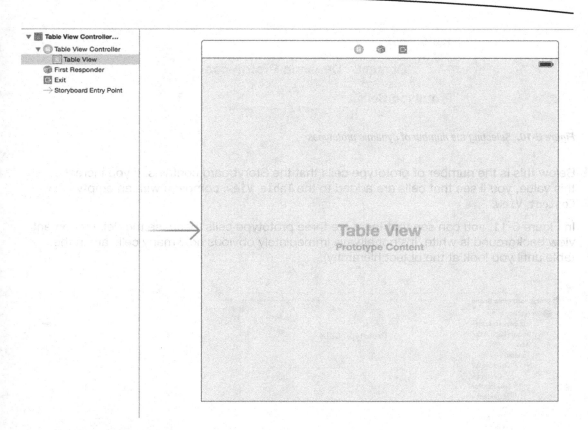

Figure 6-9. The Prototype Content section

As the name suggests, this is where you can create prototype cells that are then instantiated and dequeued by the table's dataSource.

You can use this technique to create one or more prototype cells. The main limitation is that if you have more cells than will fit in the Storyboard's Table View, they can become a bit unwieldy to manage. In this situation, you may be better off using separate XIB files.

Creating Prototype Cells

To add a prototype cell, select the Table View in the Storyboard, then switch to the Attributes Inspector, shown in Figure 6-10. In the top section, you'll see a drop-down that allows you to switch between dynamic prototypes or static cells (creating static table views is covered in Chapter 13).

Table View

Content   Dynamic Prototypes

Prototype Cells   3

Figure 6-10. Selecting the number of dynamic prototypes

Below this is the number of prototype cells that the Storyboard contains. If you increase
this value, you'll see that cells are added to the Table View, complete with an empty
Content View.

In Figure 6-11, you can see that there are three prototype cells (because the default content
view background is white, it's not always immediately obvious how many cells are in the
table until you look at the object hierarchy).

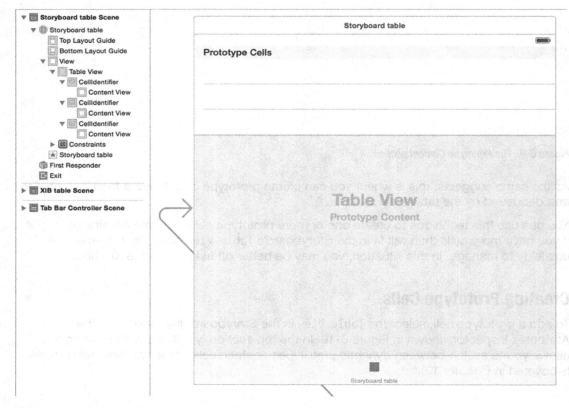

Figure 6-11. The prototype cells in the Table View

Setting Up the Prototype Cells

With the prototype cells added, now you can start configuring them. By default, they arrive in the Storyboard as instances of the Custom cell type, but you can change that by selecting the Table View Cell in the object hierarchy and choosing a different style from the Style dropdown in the Attributes Inspector.

This will update the prototype cell in the Storyboard. In Figure 6-12, there are five prototypes, with types of (from top to bottom) Basic, Right Detail, Left Detail, Subtitle, and Custom. In the screenshot from sample project, the cell identifiers have been updated to match the cell types, which you'll do in the next section.

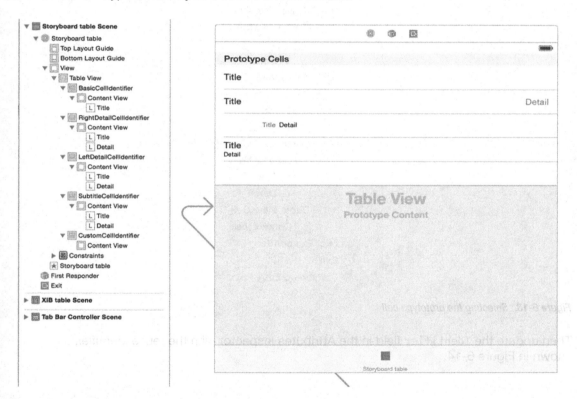

Figure 6-12. *The Table View with five prototype cells*

As you can see, the standard cell types are shown in the Storyboard with their controls. You can select this and change their styles by setting values in the Attributes Inspector.

Telling the Table View About the Prototype Cells

In order for the table view to be able to use the prototype cells, you have to provide a way of referencing which particular cell should be used for which index path value.

This is done by setting the prototype cell's `identifier` attribute in the Storyboard. When dequeuing a cell, the `dataSource` will automatically retrieve the prototype with the matching identifier from the Storyboard.

To set the prototype's identifier, select the Table View Cell object in the hierarchy, as shown in Figure 6-13.

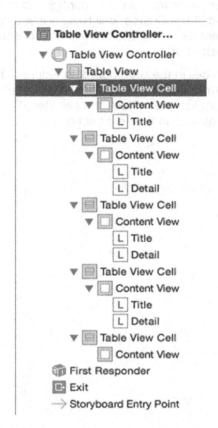

Figure 6-13. *Selecting the prototype cell*

Then update the Identifier field in the Attributes inspector with the reuse identifier, as shown in Figure 6-14.

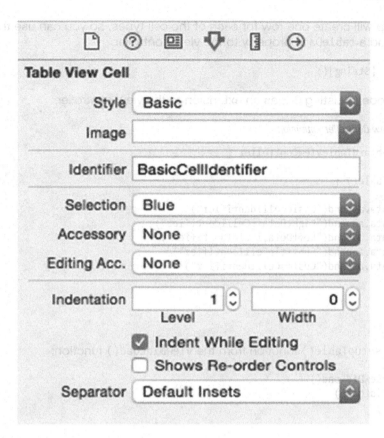

Figure 6-14. *Updating the prototype cell's Identifier*

This will also update the name of the cell in the Object tree, as shown in Figure 6-15.

Figure 6-15. *The updated prototype cell*

The sample app will create one row for each of the cell types, so you can use that as your source data. Add a `tableData` property to the view controller:

```
var tableData = [String]()
```

Now add the code in Listing 6-2 as an extension to the view controller.

Listing 6-2. The View Controller Extension

```
extension StoryboardTableViewController {

    func setupTable() {

        tableData.append("BasicCellIdentifier")
        tableData.append("RightDetailCellIdentifier")
        tableData.append("LeftDetailCellIdentifier")
        tableData.append("SubtitleCellIdentifier")
        tableData.append("CustomCellIdentifier")

    }

}
```

Finally, call the `setupTable()` function from the `viewDidLoad()` function:

```
override func viewDidLoad() {
    super.viewDidLoad()
    setupTable()
}
```

Creating and Configuring Cells

With the cell identifier set, the `cellForRowAtIndexPath:` method will now be able to create instances from your prototype. The key is to use the cell's `Identifier` attribute to create (or dequeue) the correct prototype and then configure the cell from the data model in the usual way.

Listing 6-3 shows how to do this for your newly-created cell type's `BasicCellIdentifier` cells.

Listing 6-3. The cellForRowAtIndexPath: Method

```
override func tableView(tableView: UITableView, cellForRowAtIndexPath indexPath: ↵
  NSIndexPath) -> UITableViewCell {

    let cellIdentifier = tableData[indexPath.row]

    let cell = tableView.dequeueReusableCellWithIdentifier(cellIdentifier, ↵
    forIndexPath: indexPath) as! UITableViewCell

    switch cellIdentifier {
```

```
case "BasicCellIdentifier" :
    cell.textLabel!.text = "Basic cell"

case "RightDetailCellIdentifier":
    cell.textLabel!.text = "Right detail cell"
    cell.detailTextLabel!.text = "Detail text label"

case "LeftDetailCellIdentifier" :
    cell.textLabel!.text = "Left detail cell"
    cell.detailTextLabel!.text = "Detail text label"

case "SubtitleCellIdentifier" :
    cell.textLabel!.text = "Subtitle cell"
    cell.detailTextLabel!.text = "Detail text label"

default :   // Handles CustomCellIdentifier by process of elimination
    print("The default custom cell type is empty and has no controls")

}

    return cell

}
```

This method gets the item from the data array for the current index path, and uses that as the cellIdentifier. Then it switches over the item and configures the cell accordingly. The end result looks like Figure 6-16.

Figure 6-16. The custom cells

Creating Prototype Cells in Code

Creating prototype cells in code is normally used for custom instances of UITableViewCell subclasses. If you use this approach to create "standard" UITableViewCells, you're restricted to the UITableViewStyle.Default style and won't be able to use cells with subtitles, etc.

The process is very similar to the visual methods: you register the cell class with the table view using an identifier, and then you create or dequeue an instance of the class in the cellForRowAtIndexPath: method.

Registering the Cell Class with the Table View

This must happen before the dataSource attempts to create or dequeue cells, so it is normally done as the view is set up in the viewDidLoad method or similar.

To register a cell class with the table, use the registerClass:forCellReuseIdentifier: method with the appropriate identifier.

For example, to register the UITableViewCell class with the StandardCell identifier, add the following to (for example) the tableViewController's viewDidLoad method:

```
tableView.registerClass(UITableViewCell.self, forCellReuseIdentifier: "StandardCell")
```

If you had a custom UITableViewCell subclass, you'd use this in the registerClass: forCellReuseIdentifier: method:

```
tableView.registerClass(MyCustomCellClass.self, forCellReuseIdentifier: "CustomCell")
```

To *deregister* a class for a given cellIdentifier, you pass nil to the registerClass: forCellIdentifier: method:

```
tableView.registerClass(nil, forCellReuseIdentifier: "CustomCell")
```

Creating and Configuring Cells

Once the cell classes and identifiers are registered with the table view, the cellForRowAtIndexPath: method will now be able to create instances on demand.

Use the cell's Identifier attribute to create (or dequeue) an instance of the correct class, and then configure the cell from the data model in the usual way.

Listing 6-4 shows how to do this for MyCustomCellClass cells.

Listing 6-4. The cellForRowAtIndexPath: Method

```
func tableView(tableView: UITableView, cellForRowAtIndexPath indexPath: NSIndexPath) ↵
  -> UITableViewCell {

    let cell = tableView.dequeueReusableCellWithIdentifier("CustomCell", ↵
    forIndexPath: indexPath) as! MyCustomCellClass

    // Configure the cell...
    cell.myCustomOutlet!.text = tableData[indexPath.row]

    return cell
}
```

Note that the dequeueReusableCellWithIdentifier:forIndexPath: method returns a vanilla UITableViewCell instance, so you will need to downcast this to your custom class with the as! method.

Working with Standard Cell Types

UITableViews come with four standard cell types, and for many applications these may be all you need. The four styles have constant names, which unfortunately aren't particularly descriptive:

- UITableViewCellStyleDefault
- UITableViewCellStyleValue1
- UITableViewCellStyleValue2
- UITableViewCellStyleSubtitle

This section details the four types and then shows you how to select the one you want.

Using UITableViewCellStyleDefault

As the name suggests, UITableViewCellStyleDefault is the default cell style for a standard, out-of-the-box UITableView. It provides three areas (shown in Figure 6-17):

- A UIImageView called imageView at the left end of the cell. This is optional; if an image view isn't present in the cell, the cell content will align to the left.
- A UILabel called textLabel, which holds the cell content.
- An optional UIView called accessoryView that can show one of the standard accessory view indicators, a custom image by adding a UIImageView as a subView, or a control such as a UIButton.

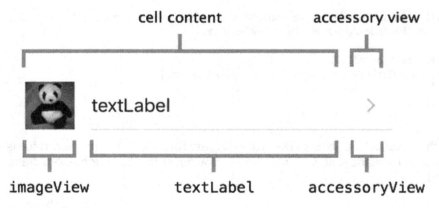

Figure 6-17. UITableViewCellStyleDefault

As with all the other standard cell styles, the textLabel can be formatted by changing the UILabel properties such as font, text alignment, and color. Although the layout of the default cells may be fixed, this formatting does enable you to apply some degree of customization.

The content of the textLabel is accessed through its `text` property:

```
cell.textLabel!.text = "textLabel"
```

Similarly, the image is set by accessing the imageView's `image` property:

```
cell.imageView!.image = UIImage(named:"panda")
```

If you're working with a prototype cell in a Storyboard, then the `UITableViewCellDefault` corresponds to `Basic` style in the Attributes Inspector (see Figure 6-18).

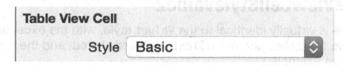

Figure 6-18. *Selecting a UITableViewCellBasic style in Interface Builder*

Using UITableViewCellStyleValue1

The `Value1` cell style is similar to the `Default` type, but includes an extra, optional `UILabel` called `detailTextLabel` and an optional `imageView`. Figure 6-19 shows an example.

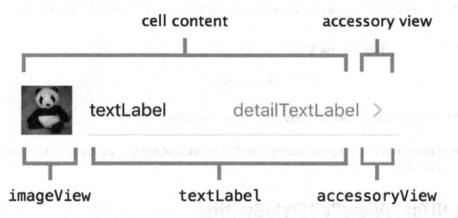

Figure 6-19. *UITableViewCellStyleValue1*

The `textLabels` will attempt to handle restricted space but won't always result in the desired effect, as shown in Figure 6-20. If the automatic results aren't acceptable, this might be a cue for you to think about implementing a custom cell style.

Figure 6-20. *Truncation of cell content*

If you're working with a prototype cell in a Storyboard, then the UITableViewCellDefault corresponds to Right Detail style in the Attributes Inspector (see Figure 6-21).

Figure 6-21. Selecting a UITableViewCellValue1 style in Interface Builder

Using UITableViewCellStyleValue2

The Value2 cell style is virtually identical to the Value1 style, with the exception that the default weight of the textLabel and detailTextLabel are altered, and there's no imageView. Figure 6-22 shows an example.

Figure 6-22. UITableViewCellStyleValue2

If you're working with a prototype cell in a Storyboard, then the UITableViewCellDefault corresponds to the Left Detail style in the Attributes Inspector (see Figure 6-23).

Figure 6-23. Selecting a UITableViewCellValue2 style in Interface Builder

I can't ever remember seeing an example of UITableViewCellStyleValue2 in the wild, but it's there if you need it.

Using UITableViewCellStyleSubtitle

The fourth default type is another variation of the other three. It combines textLabel and detailTextLabel with an optional imageView. Figure 6-24 shows this default cell with an image, and Figure 6-25 shows it without an image.

textLabel
this is a very long detail text label

Figure 6-24. UITableViewCellStyleSubtitle with an image

textLabel
this is a very long detail text label

Figure 6-25. UITableViewCellStyleSubtitle without an image

Configuring the Default Cell's Content

A `UITableViewCell` of one of the four default types has a whole range of properties that you can access to configure the content. This section presents four key properties—`textLabel`, `detailTextLabel`, `imageView`, and `contentView`—and then shows an example of using them.

textLabel

The `textLabel` property is a `UILabel`, with text that can be changed. It is generally used as the cell's main title:

```
cell.textLabel!.text = "The main cell text"
```

detailTextLabel

`detailTextLabel` is also a `UILabel`, with text that can be changed. It can act as a subtitle for the cell:

```
cell.detailTextLabel!.text = "The cell subtitle"
```

imageView

The cell's `imageView` is a `UIImageView`. It has an image property that can be passed a `UIImage`, which is then displayed in the cell:

```
if let avatar = UIImage(named:"avatar") {
    cell.imageView!.image = avatar
}
```

contentView

The cell's `contentView` is a `UIView` to which subviews can be added:

```
cell.contentView.addSubview(theView)
```

You'll look at `contentView` in much more detail in Chapter 8.

A common mistake is to try to access these properties directly:

```
cell.textLabel = "Some text"    // This won't work!
```

In order to ensure that the table is as responsive as possible, it's a good idea to make sure that any images are scaled before adding them to the cell. If cells need to rescale images before displaying them, jerky scrolling of the table can result.

Formatting Text in Default Cell Types

Here's an example of setting these properties in practice:

```
cell.textLabel!.textColor = UIColor.blueColor()
cell.detailTextLabel!.font = UIFont(name: "TimesNewRomanPSMT", size: 12)
cell.detailTextLabel!.textColor = UIColor.redColor()
```

This code results in the cell shown in Figure 6-26. I wouldn't necessarily advise using this frankly hideous combination of fonts and colors, but you get the idea.

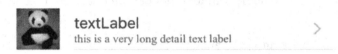

Figure 6-26. Example cell formatting

Working with Accessory Views

UITableViewCell provides three types of accessory views (well, four if you count None as a type). Accessory views are displayed at the right-hand end of the cell. You can also add your own custom accessory view. These are UIViews, which either act as a hint to the user that touching the cell will result in some kind of action or show some information about the cell state.

Tapping an accessory view causes the tableView to call the delegate's accessoryButtonTappedForRowWithIndexPath method. This allows you to trigger actions such as pushing in a new view controller.

As an alternative to using a default accessory view, you can provide a custom view of your own or place a control such as a UIButton into a custom view.

Using UITableViewCellAccessoryDisclosureIndicator

The DisclosureIndicator acts as a hint that touching the cell will result in another table view being displayed, to drill down into a data hierarchy. Figure 6-27 shows how this appears.

Figure 6-27. UITableViewCellAccessoryDisclosureIndicator

Using UITableViewCellAccessoryDetailDisclosureIndicator

The fact that DetailDisclosureIndicator looks like an info button is a hint that touching the cell will result in the display of more data. The display might be another table view, but could be another view of a different type.

When it's tapped, a DetailDisclosureIndicator sends the tableView:accessoryButtonTapped ForRowWithIndexPath message to the table's dataSource. Figure 6-28 shows this.

Figure 6-28. *UITableViewCellAccessoryDetailDisclosureIndicator*

Using UITableViewCellAccessoryCheckmark

The check mark, shown in Figure 6-29, shows that the cell has been selected, either by the user tapping the row or by some data field behind the scenes. This provides a way of selecting and deselecting one or more items in a list. It's a very common user interface pattern for setting configuration items, for example.

Figure 6-29. *UITableViewCellAccessoryCheckmark*

Using UITableViewCellAccessoryNone

As the name suggests, UITableViewCellAccessoryNone doesn't display any accessory view. Figure 6-30 shows an example. Setting this accessory type removes any previously set accessory. You might use this view because there's no further information below this level—or because the cell was previously selected and showed a UITableViewCellAccessoryCheckmark.

Figure 6-30. *UITableViewCellAccessoryNone*

Setting the Accessory View Type

The cell's accessory view is set with the `accessoryType` property:

```
cell.accessoryType = UITableViewCellAccessory.Checkmark
```

The code in Listing 6-5 shows how you might toggle a check mark on and off, depending on the value of some data.

Listing 6-5. Toggling a Cell's Accessory Type

```
let dataItem = tableData[indexPath.row]

if dataItem == "some string that indicates a checkmark is needed" {

  cell.accessoryType = UITableViewCellAccessory.Checkmark;

} else {

  cell.accessoryType = UITableViewCellAccessory.None;

}
```

Apple provides guidelines about which accessory type should be used for what purpose. Although I've never heard of an app being rejected from the App Store because disclosure indicators were used in a nonstandard way, doing so runs the risk of confusing your users. It's probably best to stick with the default behaviors unless there's a very good reason not to.

Using an Accessory View to Show Cell Selection State

Using the presence or absence of a cell accessory view is a perfectly valid way of showing whether a cell is selected. But there is a "gotcha" that can very easily get you if you're not careful.

Think back to the model-view-controller pattern for a moment. Cells are views, and the data that populates the cell exists in the model(s). When you switch a selection indicator on and off, you're doing that to the view—*not* the model.

Cells themselves don't have state. Remember, even in a `tableView` of 99,999 rows, only about 11 cells are created. If you want the selection state to persist the next time that data point is displayed, you *must* update the external data model and then set the selection indicator accordingly.

Similarly, if you set the accessory view state of a cell that is then recycled from the cache, it'll arrive back at the table in the same state it had when the cell was dumped into the cache. That's why it's important to reset accessory views (and later, any controls or views that you've included in your custom cells) every time a row is updated.

Listing 6-6 presents a code snippet from one of my apps, a networked game called TeaWars, that demonstrates this in practice. The table displays a list of peer devices. In the next step, the user can select the ones they want to connect to. Tapping the row fires the didSelectRowAtIndexPath method, which adds that client ID to an NSMutableArray called listOfPlayers.

Listing 6-6. Toggling Cell Selection

```
func tableView(tableView: UITableView, cellForRowAtIndexPath indexPath: NSIndexPath)
-> UITableViewCell {

  let cell = tableView.dequeueReusableCellWithIdentifier(kCellIdentifier,
  forIndexPath:indexPath)

    // Retrieve the ID of the relevant connected client
    let peerID = sessionManager.connectedClients[indexPath.row]

    // Retrieve the displayName of the peer
    cell.textLabel.text = sessionManager.gkSession.displayNameForPeer(peerID)

    // If this peerID is contained in the listOfPlayers, it's been selected
    // so show the checkmark in the cell

    if listOfPlayers.containsObject(peerID) {

        cell.accessoryType = UITableViewCellAccessory.Checkmark

    } else {

        // The peer ID isn't in the list, so it's not selected
        cell.accessoryType = UITableViewCellAccessory.None

    }

    return cell
}
```

As the cells are popped and pushed in and out of the cache, the cellForRowAtIndexPath method checks whether the peer exists in the listOfPlayers array. If it does, it must have been selected, so the cell needs a UITableViewCellAccessoryCheckmark. (The _sessionManager object handles the network communication, so it's not really relevant to this example.)

Creating Custom Accessory Views

Because the cell's accessoryView is an instance of UIView, it's a pretty trivial task to assign your own custom UIView to the cell:

```
if let image = UIImage(named: "imageName") {
    cell.accessoryView = UIImageView(image: image)
}
```

As with the cell's imageView, it's best to make sure any accessoryView image is sized and scaled correctly first. You're not just restricted to images, though; the accessoryView can be a useful place to insert controls such as UIButtons.

Creating and Reusing Cells

Having looked at the various default cell styles that are available, you're probably impatient to start creating custom cell styles of your own. Before you move on to that, though, it's a good idea to explore in more detail how cells are created and managed by the table view itself. Creating custom cells is often a process of knowing when to intervene in the "standard" processes, so knowing what those processes are will help you to figure out what's going on and why.

Memory Limitations

iOS devices pack a lot into small packages. But even though the iPhone and iPad have something like 256,000 times the memory of the Apollo Lunar Module's onboard computer, memory is still a constraint. The small form factor of the devices means there's a limit to the amount of RAM that can be crammed into the casing. As an iOS developer, you need to remain aware of the memory footprint of your apps.

Apps with very small tables, like the SimpleTable app, don't pose much of a problem; you had only 10 rows. But if the app's data comes from a bigger source, you could have thousands—if not millions—of rows. Dealing with that data en masse could quickly overwhelm the limited memory that iOS devices have.

Speed and Smoothness

When the first generation iPhone was first launched back in 2007, one thing that reviewers were consistently blown away by was the smoothness of the interface. Flick a table view, and it smoothly scrolls up and down—no stuttering, hesitation, or jerkiness. Interfaces that don't respond smoothly are *incredibly* obvious to the user (and jerky interface response is one of the main criticisms of iPhone and iPad rivals).

Making content move around smoothly onscreen isn't too big a challenge to today's powerful graphics processors. Making a table (or indeed, any scrolling interface) run smoothly mainly requires that data can be retrieved fast enough to be moved onto the screen, without the screen having to wait for it. Delays in fetching data manifest themselves as stuttering or hesitating scrolling views.

Just-in-Time Creation and Recycling

So, how does iOS deal with limited memory and a need for smoothness and speed? The solution to both problems is ingenious. UITableViews take advantage of an important fact: although a table might have thousands of cells, only a few are visible to the user at any one time.

First, UITableViews use a *just-in-time* approach to creating cells. A new cell is created just before it's required. Each cell is then ready to be displayed, but not so soon that the device memory becomes clogged with cells that aren't yet needed.

Second, after a cell is no longer visible, it's *dequeued* into a cache for reuse. Taking a preexisting cell and updating its content is both quicker and less memory-intensive than creating a brand new one. Instead of creating a brand new cell, the tableView will dequeue and recycle an existing cell, updating its content just before it is displayed onscreen.

The Table View's "Conveyor Belt"

All this can seem a little abstract, so a visual analogy can help. You can think of the tableView as something like a conveyor belt inside a box, as shown in Figure 6-31. The user can move the belt backwards and forwards with a control button. A small section of the belt is visible through a window in the top of the box.

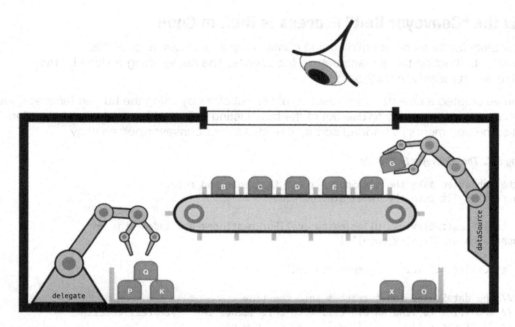

Figure 6-31. The cell production process

The conveyor belt has slots into which different types of cells can be placed. As the cells reach either end of the conveyor belt, they fall off and are sorted into a series of boxes underneath the belt, one box for each different type of cell.

Inside the box, and next to the conveyor, stand two robots. One robot – called dataSource - is responsible for putting cells onto either end of the tray, and other – called delegate - stands ready to tweak the attributes of a cell when required.

Also in the cell is a set of templates for cells; depending on how the table is set up, these might have come from a Storyboard or XIB file, or they might be a description contained in a UITableViewCell subclass.

Just before the user winds the belt to move an empty slot underneath the window, the dataSource robot checks with the model to see what kind of cell is required. Armed with this knowledge, it will look in the relevant tray to see if there are any spare cells lying around.

If the tray is empty, the dataSource robot will quickly create an empty new one by copying from the relevant template. If there is a spare cell lying around in the tray, the robot will pick it up and get it ready to put it onto the conveyor belt.

Immediately before the cell gets placed onto the conveyor belt, the robot checks with the table's model to find what information should be contained in this cell. It writes the content into the cell, and the first arm places it into the slot just in time for the cell to be scrolled into view.

If the user interacts with a cell on the conveyor belt, the delegate robot is responsible for reacting. It might colour in the contents of the cell, or ask the view controller to pop up an alert view or push in a new view.

How the "Conveyor Belt" Process Is Built in Code

Fortunately for those of us building and configuring table views, a lot of this conveyor-belt action takes place behind the scenes. The heavy lifting is done by the cellForRowAtIndexPath method.

If you've created a new UITableViewController subclass by using the built-in template, the subclass is virtually ready to use out of the box. Listing 6-7 provides the template version with some comments I've added so that it relates to our conveyor-belt analogy.

Listing 6-7. The "Conveyor Belt" Code

```
// the tableView asks the dataSource robot to create and return
// a cell to fit into the indexPath.row slot

func tableView(tableView: UITableView, cellForRowAtIndexPath indexPath: ↵
NSIndexPath) -> UITableViewCell {

    let CellIdentifier = "MyImpressiveCell"

    // the dataSource robot reaches into the tray
    // and tries to find an old cell with cell identifier "MyImpressiveCell"
    // If it can't find one, it will create a new one

    let cell = tableView.dequeueReusableCellWithIdentifier(CellIdentifier], ↵
    forIndexPath: indexPath) as! UITableViewCell

    // The dataSource robot now sets up the cell
    // Configures the cell...
    cell.textLabel!.text = "cell contents..."

    // and hands it over to the tableView robot
    return cell

}
```

Identifying Cells with the cellIdentifier

It's important to bear in mind that it's possible to display a potentially unlimited range of cell types in the same tableView. Later you'll exploit this to create highly customized tables. The tableView, therefore, needs some way of identifying each different cell type, which is the job of the cellIdentifier.

The CellIdentifier is simply an arbitrary String that is unique to each cell type. When a new cell is created, it's "tagged" with the cellIdentifier. Behind the scenes, the dataSource uses this cellIdentifier to do the following:

- Drop the discarded cell into the right queue for later reuse
- Retrieve a cell of the right type from a queue when the tableView requests a new cell

Figure 6-32 shows a somewhat contrived example with two cell types alternating on odd and even rows.

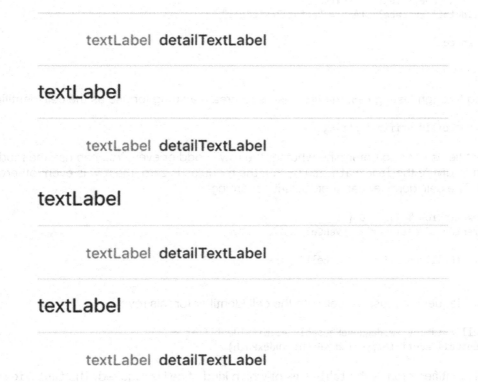

Figure 6-32. Cell alternation

The table was produced by the code in Listing 6-8.

Listing 6-8. Creating Alternating Cell Types

```
func tableView(tableView: UITableView, cellForRowAtIndexPath indexPath: NSIndexPath) ⏎
 -> UITableViewCell {

    var currentCellIdentifier: String

    if (indexPath.row % 2) == 0 {
        currentCellIdentifier = "EvenCell"
    } else {
        currentCellIdentifier = "OddCell"
    }

    var cell = tableView.dequeueReusableCellWithIdentifier⏎
  (currentCellIdentifier,forIndexPath: indexPath)

    cell.textLabel!.text = "textLabel"
    cell.detailTextLabel!.text = "detailTextLabel"

    return cell

}
```

Stepping through Listing 6-8, the first task is to create a string for use as the cell identifier:

```
var currentCellIdentifier: String
```

The identifier is used to determine whether the row is odd or even. You can use the modulo function to divide the `indexPath.row` by 2. If the modulus is zero, the row is even; otherwise, it's odd. The cell identifier can then be set accordingly:

```
if (indexPath.row % 2) == 0 {
    currentCellIdentifier = "EvenCell"
} else {
    currentCellIdentifier = "OddCell"
}
```

You then dequeue a reusable cell with the cell identifier for this row:

```
    var cell = tableView.dequeueReusableCellWithIdentifier ⏎
  (currentCellIdentifier,forIndexPath: indexPath)
```

The cell identifier informs the `tableView` of which kind of cell is required. The `tableView` will take care of either returning an already-existing cell for recycling or creating a new one from scratch if there isn't a spare waiting around.

Having been handed the right kind of cell, then it's simply a case of configuring it:

```
cell.textLabel!.text = "textLabel"
cell.detailTextLabel!.text = "detailTextLabel"
```

Finally, you return it to the `tableView`:

```
return cell
```

Side Effects of Cell Reuse and Caching

Although caching and reusing cells dramatically reduces memory use and speeds up the table, some potential side effects can cause problems. When the unused cells are dumped into the queue, they're queued *as is*. In other words, their content and attributes remain in exactly the same state as when the cell was created.

This can cause interesting display issues, with seemingly "old" cells creeping into the middle of the table. This can be reasonably obvious when it happens with cell data, but it can often catch you unawares if you're customizing other cell attributes such as selection state.

To prevent this, it's vitally important to reset the cell's content every time it's used—regardless of whether it's a new or dequeued cell.

There are three places where you can amend cell content:

- `prepareForReuse`: This method gets called on the cell in the background just before it's returned to the delegate by `dequeueReusableCellWithIdentifier`. You can override this method if needed, but for performance reasons Apple recommends that you reset only noncontent cell attributes here (editing and selection properties, for example). You can change content in `cellForRowAtIndexPath`.

- `cellForRowAtIndexPath`: As you've already seen, this is where you'll do most of the cell's configuration—setting content items based on the data returned by the `tableView`'s model and so on.

- `willDisplayCell:forRowAtIndexPath`: After the cell is created with `cellForRowAtIndexPath`, there's one last chance to tweak it before the `tableView` actually draws it to the screen. Just before this happens, the `tableView` will tell the delegate that it's about to draw a cell for a particular row—and at this point, you can change state-based properties such as selection and background color.

One technique I have seen suggested on forums is to create each cell with a unique `cellIdentifier`. Although this may work for very small tables, it's an incredibly bad idea if you're populating a table with a significant number of cells. By creating unique `cellIdentifiers`, you're preventing the caching and reuse of cells, so the memory footprint of your app will be significantly higher than it otherwise would be.

Summary

In this chapter, you looked in depth at how cells are structured, created, and reused. You also saw how cells can be configured beyond their default look by using just the default elements. Successfully customizing cells depends on knowing when to override the default processes, so you learned how the table view creates and manages cells for you.

By understanding what's possible with basic customizations, you can then use this information to go further. In Chapter 7, you'll use this knowledge to build completely customized cells, and you'll build on this further in Chapter 8. In Chapter 9, you'll improve the way that your users can interact with cells.

Improving the Look of Cells

Using UITableView's built-in standard cell types is a great way to get up and running quickly. But pretty soon you're going to run up against the limitations of the standard look and feel, and you'll want to move beyond the typical layouts.

If you're working with a UICollectionView, you don't have any standard cells in the first place, so you're going to need to customize them yourself from the outset.

Creating and using custom cells isn't difficult, and builds on all the topics that we've covered so far. There are four main ways of customizing cells:

- Add subviews to the cell's contentView in code.

- Create prototype cells in a Storyboard.

- Create a custom cell in a XIB by using Interface Builder.

- Create a custom subclass of UITableViewCell or UICollectionViewCell.

The four functions complement each other, and apply to both table and collection views with some minor differences. In this chapter, you'll look at the first three. Then in Chapter 8, you'll take a detailed look at custom subclasses.

The three approaches in this chapter are different ways to achieve much the same result, but there's a certain amount of commonality between them. This chapter's examples include some repetition in order to compare the three techniques.

Customizing Cells

When it comes to customizing cells, you can take four approaches:

- Add subviews to the cell's contentView in code.

    The entire content of the cell can be accessed through the contentView property. When the cell is dequeued by the cellForRowAtIndexPath or cellforItemAtIndexPath functions, you can create and add your controls as subviews to contentView.

If you're dealing with UITableViewCell, your new subviews can work alongside the built-in subviews, or you can ignore the built-in subviews completely. If you don't set the built-in subviews, they will not be inserted into the cell.

■ Create a prototype cell in a Storyboard.

Using a Storyboard in Interface Builder, you can lay out the cell controls visually in a prototype cell. These provide a "template" that the dataSource can use to create cells. You register the template for use when you set up the table or collection view.

When the cell is created by the dataSource, it's possible to programmatically set the properties of the custom controls.

■ Create a custom cell in a XIB by using Interface Builder.

Using Interface Builder, you can lay out the cell controls visually in a XIB, and then load that file when the cell is registered with the table or collection view.

Then with a bit of additional code to access your custom controls, it's possible to set their values programmatically in the relevant dataSource function.

■ Create a cell subclass and override layoutSubviews.

As an alternative to Interface Builder's visual approach, you can subclass the cell class and lay out the custom cell's content in code—either overriding the layoutSubviews function or drawing the cell with drawRect.

Which Function Should I Use?

The short answer is—it depends! There's no right or wrong way to customize cells. Which approach is best depends on a combination of what you're trying to achieve, how comfortable you are working with code versus laying out views visually (and vice versa), and how quickly you need to get your code up and running.

Adding Subviews to the Cell's contentView

The cell's contents sit inside a UIView called contentView. With a UITableViewCell, you also get an accessory view, shown in Figure 7-1. A UICollectionViewCell has an empty contentView, shown in Figure 7-2.

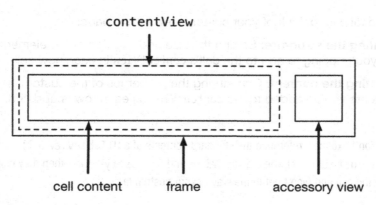

Figure 7-1. The layout of a UITableViewCell

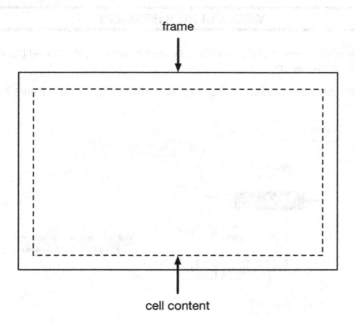

Figure 7-2. The layout of a UICollectionViewCell

Although `contentView` itself is read-only—meaning you can't replace it—you can add and remove subviews to and from it.

These subviews can be any control or component that inherits from `UIView` itself, including labels, controls, text fields, images, and so on.

You add a custom view when a new cell is created for the first time. This view will then be in place if and when the cell is subsequently recycled.

This means that if you're adding content into the custom view that will vary with each item—a label, an image, and so on—they need to be set for each and every item. The implication here is that you need to be able to reach back inside the custom view, as it were, to access the properties in order to set them.

The approach to take is to think of your custom view in two parts:

- **Creating the structure**: Setting the size and position of the elements that you're going to add to the cell's contentView in each new cell.

- **Updating the content**: Configuring the properties of the custom elements you've added to the contentView as each row is updated.

> **Tip**   If you don't explicitly reference the standard contents of a UITableViewCell —textLabel, detailTextLabel, imageView, and accessoryView—then they won't be inserted into the cell and won't get in the way of your custom layout.

VIEWS AND THEIR HIERARCHY

One aspect of iOS that often causes confusion is how UIViews relate to each other. All this talk of adding subviews—but to where? And what?

The key concept to understanding UIViews is that they form a hierarchy, shown in Figure 7-3.

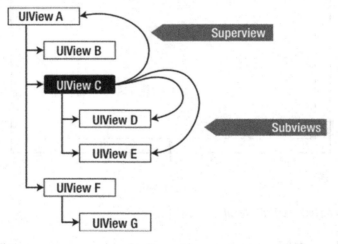

Figure 7-3. The view hierarchy

Each UIView can have a parent—or superView—and one or many subViews. Visibility of subViews is tied to their superView, so setting the visibility of UIView C to hidden will cause UIViews D and E to disappear.

Each UIView has a property called subViews, which is an Array containing any UIViews for which this UIView instance is the parent, or superView; see Figure 7-4.

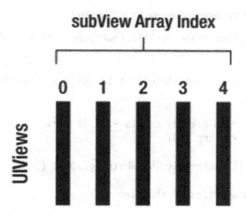

Figure 7-4. Views in a subView array

You can access each `subView` for a `UIView` by iterating through its array of `subViews`:

```
for theSubView in parentView.subViews {
  // do something to theSubView
}
```

Similarly, each `UIView` has a `superView` property that is a reference to the "parent" view. In Figure 7-3, the `superView` of view `C` is view `A`, and view `C` has two views in its `subViews` array: `views` `D` and `E`.

If you're creating complex layouts with multiple views, subviews, and superviews, it's worth keeping some diagrams to show how each view relates to the others. That can prevent much confusion later.

Creating the Elements in the Cell

The first step has to take place as each cell is created. This occurs in the relevant `dataSource` function, either `tableView:cellForRowAtIndexPath`, shown in Listing 7-1, or `collectionView:itemForRowAtIndexPath:`, shown in Listing 7-2.

Each listing shows the basic technique:

- First, check whether the subview that you want to add exists (in case you're recycling an already-existing cell).

- If the subview already exists, configure the properties that you want to control.

- If the subview doesn't exist, create and add it to the cell's `contentView`, and then configure it.

Listing 7-1. Adding and Configuring a Custom Subview for UITableView

```
func tableView(tableView: UITableView, cellForRowAtIndexPath ⏎
 indexPath: NSIndexPath) -> UITableViewCell {

    let cell = tableView.dequeueReusableCellWithIdentifier("CellIdentifier",⏎
 forIndexPath: indexPath)

    // Check if the custom view already exists - if it does,
    // we're recycling an existing cell

    if let customView = cell.contentView.viewWithTag(1000) {

        // customize the properties of the view

    } else {

        // create the custom view and set the tag value
        let customView = UIView(frame: cell.contentView.frame)
        customView.tag = 1000

        // customize the custom view's properties
        ...

        // add the custom view to the cell's contentView
        cell.contentView.addSubview(customView)

    }

    // return the cell to the tableView
    return cell

}
```

Listing 7-2. Adding and Configuring a Custom Subview for UICollectionView

```
func collectionView(collectionView: UICollectionView, cellForItemAtIndexPath ⏎
 indexPath: NSIndexPath) -> UICollectionViewCell {

    let cell = collectionView.dequeueReusableCellWithReuseIdentifier(reuseIdentifier,⏎
 forIndexPath: indexPath)

    if let customView = cell.contentView.viewWithTag(1000) {

        customView.backgroundColor = UIColor.redColor()

    } else {

        let customView = UIView(frame: cell.frame)
        customView.tag = 1000
```

```
    customView.backgroundColor = UIColor.redColor()
    cell.contentView.addSubview(customView)

}

return cell
}
```

Updating the Content in a Customized Cell

The preceding code will ensure that every new cell will be created with a UIView inside it, ready for configuration as each row is updated.

At this point, you meet what might seem like a bit of a stumbling block. After the subviews that you created are inserted into the cell's contentView, you can no longer access them directly to update them. They're effectively subsumed into the cell's contentView, which doesn't have any properties or outlets that you can use to update them.

This is where the tags come in. Updating the content is a two-step process.

1. Get a reference to the custom label and imageView inside the cell's contentView, which you do by referencing their tags.

2. Update the content of the controls.

Tagging Controls in the Cell

Every UIView control has an associate tag property, which can be set either in Interface Builder or dynamically in code. The tag is simply an Int value that uniquely identifies each element—with one very important caveat: you're in charge of the tag's uniqueness.

Let me say that again, for emphasis. The *control doesn't care about what its* tag *value is*, and *the view doesn't care if the* tag *is unique*. If you need to identify each control uniquely, the tags need to be unique. You can get some very strange results if that's not the case.

Setting the tag of a control can be done in code:

```
myControl.tag = 1050
```

Alternatively, you can use the View section of the Attributes Inspector (shown in Figure 7-5) if you're working with Interface Builder.

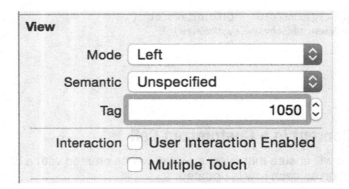

Figure 7-5. Setting a control's tag

There are a couple of tricks I use to keep track of control tags within XIB files:

- Start the numbering at a large value, and leave "space" in the numbering for additional tags. I've gotten into the habit of starting tag numbering at 1000, and incrementing by 10 for each tag.

- Keep the tag numbering consistent with the layout of the XIB. For example, if you have four UILabels in a line, give the top one the tag 1000, the second 1010, the third 1020, and so on.

After you've finished with the XIB file, the next challenge is keeping track of tag numbers in your classes. This is where enumerations come into their own.

Enumerations (enums) allow you to associate integer values with what are effectively text labels. One way of thinking about them is as a kind of compile-time global find-and-replace (this will make Swift purists wince, though.)

enums need to be defined before they're used. I tend to put them at the top of my view classes files so I know where to find them:

```
enum kCellControl: Int {
    case NameLabel = 1050
    case StreetLabel = 1060
    case UserImage = 1070
}
```

Then as the file is compiled, any instances of the enum (in this case kCellControl.NameLabel) will be replaced by whatever integer follows. So this code

```
if let myLabel = cell.contentView.viewWithTag ↵
(kCellControl.NameLabel.rawValue) as? UILabel {
    myLabel.text = "Label text"
}
```

will be interpreted by the complier as

```
if let myLabel = cell.contentView.viewWithTag(1050) as? UILabel {
    myLabel.text = "Label text"
}
```

Starting an enum with k just indicates it's a constant. You don't *need* to do this, but you'll see this done a lot in Apple code that defines constants. It's a hangover from days of yore.

By using enums inline in your code rather than the actual tag values themselves, you're doing several things:

- You're making your code significantly more readable, because it's far more obvious what the control does.

- You're making any use of the wrong tag much more obvious.

- You're providing a record of all your tags at the top of your class (or wherever you choose to place them), keeping everything neatly together.

Casting Controls

You'll notice that the line that creates your UILabel has a slightly strange syntax. You're *casting* the UIView with the tag 1050 into a UILabel. If this is something new to you, fear not—it's not as arcane as it sounds.

The viewWithTag function returns a UIView, which will respond to all the functions defined for the UIView class. The problem is that the view with tag 1050 is actually a UILabel, and you want to set its textLabel property.

UIView doesn't have a text property. If you try to send a text message to an instance of UIView, the compiler will (rightly) complain that the UIView won't respond, and the program will crash when the message is sent.

The work-around is something of a cheat. What you're doing in the line

```
if let myLabel = cell.contentView.viewWithTag(1050) as? UILabel
```

is telling the compiler that the view with tag 1050 is actually a UILabel, and that you want to access it as such. Technically speaking, you're casting it from a UIView to an optional UILabel.

If the view with the tag 1050 can be cast to a UILabel, then it will be; if not, then it will be returned as nil. By using the if let syntax to unwrap the optional, you can be sure that you are dealing with a UILabel, and you can set the text property:

```
myLabel.text = "Some custom text"
```

Creating Custom Cells Visually As Prototypes In A Storyboard

Prototype cells are a way of designing custom cells in Interface Builder, but without the overhead of creating and managing separate XIB files. They can be used for both table and collection views, and keep everything neatly together in the table or collection view object in the Storyboard.

You can think of prototype cells as blueprints. You create one prototype for each type of cell that you need, add the cell controls and lay them out, and then at runtime update the controls from the data model.

The controls in prototype cells can be accessed by the view controller by referencing them directly with tags, or via the outlets in a `UITableViewCell` or `UICollectionViewCell` subclass.

Dynamic cells, as the name suggests, will be updated at runtime with content obtained from the table or collection view's data model. They are supported in both table and collection views.

`UITableViews` are slightly different, and also offer static cells. Static cell subviews are not updated at runtime. They can be a flexible way of creating user interfaces for app components such as preference settings, or for layouts that exploit the scrolling features of table views.

Creating Prototype Dynamic Cells

Prototype dynamic cells are added to table views in Storyboards. When you first add a `UITableViewController` object into a Storyboard, you'll see that it arrives with one empty prototype cell (see Figure 7-6).

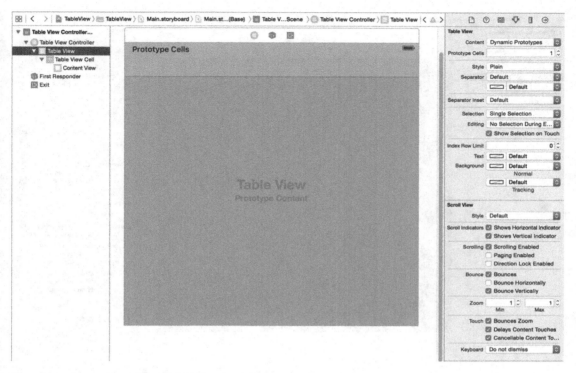

Figure 7-6. *A prototype cell in a UITableViewController*

A `UITableView` is slightly different, in that it arrives in the Storyboard empty (shown in Figure 7-7).

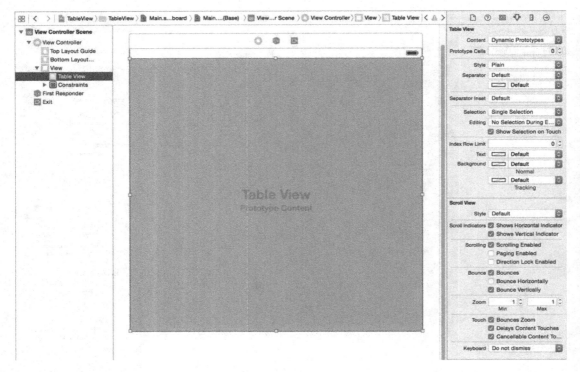

Figure 7-7. A UITableView embedded inside a UIViewController

`UICollectionView` provides a single prototype cell regardless of whether you're adding a `UICollectionView` inside a `UIViewController` or a `UICollectionViewController`.

Regardless of whether you're using a `UITableViewController` or a `UITableView` inside a `UIViewController`, you can control the number of prototype cells by changing the control in the Attributes Inspector (shown in Figure 7-8).

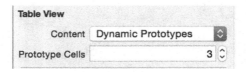

Figure 7-8. Altering the number of prototype cells in a table view

`UICollectionView` is similar, as shown in Figure 7-9.

Figure 7-9. Altering the number of prototype items in a collection view

For each prototype that you create, you need to provide it with a cell or item identifier so that the `tableView:cellForRowAtIndexPath` or `collectionView:cellForItemAtIndexPath` knows which prototype to use when required.

You add this in the Attributes Inspector. Figure 7-10 shows the `UITableView` cell identifier, while Figure 7-11 shows the `UICollectionViewCell` identifier.

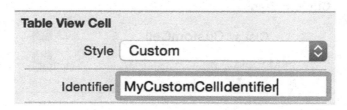

Figure 7-10. Setting the custom cell identifier for a prototype table view cell

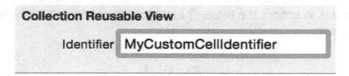

Figure 7-11. Setting the custom item identifier for a prototype collection view cell

Customizing Prototype Table View Cells

Table view cells can be instances of one of the four standard cell types:

- **Basic** (single `titleLabel` at the left)
- **Right detail** (`titleLabel` at the left, `detailTextLabel` on the right)
- **Left detail** (`detailTextLabel` on the left, `titleLabel` on the right)
- **Subtitle** (`titleLabel` on top, `detailTextlabel` below)

If these don't fit your requirements, you have two options:

- Select the `Custom` cell type, lay out the controls from scratch, and access them using their `tag` property.
- Create a custom `UITableViewCell` subclass, select the `Custom` cell in the Storyboard, lay out the controls from scratch, and link them to outlets in your custom class.

Both processes are shown in detail later in this chapter.

Prototype Cells and Custom UITableViewCell Subclasses

Custom cell subclasses allow you complete control over their content. You can lay out the prototype cell in the Storyboard, and then connect the cell's controls to outlets in the custom `UITableViewCell` subclass. When the cell is dequeued, you can set the outlet properties so that the cell displays your data.

To add a prototype of a custom cell, you first need to add a prototype cell to the table view contained in the Storyboard, as you did above.

Then, you need to set the cell's Custom Class property in the Identity Inspector, as shown in Figure 7-12.

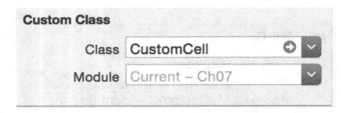

Figure 7-12. Setting the cell's class

Now you can connect the controls in the cell to the outlets in the UITableViewCell subclass. Figure 7-13 shows this in action: the UILabel in the cell is connected to the nameLabel outlet in the CustomCell class.

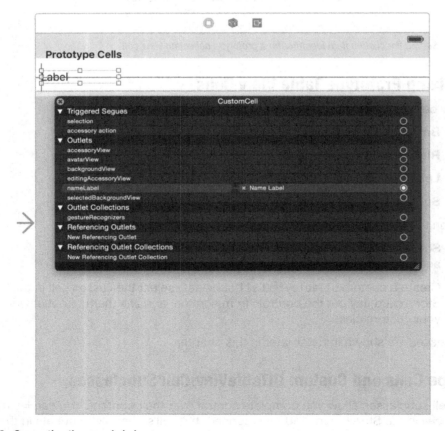

Figure 7-13. Connecting the nameLabel

When the cell is dequeued in the `tableView:cellForRowAtIndexPath:` function, you need to cast the dequeued cell to an instance of the subclass:

```
let cell = tableView.dequeueReusableCellWithIdentifier("CustomCell",
    forIndexPath: indexPath) as! CustomCell
```

This will enable you to access the connected outlets:

```
cell.nameLabel.text = tableData[indexPath.row]
```

Setting Prototype Cell Heights

The standard table cell has a standard height of 44 points, but you have flexibility to change this, either globally, or on a per-row basis. However, if you change the row height in the prototype cells, you also need to make sure that this is set at runtime. You have two options:

- Set the row height globally for all rows in the table.
- Set the row height on a per-row basis.

To change the row height in the prototype, you can either drag the resizing handle at the bottom of the cell, or set the row height value in the Size Inspector, as shown in Figure 7-14.

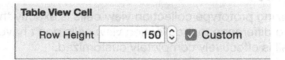

Figure 7-14. Setting the row height in the Size Inspector

Regardless of which approach you use, you will then need to set the row height in code. You can do this for *all* cells in the table, by setting the `tableView`'s `rowHeight` property:

```
tableView.rowHeight = 150.0
```

Alternatively, you can implement the `UITableViewDelegate` function:

```
func tableView(tableView: UITableView, heightForRowAtIndexPath indexPath:
    NSIndexPath) -> CGFloat {
    return 150.0
}
```

Implementing the `heightForRowAtIndexPath:` function provides the flexibility to return different heights for different sections or rows.

Setting Variable Cell Heights

If your table design involves varying heights of cells, you can potentially improve the performance of your table by implementing the `tableView:estimatedHeightForRowAtIndexPath:` function.

This is used by the table view when calculating its total height. If you have a lot of cells with complex layouts, calculating the height upfront can take time. The estimated row height gives the table view enough information to make an attempt at calculating the total content height, but allows it to defer detailed calculation until absolutely necessary.

To implement this, you need to do two things. First, set the `tableView`'s `rowHeight` property to `UITableViewAutomaticDimension`:

```
tableView.rowHeight = UITableViewAutomaticDimension
```

Then implement the `tableView:estimatedHeightForCellAtIndexPath:` function:

```
func tableView(tableView: UITableView, estimatedHeightForRowAtIndexPath↵
 indexPath: NSIndexPath) -> CGFloat {
    return 80
}
```

Using this approach allows you to exploit the power of AutoLayout when laying out prototype cells, without needing to implement the heavy lifting involved in calculating the height of cells yourself.

Customizing Prototype Collection View Cells

The process of customizing prototype collection view cells is exactly the same as that for table view cells, with the difference that collection view cells don't have standard types. Each collection view cell is effectively completely customized.

As with table view cells, you've got two options: lay out controls and access them through tag properties; or make connections to outlets in a custom `UICollectionViewCell` subclass.

Setting the Size of Prototype Collection View Cells

The size of collection view cells is controlled by the collection view's layout. If you're using a flow layout, you can set either set this in the `UICollectionViewFlowLayout` that's attached to the collection view in the Storyboard, or do so in code.

Figure 7-15 shows how the item size is controlled in the Storyboard.

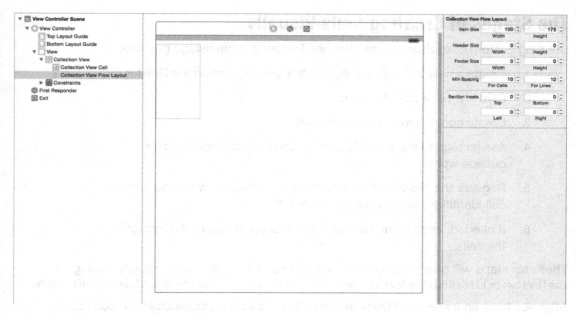

Figure 7-15. *Setting the item size in the Storyboard*

Alternatively, if you're creating a `UICollectionViewFlowLayout` or `UICollectionViewLayout` in code, you can set the item size in two ways:

- Globally for all items controlled by this layout by setting the `itemSize` property:

```
myCustomLayout.itemSize = CGSizeMake(100, 175)
```

- On an item-by-item basis when calculating the `UICollectionViewLayoutAttributes`.

This process is covered in detail in Chapters 15 and 16.

Creating Custom Cells Visually Using Interface Builder

Adding subviews to the cell's `contentView` can quickly lead to a lot of code—and unless you're good at mentally translating between the cell's layout and the coordinates in the code, that code can be difficult to follow.

An alternative approach is to use the power and flexibility of Interface Builder to create a custom cell in a NIB file, and use this to create a completely customized cell whenever a new one is required.

I don't subscribe to the school of thought that maintains, *"Real developers don't use visual tools."* If you find it quicker and easier to design your custom cells with a visual layout tool (and subject to the following caveat), go right ahead. What counts, after all, is getting the job done.

The Stages of Creating Cells Visually

Creating custom cells visually with Interface Builder is a multistage process:

1. Create a new XIB file, and lay out the cell using Interface Builder.

2. Give the cell a cell identifier.

3. Create controls inside your new cell.

4. Assign tags to the controls so they can be accessed from the outside world.

5. Register the XIB file with the table or collection view for use with the cell identifier that you created in step 2.

6. If needed, implement the functions needed to handle the size of the cells.

These six steps will give you a custom cell that can be created when required using the `tableView:cellForRowAtIndexPath` or `collectionView:cellForItemAtIndexPath:` functions.

After you have an instance of that custom cell, you can then manipulate the controls according to the values of the data in your table's model.

Laid out like this, it seems like a lot of work. In reality, it's a very quick process to get the housekeeping tasks out of the way so you can get on with creating the cell itself.

Creating a New XIB File

First, you need a new XIB file. From the File menu, choose the New File option, or type Command + N.

From the templates (shown in Figure 7-16), select the User Interface section in the sidebar, and then the Empty view option. Tap Next, and give the XIB file a name.

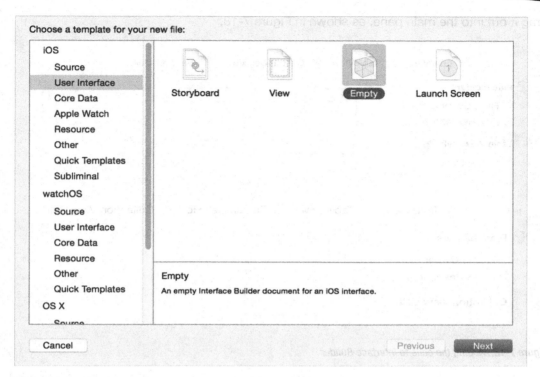

Figure 7-16. Creating the new view

The XIB will initially be empty, so the next task is to drag a cell into the main pane. In the Object Browser, select a Table or Collection View Cell (Figure 7-17).

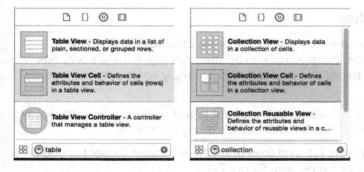

Figure 7-17. Selecting a Table or Collection View Cell

Drag it out into the main pane, as shown in Figure 7-18.

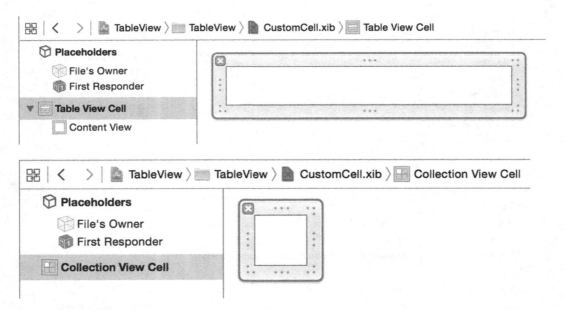

Figure 7-18. *Adding the cells to Interface Builder*

Because these cells are subclasses of UIView, you can drag and drop other controls into them in exactly the same way as if you were creating a full-screen view. However, before you get carried away, there are a couple of housekeeping activities you could get out of the way first.

Setting Up the Cell's Identifier

In previous code samples, you saw how reuseIdentifiers are used to keep track of dequeued cells for reuse. In the code, this is simply an arbitrary String. If there's only one type of cell to keep track of, I tend to call this cellIdentifier simply so its purpose is really obvious.

When you're creating cells in Interface Builder, it's important to associate whatever the reuse identifier is going to be with the kind of custom cell that it's going to refer to.

If you select the Cell item in the Objects list, and then open the Attributes Inspector, you'll see an Identifier option at the top of the list (see Figure 7-19).

Figure 7-19. *Setting the cell reuse identifier*

Creating the Cell's Content

Finally, after all that, you're ready to start laying out the cell's contents. Because the cell is an instance of UIView, you can put in a cell pretty much anything you can put in a plain ole' UIView, and position it with AutoLayout constraints.

Your choice is limited only by your imagination, what the cell needs to do, and the controls at your disposal. Figures 7-20 and 7-21 show a very simple layout that will be used in the next steps of this example.

> **Tip**   You're not limited to static content such as UILabels and UIViews. You can also place controls such as UIButtons, UISwitches, and UISliders into cells

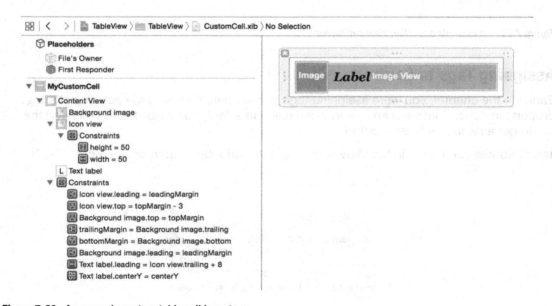

Figure 7-20. *An example custom table cell layout*

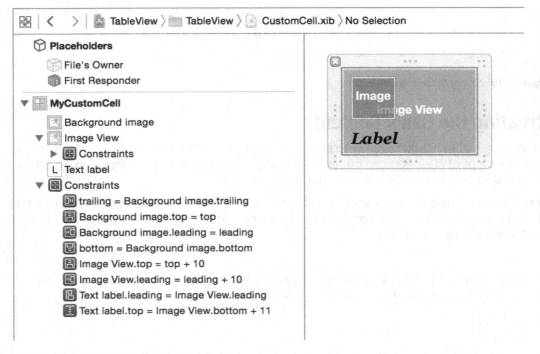

Figure 7-21. An example collection view cell layout

Assigning Tags to Controls

Earlier in the chapter, you were assigning tags to cell content by setting each object's `tag` property in code. That's not an option when using Interface Builder because you need the tag to get a reference to the control.

Tag attributes can be set in the View section of the Attributes Inspector (see Figure 7-22).

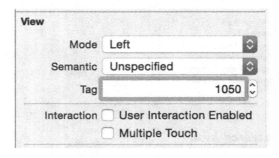

Figure 7-22. The Tag field in the Attributes Inspector

This has the same effect as

```
myControl.tag = 1050
```

has in code.

Registering the Cell

Once you've created the cell in a XIB file, you need to inform the table or collection view that you want to use it in conjunction with the cell reuse identifier that you set up. The function is identical for both table and collection view:

```
tableView.registerNib(UINib(nibName: "MyCustomCell", bundle: nil), ↵
 forCellReuseIdentifier: "MyCustomCell")

collectionView.registerNib(UINib(nibName: "MyCustomCell", bundle: nil), ↵
 forCellReuseIdentifier: "MyCustomCell")
```

This *must* happen *before* your view makes any attempt to dequeue a cell for use. Failure to do this will cause a runtime crash. One way of ensuring that this happens is to put the registration code in the viewDidLoad function of the viewController that manages the table or collection view:

```
override func viewDidLoad() {
    super.viewDidLoad()

    tableView.registerNib(UINib(nibName: "TableCustomCell", bundle: nil), ↵
  forCellReuseIdentifier: "MyCustomCell")

}
```

Controlling Cell Sizes

The cell objects that you dragged out into the Interface Builder arrived with standard sizes, but it's unlikely that these are going to be right for the interface that you're designing.

Collection View Cell Sizes

Controlling the size of the collection view cell for a given index path is the responsibility of the collection view's layout object. These are instances of UICollectionViewLayout, either as the specialized line-oriented subclass UICollectionViewFlowLayout, or as a custom layout that you implement from scratch.

The processes involved in this are covered in detail in Chapter 16 for flow layouts and Chapter 17 for custom layouts.

Table View Cell Sizes

Table views are slightly easier to deal with because you can only control the height of cells; their width is controlled by the width of the table view itself. However, cells can vary in height, so you will need to tell the table view how to handle this.

There are two approaches:

- Set a fixed height for the cell, and use AutoLayout to arrange the controls inside.

- Allow the cell height to vary, and implement one or both of the two height-related functions of the `UITableViewDelegate`.

Setting a Fixed Height

If all cells that will ever be displayed in the table view have the same height, then you should fix the cell height to maximize the table's performance. You can do this in one of two ways:

- Programmatically, by setting the `rowHeight` property for the table view with

  ```
  tableView.rowHeight = 100.0
  ```

  This overrides the cell height that you set in Interface Builder.

- By setting the table view's `rowHeight` property in the Size Inspector in Interface Builder, as shown in Figure 7-23.

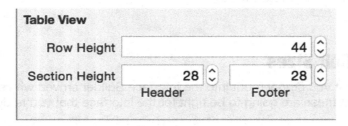

Figure 7-23. Setting the table's row height in Interface Builder

Setting Variable Row Heights

If the content of your cells demand it, you can display tables with rows of varying heights. However, with great flexibility comes great responsibility: varying row height can have a significant impact on the performance of your table views.

The reason for this lies in the fact that `UITableView` is a specialized subclass of `UIScrollView`. The frame of the scroll view provides a "window" into a (potentially) much larger content view, so one of the key setup calculations that you need to implement in order to display a scroll view is the overall content size. This is shown in Figure 7-24.

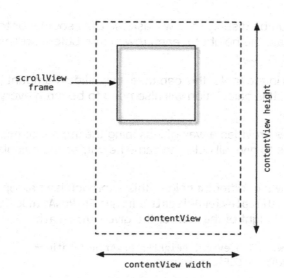

Figure 7-24. *The relationship between UIScrollView's frame and content size*

One way of thinking of UITableView is as a UIScrollView with a contentView that has the same width as the frame, but with a height that can vary with the number of cells that need to be displayed. This is shown in Figure 7-25.

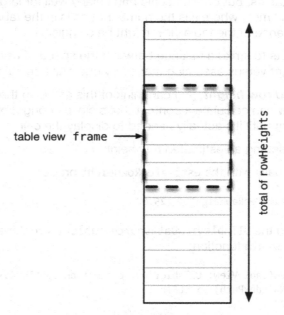

Figure 7-25. *The relationship between a table view's frame and total row height*

Before the table view can be displayed, it will ask the data source for total number of rows in the table, then calculate the height for each row in turn before adding them all together to get the total height for the table.

If there are a lot of cells in the table, this can take a significant amount of time. If the data source is dynamic, this calculation will also need to be rerun every time the table's underlying data changes.

Fortunately, UITableView provides a way of lessening the impact of this. The simplest option, which you saw above, is to give all cells the same height, so the calculation is just (number of rows x row height).

If your table will have rows of different height, this approach isn't an option. The other extreme is to implement UITableViewDelegate's heightForRowAtIndexPath: function to calculate and return the height of the row for the given indexPath:

```
func tableView(tableView: UITableView, heightForRowAtIndexPath ↩
    indexPath: NSIndexPath) -> CGFloat {

    // calculate height of row here
    return height

}
```

This works for smaller tables, but doesn't scale particularly well for larger ones because this function will be called n times, where n is the number of cells in the table. If the calculation is expensive, the performance of the table view might be sluggish.

The third option attempts to strike a balance between the speed of assuming that all cells will have the same height versus assuming that every one must be calculated individually.

By setting an **estimated row height**, you can think of this as being the average across all the cells. The table view can calculate a content that's close enough, but defer the detailed calculation of row height until it's actually needed to display the cell.

There are two ways of setting an estimated row height:

- Setting it globally with the estimatedRowHeight property:

  ```
  tableView.estimatedRowHeight = 125.0
  ```

- Implementing the UITableViewDatasource tableview:estimatedHeight ForRowAtIndexPath function:

  ```
  func tableView(tableView: UITableView, estimatedHeightForRowAtIndexPath ↩
   indexPath: NSIndexPath) -> CGFloat {
      return 125.0
  }
  ```

The second option is more flexible, in that it can return different estimated row heights for different tables and/or sections.

> **Note**   Implementing one of these approaches doesn't eliminate the need to calculate
> the exact row height before the cell can be displayed. You'll still need to do this in the
> `cellForRowAtIndexPath:` function, based on the actual cell contents retrieved from the
> data model.

Handling Cell Resizing in Tables

In Chapter 12, you will look at the various changes that take place when selecting and
editing table content—and will spend a lot of time looking at the controls that are added to
the cell when the table goes into editing mode.

This begs the question: how should a customized cell react to changes in shape, either
because of the table entering editing mode, or because the entire device has been rotated?

There are two kinds of events that can cause cell resizing:

- Putting a table into editing mode, which causes the editing and/or
  reordering controls to be displayed.
- Rotating the device so that the size class changes.

Both types of events will cause the cells to resize—in the first instance because the cell
needs to display more "furniture," and in the second because the cell has to adapt to a new
table width.

As you saw earlier, the table goes into editing mode when the `setEditing:animated` function
is called. At this point, if the cell is editable (and/or the row can be rearranged), the additional
cell controls are inserted.

Figure 7-26 shows how a table changes.

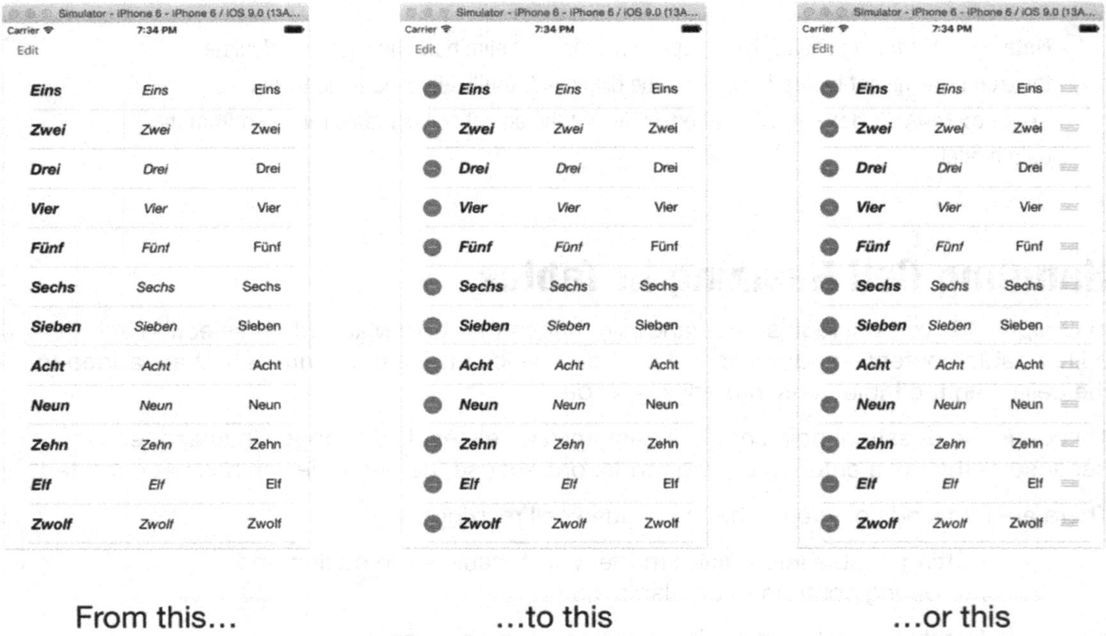

From this...   ...to this   ...or this

Figure 7-26. Changing from normal to editing mode

The deletion or insertion control appears at the left end of the cell, and the rearrangement control (if applicable) appears at the right. This means that the content of the cell has to move right to accommodate the deletion or insertion control, and potentially shrink to accommodate the rearrangement control.

When the deletion/insertion controls appear, the row appears to move right, with the accessory view moving off-screen if applicable. In both situations, the cells' contentViews will automatically alter the width value of their frames.

The good news is that AutoLayout will take care of rearranging the cell contents for you.

Figures 7-27 through 7-29 show the AutoLayout constraints in use in this example.

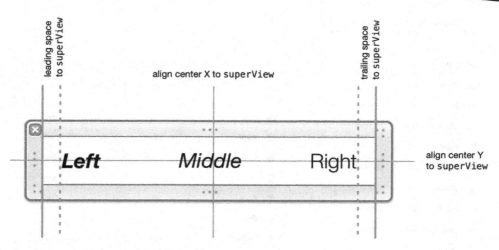

Figure 7-27. *The AutoLayout constraints in the cell*

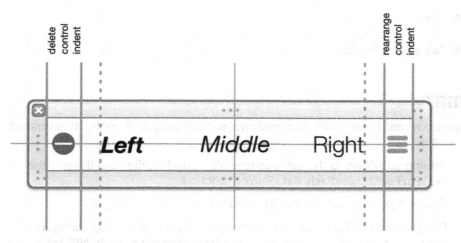

Figure 7-28. *The cell in "edit" and "rearrange" modes*

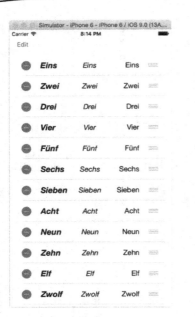

Figure 7-29. *Cells adapting to rotation*

Summary

This chapter covered three of the four main ways of creating and configuring custom `tableView` cells:

- Adding subviews to the cell's `contentView`, and configuring them in the `cellForRowAtIndexPath` `dataSource` function

- Creating prototype cells in a Storyboard

- Designing a cell from scratch by using Interface Builder and configuring the custom controls in code when the cell is loaded from its NIB file

The fourth approach—which is the most flexible, but also the one that requires the most work to set up—is to create a custom subclass for each type of cell that your `tableView` requires. This is covered in Chapter 8.

Chapter 8

Creating Custom Cells with Subclasses

In Chapter 7, you looked at two of the three main ways of creating and configuring custom table view and collection view cells:

- Adding subviews to the cell's built-in `contentView`

- Creating a custom cell from scratch and instantiating it from a XIB file

The third approach, which provides the greatest flexibility, albeit at the cost of slightly more complexity, is to create a custom subclass of `UITableViewCell` or `UICollectionViewCell`.

The main reasons for using this approach are that you need multiple types of cells in the same table or collection view, or in the case of table views, you want a level of control over the contents that is awkward to achieve by adding subviews.

In this chapter, you will look at the different ways of creating custom cells with `UITableViewCell` and `UICollectionView` subclasses:

- How to subclass `UITableViewCell` and `UICollectionViewCell`

- Using subclasses with XIB files

- Handling selection in cell subclasses

- Customizing the cell by overriding `layoutSubviews`

- Creating cells with a custom `contentView`

- Improving your app's architecture with the Model-View-View Model pattern.

Why Create a Custom Cell Subclass?

Creating a custom cell through the approach of using a custom subclass gives you complete flexibility over the layout. You're starting with a blank canvas (or blank view, at least), so how the cell looks is entirely up to you.

The trade-off is that this function is slightly more complex. For a start, you have to create a custom subclass of either UITableViewCell or UICollectionView. However, don't let that put you off; my experience is that it's all too easy to spend significant amounts of time trying to get the desired results using one of the "lighter" functions, when in fact it would have been quicker to reach straight for a custom subclass.

Creating custom subclasses also enables the creation of multiple types of cells in the same table. This can give your visual design a much greater degree of freedom than if you had to shoehorn dissimilar data into a single cell type.

As you'd expect, there are two approaches you can use: the "visual" approach, involving creating a custom cell in Interface Builder, and the "code" approach, which creates and configures the cell entirely in code.

Both processes, though, have a couple of common steps at the outset.

The Process of Creating Custom Cells

Creating custom cells with subclasses is a multi-stage process, with two common steps at the outset regardless of which approach you're taking.

1. With a pencil and paper, design the layout of your custom cell. This isn't a compulsory step, but having an idea of how the cell will fit together on paper tends to pay dividends in the long run.

2. Create a class for each type of custom cell that inherits from UITableViewCell or UICollectionViewCell and implement properties for the dynamic view objects that you are going to create in your cell, and any properties that you need to set from outside the cell.

Then, you have a choice of two visual approaches:

■ Build your cell as a XIB in Interface Builder, and populate it with the view objects that you need: labels, views, images, and so on.

■ Build the cell as a prototype cell in your Storyboard, populating it with view objects as you would in a XIB.

Or a code-based approach:

■ In the custom subclass, lay out the cell in code by overriding the initialization function–init(style:reuseIdentifier)–and add controls to the contentView.

Then, the final common steps:

3. Add any custom initialization to the layoutSubviews function that the cell needs in order to function.

4. When the table needs to fill a row with a custom cell, instantiate an instance of your custom UITableViewCell or UICollectionView subclass in the dataSource, and set the dynamic properties according to the data.

5. Rinse and repeat as required!

As you can see, it's really not all that complicated a process. Keep in mind a couple of subtleties as you build your custom cell (see the note below for details) and you'll find that this is actually a quick and flexible process.

SOME PERFORMANCE-RELATED FACTORS TO BEAR IN MIND

When creating a subclasses of UITableViewCell or UICollectionView, there are a couple of performance-related factors to bear in mind in order to maximize the performance of your table:

- **Be wary of building cells that are expensive for the graphics engine to render**. Although the GPUs (graphics processing units) built into the iPhone and iPad provide breathtaking performance considering the size of the devices, they aren't infallible. In particular, be careful with transparency and alpha values. If the GPU has to calculate how much of a lower layer can be seen through the transparency mask of an upper layer, this can result in a serious performance hit. This is covered in more detail in Chapter 9.

- **Don't violate the principles of MVC.** Your custom cell is a view, and as such should only be concerned with displaying content. If you need to undertake any kind of code-based configuration of that content (concatenating strings or adding values, for example), this should take place in the datasource, not in the view.

Having mentioned these two caveats, don't let them put you off trying to push the boundaries of what's possible. The members of the iOS device family are high-performance little beasts, so you'll most likely be surprised at what's possible before you start to push at the limits of their capabilities.

Custom Cells with XIBs

In this section, you'll look at the process of designing custom cell subclasses in conjunction with Interface Builder and XIBs.

Designing Your Cell

When designing a custom cell, I put down my Magic Mouse and reach for a pencil and some (squared) paper. That's what works for me–your approach may differ–but I find that if I start trying to design a cell in Interface Builder, two problems quickly emerge.

Firstly, Interface Builder tends to push me in the direction of "pixel perfection" before I've decided on what the cell is actually going to do. The fact that you can (relatively) easily line things up exactly means it's very tempting to spend your time doing just that, at the expense of thinking about the overall design.

Secondly, I become frustrated by the limitations of Interface Builder quite quickly. It looks like it should have the same level of fine-detailed control over layout as a tool like Photoshop, but it simply doesn't. If laying out designs in Photoshop is precision surgery with a scalpel, then Interface Builder can sometimes feel like painting a brick wall with a broom.

Note   To illustrate the process of creating custom cells, and using multiple types of cells in the same table, we'll create a somewhat-contrived example with two types, one cell type for even-numbered rows and one cell type for odd-numbered rows.

Creating the Class for the Custom Cell

The new custom cells that you will create will be instances of a subclass of UITableViewCell or UICollectionViewCell. This means that when you create them, they will have all the functionality of a "standard" cell, but with the opportunity to add additional functions of your own.

To illustrate this process, you'll create two UITableViewCell subclasses, which you'll refer to as OddCell and EvenCell, so that eventually the table will have two distinct types of cells with differing layouts.

The process is virtually identical for UICollectionView, but you'll look at this specifically later in the chapter.

Creating the Subclasses

The first step is to create the subclasses (Figure 8-1). In Xcode, Ctrl-click the group in which you want to create the new class and select New File from the pop-up window.

Then, select the Cocoa class icon from the Source group, and click Next, as shown in Figure 8-1.

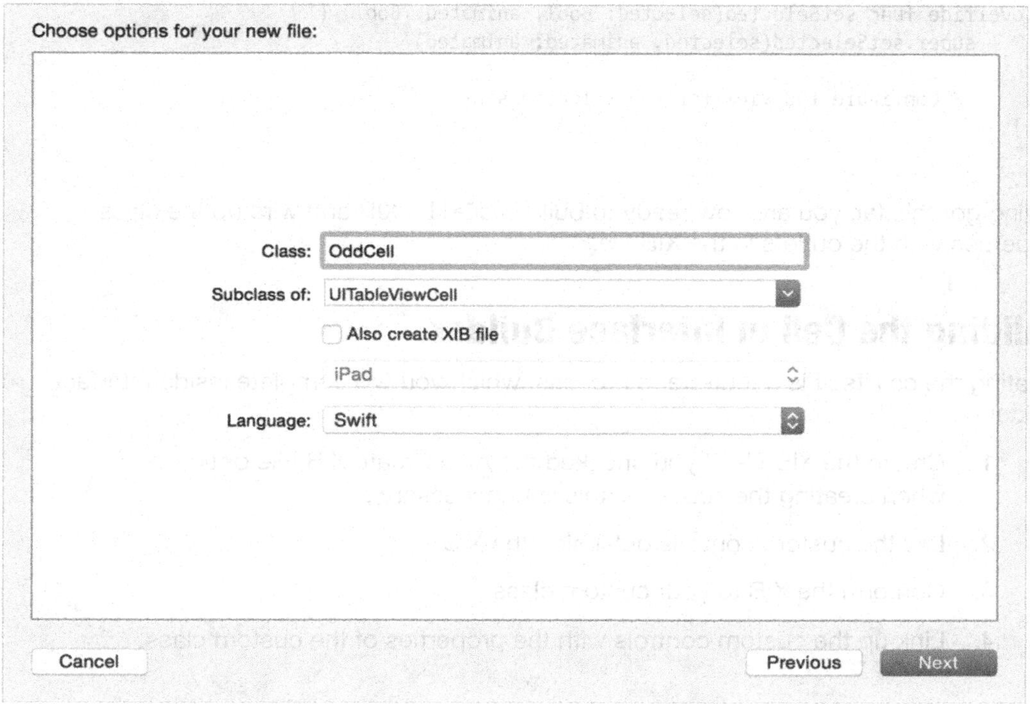

Figure 8-1. *Creating a new subclass*

The next screen allows you to choose which superclass your new class is going to belong to. Select UITableViewCell from the drop-down menu.

Call your new class OddCell and save it. You'll now see the class file for OddCell.

Now, you need to create properties for the custom controls within the cell (Listing 8-1).

Listing 8-1. The OddCell Class

```swift
import UIKit

class OddCell: UITableViewCell {

    @IBOutlet var backView: UIImageView!
    @IBOutlet var iconView: UIImageView!
    @IBOutlet var cellTitle: UILabel!
    @IBOutlet var cellContent: UILabel!

    override func awakeFromNib() {
        super.awakeFromNib()
        // Initialization code
    }
```

```
override func setSelected(selected: Bool, animated: Bool) {
    super.setSelected(selected, animated: animated)

    // Configure the view for the selected state
}
}
```

Having got this far, you are now ready to build OddCell's XIB and wire up the class's properties with the outlets in the XIB file.

Building the Cell in Interface Builder

Creating the cell itself is a four-stage process, which you will complete inside Interface Builder.

1. Create the XIB file (if you checked the Also Create XIB File option when creating the subclass, this is unnecessary).

2. Lay the custom controls out inside the XIB.

3. Conform the XIB to your custom class.

4. Link up the custom controls with the properties of the custom class.

Creating the XIB File

In Xcode, Ctrl-click the group in which you want to create the new XIB and select New File from the pop-up window.

Then, select the User Interface section in the iOS group, and select the View icon from the list of templates (Figure 8-2).

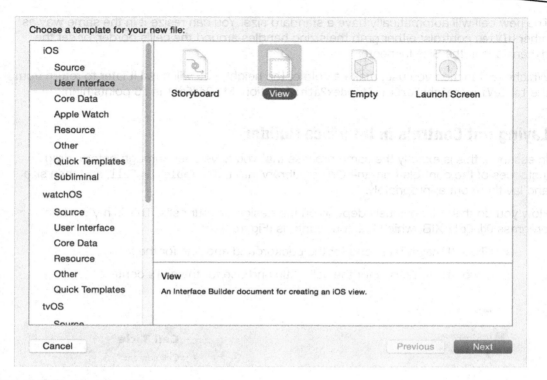

Choose a template for your new file:

Figure 8-2. Choosing a template

Then you need to provide a name for the cell (I'm calling it OddCell for consistency) and click Create to save it.

The new view will open up in Interface Builder, with a blank view. Xcode has assumed that this is a view with a size class of Any, Any, which is not what you want. So somewhat counter-intuitively, the first thing you need to do after creating the new view is delete it.

Highlight the icon for the view in the left-hand Document Outline, and press delete. You now have a completely empty Interface Builder pane.

This is the point when you create the new cell. Midway down the list of objects in the Utilities area is the Table View Cell. Drag this out into the center pane, and you have replaced the full-window view with a table view cell (Figure 8-3).

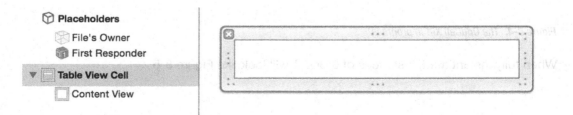

Figure 8-3. The new empty cell

The new cell will automatically have a standard size. You can resize it in the same way as other UIView controls: either grab the sizing handles around the cell's border, or set the dimensions in the Size Inspector.

Whichever function you use, make a note of the height; you will need it later to return from the tableView:heightForCellAtIndexPath: function. My OddCell is 70 points high.

Laying Out Controls in Interface Builder

In essence, this is exactly the same process that you have been through before: drag instances of the controls from the Object Library into the UITableViewCell, and then size and lay them out appropriately.

How you do this will obviously depend on the design of your cells. This is my work-in-progress OddCell XIB, which has four controls (Figure 8-4):

- Two UIImageViews, one for the background and one for the icon
- Two UILabels, one for the cell's title and one for the cell's content

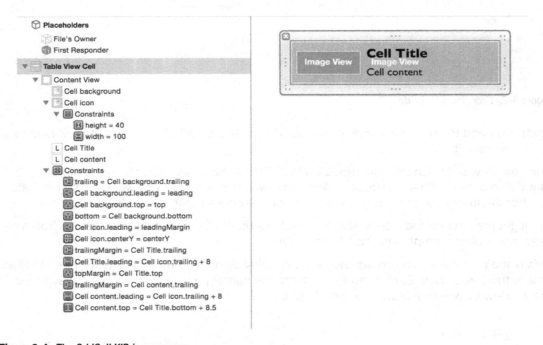

Figure 8-4. The OddCell XIB in progress

When fully instantiated, instances of OddCell will look like Figure 8-5.

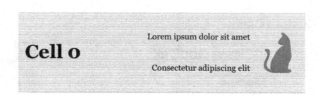

Figure 8-5. The OddCell

Conforming the Cell to the Custom Class

This step is required if you didn't create the XIB file when you created the custom class. If you did, the cell in the XIB file will be an instance of the correct subclass and you can skip straight to the next section.

If not,, the cell is an instance of UITableViewCell. In your custom class, which itself is a subclass of UITableViewCell, you have created a raft of outlets for custom controls.

The problem is that because your custom class is a *subclass* of UITableViewCell, the parent class neither knows nor cares about the outlets and properties that you created. In order to connect the controls inside the cell up to the outlets in the custom subclass, you are going to have to conform the cell to the subclass.

Fortunately, this is probably the simplest part of the whole process. In the Objects section, highlight the Table View cell icon (shown in Figure 8-6).

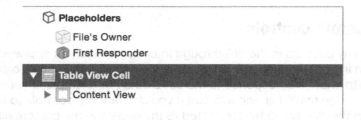

Figure 8-6. The Objects section

Then switch over to the Identity Inspector, and expand the Custom Class section if it isn't visible. At the moment, it'll show that the cell is inheriting from UITableViewCell.

What you need to do is to change this so that the cell's class is your custom subclass of UITableViewCell. Overtype the contents of the Custom Class section, and Xcode will autocomplete the field with the name of the UITableViewCell subclass (Figure 8-7).

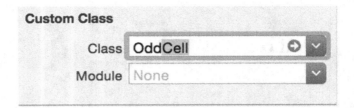

Figure 8-7. Changing the cell's owner

> **Tip**   There will probably come a point in your table-building career when your app crashes as soon as your custom table is loaded, with an error that looks something along the lines of this:
>
> 2015-11-05 19:58:13.263 myApp[6042:f803] *** Terminating app due to uncaught exception 'NSUnknownKeyException', reason: '[<UITableViewCell 0x6895790> setValue:forUndefinedKey:]: this class is not key value coding-compliant for the key cellSubtitle.'
>
> Don't panic. This is almost certainly the result of something going wrong with the connections of the cell controls. Check that you've made the connections from the custom cell, and not the file's owner.

Linking Up Custom Controls

If you've created any controls in the cell through Interface Builder, as opposed to instantiating them in code, then these will currently be sitting in the cell as orphans. If they're not going to change in response to the cell's data (for example, if you've got a static background view), then that's fair enough. But if you *do* want the controls to reflect the data in the model, then they'll have to be connected to the outlets in the custom class.

This will be familiar by now. Ctrl-click on the Custom Cell in the Objects list to reveal the Outlets HUD, and drag from the circle out to the control in the cell itself, as shown in Figure 8-8.

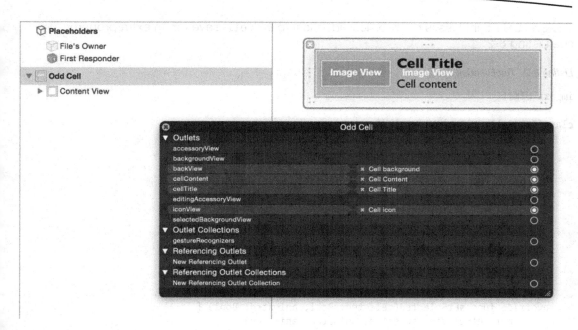

Figure 8-8. *The Outlets HUD*

Repeat this for all the dynamic controls that you've inserted into the cell.

> **Note** Because this custom cell is a subclass of `UITableViewCell`, it inherits all `UITableViewCell`'s properties such as `accessoryView` and `backgroundView`.

Creating the EvenCell

In this example, the `EvenCell` class is not too dissimilar to the `OddCell` class, but of course you've got free rein to create cells that are radically different if your app requires that.

Instances of `EvenCell` will look like Figure 8-9.

Figure 8-9. *The EvenCell*

The EvenCell subclass is more-or-less identical to OddCell, save for an extra property; see Listing 8-2.

Listing 8-2. The EvenCell Subclass

```
import UIKit

class EvenCell: UITableViewCell {

    @IBOutlet var backView: UIImageView!
    @IBOutlet var iconView: UIImageView!
    @IBOutlet var cellTitle: UILabel!
    @IBOutlet var cellMainContent: UILabel!
    @IBOutlet var cellOtherContent: UILabel!

    override func awakeFromNib() {
        super.awakeFromNib()
        // Initialization code
    }

    override func setSelected(selected: Bool, animated: Bool) {
        super.setSelected(selected, animated: animated)

        // Configure the view for the selected state
    }

}
```

Setting the Cell Heights

Unless you tell it otherwise, the tableView assumes that it will be dealing with cells that have a standard height of 44 points. Because the custom cell types you just created don't have standard sizes, you will need to implement the UITableViewDelegate's tableView:heightFor RowAtIndexPath: function in order to get cells of the correct size.

If you miss this function, your table will still work, but it will attempt to cram the cells into a height of 44 points, and their contents will be cropped.

The tableView:heightForRowAtIndexPath: function is shown in Listing 8-3. It simply checks whether the indexPath is odd or even, and then returns the appropriate height measurement as a CGFloat.

Listing 8-3. The tableView:heightForRowAtIndexPath: Function

```
extension ViewController: UITableViewDelegate {

    func tableView(tableView: UITableView, heightForRowAtIndexPath ↵
    indexPath: NSIndexPath) -> CGFloat {

        if (indexPath.row % 2 == 0) {
            return EvenRowHeight
        }
```

```
        return OddRowHeight

    }

}
```

Because values like row height are important to the interface being drawn successfully, it's often helpful to store them in constants:

```
let OddRowHeight: CGFloat = 70.0
let EvenRowHeight: CGFloat = 100.0
```

Creating Instances of the Custom Cells

Having gone to all the trouble of creating custom subclasses, and designing the layout of your custom cells, there comes a point where you will want to create actual instances of them.

It shouldn't come as a surprise to learn that this takes place in our old friend the `tableView:cellForRowAtIndexPath:` function. Whereas up until now you have been creating instances of standard `UITableViewCells`, now you are going to ring the changes slightly, and create instances of one of your custom classes.

This example is also slightly more sophisticated, in that there are two types of cells. The implication here is that there will be some kind of conditional code to choose which type of cell to create.

Before any cell types can be created, though, you need to register the XIB files that you created with the `tableView` so that they can be created or dequeued as required.

To keep the view controller organized, you can place this process in an extension, and call the function from `viewDidLoad:`. The configuration function is shown in Listing 8-4.

Listing 8-4. Configuring the Table

```
extension ViewController {

    func configureTable() {
        tableView.registerNib(UINib(nibName: "OddCell", bundle: nil), ⏎
  forCellReuseIdentifier: OddCellIdentifier)
        tableView.registerNib(UINib(nibName: "EvenCell", bundle: nil), ⏎
  forCellReuseIdentifier: EvenCellIdentifier)
    }

}
```

Cell identifiers are important because they can be used in several places, so again these are defined as constants:

```
let OddCellIdentifier = "OddCellIdentifier"
let EvenCellIdentifier = "EvenCellIdentifier"
```

Finally, call the configuration function from `viewDidLoad`:

```
override func viewDidLoad() {
    super.viewDidLoad()
    configureTable()
}
```

Having registered the XIBs, now they can be used in the `tableView:cellForRowAtIndexPath:` function.

Here's the first pass in Listing 8-5. The `tableData` and `phraseData` properties are just Arrays of Latin boilerplate phrases that you created earlier from the `viewDidLoad:` function.

Listing 8-5. Returning Custom Cells from the tableView:cellForRowAtIndexPath: Function

```
func tableView(tableView: UITableView, cellForRowAtIndexPath indexPath: NSIndexPath)
 -> UITableViewCell {

    let remainder = indexPath.row % 2

    switch remainder {

    case 0:

        let cell = tableView.dequeueReusableCellWithIdentifier(EvenCellIdentifier,
    forIndexPath: indexPath) as! EvenCell

        cell.iconView.image = UIImage(named: "cat")
        cell.backgroundColor = UIColor(patternImage: UIImage(named: "evenBackground")!)
        cell.cellTitle.text = "Cell \(indexPath.row)"
        cell.cellMainContent.text = tableData[indexPath.row]
        cell.cellOtherContent.text = tableData[indexPath.row + 1]
        return cell

    default:

        let cell = tableView.dequeueReusableCellWithIdentifier(OddCellIdentifier,
            forIndexPath: indexPath) as! OddCell

        cell.iconView.image = UIImage(named: "dog")
        if let patternImage = UIImage(named: "oddBackground") {
            cell.backgroundColor = UIColor(patternImage: patternImage)
        }
        cell.cellTitle.text = "Cell \(indexPath.row)"
        cell.cellContent.text = tableData[indexPath.row]
        return cell
    }

}
```

It's not too dissimilar to a standard `tableView:cellForRowAtIndexPath:` function, but there are some changes:

```
let remainder = indexPath.row % 2;
```

`remainder` is the remainder after dividing the row number by 2. If it's 0, the row is an even one; if `remainder` is 1, it's odd.

This allows you to create instances of the appropriate custom cell by switching between odd and even cells:

```
switch remainder {

    case 0:

        let cell = tableView.dequeueReusableCellWithIdentifier(EvenCellIdentifier, ↵
    forIndexPath: indexPath) as! EvenCell

        ... configure cell here ...

        return cell

    default:

        let cell = tableView.dequeueReusableCellWithIdentifier(OddCellIdentifier, ↵
forIndexPath: indexPath) as! OddCell

        ... configure cell here ...

        return cell
    }
```

Configuring the individual cells depends on the outlets that you created in the XIB, such as the `OddCell`:

```
cell.iconView.image = UIImage(named: "dog")
if let patternImage = UIImage(named: "OddBackground") {
    cell.backgroundColor = UIColor(patternImage: patternImage)
}
cell.cellTitle.text = "Cell \(indexPath.row)"
cell.cellContent.text = tableData[indexPath.row]
```

Creating instances of `EvenCell` is much the same process, which results in a `tableView` that looks like Figure 8-10.

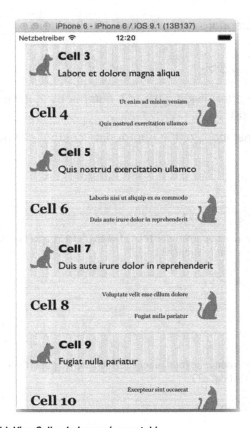

Figure 8-10. Two different UITableViewCell subclasses in one table

Handling Selection in Custom Cells

If you change the cell's backgroundView property, chances are you'll also need to control the way the cell is highlighted when it's selected.

Cell selection is controlled by UITableViewCell's selectionStyle property. This can be in one of four states:

- UITableViewCellSelectionStyleNone
- UITableViewCellSelectionStyleBlue
- UITableViewCellSelectionStyleGray
- UITableViewCellSelectionStyleDefault

When the selectionStyle value is set to None, there are no visible changes, but the other three causes the cell's background to appear to be filled with a solid color.

The cell also has two background views that sit behind the contentView: backgroundView, which is shown by default, and selectedBackgroundView, which sits between backgroundView and contentView (and isn't displayed by default).

This arrangement is shown in Figure 8-11.

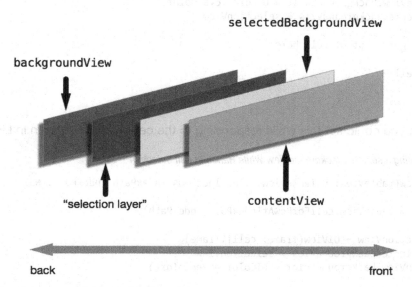

Figure 8-11. The arrangement of views inside the cell

The "selection layer" that's controlled by the selectionStyle property sits in front of the backgroundView, so if you've changed the backgroundView, it will be obscured by the default selection coloring when the cell is selected.

That might be OK, but if you want a background other than solid blue or gray, you need to change the selectedBackgroundView property. This sits behind contentView, but in front of the "selection layer," so instead of seeing the solid default color, you see whatever is in the selectedBackgroundView.

This could be a solid color, such as

```
let redView = UIView(frame: cell.selectedBackgroundView.frame)
redView.backgroundColor = UIColor.redColor()
cell.selectedBackgroundView = redview
```

This selectedBackgroundView will need to be added to the cell. You could do this before any selection takes place (for example, in the cellForRowAtIndexPath: function, as shown in Listing 8-6).

Listing 8-6. Setting the selectedBackgroundView in cellForRowAtIndexPath:

```
func tableView(tableView: UITableView, cellForRowAtIndexPath indexPath: NSIndexPath) ↵
 -> UITableViewCell {

    let cell = tableView.dequeueReusableCellWithIdentifier("CellIdentifier", ↵
    forIndexPath: indexPath)
```

```
    let selectionView = UIView(frame: cell.frame)
    selectionView.backgroundColor = UIColor.cyanColor()
    cell.selectedBackgroundView = selectionView

    ... configure rest of cell here ...

    return cell

}
```

Alternatively, you could set this while responding to the cell selection (shown in Listing 8-7) .

Listing 8-7. Adding a selectedBackgroundView While Handling Cell Selection

```
func tableView(tableView: UITableView, didSelectRowAtIndexPath indexPath: NSIndexPath) {

    let cell = tableView.cellForRowAtIndexPath(indexPath)

    let selectionView = UIView(frame: cell!.frame)
    cell?.selectedBackgroundView = selectionView
    selectionView.backgroundColor = UIColor.greenColor()

}
```

Of course, you're not restricted to using solid colors to indicate selection if your design calls for something a bit more imaginative. Here's how you could use an image:

```
let selectedImageView = UIImageView(frame: cell.frame)
if let selectedImageView.image = UIImage(named: "SelectedCellBackground") {
    cell.selectedBackgroundView = selectedImageView
}
```

This will obscure the "selection layer" so you can control the background appearance of your custom cell.

Custom Cells in Code

Laying out cells visually will take you so far, but if you prefer a code-based approach you can override the init(style:reuseIdentifier:), and then use the layoutSubviews function in the custom cell subclass or add AutoLayout contraints, which allows you to lay out a completely custom cell.

The Process of Custom Cells in Code

The process of creating custom cells in code has six stages:

- Create a custom subclass of UITableViewCell or UICollectionViewCell for each type of cell that you need.

- Create properties in the class to pass data into the cell.

- Lay out the cell's controls by overriding the init(style:reuseIdentifier:) function (for a UITableViewCell) or init(frame:) for a UICollectionViewCell.

- Override the layoutSubviews function to update the cell's controls with the values passed into the cell properties.

- Optionally, override the prepareForReuse() function to update the cell's controls just before the cell is displayed

- Register the cell class for use by the table or collection view.

- Implement the standard datasource function to dequeue cells as instances of your new custom cell subclass.

In this section, you'll build a table view and a collection view that use custom cells to display the simple layouts shown in Figure 8-12.

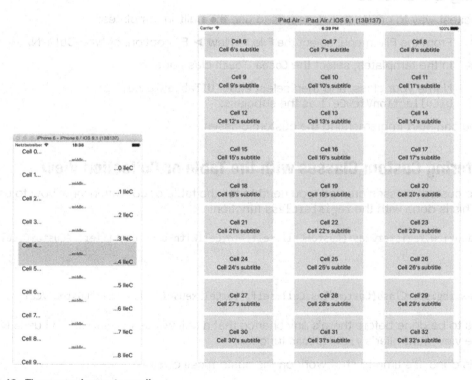

Figure 8-12. The apps using custom cells

Creating Custom Subclasses

In order to create cells with custom subclasses, you need to override the appropriate init function:

- init(style:reuseIdentifier:) for a UITableViewCell
- init(frame:) for a UICollectionViewCell

And the common init function:

- init(coder:)

Although you must provide an implementation of this last function in order to satisfy the compiler, it won't actually get called using your cell creation process.

Creating the Classes

The quickest way to create the classes is to use the built-in templates:

- From the File menu, select the File ➤ New ➤ File option, or type Ctrl + N.
- In the templates, select the Cocoa Touch class option.
- Name your class, and then select either UITableViewCell or UICollectionViewCell as the subclass.

Now you can start implementing the custom classes.

Registering Custom Classes with the Table or Collection View

With the custom classes created, you need to tell the table or collection view how to use them. This is done with the registerClass function:

```
collectionView.registerClass(CustomCell.self, forCellWithReuseIdentifier: "CustomCVCell")
```

or

```
tableView.registerClass(CustomClassCell.self, forCellReuseIdentifier: "CustomTVCell")
```

This has to be done before there's any chance that a cell will be dequeued, so I usually call it from the view controller's viewDidLoad function.

With this done, it's time to start work on the custom cell classes.

The init Functions

The init(style:reuseIdentifier:) and init(frame:) functions are called when the datasource creates an instance of the cell; it's here that you draw the cell contents.

> **Note**   You might be surprised to find that the `init` functions will only be called a few times throughout the lifecycle of the table or collection view, even if your control has thousands of cells. That's down to the caching and dequeuing mechanism of the two controls; by recycling previously-created cells, the number of expensive setup operations can be kept to a minimum.

The Table View Cell's init Function

First, let's add the properties that the class is going to need:

```
var cellTitle: String?
var cellSubtitle: String?

var leftLabel: UILabel!
var middleLabel: UILabel!
var rightLabel: UILabel!
```

The two `String?` properties will be set with the data model's object; while the three labels will display the data.

Now, get the `init(coder:)` function out of the way:

```
required init?(coder aDecoder: NSCoder) {
    super.init(coder: aDecoder)
}
```

Now you can implement the `init(style:reuseIdentifier:)` function; it isn't much more complicated at this stage:

```
override init(style: UITableViewCellStyle, reuseIdentifier: String?) {

    super.init(style: style, reuseIdentifier: reuseIdentifier)
    setupViews()

}
```

To help reduce code repetition, implement a helper function that creates the `UILabel`, shown in Listing 8-8. It's the same for both table and collection view.

Listing 8-8. The Label Helper Function

```
func drawLabel() -> UILabel {

    let cellTitleLabel = UILabel(frame: CGRectZero)
    cellTitleLabel.translatesAutoresizingMaskIntoConstraints = false
    cellTitleLabel.sizeToFit()

    return cellTitleLabel

}
```

The heavy lifting is done by the setupViews() function, shown in Listing 8-9.

Listing 8-9. The setupViews() Function

```
func setupViews() {

    // Setup title label
    leftLabel = drawLabel()

    let vLeftLabelConstraint = NSLayoutConstraint(item: leftLabel, attribute: ↵
NSLayoutAttribute.Top, relatedBy: NSLayoutRelation.Equal, toItem: self.contentView, ↵
attribute: NSLayoutAttribute.Top, multiplier: 1.0, constant: 0)

    let hLeftLabelConstraint = NSLayoutConstraint(item: leftLabel, attribute: ↵
NSLayoutAttribute.Left, relatedBy: NSLayoutRelation.Equal, toItem: self.contentView, ↵
attribute: NSLayoutAttribute.Left, multiplier: 1.0, constant: 10)

    // Setup middle label
    middleLabel = drawLabel()

    let vMiddleLabelConstraint = NSLayoutConstraint(item: middleLabel, attribute: ↵
NSLayoutAttribute.CenterY, relatedBy: NSLayoutRelation.Equal, toItem: ↵
self.contentView, attribute: NSLayoutAttribute.CenterY, multiplier: 1.0, constant: 0)

    let hMiddleLabelConstraint = NSLayoutConstraint(item: middleLabel, attribute: ↵
NSLayoutAttribute.CenterX, relatedBy: NSLayoutRelation.Equal, toItem: ↵
self.contentView, attribute: NSLayoutAttribute.CenterX, multiplier: 1.0, constant: 0)

    // Setup subtitle label
    rightLabel = drawLabel()
    rightLabel.text = "...middle..."
    rightLabel.font = UIFont(name: "Georgia", size: 11.0)
    rightLabel.sizeToFit()

    let vRightLabelConstraint = NSLayoutConstraint(item: rightLabel, attribute: ↵
NSLayoutAttribute.Bottom, relatedBy: NSLayoutRelation.Equal, toItem: ↵
self.contentView, attribute: NSLayoutAttribute.Bottom, multiplier: 1.0, constant: 0)

    let hRightLabelConstraint = NSLayoutConstraint(item: rightLabel, attribute: ↵
NSLayoutAttribute.Right, relatedBy: NSLayoutRelation.Equal, toItem: ↵
self.contentView, attribute: NSLayoutAttribute.Right, multiplier: 1.0, constant: -10)

    self.contentView.addSubview(leftLabel)
    self.contentView.addSubview(middleLabel)
    self.contentView.addSubview(rightLabel)

    self.contentView.addConstraints([vLeftLabelConstraint, hLeftLabelConstraint, ↵
        vMiddleLabelConstraint, hMiddleLabelConstraint, ↵
        vRightLabelConstraint, hRightLabelConstraint])

}
```

Working through this, you create each `UILabel` in turn by calling the helper function. Then there are horizontal and vertical AutoLayout constraints for each one.

The labels are added to the cell's `contentView`, and then the layout constraints are added to the container.

The Collection View's init Function

If you're building a `UICollectionViewCell` subclass, the process is very similar to that for `UITableViewCell`.

Here's the init function:

```
override init(frame: CGRect) {
    super.init(frame: frame)

    setupViews()

}
```

The `drawLabel()` function is exactly the same as Listing 8-8, and the `setupViews()` function is shown in Listing 8-10.

Listing 8-10. The setupViews() Function for the Collection View Cell

```
func setupViews() {

    // Setup title label
    titleLabel = drawLabel()

    let vTitleConstraint = NSLayoutConstraint(item: titleLabel, attribute: ↵
NSLayoutAttribute.CenterY, relatedBy: NSLayoutRelation.Equal, toItem: ↵
self.contentView, attribute: NSLayoutAttribute.CenterY, multiplier: 1.0, constant: 0)

    let hTitleConstraint = NSLayoutConstraint(item: titleLabel, attribute: ↵
NSLayoutAttribute.CenterX, relatedBy: NSLayoutRelation.Equal, toItem: ↵
self.contentView, attribute: NSLayoutAttribute.CenterX, multiplier: 1.0, constant: 0)

    self.contentView.addSubview(titleLabel)

    // Setup subtitle label
    subtitleLabel = drawLabel()

    let hSubtitleConstraint = NSLayoutConstraint(item: subtitleLabel, attribute: ↵
NSLayoutAttribute.CenterX, relatedBy: NSLayoutRelation.Equal, toItem: ↵
self.contentView, attribute: NSLayoutAttribute.CenterX, multiplier: 1.0, constant: 0)

    let vSubtitleConstraint = NSLayoutConstraint(item: subtitleLabel, attribute: ↵
NSLayoutAttribute.Top, relatedBy: NSLayoutRelation.Equal, toItem: titleLabel, ↵
attribute: NSLayoutAttribute.Bottom, multiplier: 1.0, constant: 5)
```

```
self.contentView.addSubview(subtitleLabel)

self.contentView.backgroundColor = UIColor.cyanColor()

// Apply constraints
self.contentView.addConstraints([vTitleConstraint, hTitleConstraint, ↩
hSubtitleConstraint, vSubtitleConstraint])

}
```

Here you're creating each label in turn from the helper function and then setting up some AutoLayout constraints. Once the labels have been added to the contentView, the constraints can be applied.

Overriding the layoutSubviews Function

The layoutSubviews function is called on the cell when it's dequeued; it's a opportunity to tweak the layout and look of the cell before it's drawn, and also to set the content of any controls based on the data model passed into the cell.

To show how this works in practice, let's look at the cellForItemAtIndexPath: function from the collection view app's viewController class, in Listing 8-11.

Listing 8-11. The Collection View's cellForItemAtIndexPath: Function

```
func collectionView(collectionView: UICollectionView, cellForItemAtIndexPath ↩
indexPath: NSIndexPath) -> UICollectionViewCell {

    let cell = collectionView.dequeueReusableCellWithReuseIdentifier("CustomCVCell", ↩
forIndexPath: indexPath) as! CustomCell

    cell.cellTitle = cvData[indexPath.row]

    return cell

}
```

You've seen this pattern before. You're dequeuing a cell with the cell identifier, and then downcasting it to an instance of your custom class.

This allows you to access the properties of the cell and pass in the relevant object from the data model, before returning the cell to the collection view.

Listing 8-12 shows the equivalent for the table view app.

Listing 8-12. The Collection View's cellForItemAtIndexPath: Function

```
func tableView(tableView: UITableView, cellForRowAtIndexPath indexPath: NSIndexPath) ↵
-> UITableViewCell {

    let cell = tableView.dequeueReusableCellWithIdentifier("CustomTVCell", ↵
    forIndexPath: indexPath) as! CustomClassCell

    cell.cellTitle = "Cell \(tableData[indexPath.row])..."
    cell.cellSubtitle = "...\(tableData[indexPath.row]) lleC"

    return cell

}
```

Behind the scenes, the cell's `init` and `layoutSubviews` functions are being called:

- The init function is called when a new instance of the cell is instantiated. This will only happen when the first few cells are created; after that, the table or collection view will cache cells for reuse once they scroll off the top or bottom of the view.

- The layoutSubviews function is called just before the cell is displayed, so this is where you update the cell controls to display the data that was passed into the cell when it was dequeued.

Overriding the prepareForReuse Function

The `prepareForReuse()` function is called just before the cell is returned from the `dequeueReusableCellWithIdentifier:` or `dequeueReusableViewWithIdentifier:` functions.

It's a last chance to clean the cell up before it's reused, but there are a couple of things to bear in mind when overriding this function:

- Always make sure that you call the superclass implementation at the start of the function with `super.prepareForReuse()`

- Only use this function to reset non-content properties of the cell – alpha, editing or selection properties. Using it to change content-related outlets can have an adverse impact on performance.

Improving the App's Architecture with MVVM

UITableView and UICollectionView are complex beasts, and rely on a lot of "moving parts" to function: table and collection view objects, cells, datasources, delegates, and view controllers. All them have to coordinate to produce the desired effect.

The number of moving parts can lead to blurred responsibilities within your app's classes. For example, a very common pattern that you've seen several times so far is where a UIViewController acts as the dataSource and delegate for a table or collection view.

There's nothing wrong with this per se, but a class that does several things is usually regarded as a code smell: it's harder to write, harder to understand after you've written it, harder to test, and harder to debug.

One of the most important design patterns in object- oriented software is the single responsibility principle, which can be summed up as "do one thing, and do it well." The model-view-view model (or MVVM) approach is one way of attempting this.

The Model-View-View Model Approach

To understand the MVVM model, it's worth starting by looking at the "traditional" approach to structuring a table view project.

> **Note**   I'm going to illustrate the MVVM approach with a UITableView example, but everything that applies to MVVM in a table view context also applies to MVVM and UICollectionViews.

The split between controller and view is reasonably obvious: the table is the view, and the view controller that acts as the table's datasource and delegate is the controller.

But views are a little more complicated than that; cells are also view objects, and the data source has to be aware of cells in order to configure them in the tableView:cellForRow ↵ AtIndexPath: function. This means that the datasource has to be concerned with the internal structure of the cells so it can set outlets.

If you change your data model, you must change both cell and datasource. If you have multiple cell types, your cellForRowAtIndexPath: function can quickly become messy with if-then statements checking which kind of cell is being configured. Big, complex logic statements like this are a code smell: hard to read, hard to understand, hard to test, and hard to debug.

MVVM changes this approach radically, but with one very simple change.

You start by focusing the responsibility of the datasource. It does two things: gets the relevant object from the underlying data model, and passes it to a cell before handing the cell off to the table. It neither knows nor cares about the internal structure of the cell; as far as the datasource is concerned, the cell has a single property that can be set, the view model.

The view model is the object that contains all the data that the cell will require to configure itself. In an address book app, this might be a Contact object containing name, phone numbers, and email addresses. Crucially, it's not tailored in any way to the specific needs of the cell. Even if the cell will only be displaying phone numbers, you pass the whole Contact object into the cell subclass.

Figure 8-13 shows how the model, the view model, and the controllers interrelate.

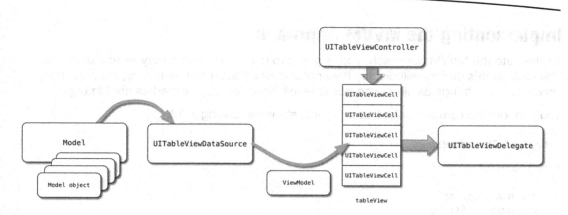

Figure 8-13. *The model-view-view model relationship*

The cell is responsible for managing its own layout. It will take the relevant attributes of the view model, say the phone number fields, and ignore the others. It will use the relevant attributes to set up its view outlets, text field contents, and so on, as well as handling AutoLayout constraints and so on. You can even go one stage further and use a property observer so that the layout processes are triggered automatically whenever the view model property is set.

Advantages and Disadvantages of MVVM

Employing a model-view-view model approach brings several advantages:

- The data source class of the table view no longer needs to be aware of the internal structure of the cell.

- Cell types can be swapped in and out much more easily, with significantly less code in the datasource class.

- It becomes much easier to update and adapt cells. Again, there's no need to keep the datasource and cell classes in sync.

- It makes testing cell subclasses much easier, as you don't need to wrangle the datasource class to generate and feed model objects in the cell instance during the test.

The MVVM approach does have a couple of drawbacks, however:

- It's not a "standard" Apple design pattern, so there's no "native" implementation to use as a starting point.

- The division of responsibilities is offset by the need for some more "moving parts." Your cell classes need to be more complex than they would be if they were simpler "passive" components.

Even with these disadvantages, I'm firmly of the opinion that MVVM is a useful design pattern that can make your table and collection views a lot easier to configure and maintain.

Implementing the MVVM Approach

To illustrate the MVVM approach, you're going to use it to power a very simple example. The table in this project will display the contents of a Contact object: name, number, and notes. To keep things as simple as possible, all three Contact properties are Strings.

You'll model the Contact object as a Struct, shown in Listing 8-13.

Listing 8-13. The Contact struct

```
struct Contact {

    var name: String?
    var number: String?
    var notes: String?

    init(name: String, number: String, notes: String) {
        self.name = name
        self.number = number
        self.notes = notes
    }

}
```

The Contacts will be stored in an Array that is set up by a function called from the table view controller's viewDidLoad function (shown in Listing 8-14).

Listing 8-14. The setupDate Function

```
extension ViewController {

    func setupData() {

        for index in 1...10 {

            let contact = Contact(name: "Name \(index)", number: "\(index)", notes:↵
 "The notes for contact \(index)")
            tableData.append(contact)

        }

    }

}
```

The cells displayed in the table are instances of a custom UITableViewCell subclass called ContactCell (shown in Listing 8-15).

Listing 8-15. The ContactCell Class

```
import UIKit

class ContactCell: UITableViewCell {

    @IBOutlet var nameLabel: UILabel!
    @IBOutlet var numberLabel: UILabel!
    @IBOutlet var descriptionLabel: UILabel!

}
```

The three outlets are connected to UILabel controls in the prototype cell in the Storyboard, as shown in Figure 8-14.

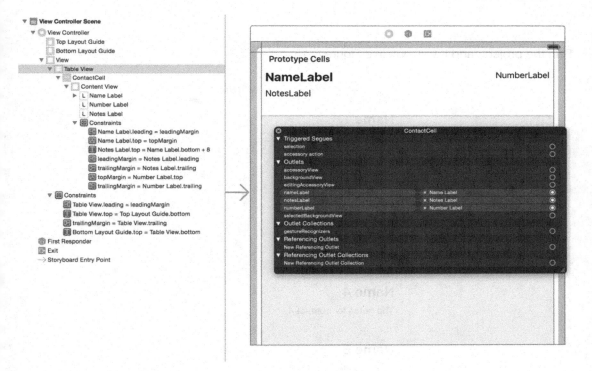

Figure 8-14. The prototype cell

With everything wired together, you can turn your attention to setting up the UITableViewDataSource functions to configure and feed the cells to the table.

Up to now, you've used a very standard approach that uses the cellForRowAtIndexPath: function to configure the cell. This is show in Listing 8-16.

Listing 8-16. The Standard cellForRowAtIndexPath: Function

```
func tableView(tableView: UITableView, cellForRowAtIndexPath indexPath: NSIndexPath) -> ↵
UITableViewCell {

    let cell = tableView.dequeueReusableCellWithIdentifier("ContactCell", forIndexPath: ↵
indexPath) as! ContactCell

    let contact = tableData[indexPath.row]

    cell.nameLabel.text = contact.name
    cell.numberLabel.text = contact.number
    cell.descriptionLabel.text = contact.notes

    return cell

}
```

Run the project, and it will look like Figure 8-15.

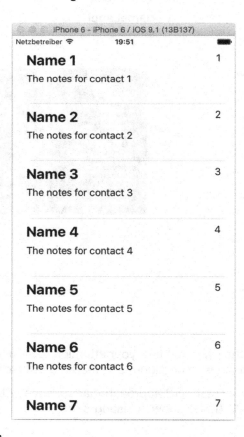

Figure 8-15. The running project

There shouldn't be any surprises about the approach here. You're dequeuing a cell as an instance of ContactCell, getting the Contact object from the data model, and populating the cell outlets with the contents of the Contact's properties.

However, it's also possible to see some of the pitfalls of this approach:

- You've blurred the separations of concern between the cell subclass and the view controller, because the view controller is directly referencing the cell outlets.

- Any changes in the cell subclass or Contact object have to be reflected in the table view controller.

- If you want to test the cell subclass, you must figure out a way to wrangle the view controller so that you can populate the cell's outlets.

Surely there has to be a more efficient way. Good news! There is.

Converting the Project to an MVVM Approach

You're going to convert the project to an model-view-view model approach by passing the Contact object directly to the ContactCell instance, and letting the cell configure itself..

The view controller won't know, or care, what outlets the cell has. Instead, you'll update the cellForRowAtIndexPath: function to remove all references to the cell outlets.

This is an example of an approach known as *dependency injection*: the ContactCell has a *dependency* on the Contact object to populate its outlets, and you're going to *inject* that Contact object into the ContactCell immediately after you've dequeued it.

Listing 8-17 shows what the updated cellForRowAtIndexPath: function looks like.

Listing 8-17. The Updated cellForRowAtIndexPath: Function

```
func tableView(tableView: UITableView, cellForRowAtIndexPath indexPath: NSIndexPath) ↵
 -> UITableViewCell {

    let cell = tableView.dequeueReusableCellWithIdentifier("ContactCell", ↵
  forIndexPath: indexPath) as! ContactCell

    let contact = tableData[indexPath.row]

    cell.contact = contact

    return cell

}
```

Straight away you can see that the function is much more streamlined, and the difference would be even more dramatic if the cell was more complex than this admittedly trivial example.

However, this won't compile as it stands. You need to make some changes to the CustomCell class to allow it to accept the injection of the Contact dependency.

Listing 8-18 shows the initial changes.

Listing 8-18. The ContactCell Class Updated to Receive an Injected Contact

```
import UIKit

class ContactCell: UITableViewCell {

    var contact: Contact?

    @IBOutlet var nameLabel: UILabel!
    @IBOutlet var numberLabel: UILabel!
    @IBOutlet var notesLabel: UILabel!

}
```

This gets you part of the way, but if you run the project now you'll see that the cells aren't displaying any data. Figure 8-16 shows the effect.

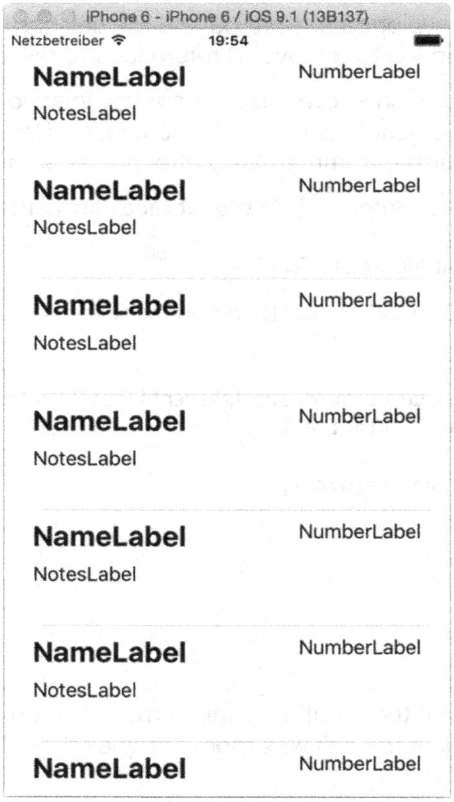

Figure 8-16. Cells no longer being updated

Previously, you were setting the text property of the UILabels in the cellForRowAtIndexPath: function, but as this no longer happens, the cells are no longer updated.

You need to find some way to set the label properties once more.

One option would be to override the UITableViewCell's layoutSubviews function, and set the outlets there. Listing 8-19 shows how you could do that.

Listing 8-19. Using layoutSubviews to Update the Outlets

```
override func layoutSubviews() {
    nameLabel.text = contact?.name
    numberLabel.text = contact?.number
    notesLabel.text = contact?.notes
}
```

Although this would certainly work, there is a disconnect between setting the Contact property in the cell and updating the outlets. Is there a way of tying the two things closer together?

As it turns out, there is. Swift class and struct properties allow you to attach property observers. These are inline functions that are called whenever a property is set, and they allow you to perform arbitrary tasks every time you access a property to set it.

There are two property observers available to us:

- willSet is called just before a value is stored in the property.
- didSet is called just after a value is stored in the property.

This means you can use the cell's contact property's didSet observer to update the outlets with the values of the Contact object that's just been injected into the CustomCell instance.

Listing 8-20 shows the updated CustomCell class.

Listing 8-20. The Updated CustomCell Class

```
import UIKit

class ContactCell: UITableViewCell {

    var contact: Contact? {

        didSet {
            nameLabel.text = contact?.name
            numberLabel.text = contact?.number
            notesLabel.text = contact?.notes
        }
    }

    @IBOutlet var nameLabel: UILabel!
    @IBOutlet var numberLabel: UILabel!
    @IBOutlet var notesLabel: UILabel!


}
```

Here, you're using the `didSet` observer to update the `nameLabel`, `numberLabel`, and `notesLabel` outlets with the relevant property from the `Contact` object. Whenever a new `Contact` object is passed in, such as when a `ContactCell` is dequeued in the `cellForRowAtIndexPath:` function, the cell outlets will be updated automatically.

Having updated the `ContactCell` class, run the project again, and you'll see the rows being populated once more, as shown in Figure 8-17.

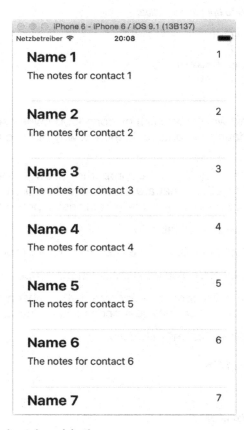

Figure 8-17. Cells updated after dependency injection

Summary

In this chapter, you saw how to create your own custom subclass of `UITableViewCell` to give you the ultimate in control over the appearance and functions of your cells.

There's a range of approaches that you can use to tackle custom cells:

- Combine a custom subclass with a XIB file.

- Replace the need for a XIB file by building the cell entirely in code.

- Modify a standard cell type by overriding `layoutSubviews`.

Choosing the approach to take is a case of trading off the level of control you need over the cell against the complexity and additional code overhead of each technique. Another factor is performance; custom subclasses allow you to take advantage of various techniques that can speed up the performance of your table views.

Chapter 9

Improving Interaction

So far, the cells that you have been creating have been relatively static: the user's interaction with them has been limited to tapping for selection and editing.

That's not all you can do with cells, though, so this chapter looks at some of the tricks you can use to make table and collection views truly interactive:

- Embedding custom controls including buttons, switches, and sliders within the cell

- Implementing the widely used pull-to-refresh functionality

- Adding gesture recognizers to cells to support double taps and so on

- Implementing search within the contents of the view

No matter how interactive the view is, however, it's not going to deliver a good user experience if it's not responsive. Although we've been covering best-practice as we've gone along in earlier chapters, this chapter finishes up by looking at a checklist of ways to ensure that you squeeze maximum performance from your table and collection views.

> **Note** The techniques in this chapter are broadly identical for both `UITableView` and `UICollectionView`. However, if it's something that's specific to just `UITableView` I'll use "table view"; if it's something specific to `UICollectionView` I'll use "collection view"; and when it's common to both I'll use "view".

Embedding Custom Controls into Cells

Up to now, you've been mainly concerned with creating and presenting largely static views. Although you've created cells that present dynamic data, the cells themselves have so far only responded to the basic taps and swipes associated with editing, deleting, and sorting.

Because both `UITableViewCell` and `UICollectionViewCell` are subclassed of `UIView`, this allows you to do pretty much anything you can do with a "standard" `UIView`. This includes embedding custom controls such as buttons, sliders, and switches as subviews, and having them respond to user actions.

To begin with, here's a really trivial example. Each cell contains a `UIButton` that pops up an alert view when it's tapped, as shown in Figure 9-1.

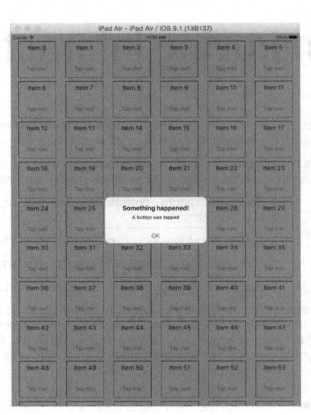

Figure 9-1. Really simple buttons

There are two approaches that you can use to implement this kind of functionality:

- A simple approach, which inserts a button directly into the cell when the cell is first created
- A more robust approach, which uses a custom cell class and delegation.

In this section, we'll look at the simple approach; and then build up to a more robust solution in the next section.

A Simple Approach – Adding a Button Directly To The Cell

I'm not going to go into detail about the main aspects of creating the table or collection view — that's pretty familiar by now—but there are two things you need to do in order to create the button and the alert view.

Creating an Alert View

The first is to create a function to display the alert view when one of the buttons is tapped; this should go in an extension of the view controller. Listing 9-1 shows the table version.

Listing 9-1. The didTapButtonInCell: Method

```
func didTapButtonInCell(sender: UIButton) {

    let alert = UIAlertController(title: "Something happened!", message: "A button was⏎
tapped", preferredStyle: .Alert)
    let action = UIAlertAction(title: "OK", style: .Default, handler: nil)

    alert.addAction(action)

    self.presentViewController(alert, animated: true, completion: nil)

}
```

Creating the Buttons

Having created the didTapButtonInCell function, you need to add the buttons to the cells and connect them to this method.

Create a function called addButtonToCell. Listing 9-2 shows the table view version.

Listing 9-2. The addButtonToCell Method for a Table View

```
func addButtonToCell(cell: UITableViewCell) {

    guard cell.contentView.viewWithTag(1000) == nil else {
        return
    }

    let button = UIButton(type: UIButtonType.RoundedRect)
    button.tag = 1000
    button.setTitle("Tap me!", forState: UIControlState.Normal)
    button.sizeToFit()
    button.translatesAutoresizingMaskIntoConstraints = false

    button.addTarget(self, action: "didTapButtonInCell:", forControlEvents: ⏎
UIControlEvents.TouchUpInside)
```

```
  let vConstraint = NSLayoutConstraint(item: button, attribute: ↵
NSLayoutAttribute.CenterY, relatedBy:
  NSLayoutRelation.Equal, toItem: cell.contentView, attribute: ↵
NSLayoutAttribute.CenterY, multiplier: 1.0, constant: 0)

  let hConstraint = NSLayoutConstraint(item: button, attribute: ↵
NSLayoutAttribute.Right, relatedBy: NSLayoutRelation.Equal, toItem: ↵
cell.contentView, attribute: NSLayoutAttribute.Right, multiplier: 1.0, constant: 0)

  cell.contentView.addSubview(button)
  cell.contentView.addConstraints([vConstraint, hConstraint])

}
```

The collection view function needs a slightly different definition:

```
func addButtonToCell(cell: UICollectionViewCell) {
```

The first section of the function checks whether there's already a button in the cell:

```
guard cell.contentView.viewWithTag(1000) == nil else {
    return
}
```

The guard statement checks if there's a UIView or a UIView subclass in the cell's contentView that is tagged with 1000. Unless the result of the viewWithTag() function is nil, the function will return, because there's already a button created and it doesn't need to be added.

If on the other hand there *isn't* already a button in the cell, the next section of the function creates an instance of a UIButton, sets the title, and then resizes it to fit:

```
let button = UIButton(type: UIButtonType.RoundedRect)
button.setTitle("Tap me!", forState: UIControlState.Normal)
button.sizeToFit()
button.translatesAutoresizingMaskIntoConstraints = false
```

Then you link the button with the function by adding a target to the button:

```
  button.addTarget(self, action: "didTapButtonInCell:", forControlEvents: ↵
UIControlEvents.TouchUpInside)
```

Next, you need a couple of AutoLayout constraints to position the button. Here's the positioning for the table view:

```
  let vConstraint = NSLayoutConstraint(item: button, attribute:↵
NSLayoutAttribute.CenterY, relatedBy: NSLayoutRelation.Equal, toItem: ↵
cell.contentView, attribute: NSLayoutAttribute.CenterY, multiplier: 1.0, constant: 0)

  let hConstraint = NSLayoutConstraint(item: button, attribute: ↵
NSLayoutAttribute.Right, relatedBy: NSLayoutRelation.Equal, toItem: ↵
cell.contentView, attribute: NSLayoutAttribute.Right, multiplier: 1.0, constant: 0)
```

The positioning for a collection view is slightly different:

```
    let vConstraint = NSLayoutConstraint(item: button, attribute:↵
NSLayoutAttribute.CenterX, relatedBy: NSLayoutRelation.Equal, toItem: ↵
cell.contentView, attribute: NSLayoutAttribute.CenterX, multiplier: 1.0, constant: 0)

    let hConstraint = NSLayoutConstraint(item: button, attribute: ↵
NSLayoutAttribute.Bottom, relatedBy: NSLayoutRelation.Equal, toItem: ↵
cell.contentView, attribute: NSLayoutAttribute.Bottom, multiplier: 1.0, constant: -10)
```

Finally, you can add the button to the cell:

```
cell.contentView.addSubview(button)
```

And add the layout constraints:

```
cell.contentView.addConstraints([vConstraint, hConstraint])
```

Adding the Buttons to Cells

Adding the buttons to the cells requires an update to either the
`tableView:cellForRowAtIndexPath:` or `collectionView:cellForItemAtIndexPath:` functions.

The first part of the function is standard – here there's a label in the cell with the tag 2000, which is used to display the row count.

To insert the button into the cell, add a call to the `addButtonToCell(:_)` function. Listing 9-3 shows the collection view version.

Listing 9-3. Adding the Buttons to Cells

```
func collectionView(collectionView: UICollectionView, cellForItemAtIndexPath ↵
indexPath: NSIndexPath) -> UICollectionViewCell {

    let cell = collectionView.dequeueReusableCellWithReuseIdentifier("CellIdentifier",↵
    forIndexPath: indexPath)

    let label = cell.contentView.viewWithTag(2000) as! UILabel
    label.text = "Item \(cvData[indexPath.row])"

    addButtonToCell(cell)

    cell.layer.borderColor = UIColor.blackColor().CGColor
    cell.layer.borderWidth = 1.0

    return cell

}
```

Reacting to Individual Controls

Impressive as this example might seem, there's one significant limitation. Each button is tied to the same method, so it isn't possible to do something that is related to a specific cell. A very simple example might be to pop up an alert view containing the indexPath of the button's cell.

To do this, you need to update the didTapButtonInCell: function, as shown in Listing 9-4.

Listing 9-4. Reacting to Individual Cells

```
func didTapButtonInCell(sender: UIButton) {

    let cell = sender.superview!.superview as! UICollectionViewCell
    let indexPathAtTap = collectionView.indexPathForCell(cell)

    let alert = UIAlertController(title: "Something happened!", message: "A button was
    tapped at row \(indexPathAtTap?.row)", preferredStyle: .Alert)
    let action = UIAlertAction(title: "OK", style: .Default, handler: nil)

    alert.addAction(action)

    self.presentViewController(alert, animated: true, completion: nil)

}
```

You'll notice something slightly strange about the first line. You're getting the superview of the superview of the button.

That's because the button sits inside the cell's contentView, which sits inside the cell. Figure 9-2 shows how the elements fit together.

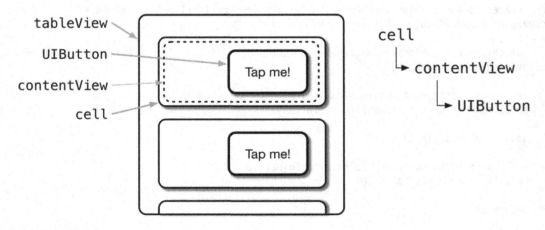

Figure 9-2. How the cell views fit together

Putting this all together, you now have a set of cells with buttons that trigger row-specific actions, shown in Figure 9-3.

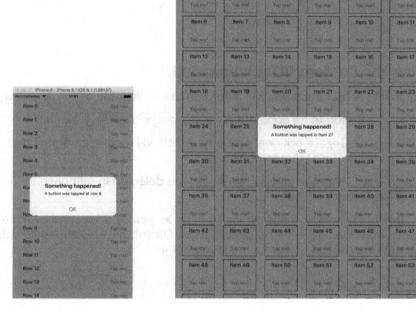

Figure 9-3. The row-specific alertView

A More Robust Subclass-based Approach

Although it works, the simple approach has a major flaw – it relies on the button being in exactly the right place in the cell's view hierarchy. If that changes for any reason, you would have to ensure that the `didTapButtonInCell:` function was updated to match.

A less hacky approach is to use a custom cell subclass which calls back to a delegate in order to react to the tap on the button.

This involves making some changes to the project as it stands:

- Declaring a protocol to define the interaction between the cell and the view controller.

- Implementing a custom `UITableViewCell` subclass which has a delegate property, and adds a button which makes a call to the delegate when it is tapped.

- Amending the Storyboard to use instances of the custom `UITableViewCell` subclass

- Updating the view controller to set the cell's delegate as the cell is instantiated; and handle the delegate callback from the cell.

Declaring the Protocol

To declare the protocol, you'll need to add it to the very top of the view controller, as shown in Listing 9-5:

Listing 9-5. The Delegate Protocol Declaration

```
protocol InCellButtonProtocol {
    func didTapButtonInCell(cell: ButtonCell)
}
```

Implementing the Custom UITableViewCell

The custom UITableViewCell subclass will differ from a vanilla table cell in three ways:

- ▣ It will add a button to its contentView in the awakeFromNib() function

- ▣ It will have a delegate optional property, which will require an object that conforms to the InCellButtonProtocol

- ▣ It will have an IBAction function that calls the delegate in response to taps in the button.

Start by adding a new class for the custom cell – File ➤ New ➤ File, and select the Cocoa Touch class option from the Source templates. Call the file ButtonCell, and make sure that it is a subclass of UITableViewCell, as shown in Figure 9-4:

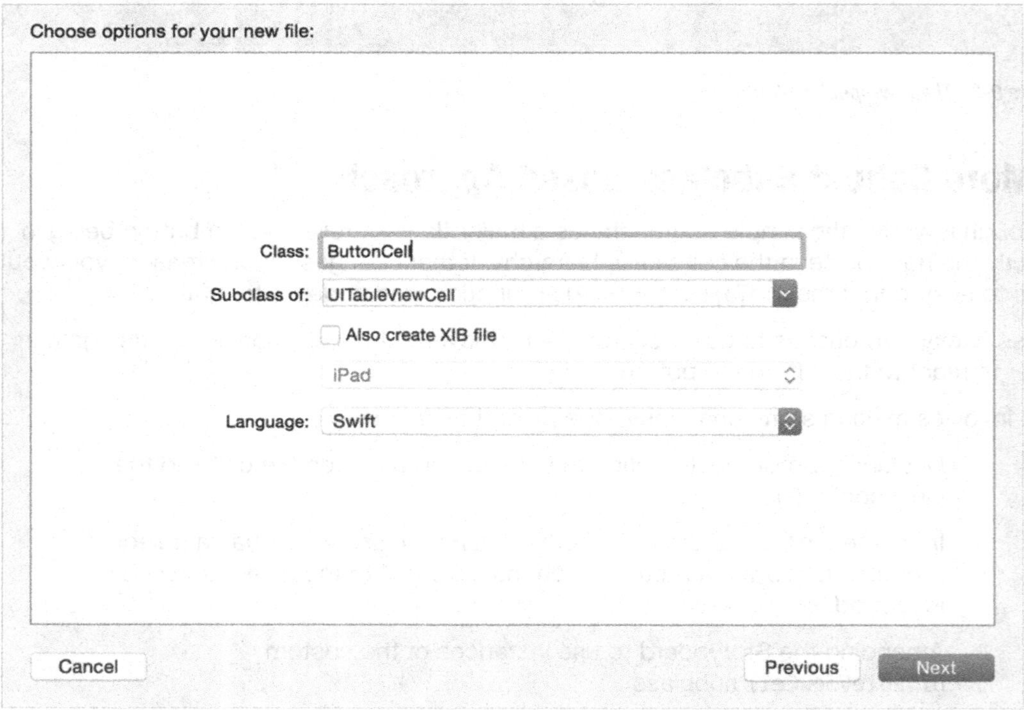

Choose options for your new file:

Class:	ButtonCell
Subclass of:	UITableViewCell
	☐ Also create XIB file
	iPad
Language:	Swift

Cancel   Previous   Next

Figure 9-4. Adding the cell subclass

Adding the Button to the Cell's ContentView

To add the button to the cell's `contentView`, you'll override the `awakeFromNib()` function – this is called when the cell is retrieved from the Storyboard in the `cellForRowAtIndexPath:` function.

As things stand, there will be a stub function in the ButtonCell class, as shown in Listing 9-6:

Listing 9-6. The Stub awakeFromNib() Function

```
override func awakeFromNib() {
    super.awakeFromNib()
    // Initialization code
}
```

Update this function as shown in Listing 9-7 – this is based on the code which you saw in the previous section, but with some updates that are detailed below.

Listing 9-7. The Updated awakeFromNib() Function

```
override func awakeFromNib() {
    super.awakeFromNib()
    // Initialization code

    let button = UIButton(type: UIButtonType.RoundedRect)
    button.setTitle("Tap me!", forState: UIControlState.Normal)
    button.sizeToFit()
    button.translatesAutoresizingMaskIntoConstraints = false

    button.addTarget(self, action: "didTapButton:", forControlEvents: UIControlEvents.TouchUpInside)

    let vConstraint = NSLayoutConstraint(item: button, attribute: NSLayoutAttribute.CenterY,
    relatedBy:
        NSLayoutRelation.Equal, toItem: self.contentView, attribute: NSLayoutAttribute.
        CenterY, multiplier: 1.0, constant: 0)

    let hConstraint = NSLayoutConstraint(item: button, attribute: NSLayoutAttribute.Right,
relatedBy: NSLayoutRelation.Equal, toItem: self.contentView, attribute: NSLayoutAttribute.
Right, multiplier: 1.0, constant: 0)

    self.contentView.addSubview(button)
    self.contentView.addConstraints([vConstraint, hConstraint])

}
```

There are a couple of differences – firstly, the button has no `tag` set, and secondly, the added target is the cell instance itself:

```
button.addTarget(self, action: "didTapButton:", forControlEvents: UIControlEvents.
TouchUpInside)
```

Otherwise, everything is the same – the button is created; the title is set; it is sized to fit the text; the attributes are created; and added to the cell.

Adding a Delegate Property

When the button is tapped, it will call back to the delegate which is responsible for implementing whatever action should take place.

In order for this to happen, add a delegate property to the ButtonCell class:

```
var delegate: InCellButtonProtocol?
```

This declares that the delegate is an optional that conforms to the InCellButtonProtocol.

Adding the Code to Handle a Button Tap

The action that we added to the button in the awakeFromNib() function calls the ButtonCell's didTapButton: function, which you need to add. This is shown in Listing 9-8:

Listing 9-8. The didTapButton: function

```
func didTapButton(sender: AnyObject) {
    if let delegate = delegate {
        delegate.didTapButtonInCell(self)
    }
}
```

This simple checks if there is a delegate set, and calls the didTapButtonInCell: function if there is, passing a reference to itself as the parameter.

This is all the changes that are needed in the ButtonCell class. Now there's a change required in the Storyboard.

Updating the Storyboard

Switch to the Storyboard, and update the prototype cell so that is an instance of ButtonCell. In the Identity Inspector, click into the Class field in the Custom Class section, and add ButtonCell as shown in Figure 9-5:

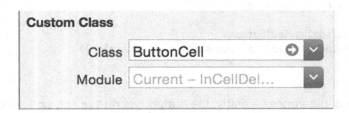

Figure 9-5. Updating the Cell's Class

Updating the View Controller

Now it's time to update the ViewController to use the new cell class, and react to calls from the cell.

Firstly, conform the ViewController class to the InCellButtonProtocol by updating the class declaration:

```
class ViewController: UIViewController, InCellButtonProtocol {
```

Then add the didTapButtonInCell: function as shown in Listing 9-9:

Listing 9-9. The didTapButtonInCell: Function

```
func didTapButtonInCell(cell: ButtonCell) {

    let indexPathAtTap = tableView.indexPathForCell(cell)

    let alert = UIAlertController(title: "Something happened!", message: "A button was ↵
    tapped at row \(indexPathAtTap!.row)", preferredStyle: .Alert)
    let action = UIAlertAction(title: "OK", style: .Default, handler: nil)

    alert.addAction(action)

    self.presentViewController(alert, animated: true, completion: nil)

}
```

This is similar to the previous version, but the cell parameter is an instance of the ButtonCell class.

Next, update the cellForRowAtIndexPath: function so that it matches Listing 9-10:

Listing 9-10. The Updated cellForRowAtIndexPath: Function

```
func tableView(tableView: UITableView, cellForRowAtIndexPath indexPath: NSIndexPath) -> ↵
UITableViewCell {

    let cell = tableView.dequeueReusableCellWithIdentifier("CellIdentifier", forIndexPath: ↵
    indexPath) as! ButtonCell
    cell.textLabel?.text = "Row \(tableData[indexPath.row])"

    if cell.delegate == nil {
        cell.delegate = self
    }

    return cell
}
```

This hasn't changed much – but instead of calling the addButtonToCell: function, the cell's delegate is being set as a reference to the view controller itself.

At this point, you can also clean up the view controller a bit by removing the now-redundant addButtonToCell: function.

If you run the project again, you'll see that the functionality is exactly the same as it was previously. The difference is that we've refactored the code to implement an architecture that is much cleaner than before:

■ There is now a separation of concerns between cell and view controller.

■ The code to handle interaction with the button is much more robust, with no reference to the cell's view hierarchy.

■ The project has become more adaptable, as it is now possible to implement the cell's delegate functionality in a class other than the view controller.

Adding Gestures to Cells

You're not limited to adding controls to cells; you can also enable additional functionality by attaching gesture recognizers. As you will see in the next section, this opens up the possibility of adding swipe gestures to expose additional information. A simpler interaction is to add the ability to double-tap a cell in order to trigger some action or transformation.

Listing 9-11 shows how to add a double-tap recognizer to each cell in the cellForRowAtIndexPath: function.

Listing 9-11. Adding a gestureRecognizer to Each Cell

```
func tableView(tableView: UITableView, cellForRowAtIndexPath indexPath: NSIndexPath) ↩
 -> UITableViewCell {

    let cell = tableView.dequeueReusableCellWithIdentifier("CellIdentifier", ↩
  forIndexPath: indexPath)

    cell.textLabel?.text = "Row \(tableData[indexPath.row])"

    if cell.gestureRecognizers?.count != 1 {
        let tapRecognizer = UITapGestureRecognizer(target: self, action: ↩
    "didDoubleTapInCell:")
        tapRecognizer.numberOfTapsRequired = 2
        cell.addGestureRecognizer(tapRecognizer)
    }

    return cell
}
```

Having added the double-tap recognizer to the cell, you'll probably want to be able to distinguish which cell has been tapped. Here's how you can access the cell in the example didDoubleTapCell: function:

```
func didTapButtonInCell(sender: AnyObject) {

    let recognizer = sender as! UITapGestureRecognizer
    let cell = recognizer.view as! UITableViewCell
    let indexPathAtTap = tableView.indexPathForCell(cell)

    ... do something with cell here ...

}
```

The UIGestureRecognizer instance that responded to the interaction is passed through to the function as sender. This has a view property that's a pointer to the UIView object to which the gesture recognizer was attached.

In this case, it's the cell, so the sender.view property can be cast to an instance of UITableViewCell, at which point you can treat it as the cell that it is.

Obviously you're not restricted to just tap gestures: pinches, pans, rotations, long presses, and swipes are all available. Some of these will work better in the limited size of a cell than others, though, so some careful experimentation is called for in order to get the best overall user experience. You may find that some multi-touch gestures are only practical on the larger user interface of the iPad.

Adding Pull-to-Refresh to Table Views

Pull-to-refresh is an action that triggers a refresh of a table's data in response to the user pulling the table *down past the top*, and then letting go. Instead of springing straight back, they'll see an activity indicator. Once the data has been updated (or sometimes, if the network call times out) the table "springs" back up again, and the contents get refreshed.

It's a brilliant piece of interface design–but actually not one originally created by Apple. It first appeared in a third-party Twitter client; was quickly implemented as a number of open-source controls; and eventually found its way into the official iOS SDK.

It's also very easy to implement. The easiest option is when you're using a UITableViewController, but it's also possible to implement if you have a table view inside a standard UIViewController. We'll look at both approaches in order.

Implementing Pull-to-Refresh with UITableViewController

In this example, I'm assuming that you're using a UITableViewController instance in a Storyboard, as shown in Figure 9-6.

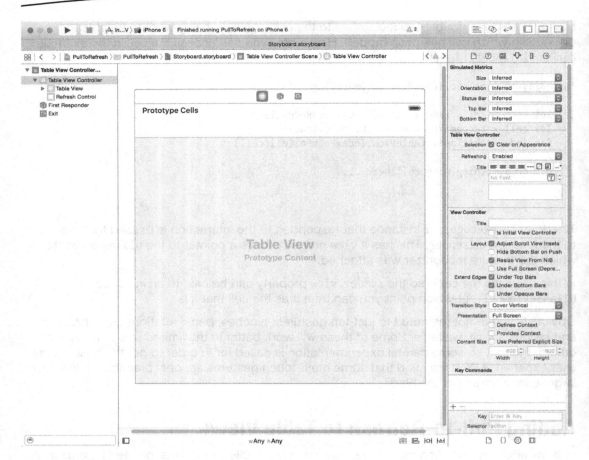

Figure 9-6. A UITableViewController in the Storyboard

Adding the Refresh Control

In the Attributes Inspector, there's a drop-down option for Refreshing. Select the Enabled option, as shown in Figure 9-7.

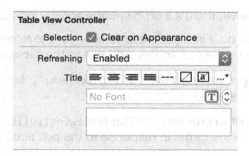

Figure 9-7. *Setting the Refreshing option*

If you run the project now, you'll see that you can pull down on the table, and the activity indicator appears at the top, as shown in Figure 9-8.

Figure 9-8. *Pull-to-refresh in the table view*

Although this looks impressive, there's a problem: the activity indicator doesn't disappear!

There's a little more work to do. First, you need to connect the refresh control to a function in response to being invoked by the pull action. Add this to the viewDidLoad function:

```
refreshControl?.addTarget(self, action: "didPullRefresh:", forControlEvents:  ⏎
UIControlEvents.ValueChanged)
```

The refreshControl is a built-in property of UITableViewController. Here, you're adding the didPullRefresh: function as the target in response to the pull action.

Implementing the pullToRefresh Function

Add a new function, as shown in Listing 9-12.

Listing 9-12. The pullToRefresh Function

```
func didPullRefresh(sender: UIRefreshControl) {

    tableData.append(tableData.count)
    tableView.reloadData()

    sender.endRefreshing()

}
```

This function does three things:

- It adds another entry to the end of the tableData array.
- It forces the table to reload the data from the model.
- It stops the UIRefreshControl from spinning, and animates its removal.

This is an extremely trivial example. What you would be far more likely to do in practice is call some kind of network manager function to retrieve information from an API.

If you run the app again, you'll see that the activity indicator appears, followed by a new entry at the end of the table. Once the table has been refreshed, the activity indicator is animated off the top of the view.

Adding a UIRefreshControl to a Table View

The process in the previous section was predicated on using a UITableViewController. If instead you have a plain UITableView embedded inside a UIViewController, the process is a little more involved.

The extra steps required are to

- Add a property for a UIRefreshControl to the view controller class.
- Instantiate the UIRefreshControl and give it an action.
- Add the newly-instantiated UIRefreshControl to the table view.

Adding the UIRefreshControl Property

This is simple a case of adding a property to the `UIViewController`:

```
var refreshControl: UIRefreshControl!
```

Instantiating the Refresh Control

Before it can be used, the property needs to be instantiated. Since this needs to be done before it's used, one obvious place to do this is in the viewController's `viewDidLoad` function:

```
override func viewDidLoad() {
    super.viewDidLoad()

    ... setup the table and data ...

    refreshControl = UIRefreshControl()
    refreshControl.addTarget(self, action: "didPullRefresh:", forControlEvents: ↩
    .ValueChanged)
    tableView.addSubview(refreshControl)

}
```

Here, you're setting up the table and its data, and then instantiating the `refreshControl` property:

```
refreshControl = UIRefreshControl()
```

With that done, you can set the `didPullRefresh:` function as the action for a `valueChanged` event. This event is triggered by the pull-down interaction on the table:

```
    refreshControl.addTarget(self, action: "didPullRefresh:", forControlEvents: ↩
    .ValueChanged)
```

With the function linked to the `refreshControl`, you simply add it to the `tableView`:

```
tableView.addSubview(refreshControl)
```

The end result is exactly the same as if you'd used a `UITableViewController` and set up its in-built `refreshControl` property.

Searching in Tables and Collection Views

If you've got a view displaying any significant amount of data, you owe it to your users to give them the means to navigate around easily. There's nothing more frustrating than having to scroll through hundreds of entries in search of the one that you're after.

Previously you looked at adding indexes to the `tableView`; that's a good way of letting the user jump between sections. But sometimes even that's not enough. Wouldn't it be much better if you could provide a means of searching the content of the table so the user could find the row for which they were looking?

Fortunately for us, the iOS SDK includes the `UISearchBar` class and its associated delegate protocols. This class makes implementing search in table views almost trivially easy; building the same functionality from scratch would be significantly more work.

The `UISearchBar` class operates in exactly the same way for both table and collection views. This example will focus on searching within a `UITableView`, but the processes are identical between the two controls.

Adding a Search Bar to the Table

The `UISearchBar` provides a styled text field that you can add to your interface as required. The normal layout for a table view is to put the search back at the top, although there's nothing to stop you putting somewhere else.

You can embed the search bar within in the table itself, in which case it will scroll with the table (shown in Figure 9-9).

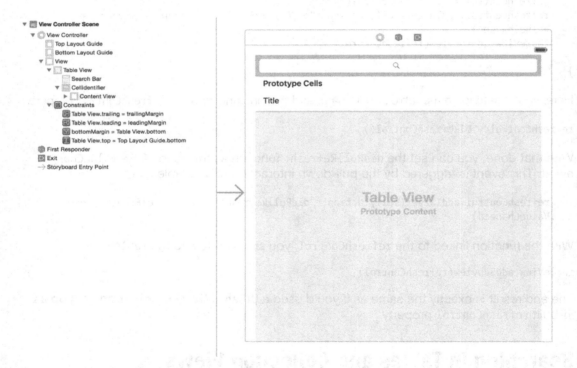

Figure 9-9. The search bar placed within the table

In this situation, the search bar will scroll with the table. If you want it to remain "anchored" at the top, you can place it outside the table, as shown in Figure 9-10.

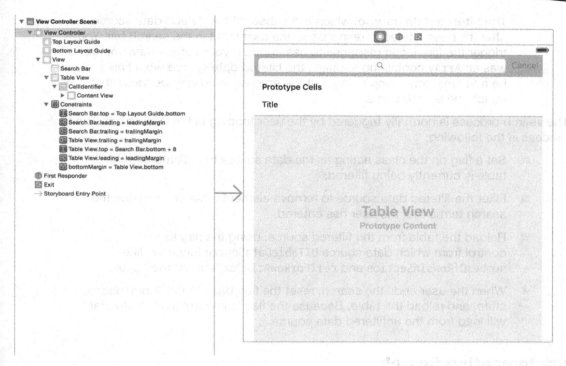

Figure 9-10. The search bar placed above the table

You can use AutoLayout constraints to set up and secure the place of the search bar within your layout.

Regardless of where the `UISearchBar` is placed, it's important that its delegate outlet is connected.

You can do this visually, by Ctrl-clicking in the bar and dragging over to the relevant controller object in the Document Outline to connect the `delegate` outlet; or programmatically by setting the `delegate` property:

```
searchBar.delegate = self
```

How Search Works

The basic principle of table view search is that the table has two data sources:

- The **default data source**, which contains all the data that the table will display. This is implemented in the same way as you've been doing throughout the book so far. For example, it might be an `Array` containing `Strings`.

■ The **filtered data source**, which is a subset of the default data source after it's been filtered in response to the user input in the search bar. You trigger the filtering in response to user input. If your default data source was an Array containing Strings, the filtered data source would also be a String-containing Array, but the entries would only be those that match the search terms.

The search process is normally triggered by the user tapping in the Search bar. The typical process is the following:

■ Set a flag on the class acting as the data source to indicate that the table is currently being filtered.

■ Filter the filtered data source to remove elements that don't match the search terms that the user has entered.

■ Reload the table from the filtered source, using the flag to control from which data source UITableDataSource functions like numberOfRowsInSection and cellForRowAtIndexPath get their data.

■ When the user ends the search, reset the flag back to the "normal table" state, and reload the table. Because the flag is in normal mode, the table will load from the unfiltered data source.

Implementing Search

Let's work through the process of wiring up a search bar and filtering a data source. For the purposes of this exercise, you're going to use an Array of Strings as the table's data source and filter based on the text that you type in the search bar.

You can use whatever source data you like, but the sample project for this chapter uses a list of German spa towns (there's lots of them!) It looks like Figure 9-11.

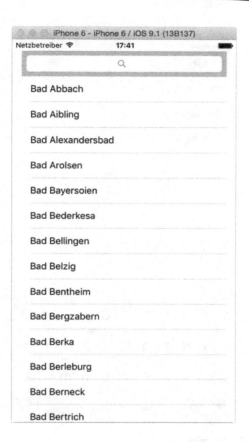

Figure 9-11. The running app

As you type in the search bar, the list will be filtered using a case-insensitive substring search and the table update (shown in Figure 9-12).

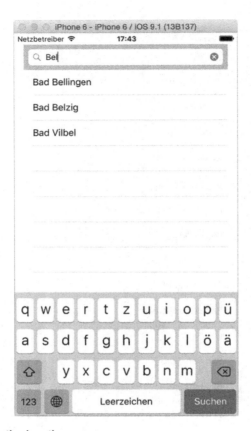

Figure 9-12. A basic search function in action

I'll assume that you've

- Built a basic table that displays items from an Array of Strings.
- Added a UISearchBar at the top of the table view, and connected its delegate outlet to the view controller managing the table.
- Added an IBOutlet property called searchBar to the view controller, and connected this to the UISearchBar in the Storyboard.

The first stage is to add two additional properties to the view controller class:

```
var filteredTableData = [String]()
```

This is an array to hold the list of filtered results, and will be used to feed the table while it's in search mode:

```
var searchActive: Bool = false
```

The searchActive flag will be used by the UITableViewDatasource methods to determine whether they should use the filtered or unfiltered data model.

With those properties in place, the next stage is to set up the UISearchBarDelegate.

Implementing the UISearchBarDelegate Functions

Add the UISearchBarDelegate functions to an extension of the view controller. Listing 9-13 shows the first two functions to add.

Listing 9-13. Implementing the UISearchBarDelegate Functions

```
extension ViewController: UISearchBarDelegate {

    func searchBarTextDidBeginEditing(searchBar: UISearchBar) {
        searchActive = true
    }

    func searchBarTextDidEndEditing(searchBar: UISearchBar) {
        searchActive = false
        tableView.reloadData()
    }

}
```

The searchBarTextDidBeginEditing function simply sets the searchActive flag to true.

The searchBarTextDidEndEditing function does the opposite, and then forces the table to reload, so that it contains unfiltered data once more.

Now it's time for the function that will handle the actual searching, shown in Listing 9-14 – this will also go inside the UISearchBarDelegate extension.

Listing 9-14. The searchBar:textDidChange Function

```
func searchBar(searchBar: UISearchBar, textDidChange searchText: String) {

    if searchText.characters.count == 0 {
        searchActive = false
        tableView.reloadData()
        return
    }

    searchActive = true

    filteredTableData = tableData.filter({( spaTown: String) -> Bool in

        let spaRange = Range(start: spaTown.startIndex, end: spaTown.endIndex)

        let stringMatch = spaTown.rangeOfString(searchText,  ↵
            options: NSStringCompareOptions.CaseInsensitiveSearch,  ↵
            range: spaRange,  ↵
            locale: NSLocale.autoupdatingCurrentLocale())

        return stringMatch != nil

    })

    tableView.reloadData()

}
```

This looks a bit intimidating at first, but it's not as bad as it seems.

The first part checks whether the user has cleared the search field. If there are no characters in the searchText, you assumed that searching has completed. The searchActive flag is set to false, you reload the table to show the unfiltered data, and then return:

```
if searchText.characters.count == 0 {
    searchActive = false
    tableView.reloadData()
    return
}
```

If there are characters in the searchString, then it's game on.

First, you set the searchActive flag to true so that the UITableViewDelegate method will use the filteredTableData array (you'll implement this in a moment):

```
searchActive = true
```

Now comes the actual filtering. Here, you're using the Array filter function to step through the tableData array and place any Strings that match the searchText into the filteredTableData array.

The filter function steps through each entry in turn, and passes it as the spaTown parameter to a closure that returns a Bool. If the returned Bool is true, then the entry is added to the filteredTableData array. If it's false, the entry is ignored.

The closure starts by creating a Range from the spaTown parameter:

```
let spaRange = Range(start: spaTown.startIndex, end: spaTown.endIndex)
```

It then uses the rangeOfString function to look through the spaTown string to see if the contents of searchText appear anywhere. For example, if the spaTown contained "Bad Marianberg" then a searchText containing "enb" would match:

```
let stringMatch = spaTown.rangeOfString(searchText, ↵
        options: NSStringCompareOptions.CaseInsensitiveSearch, ↵
        range: spaRange, ↵
        locale: NSLocale.autoupdatingCurrentLocale())
```

The options ensure that the search is case-insensitive, and the locale ensures that locale-specific factors such as accented characters are handled correctly.

If a match is found, the rangeOfString function returns the range of characters in the spaTown string where it was found. If there's no match, it returns nil.

You can use this to decide whether to return a true or false to the filter function. If nothing was found, it'll have a range of nil and can return false. If something was found, then it'll return true so that the spaTown will be added to the filteredTableData array.

Finally, having filtered the tableData array, you call the table's reloadData() function to force it to reload.

Updating the UITableViewDatasource Functions

If you run the project now, you can enter text into the search box, but you won't see any difference in the data that the table displays.

This is because the table is loading its data from the `tableData` array regardless of whether it's in search mode or not. You need to update the `UITableViewDelegate` function to use the right data source.

There are two functions that need to be updated. Listing 9-15 shows `tableView:numberOf RowsInSection:`

Listing 9-15. The Updated tableView:numberOfRowsInSection: Function

```
func tableView(tableView: UITableView, numberOfRowsInSection section: Int) -> Int {

    if searchActive {
        return filteredTableData.count
    }

    return tableData.count
}
```

It's actually very simple. If the table is in `searchActive` mode, then the number of rows is derived from the `filteredTableData` array; if not, the number of rows is derived from `tableData` as normal.

Listing 9-16 shows the updated `tableView:cellForRowAtIndexPath:` function. It uses the same approach: if the table is being searched, use the `filteredTableData` array as the data mode; if not, use `tableData`.

Listing 9-16. The Updated tableView:cellForRowAtIndexPath: Function

```
func tableView(tableView: UITableView, cellForRowAtIndexPath indexPath: NSIndexPath) ↩
  -> UITableViewCell {

    let cell = tableView.dequeueReusableCellWithIdentifier("CellIdentifier", ↩
  forIndexPath: indexPath)

    if searchActive {
        cell.textLabel!.text = filteredTableData[indexPath.row]
    } else {
        cell.textLabel!.text = tableData[indexPath.row]
    }

    return cell
}
```

There's one other piece of housekeeping to do before things are completely finished. In the `UISearchBarDelegate` extension, add the function shown in Listing 9-17.

Listing 9-17. The searchBarCancelButtonClicked Function

```
func searchBarCancelButtonClicked(searchBar: UISearchBar) {
    searchBar.text = ""
    searchBar.resignFirstResponder()
    searchActive = false
}
```

This clears the search bar, dismisses the keyboard, and sets the searchActive flag to false in response to the user tapping the Cancel button in the Search Bar.

You haven't actually set the Cancel button up so far, so switch back to the Storyboard, highlight the Search Bar, and select the Shows Cancel Button option in the Attributes Inspector (shown in Figure 9-13).

Figure 9-13. The Shows Cancel Button option

If you run the project again, you'll see a working Search function complete with a Cancel function that dismisses the keyboard and reloads the table with the full data set (Figure 9-14).

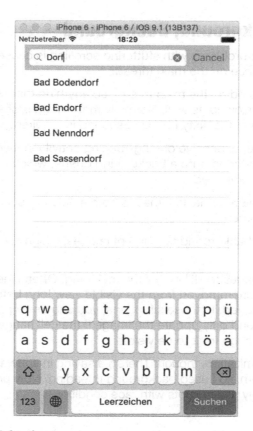

Figure 9-14. The working search function

Happy, Healthy Tables

If the overall user experience of the iOS device family had to be boiled down to a single adjective, I'd go for "smooth." Everything about the interface of well-written apps moves without hesitation, stuttering, or jerkiness. Get it right, and the overall impression is that of a precision, well-oiled device.

Table views have a lot of moving parts, so if that level of smoothness is going to go wrong anywhere, it could be here. Although the `UITableView`, `UICollectionView` and their supporting classes are designed and written for performance, it *is* possible to build table and collection views that don't perform well, especially if you lose sight of some basic best practices.

In this section, we take a look at some things you can do—both quick fixes, and some more in-depth—to make sure that your views perform as well as they possibly can.

Background, Background, Background

One of the most common problems with stuttering scrolling is caused by expensive and slow processing taking place on the main thread.

The iOS interface is rendered on the main thread, so anything that slows this down will cause the interface to be slowed as well. Normally that's not a problem, but scrolling is one situation where every one of the sixty frames a second is required.

As a general rule of thumb, expensive or long-running activity–network requests in particular–should be dispatched onto a background queue, which calls back to the main thread when the work is completed.

This is often an issue if you're retrieving images from a network source. There are a couple of techniques you can use here:

- Asynchronous background fetching of images, which are then updated once retrieved.

- Placeholder images to "fill in" for the real thing. Often when scrolling a view, the cells are removed from the visible view long before the image can be downloaded. In those situations, you can use a placeholder image initially, and only update the image if the cell hangs around on the screen long enough for it to be visible.

Beware of premature optimization, though. There's a saying in software engineering that goes "I had a bottleneck problem, so I used background threading. Now problems two have I." It's very easy to get completely tied in knots with race conditions.

Are the Cells Cached?

Building cells is expensive in processing terms, so the UITableView and UICollectionView classes provide caching and dequeuing functionality to allow constructed cells to be reused. This can make a dramatic difference if you've got more rows than can fit on the screen.

The two places to check are the tableView:cellForRowAtIndexPath: or collectionView:cellForItemAtIndexPath: methods. For maximum efficiency, you should be doing one of three things:

- Dequeuing an existing reusable cell before creating an new instance:

```
let cell = [tableView ↵
dequeueReusableCellWithIdentifier:CellIdentifier];
```

- Registering a class for the cell:

```
tableView.registerClass(MyCell.self, forCellReuseIdentifier: ↵
"MyCustomCell")
```

- Registering a nib file containing the cell layout:

```
tableView.registerNib(UINib(nibName: "MyCell", bundle: nil), ↵
forCellReuseIdentifier: "MyCustomCell")
```

The only exceptions to the first rule are if you're dealing with a static table or if you'll never have more cells than will fit into the visible area. In the later situation you can probably get away without cached cells because they'll always remain visible.

Do Your Table Cells Have Varying Heights?

Behind the scenes, UITableView uses the cell height to build a number of elements relating to the "chrome" of the table. When all cells in the tableView are the same height, this can be done relatively cheaply, but if the cell height varies, these calculations get repeated every time a new cell is created.

To extract the last ounce of speed from a table view, it's most efficient to keep the cell heights identical. Whether this is possible is going to vary from project to project, of course, but if your cell heights only vary within a limited range, you may find you're better off designing them with a single consistent height and managing the differences within the internal cell layout.

If that's not possible, implement UITableViewDelegate's tableView:estimatedHeightForCell: function to return an estimated height. The table will use this value to calculate the full content area by assuming that all cells will have this height, and defer the exact calculation until the very last moment possible.

It's not a get-out-jail-free card—you can run into problems if your estimated row height is wildly different from the actual value—but this function can help.

Cutting the Cost of Compositing

The iPhone and iPad have incredibly powerful GPUs considering the limitations of the form factor and battery constraints. Even so, they do have limits, and one thing that pushes at those limits is drawing views with transparency.

The reason is fairly apparent when you think about it. Put crudely, the device builds the view front-to-back and if a front layer is opaque, it doesn't need to bother with even considering what lies behind it when rendering the screen.

Create a layer with transparent pixels, though, and that calculation has to take place, and the more calculations that are needed, the slower the rendering process will become.

Life would be great if all elements of a view could be opaque, but of course it's never that simple. Gradients, drop shadows, and the like are all illusions that are only possible thanks to transparency, so a purely opaque interface would be a pretty dull one.

The key to maximum application performance is to use transparency only where it's needed. This then poses another dilemma: how can you tell what's transparent and what isn't? Fortunately, there's a tool that can help.

Checking Transparency in the Simulator

The Simulator has some often-overlooked tools that allow you to peer deep inside the interface of your apps. One of the features that it provides enables the visualization of the level of transparency and blending in your views, which can then be used to fine-tune your interfaces.

- `Color blended layers` highlights multiple view layers that are drawn on top of each other. Red layers indicate where there are transparent areas that need to be blended with lower layers, while green shows opaque areas that don't need blending.

  It's not always possible to completely remove blended layers, but if you're having problems with rendering speeds and there's a lot of red showing, it is worth digging further to see if the interface can be rejigged to remove as much blending as possible.

- `Color copied images` indicates images that have a color format that the GPU can't handle directly. In this situation, the rendering will be handled by the CPU. That's doubly-expensive because it uses resources that will be needed elsewhere, and the CPU is not optimized for image processing.

- `Color misaligned images` highlights images with bounds that don't align to pixel boundaries. This causes additional rendering to be needed, which can slow things down.

  This is often caused by mis-sizing of assets between @2x and @3x sizes. Check to see if there are the image assets with sizes that have odd numbers of pixels, and resize them to even numbers if necessary.

- `Color offscreen-rendered` highlights layers that have been rendered separately to the main screen. This is something that can happen automatically, so it's not always an indication of a problem per-se, but it's caused by applying masks to layers, so this may be something to look for in an effort to optimize your interfaces.

Figure 9-15 shows an example of this highlighting in action, in the iOS Calendar app – what's interesting to note is that even an app which has been built and optimized by Apple engineers still has a certain amount of blending going on. That's because it's not necessarily a bad thing per se – the key to optimizing performance is to aim for as little as possible.

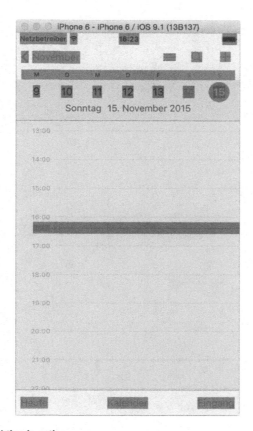

Figure 9-15. View blend highlighting in action

Graphics processing and image optimization is a complex subject. There are some excellent deep-dives into the problems and pitfalls available in WWDC videos on the Developer Portal which are well-worth checking out.

Summary

In this chapter, you looked at bringing your table views to life by transforming cells from static displays of data through adding some interaction to the cells. There's a range of ways to do this:

- Embedding custom controls such as buttons, switches, and sliders within the cell

- Implementing pull-to-refresh functionality

- Adding gesture recognizers to cells to support double taps and so on

- Implementing search within the table's contents

Finally, you looked at some of the processes to ensure that the performance of your table views is as slick as possible.

Chapter 10

Using Tables for Navigation

Navigation controllers are an almost ubiquitous feature of the iOS user interface. They enable a user to manage the navigation through a hierarchy of content, moving through the tree of content items in a simple and consistent way.

Examples of this kind of user interface pattern abound. The iPhone's built-in Contacts app is a classic example. Contacts are displayed in a table view, and tapping a row pushes in a view showing the details, as you can see in Figure 10-1.

Figure 10-1. *The built-in iPhone Contacts app*

This user interface pattern is so common that the iOS SDK provides a controller for this specific purpose, which handles the heavy lifting of the navigation for you. This chapter will show you how to create and configure a navigation-based app with `UINavigationController`.

This is done in five steps.

1. Create the skeleton structure of the app.

2. Create some example data to feed the `UINavigationController`.

3. Build the detail view.

4. Link the `UINavigationController` with the detail view.

5. Tweak the `UINavigationController` to customize its appearance.

The approach that I take here is a little unusual, in that you would often create a navigation controller-based app using the template that Xcode provides. That's fine, but the template does a lot for you, and it hides significant details about how the various pieces fit together.

Building the app from scratch, by contrast, will give you a good understanding of the anatomy of a navigation controller.

The Navigation Controller Interface Pattern

The way in which navigation controllers fit together with the application structure always reminds me of Russian dolls. Views fit inside controllers, which fit inside windows; at first it can seem unfeasibly complicated.

Navigation controllers act in a similar way to the page history and forward and back buttons of a web browser. As you visit each new page, that page is added to the browser's history. The forward and back buttons allow you to move up and down the list of pages that you've visited. That's the pattern used by the Contacts app, shown in Figure 10-2.

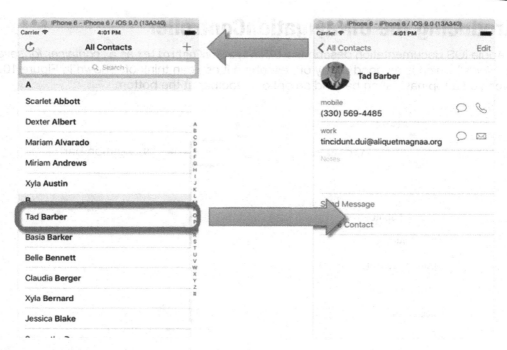

Figure 10-2. *Pushing and popping views*

Instead of a list of pages, the navigation controller is basically a stack of view controllers. The top-most view controller in the stack is visible, so in order to display a new view controller, you push that onto the top of the stack. Visually, the new view controller usually appears to slide in from the right, as in Figure 10-3.

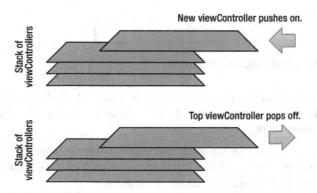

Figure 10-3. *Pushing and popping view controllers into the navigation controller stack*

When you want to navigate "backwards," you pop the current view controller off the stack to expose the one underneath. The top-most view controller usually appears to slide off to the right.

Introducing the UINavigationController

The Apple iOS documentation describes a `UINavigationController` as a "*container for several other views*" which is as good a way of describing it as I can think of. Shown in Figure 10-4, it gives you a top navigation bar and an optional toolbar at the bottom.

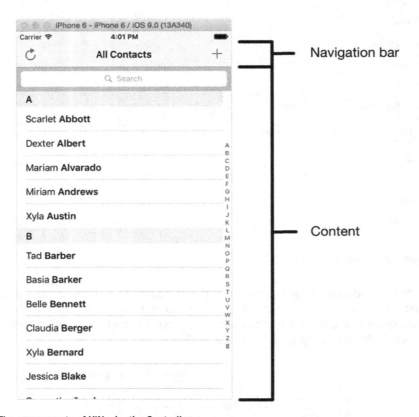

Figure 10-4. The components of UINavigationController

There's also space for bar button items on the navigation bar. Between the top and bottom bar there's a space for your custom content to be loaded into: it's into this space that you'll push and pop view controllers.

Interacting with the content inside the view controllers—tapping on a row, tapping on a button, and so on—is the cue to call the `UINavigationController`'s `pushViewController:animated:` and `popViewController:animated:` functions.

As well as moving through the stack of view controllers one by one, you can also head straight to the top of the stack by calling the `UIViewController` class's `popToRootControllerAnimated:` function.

And finally, pushing (or popping) to a specific view controller is achieved by the `popToViewController:animated` function, which takes a parameter of type `UIViewController` through which you can indicate which controller you're after.

> **Note**   Although using `UITableViews` with `UIViewControllers` is far and away the most common scenario, it's worth remembering that the view controllers you push and pop can be *any* kind of view controller.
>
> You're not restricted to using a table at the top level; you could just as easily push in the next view by tapping on, say, a `UIButton` as you could by tapping on a row in a `tableView`. Use whatever will provide the user experience that you're trying to deliver.

THE NAVIGATION CONTROLLER EXAMPLE APPLICATION

Illustrating the function of the `UINavigationController` really calls for an example application that is a bit more complex than the simple apps that I've been using as the examples so far. To do this, I've built a relatively simple app to use as the basis of this chapter. It's far from being something that you'd want to buy from the App Store, but it'll do for these purposes.

If you've got kids (or even if you haven't and you've got friends who do), you know that one of the most important decisions you can make before the little bundle of joy arrives is deciding on a name. Get it wrong, and you could condemn your offspring to an educational lifetime of teasing in the playground. Don't get it right, and Great Aunt Agatha will cut you out of her will for not continuing the family tradition of naming all first-born males Algernon.

To help you navigate through this minefield, what you need (of course!) is an iOS app: enter the oh-so-imaginative titled Baby Names. Although this most emphatically won't win any awards for either design or ground-breaking functionality, it gives us something to work with.

Creating a Navigation Controller App

Probably because navigation controller-based apps are so common, most versions of Xcode so far have shipped with a template for creating this type of app. It provides much of the plumbing ready-made to speed you on your way. You also get a lot of functionality for free if you use a `UITableViewController` object in a Storyboard.

While that's great, you're going to take the back-to-basics approach, and build the app entirely by hand. That's not because there's anything wrong with the app templates, but if you start from scratch you'll end up with a much better feel for how all the pieces fit together.

Start by creating a new app in Xcode (File ➤ New ➤ New Project) that uses the Single View Application template, as shown in Figure 10-5.

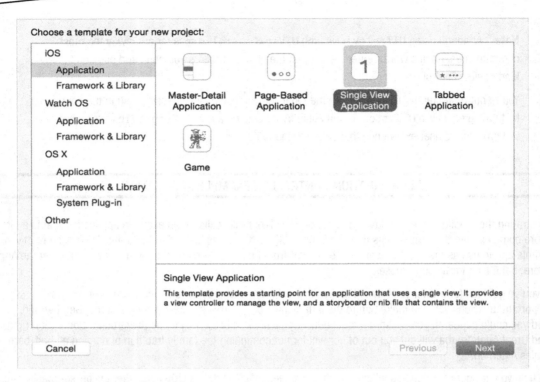

Figure 10-5. Xcode's new application dialog

> **Tip**   The selection of default templates that ship with Xcode tends to alter from version to version (this book was written using Xcode 7.1).
>
> Your version of Xcode may look different from this, but among the templates there'll be one that creates a skeleton application with a single view; that's the one you're after.

Name the application `BabyNames` and save it to the folder of your choice. You'll end up with an app containing

- An app delegate, called `AppDelegate`
- A view controller, called `ViewController`
- A storyboard file, called `Main`

As you progress through building the app you will create some extra view controllers, object classes, and nib files, so you may want to set up some groups in Xcode to keep the various files organized, as displayed in Figure 10-6. It's up to you whether to do this in your apps, but I find it helps keep things organized as the project expands.

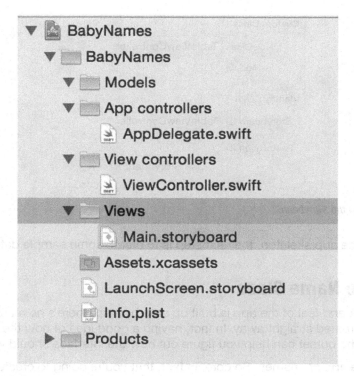

Figure 10-6. Creating groups in the app

To make keeping track of things slightly easier for yourself later, first rename the
`ViewController` to `TableViewController`.

Highlight the `ViewController` file in the Navigator, then double-click it and change the name
to `TableViewController`.

Next, change the name in the class itself, so that it looks like this:

```
class TableViewController: UIViewController {
```

Finally, open the Storyboard and select the `ViewController` in the Document Outline, switch
to the Identity Inspector in the Utilities pane and update the Class and Storyboard ID to
`TableViewController`, as shown in Figure 10-7.

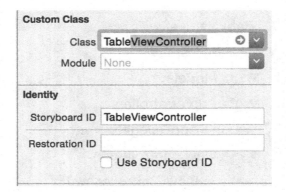

Figure 10-7. Updating the Storyboard

Having created the app skeleton, the next step is to create some sample data.

Creating the Name Class

Although the look and feel of the app is built up step by step, there's no reason why the data model can't be created straight away. In fact, having a good idea of how the data will be structured from the outset can help you figure out how the interface should work.

At the core of the app are names. So core, in fact, that you're going to create a Name struct with the following attributes (see also Figure 10-8):

- nameText: A string containing the name itself
- gender: A string containing a gender flag of M, F, or U (for unisex)
- derivation: A string containing some text about the derivation of the name
- iconName: A string containing the filename of the name's icon
- notes: A string containing some explanatory notes about the name

```
Name

nameText: String?

gender: String?

derivation: String?

notes: String?

iconName: String?
```

Figure 10-8. The Name struct

Let's get this underway. Highlight the Models group in the navigator area and Ctrl or right-click. In the context menu that pops up, select the New File option. You'll be presented with a selection of templates for the new file (see Figure 10-9).

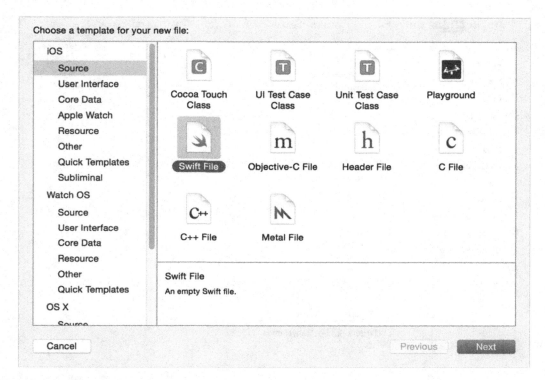

Figure 10-9. Xcode's New File templates

Select Swift File and click Next (see Figure 10-10).

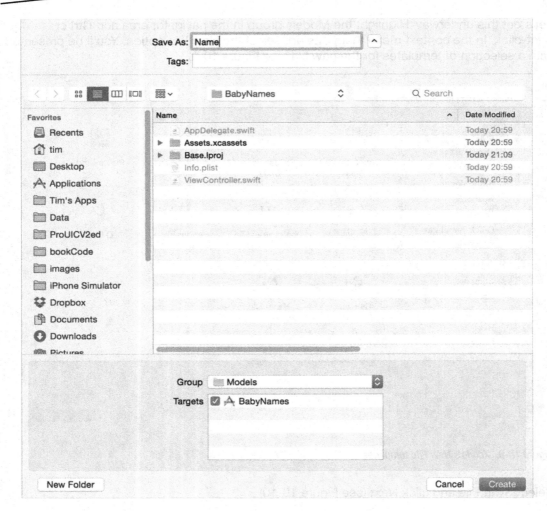

Figure 10-10. Naming the new file

Call the new file Name, click Next, and make sure that the tick-box to add the file to the BabyNames target is selected.

The new Name file will be created and appear in the navigator (Figure 10-11).

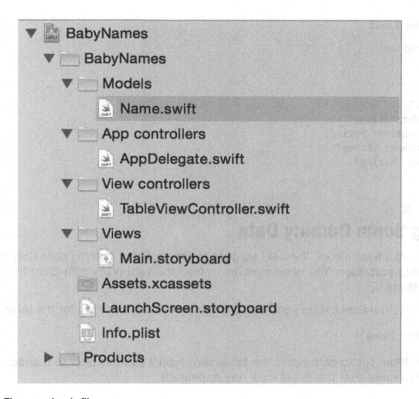

Figure 10-11. The new class's files

> **Tip**   If you ticked the "Create local git repository for this project" option when you created the project, you'll see symbols appearing to the right of filenames. They show each file's source control status. New files show a status of A (indicating they need to be added to the repository). Files with a status of M have been modified.
>
> It's out of the scope of this book, but if you're not using source control with your projects, I'd *strongly* recommend investigating it.

Now you need to configure the new struct. Open up the Name file, and add the struct's properties, as shown in Listing 10-1.

Listing 10-1. Name.swift

```
import Foundation

struct Name {

    var nameText: String?
    var gender: String?
    var derivation: String?
    var iconName: String?
    var notes: String?

}
```

Creating Some Dummy Data

Having created a Name struct, the next stage is to create some dummy data that you can use for prototyping purposes. You need a model to feed the tableView with data; this is created as the app starts up.

Switch to TableViewController, and add a property to hold an Array for the table data:

```
var tableData: [Name]!
```

Now add an IBOutlet to connect to the table view (you'll use this later to manage the highlighting of rows after the detail view has appeared):

```
@IBOutlet var tableView: UITableView!
```

Finally, add another property to hold the number of names that you want to display in the table:

```
let numberOfNames = 25
```

Initially, you're going to create instances of Name with nonsense data so you've got some data with which you can test out your app. To do this, you need to create a function called createNameWithNonsenseData that returns—well—a Name filled with random data.

Then, in the ViewController's viewDidLoad function, the tableData array will be loaded with a suitable number of nonsense Names.

You'll add the two new functions in an extension to the view controller, so that the functions relating to the view controller lifecycle are separated from your custom functions.

At the bottom of the TableViewController file, add the extension; see Listing 10-2.

Listing 10-2. Updating the TableViewController

```
import UIKit

class TableViewController: UIViewController {

    var tableData: [Name]!
    @IBOutlet var tableView: UITableView!
```

```
let numberOfNames = 25

override func viewDidLoad() {
    super.viewDidLoad()
    // Do any additional setup after loading the view, typically from a nib.
}

override func didReceiveMemoryWarning() {
    super.didReceiveMemoryWarning()
    // Dispose of any resources that can be recreated.
}

}

extension ViewController {

}
```

Now add the first new function in the extension, shown in Listing 10-3.

Listing 10-3. Creating Random Names

```
func createRandomNameWithNonsenseData() -> Name {

    // Create sample data arrays

    let namesArray = ["Abigail", "Ada", "Adelaide", "Abel", "Algernon", "Anatole",⏎
    "Barbara", "Bertha", "Brunhilda", "Barton", "Ben", "Boris", "Calista", "Cassandra",⏎
    "Constance", "Caspar", "Clive", "Corey", "Danica", "Dido", "Dora", "Darnell",⏎
    "Dexter", "Dunstan", "Duncan"]

    let genderArray = ["Boy", "Girl", "Unisex"]

    let notesArray = ["Prosperous and joyful", "A popular name in Victorian times.",⏎
    "'Bright fair one'. A term of endearment used by the Irish", "'Son of the furrows;⏎
    ploughman' One of the twelve apostles", "One who is graceful and charming",⏎
    "'Spear'. A warrior who wielded her spear to the detriment of her enemies"]

    let derivationArray = ["Celtic", "Germanic", "Old English", "Latin", "Greek"]

    let iconArray = ["icon1.png", "icon2.png", "icon3.png", "icon4.png", "icon5.png"]

    // Get counts of sample data arrays, to act as seeds
    // for the random numbers

    let nameCount = UInt32(namesArray.count)
    let genderCount = UInt32(genderArray.count)
    let notesCount = UInt32(notesArray.count)
    let derivationCount = UInt32(derivationArray.count)
    let iconCount = UInt32(iconArray.count)
```

```
    // Create a Name struct
    var thisName = Name()

    // Set some random facts
    thisName.nameText = namesArray[Int(arc4random_uniform(nameCount))]
    thisName.gender = genderArray[Int(arc4random_uniform(genderCount))]
    thisName.notes = notesArray[Int(arc4random_uniform(notesCount))]
    thisName.derivation = derivationArray[Int(arc4random_uniform(derivationCount))]
    thisName.iconName = iconArray[Int(arc4random_uniform(iconCount))]

    return thisName

}
```

> **Note** You don't need to use this data. I picked the values pretty much at random. There's enough *lorem ipsum* in the world without me adding to it!

Having gained the ability to create instances of Name filled with random data, you can now store them in the tableData array.

Add a second function to the ViewController's extension, shown in Listing 10-4.

Listing 10-4. Creating the Random Data

```
func loadRandomNames() -> [Name] {

var namesArray = [Name]()

    for _ in 0...numberOfNames {

        let thisName = createRandomNameWithNonsenseData()
        namesArray.append(thisName)

    }

    return namesArray

}
```

With the two data generation functions created, you can now use them to create the dummy data for the table. Update the viewDidLoad() function, as shown in Listing 10-5.

Listing 10-5. The updated viewDidLoad() Function

```
override func viewDidLoad() {
    super.viewDidLoad()
    // Do any additional setup after loading the view, typically from a nib.

    tableData = loadRandomNames()

}
```

Connecting Up the Table View

As it stands, the app doesn't actually display any content when it launches. Let's fix that by adding in a tableView, and getting it to load the data.

Switch to the Main storyboard, and drag in a UITableView object so that it looks like Figure 10-12.

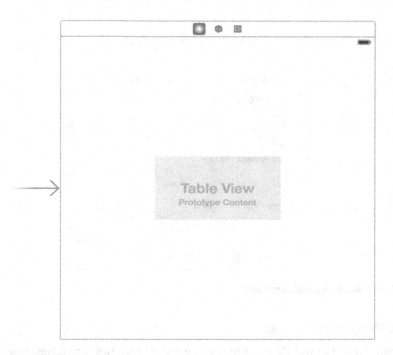

Figure 10-12. *Adding a table view to the view*

Now add some AutoLayout constraints so that it fills the entire view. Select the tableView in the Storyboard, click the Pin icon at the bottom right of the Storyboard pane, and set the constraints to the values shown in Figure 10-13.

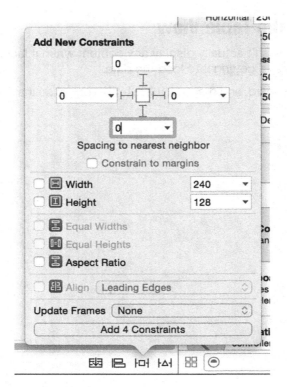

Figure 10-13. Setting the AutoLayout constraints

There are two things to note here:

■ Make sure that the Constraint lines are solid red, not a hatched line.
  Click the line to set it if that's not the case.

■ Make sure that `Constrain to Margin` option is unchecked.

Once those are set correctly, click the `Add 4 Constraints` button, and the constraints will be added, as shown in Figure 10-14.

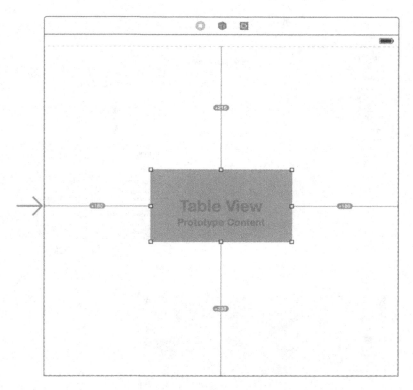

Figure 10-14. *The newly added constraints*

The yellow lines indicate that there's a discrepancy between the constraints that have been added and the display of the table in the Storyboard. To force the Storyboard to apply the constraints, click the yellow update icons, as shown in Figure 10-15.

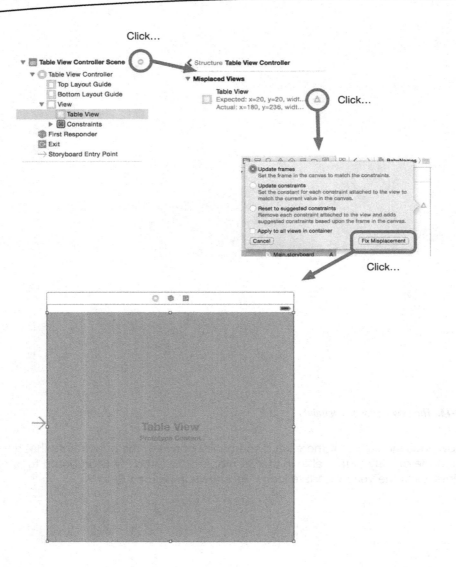

Figure 10-15. Updating the AutoLayout constraints

Now let's connect the new tableView to the view controller. Right-click the tableView in the Storyboard and drag it over to the View Controller object in the Document Outline to connect the table's dataSource and delegate outlets, as shown in Figure 10-16.

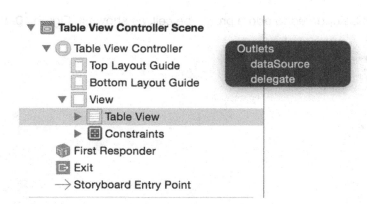

Figure 10-16. Connecting the dataSource and delegate

Now you need to connect the `tableView` outlet of the `TableViewController` to the table itself. Right-click the `TableViewController` in the Document Outline, and drag it out to the table in the Storyboard. When the HUD pops up, select the `tableView` outlet to make the connection (Figure 10-17).

Figure 10-17. Linking the tableView outlet to the table

There's one last job left to do with the `tableView`, which is to add a prototype cell and give it a `cellIdentifier` so that the view controller can use the prototype to create a new cell instance when required.

Click in the table view if it isn't already selected, then switch to the Attributes Inspector in the Utilities pane. At the top, there's the drop-down to select the table's content type; make sure this is set to Dynamic Protoypes.

Then increase the Prototype Cells to 1, as shown in Figure 10-18.

Table View	
Content	Dynamic Prototypes
Prototype Cells	1

Figure 10-18. Increasing the number of prototype cells

The table view will be updated to add a prototype cell, as shown in Figure 10-19.

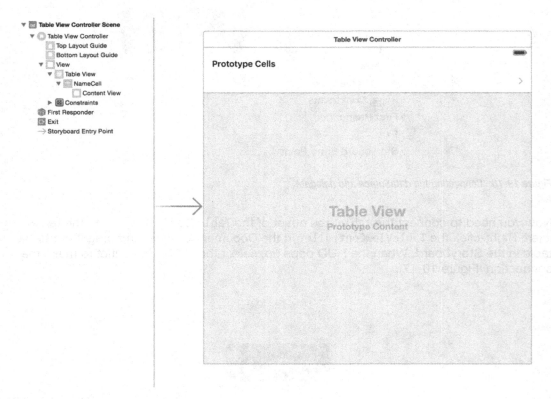

Figure 10-19. *The new prototype cell*

Click into the prototype cell at the top of the table, switch to the Attributes Inspector, and update the cell so that it has a Basic style, an identifier of NameCell and shows a Disclosure Indicator accessory, as shown in Figure 10-20.

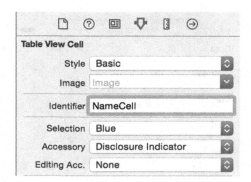

Figure 10-20. Updating the prototype cell

Now you can switch back to the TableViewController class, and create the
UITableViewDataSource functions to feed the table with its data.

Add the dataSource functions in the extension to the class at the bottom, as shown in
Listing 10-6.

Listing 10-6. Adding dataSource Functions

```
extension TableViewController: UITableViewDataSource {

    // DataSource functions

    func numberOfSectionsInTableView(tableView: UITableView) -> Int {
        return 1
    }

    func tableView(tableView: UITableView, numberOfRowsInSection section: Int) ->↵
    Int {
        return tableData.count
    }

    func tableView(tableView: UITableView, cellForRowAtIndexPath indexPath: ↵
    NSIndexPath) -> UITableViewCell {

        let cell = tableView.dequeueReusableCellWithIdentifier("NameCell",↵
        forIndexPath: indexPath)

        let name = tableData[indexPath.row]

        cell.textLabel!.text = name.nameText

        return cell

    }

}
```

Run the app to check everything's wired up correctly, and you should see a table displaying
50 random names, as in Figure 10-21.

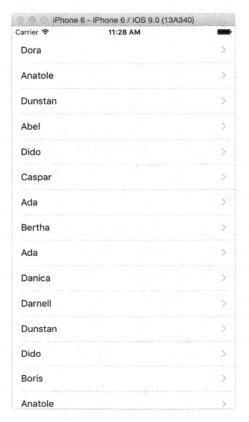

Figure 10-21. Data appears in the table!

Building the Detail View

When the users click a Name row in the table, the app will present them with a details screen with the information for that name. The UINavigationController will handle the process of pushing the detail view in, but before it can do this you need to create a details view.

Since the app is still at the proof-of-concept stage, you can make this as simple or as detailed as you like. I've made a very (very!) basic version to use as a starting point. Either way, you're going to need a new view controller.

Highlight the View controllers group in the Navigator, right-click, and add a new file. Choose the Cocoa Class item in the templates, then create a UIViewController subclass, and call the file DetailViewController.

Next, switch to the Storyboard and drag out a View Controller from the Object browser. This will add the scene to the Document Outline, as shown in Figure 10-22.

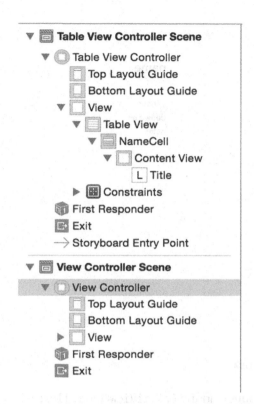

Figure 10-22. The new view controller in the Document Outline

With the new view controller in the Storyboard, you need to link it to the
DetailViewController class you just created. Highlight the View Controller item in the
Document Outline if it isn't already, then switch to the Identity Inspector. Update the Custom
Class property to DetailViewController, as shown in Figure 10-23.

Figure 10-23. Linking the View Controller to the custom class

Now you can lay out the controls in the Storyboard to display the data for the name detail.
My work of art looks like that in Figure 10-24.

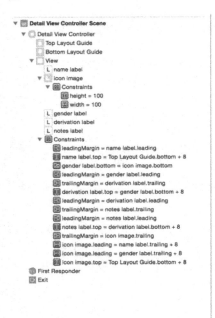

Figure 10-24. A very basic detail view

There are corresponding outlets in the `DetailViewController`:

```
@IBOutlet var nameLabel: UILabel!
@IBOutlet var genderLabel: UILabel!
@IBOutlet var derivationLabel: UILabel!
@IBOutlet var notesLabel: UILabel!
@IBOutlet var iconImageView: UIImageView!
```

> **Tip**   To allow the image view to change its aspect ratio to fit an image, you can tweak the AutoLayout constraints. Set the priority of the `height` and `width` constraints to 750, and the `vertical` and `horizontal` priorities of both `content hugging` and `content compression` to 1000.

Passing Data into the Detail View

To pass data into the detail view, you'll use a technique called *dependency injection*. That's basically a fancy term for passing in–or *injecting*–some object that the view *depends on* to configure itself, in this case the `Name` struct for the row whose detail you're displaying.

Start by adding a `displayName` property as an option to the `DetailViewController` class:

```
var displayName: Name?
```

This provides a property that the TableViewController can set when the table's row is tapped, before the detail view gets pushed in.

Then update the viewDidLoad function to set the outlets:

```
override func viewDidLoad() {

    super.viewDidLoad()

    if let displayName = displayName {

        nameLabel.text = displayName.nameText
        genderLabel.text = displayName.gender
        derivationLabel.text = displayName.derivation
        notesLabel.text = displayName.notes

        if let iconName = displayName.iconName {
            iconImageView.image = UIImage(named: iconName)
        }

    }

}
```

This unwraps the displayName property and updates the contents of the labels.

There's a subtlety to note here: all the properties of the displayName struct are optionals. That's not a problem for setting labels, because they'll be blank if the property is empty, but when creating an image, you need to use the if-let construct to safely unwrap the optional iconName string before attempting to use it to load the iconImageView.

Having created a view controller and a layout for the detail screen, this is the point where you can introduce the navigation controller.

Implementing the Navigation Controller

Implementing the navigation controller is the process of replacing the app's initial table view with a UINavigationController, then loading the table view into this.

At the moment, the initial view that's displayed is handled by the Storyboard, so there's no code in the AppDelegate to manage this. Listing 10-7 shows the current state of the AppDelegate's application:didFinishLaunchingWithOptions: function.

Listing 10-7. The Current Initial View Code

```
func application(application: UIApplication, didFinishLaunchingWithOptions ↵
launchOptions: [NSObject: AnyObject]?) -> Bool {
    // Override point for customization after application launch.
    return true
}
```

You need to update this so that it does two things:

- Creates a `UINavigationController`, and sets it as the root view of the app
- Loads the `tableViewController` as the root view of the navigation controller

A diagram or two can help make sense of this. Let's start by looking at Figure 10-25, which displays how this app currently sets up its visual interface.

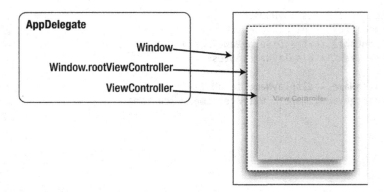

Figure 10-25. How the app delegate instantiates the user interface

The app delegate has a `window` property that is created using the bounds of `UIScreen`'s `mainScreen` property. This `window` is where the visible user interface for the app has to fit. In effect, it's a virtual reference in software to the physical screen of the device.

The `window` property has a `rootViewController` property, which you can think of as the front most slot in the window into which a view controller can be placed.

> **Caution**   There's a potential source for confusion here due to some less-than-consistent naming conventions in iOS. Both the app delegate and `UINavigationControllers` have a property called `rootViewController`.
>
> They've both got broadly similar purposes, but they're **NOT** the same thing. Make sure you know what context you're dealing with when thinking about `rootViewController` properties.

The app delegate also has a `viewController` property. An instance of the `ViewController` is instantiated from the Storyboard, and then assigned to the `viewController` property.

At this point you have two things: a way of referencing the physical screen (via the `window` property) and a `viewController` object. To make the `viewController` visible, you simply insert the `viewController` object into the window's `rootViewController` property. That's at the top of the stack, so it's the one that's visible on the device screen.

How the Navigation Controller Is Wired Up

The process for a navigation controller app is similar, but subtly different. Instead of filling the window with the viewController, you create a UINavigationController object and put that in the window. Then you take the viewController that you had to start with and put that inside the navigation controller. See what I mean about Russian dolls?

Figure 10-26 shows how this hangs together in practice.

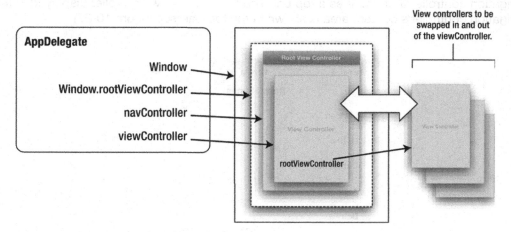

Figure 10-26. *How the navigation controller fits into the picture*

The corresponding code from the app delegate is shown in Listing 10-8.

Listing 10-8. The Updated Code

```
func application(application: UIApplication, didFinishLaunchingWithOptions ⏎
launchOptions: [NSObject: AnyObject]?) -> Bool {
    // Override point for customization after application launch.

    let storyboard = UIStoryboard(name: "Main", bundle: nil)

    let tableViewController = ⏎
  storyboard.instantiateViewControllerWithIdentifier("TableViewController") as! ⏎
  TableViewController

    let navigationController = UINavigationController(rootViewController: ⏎
  tableViewController)
    navigationController.navigationBarHidden = false

    self.window?.rootViewController = navigationController

    self.window?.makeKeyAndVisible()

    return true

}
```

Just before you run the app, make one more tweak. Switch back to the
TableViewController, and add these two lines to the viewDidLoad function:

```
title = "Baby Names"
automaticallyAdjustsScrollViewInsets = false
```

This aligns the top of the table to the bottom of the navigation bar, and sets the title.

If you run the app now, you'll see that the table is still there, but now it sits inside a
navigation controller that provides a top bar. The title of the view controller displayed in the
navigation controller's content area is shown in the top bar (see Figure 10-27).

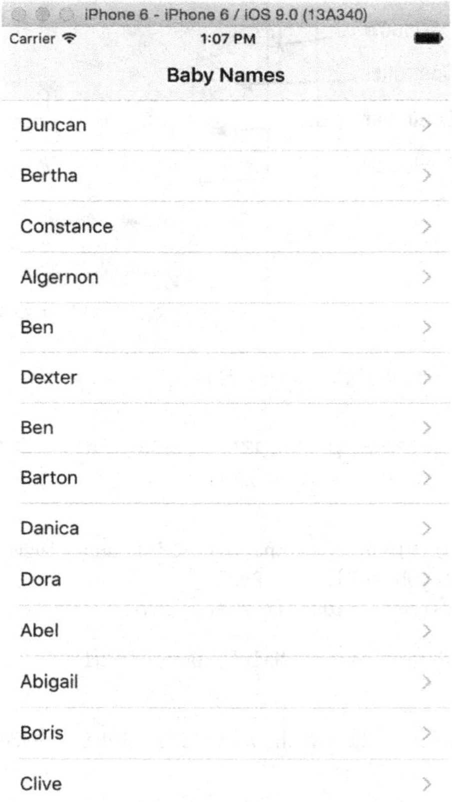

Figure 10-27. The navigation controller with the table inside

Linking the Navigation Controller and Detail Views Together

The app is getting close to being done, but tapping on the cells still doesn't cause the detail view to magically appear. In order for this to happen, you need to implement the TableViewController's didSelectRowAtIndexPath: function.

Switch to the TableViewController and update the extension so that it also implements the UITableViewDelegate protocol:

```
extension TableViewController: UITableViewDataSource, UITableViewDelegate {
```

Now implement the tableView:didSelectRowAtIndexPath: function, as shown in Listing 10-9.

Listing 10-9. The tableView:didSelectRowAtIndexPath: Function

```
func tableView(tableView: UITableView, didSelectRowAtIndexPath indexPath: ↩
  NSIndexPath) {

    let storyboard = UIStoryboard(name: "Main", bundle: nil)
    let detailView = ↩
  storyboard.instantiateViewControllerWithIdentifier("DetailViewController") as! ↩
  DetailViewController

    detailView.displayName = tableData[indexPath.row]

    navigationController?.pushViewController(detailView, animated: true)

}
```

To kick things off, you need to create an instance of the storyboard:

```
    let storyboard = UIStoryboard(name: "Main", bundle: nil)
```

Then instantiate the DetailViewController from the view controller with the appropriate Storyboard identifier:

```
    let detailView = ↩
  storyboard.instantiateViewControllerWithIdentifier("DetailViewController") as! ↩
  DetailViewController
```

When the detailView is instantiated from storyboard, it will be an instance of UIViewController, so you need to force-downcast this to an instance of DetailViewController with the as! operator so that the displayName property is available to be set.

With a newly-instantiated instance of DisplayViewController, you can inject the displayName property with the appropriate Name from the tableData array:

```
detailView.displayName = tableData[indexPath.row]
```

And then get the navigation controller inside which TableViewController sits to push in the new view:

```
navigationController?.pushViewController(detailView, animated: true)
```

Run the app now, and tap on a row: the DetailViewController will slide in from the right, and tapping the "back" button will slide it out again, as shown in Figure 10-28.

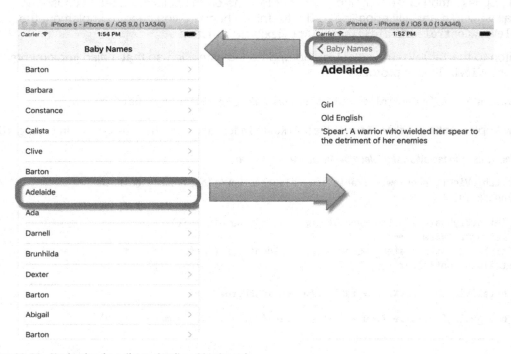

Figure 10-28. Navigation from list to detail and back again

One minor bit of housekeeping remains: when the detail view is removed and the tableView reappears, you need to deselect the previously selected row.

The TableViewController's viewWillAppear: and viewDidAppear: functions are called just before and just after the detail view is removed, so you can use the viewDidAppear: to remove the selection highlight from the row, as shown in Listing 10-10.

Listing 10-10. The viewDidAppear: Function

```
override func viewDidAppear(animated: Bool) {
    super.viewDidAppear(animated)

    if let indexPath = tableView.indexPathForSelectedRow {
        tableView.deselectRowAtIndexPath(indexPath, animated: true)
    }

}
```

First, you need to get hold of the indexPath of the currently selected row (which is the same as it was when the detail view was pushed in), and then use this to call the tableView's deselectRowAtIndexPath:animated: function.

If you pass in true as the animated: parameter, the highlight will be removed with a gentle fade effect.

Although this certainly isn't going to win any awards for user interface design, you've now got the navigation controller, table view, and detail view controllers wired up and playing nicely together.

Building Navigation Structure with Segues

So far, you've build the app's structure and navigation processes manually, which means that you created the UINavigationController in code in the AppDelegate, and the TableViewController and DetailViewController aren't connected in any way in the Storyboard.

There is an alternative way of implementing the same results, which provides a more visual indication of what's going on in the Storyboard. The end results are completely identical, so it's up to you which to implement.

To illustrate this, let's convert the app you've got at this point to use segues to manage the transition between the table and the detail views.

Embedding the Table View in a Navigation Controller

The first step is to embed the TableViewController inside a UINavigationController in the Storyboard. This is very simple: select the TableViewController in the Document Outline, and select the Embed In ➤ Navigation Controller item from the Editor menu.

This will insert a Navigation Controller into the Storyboard, and link the TableViewController with a relationship.

As you can see in Figure 10-29, the TableViewController is linked to the Navigation Controller by a relationship, and the Navigation Controller has been set as the app's initial view controller (the inward pointing arrow at the left side of the Navigation Controller).

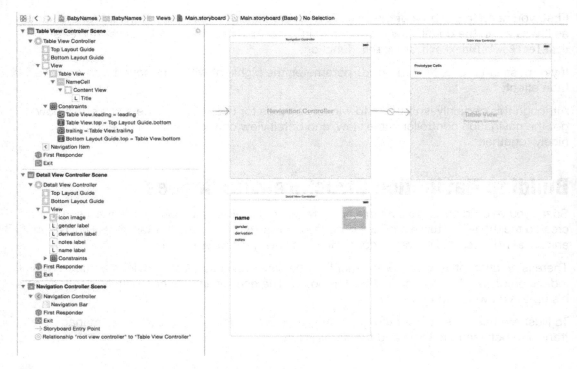

Figure 10-29. The new navigation controller in the Storyboard

All of these elements are listed below the Navigation Controller scene in the Document Outline. It's at this point in iOS development that you start to appreciate the utility of a large monitor!

The Navigation Controller scene has arrived in the Storyboard without any identifier, so you will need to set that. Select it in the Document Outline, switch to the Identity Inspector in the Utilities pane, and update the Storyboard ID to NavigationController, as shown in Figure 10-30.

Custom Class

Class | UINavigationController
Module | None

Identity

Storyboard ID | NavigationController

Restoration ID |

☐ Use Storyboard ID

Figure 10-30. Updating the Navigation Controller's identifier

Updating the App Delegate

Since you've changed the structure of the Storyboard, you'll need to update the AppDelegate to reflect the changes.

Switch to the application:didFinishLaunchingWithOptions: function, and update it to match Listing 10-11.

Listing 10-11. The Updated Application:didFinishLaunchingWithOptions: Function

```
func application(application: UIApplication, didFinishLaunchingWithOptions ↩
 launchOptions: [NSObject: AnyObject]?) -> Bool {
    // Override point for customization after application launch.

    let storyboard = UIStoryboard(name: "Main", bundle: nil)

    let navigationController = ↩
  storyboard.instantiateViewControllerWithIdentifier("NavigationController")
    navigationController.navigationBarHidden = false

    self.window?.rootViewController = navigationController

    self.window?.makeKeyAndVisible()

    return true

}
```

Here you're instantiating storyboard as before, but this time you're loading the navigation controller from storyboard rather than creating it with code. There's also no need to create an instance of the TableViewController; the links you made in storyboard take care of that for you.

Linking the Detail View to the Table View

Now that the TableViewController is embedded inside a navigation controller, you can link the TableViewController to the DetailViewController.

This is as simple as right-clicking in the prototype row in the table view, dragging the blue connection line out to the Detail View Controller, and releasing the mouse button.

At this point, you'll see the connection HUD pop up. Select the Show option, as shown in Figure 10-31.

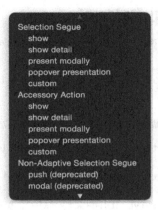

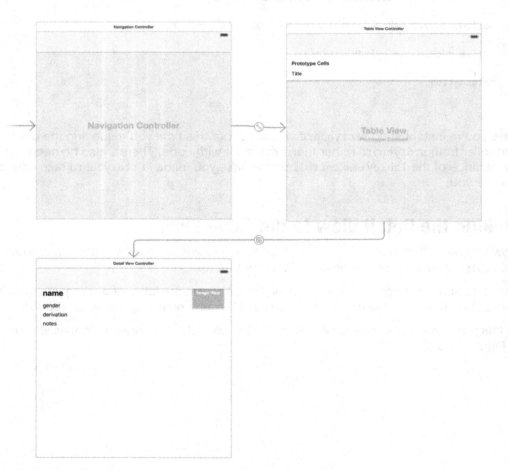

Figure 10-31. The connection HUD

A connection will be made between the two controllers (shown in Figure 10-32).

Figure 10-32. Making the connection between the TableViewController and the detail view

Once the link, or segue, has been made, you need to give it an identifier. Click it so that the line is highlighted, switch to the Identity Inspector in the Utilities pane, and give it a name of PushDetailSegue, as shown in Figure 10-33.

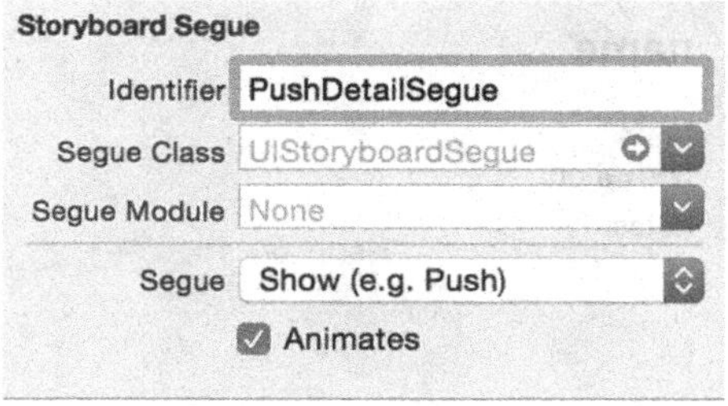

Storyboard Segue

Identifier	PushDetailSegue
Segue Class	UIStoryboardSegue
Segue Module	None
Segue	Show (e.g. Push)
	☑ Animates

Figure 10-33. *Giving the segue an identifier*

At this point, you no longer need the UITableViewDelegate function to react to selections, so switch back to the TableViewController and remove the tableView:didSelectRowAtIndex Path: function from the TableViewController extension. It should now look like Listing 10-12.

Listing 10-12. *The Updated TableViewController Extension*

```
extension TableViewController: UITableViewDataSource {

    // DataSource functions

    func numberOfSectionsInTableView(tableView: UITableView) -> Int {
        return 1
    }

    func tableView(tableView: UITableView, numberOfRowsInSection section: Int) -> ↵
    Int {
        return tableData.count
    }

    func tableView(tableView: UITableView, cellForRowAtIndexPath indexPath: ↵
    NSIndexPath) -> UITableViewCell {

        let cell = tableView.dequeueReusableCellWithIdentifier("NameCell", ↵
        forIndexPath: indexPath)

        let name = tableData[indexPath.row]

        cell.textLabel!.text = name.nameText

        return cell

    }

}
```

Run the app, and test the push from table to detail. Something's not quite right; the detail view looks like Figure 10-34.

Figure 10-34. The problematic detail view

The problem here is that you removed the function where the Name struct was passed from the TableViewController to the DetailViewController. This means that the displayName property of the DetailViewController is empty and there's nothing to update the fields with.

Before it performs a segue, the view controller executes the prepareForSegue:sender: function. This is the point where you can access the view controller that will be displayed, and pass over any data objects that the new controller will need.

In the main body of the TableViewController, add the function shown in Listing 10-13.

Listing 10-13. The prepareForSegue:sender Function

```
override func prepareForSegue(segue: UIStoryboardSegue, sender: AnyObject?) {

    if segue.identifier == "PushDetailSegue" {

        let detailViewController = segue.destinationViewController as! ↵
    DetailViewController
```

```
        if let indexPath = tableView.indexPathForSelectedRow {
            detailViewController.displayName = tableData[indexPath.row]
        }

    }

}
```

First, you check which segue is being performed. This function will be called for all segues, so it's important to make sure that the right action takes place.

Assuming that the segue that is about to be performed has an identifier of PushDetailSegue, you access its destinationViewController property and create a reference to detailViewController by force-downcasting it to an instance of the DetailViewController class. (By default, the destinationViewController property of a segue is an instance of UIViewController).

Next, you check if there is a selected row by asking the table for the indexPath of any selected row. If there *isn't* a selected row for some reason, the table view will return the optional containing nil, so it's safest to unwrap it with an if-left clause.

Then with the indexPath for the selected row, you can set the detailViewController's displayName property with the relevant item from the tableData array.

Run the app again, and this time you'll see that the detail view has been populated with the Name struct, as shown in Figure 10-35.

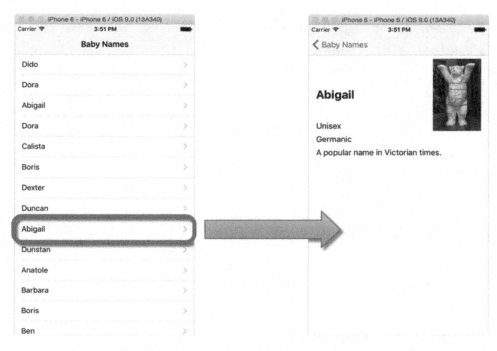

Figure 10-35. The app with a populated detail view

Summary

In this chapter you wired together a UINavigationController-based app from scratch. The app delegate loads the navigation controller. The navigation controller loads the table view. The table view provides the relevant row, and asks the navigation controller to push in the detail view for the row's content.

There are two basic ways to implement this functionality: either by wiring it up in code and using the UITableViewDelegate functions to react to selections in the table, or by using Storyboard features and reacting to segues.

Having put the structure and the basic function of the app together, you can adapt this to drive the table with any suitable model as the data source. The structure of that data will determine how you'll handle drilling into the details; by moving from table to table, it's very easy to navigate backwards and forwards in a hierarchical data structure.

Indexing, Grouping, and Sorting Tables

Although UITableView is efficient at managing large quantities of data, the user interface is constrained by the physical size of the device. By the time a table displays more than 10 or 12 rows, its labels and controls have become too small to easily work with.

If a table contains a lot of data, the user might also have to perform a lot of scrolling, which doesn't make for a good user experience. Fortunately, some UITableView facilities are available to improve the organization of the data presented by the table view.

Using Indexed Tables

An *indexed table* is fundamentally the same as a plain-style table, but with an index running down the right hand edge, as you saw in Chapter 3. Typically, this index displays letters or numbers, which the user can tap to automatically scroll the table to the relevant section, without having to scroll manually.

This is how apps such as the built-in Contacts application work. When the app opens, you're at the top of the list of names beginning with A. Tapping Z will rapidly scroll the app down to the bottom of the list.

Indexed tables rely on two elements: an array of strings to act as index entries that will be displayed down the right-hand edge, and data that is organized into sections corresponding to the index entries. In the case of the Contacts app, names are organized alphabetically in sections—a section for names beginning with *A*, a section for names beginning with *B*, and so on.

Although there needs to be a corresponding section for each entry in the index, the titles of the section headers don't have to be the same as the index strings themselves. In the Contacts app, the section headers and indexes *are* the same, but you can be more flexible if you need to be.

> **Caution**   Apple's iOS Human Interface Guidelines advise against using table indexes in conjunction with in-cell controls, because the index will tend to obscure the right-hand side of the cells.

Using Sectioned and Grouped Tables

Sections take the organized presentation of data one stage further, and introduce the concept of grouping the rows together, as you learned in Chapter 3. These can be presented either by dividing the table view by section headers or by splitting the table up into groups.

Splitting the rows into distinct groups helps break up the information, and makes it easy to see the separate groups when scrolling through a long table, as shown in Figure 11-1.

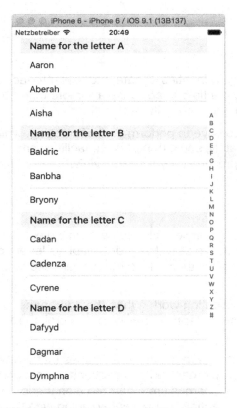

Figure 11-1. Sectioned and grouped table styles

Although the visual presentation is quite distinct, both sectioned and grouped tables use the same underlying data structure. The data for each section or group is stored in an "inner" array, which in turn is stored in an "outer" array that organizes all the sections and groups together.

> **Note** If you're using a grouped table, you wouldn't typically use an index. Although there's nothing in Apple's Human Interface Guidelines *explicitly* prohibiting it, an index does tend to look strange because of the way that it overlaps with the grouped table's background.

Creating a Simple Indexed Table

Before you dive into the complex stuff, let's put together a very simple indexed table, shown in Figure 11-2. This table consists of a list of names, one for each letter of the alphabet. The names are sorted into sections, and there's an index list for navigation.

Figure 11-2. The simple indexed table

To keep the example simple, each section has only one name, so there's no need to sort the data for each section. You'll look at sorting the rows in the next section of this chapter.

Start by creating a new project based on the Single View Application template. This will provide you with a skeleton application containing an `AppDelegate`, a view controller class, and a XIB file.

Setting Up the Basic Table

The Single View Application template gives us a very basic skeleton app, with an AppDelegate and a single view controller. At the moment, that view controller is an empty view (if you run the app at this stage, it's a blank, gray screen).

To get the initial table view up and running, you need to do two things:

1.   Add the tableView to the Storyboard.

2.   Add extensions to the view controller so that it conforms to the UITableViewDelegate and UITableViewDataSource protocols.

To add the table view, switch to the Storyboard and drag a UITableView object out into the view from the Object Browser. Add AutoLayout constraints so that it fits the entire view, as shown in Figure 11-3.

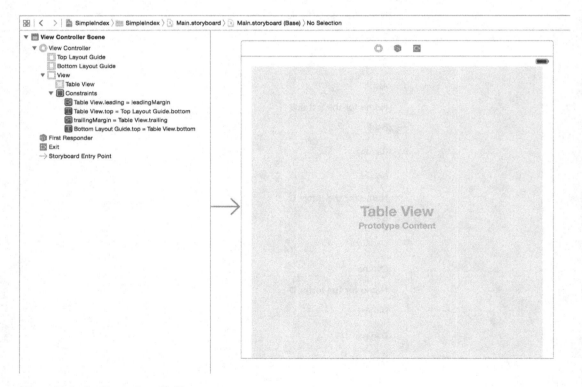

Figure 11-3. Setting up the tableView

Then connect the tableView's delegate and dataSource outlets to the viewController by dragging out from the table to the View Controller in the Document Outline.

Next, add a single Prototype cell to the table by selecting the tableView object and setting the number of Prototype Cells to 1 in the Attributes Inspector (shown in Figure 11-4).

Table View

Content   Dynamic Prototypes   ⬍

Prototype Cells   1 ⬍

Figure 11-4. Adding a prototype cell

Finally, change the Prototype cell type to Basic by selecting the row and changing the Style in the cell's Attributes Inspector, and then give it an identifier of CellIdentifier (shown in Figure 11-5).

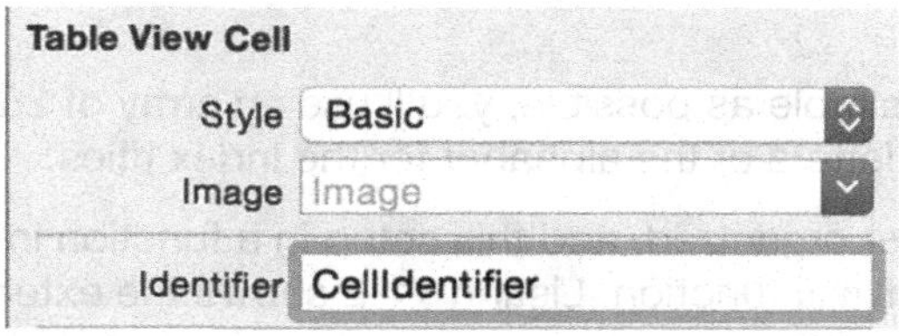

Table View Cell

Style   Basic   ⬍

Image   Image   ⌄

Identifier   CellIdentifier

Figure 11-5. Setting up the Protoype cell

That's as much as you need to do with the Storyboard for now, so switch back to the ViewController.

Creating the Source Data

To start, you're going to need two sources of data:

- The objects to display in the table rows
- The objects to display as the index titles

These will be stored in two Array properties. The view controller will also need to act as a delegate and a dataSource for the table view in an extension. Update the ViewController as shown in Listing 11-1.

Listing 11-1. The Initial Update to the View Controller

```
import UIKit

class ViewController: UIViewController {

    var tableData: [String]!
    var indexTitlesArray: [String]!

    override func viewDidLoad() {
        super.viewDidLoad()
        // Do any additional setup after loading the view, typically from a nib.
    }
```

```
    override func didReceiveMemoryWarning() {
        super.didReceiveMemoryWarning()
        // Dispose of any resources that can be recreated.
    }

}

extension ViewController {

}

extension ViewController: UITableViewDataSource {

}
```

To keep this example as simple as possible, you'll use an array of 26 names for the table data, and an array of the letters of the alphabet for the index titles.

To keep the view controller organized, add this setup in a function in an extension, which is then called in the viewDidLoad function. Listing 11-2 shows the extension, Listing 11-3 the updated viewDidLoad function.

Listing 11-2. The Extension to the View Controller

```
extension ViewController {

    func setupTableData() {

        tableData = ["Aaron", "Bailey", "Cadan", "Dafydd", "Eamonn", "Fabian",↵
    "Gabrielle", "Hafwen", "Isaac", "Jacinta", "Kathleen", "Lucy", "Maurice", "Nadia",↵
    "Octavia", "Padraig", "Quinta", "Rachael", "Sabina", "Tabitha", "Uma", "Valentin",↵
    "Wallis", "Xanthe", "Yvonne", "Zebadiah"]

        let letters = "A B C D E F G H I J K L M N O P Q R S T U V W X Y Z"

        indexTitlesArray = letters.componentsSeparatedByString(" ")

    }

}
```

The indexTitlesArray uses String's handy componentsSeparatedByString method to take a string of letters, separated by spaces, and return an array of the original string split at each space. That's a *lot* quicker than typing "a", "b", "c", and so on.

Listing 11-3. The Updated viewDidLoad() Function

```
override func viewDidLoad() {
    super.viewDidLoad()
    // Do any additional setup after loading the view, typically from a nib.

    setupTableData()

}
```

Feeding the Table with Data

To create an indexed table, the tableView's dataSource and delegate have a little bit more work to do than you've seen in previous examples.

The tableView:cellForRowAtIndexPath function is identical to ones that you've seen before, as you can see in Listing 11-4.

Listing 11-4. The tableView:cellForRowAtIndexPath Function

```
func tableView(tableView: UITableView, cellForRowAtIndexPath indexPath: NSIndexPath)↩
 -> UITableViewCell {

    let cell = tableView.dequeueReusableCellWithIdentifier("CellIdentifier",↩
    forIndexPath: indexPath)
    cell.textLabel!.text = tableData[indexPath.section]

    return cell

}
```

In previous simple tables with a single section, the number of rows in the section was the number of rows in the source data. This made the numberOfRowsInSection function very simple.

If the table's data were stored in an Array called tableData, for example, the method would look like Listing 11-5.

Listing 11-5. A Simple numberOfRowsInSection Method

```
func tableView(tableView: UITableView, numberOfRowsInSection section: Int) -> Int {
    return tableData.count
}
```

In your indexed table, you need to know how many rows will appear in each of the sections so that the numberOfRowsInSection method can return this data.

Because this is a simple example with one name per letter of the alphabet, you can hack this by simply returning 1, as shown in Listing 11-6.

Listing 11-6. The Actual numberOfRowsInSection Function

```
func tableView(tableView: UITableView, numberOfRowsInSection section: Int) -> Int {
    return 1
}
```

Having established the number of rows in each section, and created a cell for each row, there are four things you need to do to get the indexing side of things working:

- Return the number of sections in the table.

- For each section, return the title for that section's header so that it can appear above the cells.

- Return an array of strings to use as the index so that this can be displayed down the right-hand side of the table.

- For each string in the index, figure out which section that string relates to so that the table can jump to the appropriate one.

Let's tackle these one by one.

Returning the Number of Sections in the Table

To return the number of sections in the table, you need the `numberOfSectionsInTableView` function. This will be the same as the number of entries in the index titles, as shown in Listing 11-7.

Listing 11-7. The numberOfSectionsInTableView Function

```
func numberOfSectionsInTableView(tableView: UITableView) -> Int {
    return indexTitlesArray.count
}
```

Creating the Title for the Section Header

The section headers will appear above the rows in that section. The appearance of the header can be customized, but the default is a gray bar, as shown in Figure 11-6.

Figure 11-6. The default section header

You need to supply a section header for each section, but these headers don't necessarily have to be the same as the index entries.

Your section headers *will* be the same as the index entries, so you can use the section number to access the object at that index of the `indexTitlesArray`, as shown in Listing 11-8.

Listing 11-8. The titleForHeaderInSection Method

```
func tableView(tableView: UITableView, titleForHeaderInSection section: Int) ↵
  -> String? {
    return indexTitlesArray[section]
}
```

Building the Index

The index is built up from an Array of Strings. Strictly speaking, these could be of any length, but there are fairly obvious space constraints. It's best to keep the strings to no more than about three letters.

Providing the data for the index is simply a case of returning the array, as shown in Listing 11-9.

Listing 11-9. The SectionIndexTitlesForTableView Function

```
func sectionIndexTitlesForTableView(tableView: UITableView) -> [String]? {
    return indexTitlesArray
}
```

Matching the Index to the Section

When an element in the index is tapped, the tableView will automatically scroll so that the heading for the corresponding section is at the very top of the table. Fortunately, the tableView handles working out how far to scroll, but you do need to give it a helping hand by telling it which table section corresponds to which index. Listing 11-10 shows how to achieve this.

Listing 11-10. The tableView:sectionForSectionIndexTitle:atIndex Function

```
func tableView(tableView: UITableView, sectionForSectionIndexTitle title: String, ↵
  atIndex index: Int) -> Int {
    return indexTitlesArray.indexOf(title)!
}
```

Putting this all together will result in a table that looks like Figure 11-7.

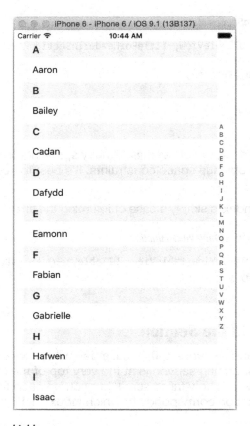

Figure 11-7. *A very simple indexed table*

It's worth noting that you don't have to use indexes and sections together. If you want an indexed table without section headers, don't implement the `tableView:titleForHeaderInSection` function, and your table will be a simple indexed one, as shown in Figure 11-8.

Figure 11-8. *An indexed table without section headings*

Similarly, you can remove the index by omitting the sectionIndexTitlesForTableView method, which will give you a table that looks like Figure 11-9.

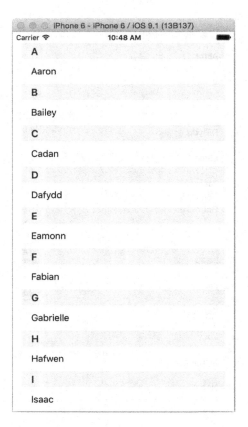

Figure 11-9. Sections with indexes

Building Practical Sectioned Tables

The simple table that you've built so far will hopefully have given you a feel for how an indexed and sectioned table fits together, but it was a very simple example. In reality, your apps are likely to have far more complex data, with correspondingly complex implementations.

In this section, you're going to build a more complex example with data that can support the table types in Figure 11-10.

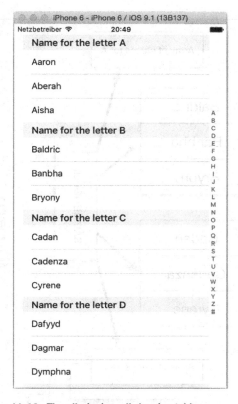

Figure 11-10. The all-singing, all-dancing tables

The app is going to implement several new features:

- Loading source data from a property list (plist) file

- Using the `UILocalizedIndexedCollation` class to automate the creation of section headers and index lists

- Creating section headers conditionally, based on the index

Creating the Data for a Table with Sections and Indexes

To feed an indexed table, you need three sets of data:

- An array of strings for the table's index

- Data for each section header

- Data for the rows in each section

The easiest way to supply the latter two is with an array of arrays. The outer array organizes the sections, and contains the inner arrays that hold the data for the rows.

The inner arrays will be sorted so that the rows appear in order. The outer array is sorted so that the sections appear in order. Figure 11-11 shows the example.

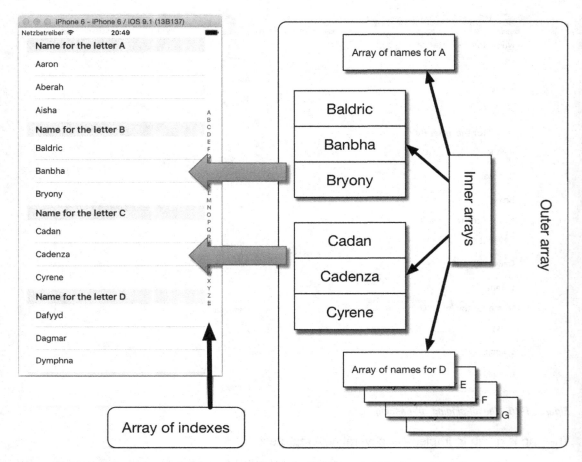

Figure 11-11. *How the table gets fed data*

The data objects in the inner arrays don't necessarily have to be ordered, but that's usually the case.

There are two ways to create the data for an indexed table:

- Manually, by creating an array of arrays yourself
- Using the `UILocalizedIndexedCollation` class to do much of the heavy lifting for you

The method you use is a matter of personal preference and the dictates of the app you're building, so I'll cover both.

Arrays of Arrays

Creating the data structure manually is a two-stage process:

1. Create the inner arrays and populate them with their objects.

2. Add the inner arrays into the outer array.

There's an implicit assumption here that you'll be adding the objects into the arrays (and the inner arrays into the outer array) in the order that you want them to appear in the table. If this isn't the case, you can sort them before they're needed. You'll look at this in a moment.

Listing 11-11 provides a very simple (and very contrived) example of how you might create an array of arrays.

Listing 11-11. The Simplest Possible Array of Arrays

```
func createArrayOfArrays() -> [Array<String>] {

    // Create the inner arrays
    let innerArrayA = ["A1", "A2", "A3", "A4"]
    let innerArrayB = ["B1", "B2", "B3", "B4"]
    let innerArrayC = ["C1", "C2", "C3", "C4"]
    let innerArrayD = ["D1", "D2", "D3", "D4"]
    let innerArrayE = ["E1", "E2", "E3", "E4"]

    let outerArray = [innerArrayA, innerArrayB, innerArrayC, innerArrayD, innerArrayE]

    return outerArray
}
```

Although this approach is perfectly functional, it's not the most flexible—especially because you're in charge of sorting the arrays into the order that they're needed.

Fortunately, iOS provides the snappily named `UILocalizedIndexedCollation` class that automates a lot of the process for us.

UILocalizedIndexedCollation

The `UILocalizedIndexedCollation` class provides some convenience functions that can help create data structures for indexed tables. To quote Apple's class reference:

> *The UILocalizedIndexedCollation class is a convenience for organizing, sorting, and localizing the data for a table view that has a section index.*

It provides a number of helper functions, including ones for sorting that you'll use shortly; and it works with an array of row objects, and sorts, organizes, and localizes the data into a form that's ready for the table view.

It's a four-stage process:

1. Create an instance of a `UILocalizedIndexCollation` object. This provides an array called `sectionTitles` that contains the alphabet for the current locale setting. (This will automatically adjust, so you don't need to worry about what it contains.)

2. Create the array structure: an outer array for the sections, and an inner array for each of your `sectionTitles`.

3. For each object in the array of row objects, use `UILocalizedIndexCollation`'s `sectionForObject` method to determine which inner array the object should be placed in.

4. After placing all the row objects into their respective inner arrays, use the `UILocalizedIndexCollation`'s `sortedArrayFromArray` method to sort the inner array into order.

In each case, `UILocalizedIndexCollation` will use the relevant locale to figure out how the row objects should be organized and sorted, which means you don't need to know your SS from your ß…

LOCALIZATION IN PRACTICE

A the name suggests, the `UILocalizedIndexedCollation` class handles a lot of the heavy lifting involved in localizing your app, and is dependent on the localization settings of your application bundle. This allows the class to handle the different ordering requirements of various languages.

For example, an app that uses US English as its locale will return 27 results in its `sectionTitles` array: one each for A to Z, and one for numbers that appear in the list as #. If you're using one of the German locales, however, you'll also automatically get an entry for characters such as Ü character—so the class can save a lot of time and effort.

iOS localization is even clever enough to support non-Latin character sets. When using the Traditional Chinese locale, for example, the class will sort the entries by the number of strokes in the Chinese character.

There is extensive support for localization in iOS, but it's a big topic in its own right. Check out the *Internationalization and Localization Guide* in the iOS documentation for more details.

All this *sounds* like a lot of work, but it's not bad as it seems. By using `UILocalizedIndexCollation`, you'll put the app in Figure 11-7 together in short order.

Creating the All-Singing, All-Dancing Table

Creating the app is a four-step process:

1. Create a new app from the Single View Application template.

2. Create some data to display in the table. To provide a bit of variety, you'll use a plist file to provide the raw data.

3. Add the `tableView` to the Storyboard file and conform the view controller class to `UITableView`'s `delegate` and `dataSource` protocols (which will be very familiar by now).

4. Extend the view controller class to implement the additional methods that handle the indexing and section handling for the table.

Creating the App from a Template

There's nothing new here. In Xcode, create a new project by choosing File New New Project, select the Single View Application template, and save the project somewhere suitable.

This will give you an `AppDelegate`, a subclass of `UIViewController` called `ViewController`, and a Storyboard file.

Creating Some Data in a plist File

If you haven't met them before, property list (commonly abbreviated as *plist*) files are a useful way of storing data in a key-value structure. They serve a practically identical purpose to JavaScript Object Notation (JSON) files, but with a couple of iOS-specific advantages:

■   Because plist files are a native iOS format, Xcode provides a nifty editor that makes creating and editing them a snap.

■   iOS can read and write to plist files significantly faster than it can to an equivalent JSON file.

Plist files are stored in the application bundle, but you can create and edit them in much the same way as you would a class or a XIB file. To create a new plist for the table data, choose File ➤ New ➤ New File, and then select the Property List option from the Resource group, as shown in Figure 11-12.

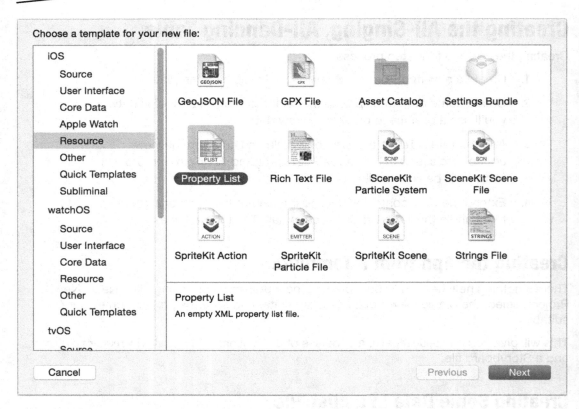

Figure 11-12. Creating a new property list file

Call the file **Names**, and click Create to create the file.

If you click the Names.plist file in the Project Explorer, you'll be presented with a blank file, with headings for Key, Type, and Value.

To create a new key-value pair, select the Root entry and Ctrl-click in the Source Editor before selecting the Add Row option, as shown in Figure 11-13.

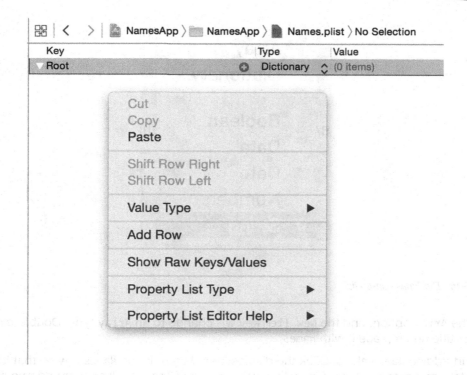

Figure 11-13. *Adding a new key-value pair*

A new, empty Key item will be added, as shown in Figure 11-14.

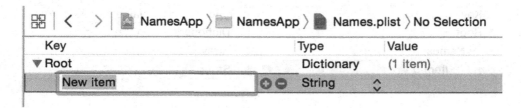

Figure 11-14. *The new key-value pair*

Various types of key-value pairs can be created, but the key thing to remember (labored pun intended) is that keys must be unique. You're going to create a list of names, so rather than a type string, you're going to need an array.

Click the drop-down arrows next to String, and you'll see a pop-up list of types, shown in Figure 11-15.

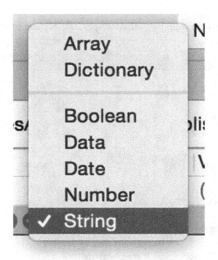

Figure 11-15. *The Types pop-up list*

Select the Array option, and the New Item key will change to an Array type. Double-click the New Item title and replace it with names.

Now start adding Name values. Click the disclosure indicator in the Names row so that it's highlighted, and press Return. A new line with a name of Item 0 will appear underneath Names, as shown in Figure 11-16.

Key	Type	Value
▼ Root	Dictionary	(1 item)
▼ Names	Array	(1 item)
Item 0	String	

NamesApp ⟩ NamesApp ⟩ Names.plist ⟩ No Selection

Figure 11-16. *Adding a new value*

In the Value field, type the first name. (I've used Aaron, but you use whatever takes your fancy.) Then press Return to save the new value. Press Return again, and you'll repeat the process.

Now you have two options: continue typing, or use the plist file from the source code in the project's repository on GitHub. If you go for the second option, you'll end up with a plist that looks like Figure 11-17.

Key	Type	Value
▼ Root	⊕ Dictionary ↕	(1 item)
▼ Names	Array	(78 items)
Item 0	String	Aaron
Item 1	String	Aberah
Item 2	String	Aisha
Item 3	String	Cadan
Item 4	String	Cadenza
Item 5	String	Cyrene
Item 6	String	Baldric
Item 7	String	Banbha
Item 8	String	Bryony
Item 9	String	Dafyyd
Item 10	String	Dagmar
Item 11	String	Dymphna
Item 12	String	Fabian
Item 13	String	Florence
Item 14	String	Frieda
Item 15	String	Eamonn
Item 16	String	Edith
Item 17	String	Eveline
Item 18	String	Gabriella
Item 19	String	Grant
Item 20	String	Gwyneth

Figure 11-17. The source code's plist file

Using the plist in Code

In order to use the data stored in the plist file, it has to be loaded and parsed before you can use it as the data source for the table view.

In the ViewController class, add an Array called tableData as a property. Now update the ViewController by adding the extension shown in Listing 11-12.

Listing 11-12. ViewController Extension

```
extension ViewController {

    func parsePlist() {
        let bundle = NSBundle.mainBundle()

        if let plistPath = bundle.pathForResource("Names", ofType: "plist"),
            let namesDictionary = NSDictionary(contentsOfFile: plistPath),
            let names = namesDictionary["Names"] {
                tableData = names as! [String]
        }
    }
}
```

Now update the viewDidLoad method to call the parseList() function, as shown in Listing 11-13.

Listing 11-13. The Updated viewDidLoad() Method

```
override func viewDidLoad() {
    super.viewDidLoad()
    // Do any additional setup after loading the view, typically from a nib.

    parsePlist()

}
```

This code performs three tasks:

- ▪ Locates the plist file in the application's main bundle
- ▪ Creates an NSDictionary from the contents of the plist file
- ▪ Loads the values held in the plist's Names array into the tableData property

Sorting Out the User Interface

Having started the creation of the data, it's time for a quick diversion into the user interface. Open the Storyboard and drag a UITableView onto the view, then add AutoLayout constraints so that it fills the full view. Then connect the delegate and dataSource outlets to the View Controller.

You have the option of setting the table's style to *plain* or *grouped*. Select the table view in the Document Outline, and then switch to the Attributes Inspector if it isn't already shown.

If you want a grouped style, you can select the Grouped option from the Table View section at the top of the Attributes Inspector, as shown in Figure 11-18. By default, you get a Plain table.

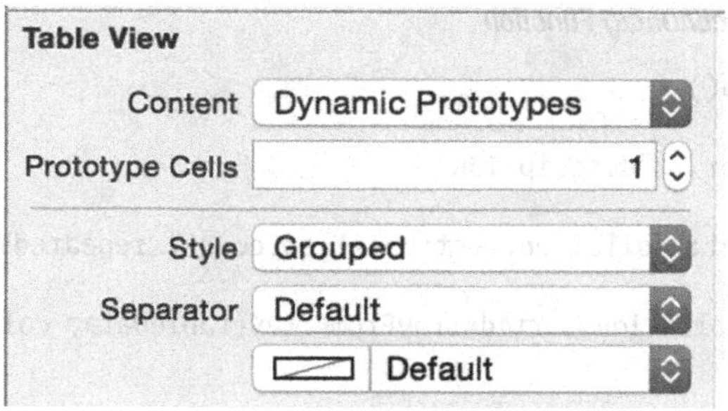

Figure 11-18. Changing the tableView's style to Grouped

Finally, you need to conform the ViewController class to the UITableViewDataSource protocol. Switch to the ViewController file and add an extension at the bottom of the file:

```
extension ViewController: UITableViewDataSource {
}
```

Extending the ViewController Class

Now it's time to start implementing the additional methods in the ViewController class to set up the table.

The first step is to create another property, this time for the UILocalizedIndexedCollation object. Add the following:

```
var collation: UILocalizedIndexedCollation.currentCollation()
```

You also need properties for two other Arrays. The first will hold the table data that is loaded from the plist file:

```
var initialTableData: [String]!
var sections: [[String]] = []
```

The second will hold the sorted data as an array of arrays, one for each element of the collection, containing the sorted names. Note the double square brackets; you're defining an array of arrays here. You could also write this as:

```
var sections: Array<Array<String>> = []
```

The end result is exactly the same, but you might find the second syntax a bit clearer.

Because there's a fair amount of code involved to set up the UILocalizedIndexedCollation, you'll put this in its own function. Add this to the ViewController extension, as shown in Listing 11-14.

Listing 11-14 The configureSectionData() Function

```
func configureSectionData() {

    let selector: Selector = "description"

    sections = Array(count: collation.sectionTitles.count, repeatedValue: [])

    let sortedObjects = collation.sortedArrayFromArray(tableData, collationStringSelector: ↵
    selector)

    for object in sortedObjects {
        let sectionNumber = collation.sectionForObject(object, collationStringSelector: selector)
        sections[sectionNumber].append(object as! String)
    }

}
```

And then call the configureSectionData() function at the end of viewDidLoad, which should look like Listing 11-15.

Listing 11-15. The Full viewDidLoad Method

```
override func viewDidLoad() {

    super.viewDidLoad()

    parsePlist()

    configureSectionData()

}
```

Let's look at the configureSectionData() function more closely.

Firstly, you're creating a selector to use to sort the contents of the array that's been loaded from the plist (in this case, description):

```
    let selector: Selector = "description"
```

The UILocalizedIndexCollation class provides a sectionTitles property that returns an NSArray of section titles relevant to the device's locale. If the device locale is set to US English, for example, sectionTitle will return the following:

```
(A,B,C,D,E,F,G,H,I,J,K,L,M,N,O,P,Q,R,S,T,U,V,W,X,Y,Z,#)
```

Other locales will differ. Swedish, for example, has additional elements:

```
(A,B,C,D,E,F,G,H,I,J,K,L,M,N,O,P,Q,R,S,T,U,V,W,X,Y,Z,Å,Ä,Ö,#)
```

You use this to create the sections array with one element for each of the section titles that the collation creates:

```
sections = Array(count: collation.sectionTitles.count, repeatedValue: [])
```

Next, you create an Array based on the data that was loaded from the plist, but sorted according to the selector:

```
let sortedObjects = collation.sortedArrayFromArray(tableData, collationStringSelector: selector)
```

Finally, you iterate across each element in the sortedObjects array, decide which section it should be in based on the collation, and add it into the corresponding inner array:

```
for object in sortedObjects {
    let sectionNumber = collation.sectionForObject(object, ↩
    collationStringSelector: selector)
        sections[sectionNumber].append(object as! String)
}
```

The sectionForObject:collationStringSelector function takes two arguments: the object that you want to allocate to the appropriate inner array, and a collationStringSelector that determines how each object should be evaluated.

Because the tableData array is full of String objects, you can use the lowercaseString method as the selector.

It returns an Int that is the index of the inner array into which the object should be placed. If the value of nameString that was being evaluated was Aaron, then this would return 0, while a value of Baldric would return 1, Cadan would return 2, and so on.

> **Note**   If you were dealing with custom objects with their own properties, you would use one of those instead. You'd need to ensure that the custom object had a String property that could be used as the collation string selector. For example, if you had a Customer object with a range of properties including a String called customerName, the call to the sectionForObject:colla tionStringSelector method might look like the following:
>
> ```
> let sectionNumber = collation.sectionForObject(theCustomer, ↩
>
>     collationStringSelector:@selector(customerName))
> ```

Having obtained the sectionNumber, you use this to get a reference to the relevant inner array and add the object object to it:

```
sections[sectionNumber].append(object as! String)
```

After you've iterated across each nameString object in the tableData array, each one will have been placed into the relevant inner array.

Configuring the Sections

With the data organized into the required structure, you're now in a position to set up the sections. There are five functions you need to implement:

- numberOfSectionsInTableView returns an Int of the total number of sections in the table (see Listing 11-16).

- titleForHeaderInSection returns an String that can be used as the title for each section (see Listing 11-17).

- sectionIndexTitlesForTableView returns an Array containing Strings for each title in the index displayed down the right-hand edge of the table (see Listing 11-18).

- numberOfRowsInSection returns the number of rows in the given section (in other words, the number of elements in the relevant inner array; see Listing 11-19).

Listing 11-16. numberOfSectionsInTableView

```
func numberOfSectionsInTableView(tableView: UITableView) -> Int {
    return sections.count
}
```

This function returns the number of entries in the sections array, which was supplied by UILocalizedIndexCollation's sectionTitles method. If the device locale is set to US English, for example, this would return 27 (the letters A to Z plus # for numbered titles).

Listing 11-17. tableView:titleForHeaderInSection

```
func tableView(tableView: UITableView, titleForHeaderInSection section: Int)
-> String? {
    return "Name for the letter \(collation.sectionTitles[section])"
}
```

This function returns a String for each section, A through #.

Listing 11-18. sectionIndexTitlesForTableView

```
func sectionIndexTitlesForTableView(tableView: UITableView) -> [String]? {
    return collation.sectionTitles
}
```

This function returns an Array of the section index titles for the table view, which are then displayed down the right-hand edge of the table. If you don't need an index (if, for example, you're using a grouped-style table), you can omit this method and an index won't be displayed.

Listing 11-19. numberOfRowsInSection

```
func tableView(tableView: UITableView, numberOfRowsInSection section: Int) -> Int {
    return sections[section].count
}
```

This method returns the number of rows that are required to be displayed in a given section. This is the count of the number of elements in the appropriate inner array, so the first step is to get a reference to the array that is the *n*th object in the outer array; and then return the number of elements in the inner array.

Finally, you'll need your old friend the `tableView:cellForRowAtIndexPath` method, shown in Listing 11-20.

Listing 11-20. tableView:cellForRowAtIndexPath

```
func tableView(tableView: UITableView, cellForRowAtIndexPath indexPath: NSIndexPath)
 -> UITableViewCell {

    let cell = tableView.dequeueReusableCellWithIdentifier("CellIdentifier",
    forIndexPath: indexPath)

    let innerData = sections[indexPath.section]

    cell.textLabel!.text = innerData[indexPath.row]

    return cell

}
```

This gets the data for the row in two stages. First, it gets a reference to the array of content for the section in question (the names for the letter), and then it gets the name string from the array based on the row.

Put all these together, and you'll end up with the table view in Figure 11-19.

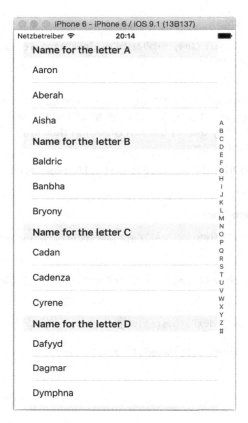

Figure 11-19. The finished table view

Creating Table and Section Header and Footer Views

Up until now, you've been customizing the section headers with simple text strings, but you don't have to stop there. The `tableView:viewForHeaderInSection` and `tableView:viewForFooterInSection` methods return `UIViews`, which means that anything you can put in a `UIView`, you can put in a section's header and footer.

Figure 11-20 shows a deliberately contrived and hideous example of where headers and footers appear and how they're repeated.

Listing 11-21 produces the section header shown in Figure 11-20.

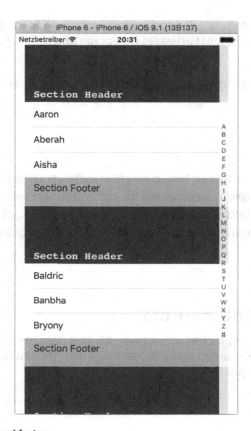

Figure 11-20. Section headers and footers

Listing 11-21. A Custom Section Header

```
func tableView(tableView: UITableView, viewForHeaderInSection section: Int) ->↵
 UIView? {

    let headerFrame = CGRectMake(0, 0, tableView.frame.size.width, 100.0)
    let headerView = UIView(frame: headerFrame)
    headerView.backgroundColor = UIColor(red: 0.5, green: 0.2, blue: 0.57, alpha: 1.0)

    let labelFrame = CGRectMake(15.0, 80.0, view.frame.size.width, 15.0)
    let headerLabel = UILabel(frame: labelFrame)
    headerLabel.text = "Section Header"
    headerLabel.font = UIFont(name: "Courier-Bold", size: 18.0)
    headerLabel.textColor = UIColor.whiteColor()

    headerView.addSubview(headerLabel)

    return headerView

}
```

If you've implemented custom header and footers, you need to inform the table of their respective heights with the heightForHeaderInSection and heightForFooterInSection methods:

```
func tableView(tableView: UITableView, heightForHeaderInSection section: Int)↵
 -> CGFloat {
    return 100.0
}
```

> **Tip**   If your header and footer view heights vary from section to section, you can improve the performance of the table by implementing the tableView:estimatedHeightForHeaderI nSection: and/or tableView:estimatedHeightForFooterInSection: functions to defer the final calculation until the point where the header and/or footer is actually needed.

Table Headers and Footers

As well as adding headers and footers to sections, it's also possible to add headers and footers to the top and bottom of the entire table; these scroll with the entire table. Figure 11-21 shows a very simple example.

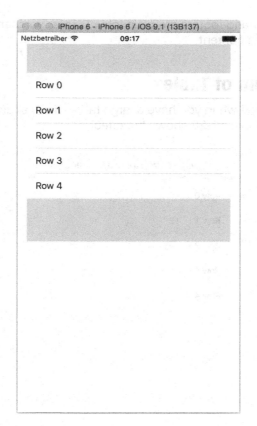

Figure 11-21. *Simple table header and footer*

Because table and header footers only need to be configured once in the lifecycle of the table, I tend to set them up in the view controller's viewDidLoad method. Listing 11-22 shows the process of setting up this example.

Listing 11-22. Setting Up the Example Table Header and Footer

```
override func viewDidLoad() {

    super.viewDidLoad()

    let headerRect = CGRectMake(0, 0, tableView.frame.size.width, 50.0)
    let headerView = UIView(frame: headerRect)
    headerView.backgroundColor = UIColor.cyanColor()
    tableView.tableHeaderView = headerView

    let footerRect = CGRectMake(0, 0, tableView.frame.size.width, 75.0)
    let footerView = UIView(frame: footerRect)
    footerView.backgroundColor = UIColor.cyanColor()
    tableView.tableFooterView = footerView

}
```

Because the table header and footers are plain 'ole UIViews, you can add subviews and use AutoLayout to your heart's content.

Tidying the Bottom of Tables

A very common occurrence when you have a large table with a short amount of content is "blank cell syndrome." Figure 11-22 shows the effect.

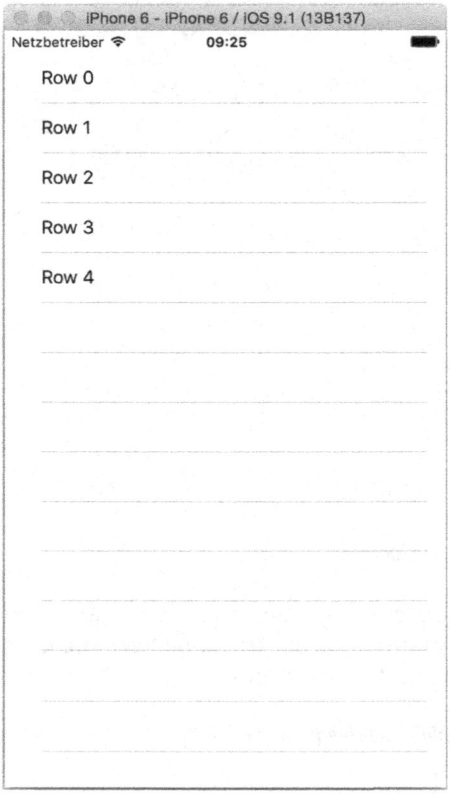

Figure 11-22. Blank cells at the bottom of a table

These extra empty cells can look a little untidy. Fortunately, there's a really easy way to clean this up.

If you add a footer view with zero height to the table, the empty cells will magically disappear. Just add this line to the viewDidLoad (or wherever you decide to set up your tableView):

```
tableView.tableFooterView = UIView(frame: CGRectZero)
```

The header will be unaffected, but you can see in Figure 11-23 that the extra blank rows have now been removed.

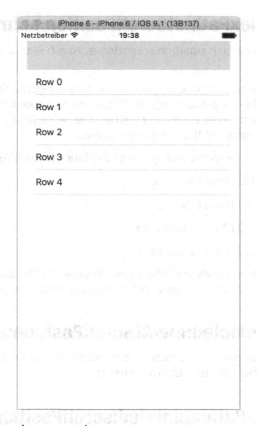

Figure 11-23. *The spare rows have been removed*

Moving the Table Programmatically

The table view scrolls around automatically in response to taps on an index entry, but it's also possible to move the table around programmatically.

> **Caution**   If you're reacting to user input through `UITableViewDelegate` methods such as
> `viewDidScroll` or `tableView:didSelectRowAtIndexPath:`, be aware that moving and
> selecting the table programmatically *won't* cause the delegate methods to be invoked, so you need
> to trigger them manually.

There are three main methods that can be used:

- `scrollToRowAtIndexPath:atScrollPosition:animated:`
- `scrollToNearestSelectedRowAtScrollPosition:animated:`
- `selectRowAtIndexPath:animated:scrollPosition:`

scrollToRowAtIndexPath:atScrollPosition:animated:

This method takes an IndexPath position—section *a*, row *b*—and scrolls to the appropriate place.

The second parameter controls where in the tableView the destination row should appear: top, middle, or bottom. There's a fourth option that aims to make the row visible with a minimum of movement. If the row is already visible, the table won't move at all. Otherwise, it will be scrolled to the nearest of the three alternatives.

You select the desired behavior by providing one of the four UITableViewScrollPosition values:

- ▩ UITableViewScrollPositionNone
- ▩ UITableViewScrollPositionTop
- ▩ UITableViewScrollPositionMiddle
- ▩ UITableViewScrollPositionBottom

The final parameter determines whether the table "zooms" to the desired row with some animation or moves there instantaneously. YES enables animations, and NO suppresses them.

scrollToNearestSelectedRowAtScrollPosition:animated:

This method is similar in terms of parameters, but will scroll the table to the nearest already-selected row, either with or without animations.

selectRowAtIndexPath:animated:scrollPosition:

This method allows a row to be selected programmatically, and optionally scrolls the table so that the selected row is located in the desired location in the tableView.

Passing in UITableViewScrollPositionNone has a different effect than with the previous two methods—the table won't scroll at all. If you want minimum scrolling, select the row with this method and then call scrollToViewAtIndexPath.

Finding the Current Scroll Position in the Table

There are occasions when you need to figure out how far down a table the user has scrolled. The solution to this task lies in the fact that UITableView is a subclass of UIScrollView, and so inherits all the properties and methods that UIScrollView provides.

The contentOffset property exposes how far from the origin the scroll view (or in this case, the table view) has been scrolled. If you had a table that was, say, 1000 pixels high when all its data was fully loaded, the contentOffset's y value would gradually increase as the user scrolled down, until it reached a maximum of 1000 pixels.

Figuring out how tall the table is going to be is a little trickier, mainly because of the way that the table view handles building rows and loading data without the need for much "manual" intervention on your part when writing the code.

The trick is to wait until the all the table's data has been loaded. In other words, the table view knows how many rows and sections it has (and therefore how tall the content is going to be). Figuring out exactly when this has happened is difficult, especially if your table's data is very dynamic, but one option is to override the table view controller's `viewDidAppear` method something like this:

```
override func viewDidAppear(animated: Bool) {
    super.viewDidAppear(animated)

    maxTableHeight = tableView.contentSize.height;
    frameTableHeight = tableView.frame.size.height;

}
```

The table view's `contentSize` property is a `CGSize`. The `height` value is the total height of the table after all the rows have been loaded. The `frame` property is the size of the table in the NIB itself.

After you have these three values, you can use them to calculate the Y position of the timestamp and to update that as the table scrolls. `UIScrollView` has a series of delegate properties, including `scrollViewDidScroll`:

```
func scrollViewDidScroll(scrollView: UIScrollView)
```

If you conform your table view's controller to the `UIScrollViewDelegate` protocol and implement this method, it'll get called every time the table is scrolled. This is the point when you can perform the calculations and redraw the `UIView` that's moving around the screen.

Summary

In this chapter, you looked at a couple of methods to improve the visual presentation of large amounts of data in table views. Breaking the data, and the table, into sections provides additional structure to the table, and indexes provide a means of quick navigation between sections.

Using the grouped table style further subdivides the information visually, which can help to emphasize the sections when scrolling around. Groups can be enhanced with header and footer views.

Chapter **12**

Selecting and Editing Content

Although some situations can be handled with read-only tables or collection views, you don't need to look too far to find others where tables need to be adaptable. Building tables that can handle selection and rearrangement—and can insert, update, and delete new rows—is a common requirement.

In this chapter, you'll look at

- How to handle selection of rows in your tables, or cells in your collection views

- How tables and collection views can be built to handle rearrangement of their data

- How tables and collection views can be used to create, edit, update, and delete items from their underlying data models

- Adding custom menus to collection views

A Recap of the Model-View-Controller Pattern

Before getting into the mechanics of selecting, inserting, and deleting with a table or collection view, you need to understand how these changes affect the underlying data that the table or collection view displays.

This means understanding the model-view-controller (MVC) architecture pattern that you met back in Chapter 5. Both `UITableView` and `UICollectionView` are examples of an MVC architecture, which separates the front-end *views* from the back-end *models*.

That separation is described by the MVC pattern, which divides the application into three areas:

- **Views**: In iOS terms, these are the views (or interfaces) that are created in Interface Builder or programmatically within the code. In UITableView or UICollectionView terms, a view is the table or collection view itself, and the cells that form the rows of the table, or items of the collection view.

- **Controllers**: These represent the application's internal logic. In other words, the controller is the class or classes that controls the display of data and interaction with the table—either because it's an entire subclass of UITableViewController or UICollectionView or because it's a UITableViewController or UICollectionView delegate and/or data source.

- **Models**: These manage the data within the application. The model can be as simple as an Array containing some Strings, or could be a full-blown Core Data setup. However complex or simple, though, it's the model that supplies the data to be displayed in the tableView or collectionView.

Figure 12-1 illustrates the MVC pattern, which you saw earlier in Chapter 5.

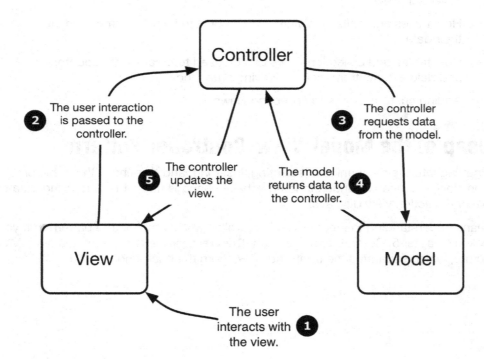

Figure 12-1. The model-view-controller pattern

As you can see, the controllers fetch and process data from the models that gets passed to the views for consumption by the user. The user interacts with the views, and the controllers handle the results of those interactions.

Why the Model-View-Controller Pattern Is Important

When working with `tableViews` or `collectionViews` that respond to user interaction in some way, it's important that you bear the MVC design pattern in mind. Cells have no memory—effectively, they're just envelopes for their contents. As soon as they're scrolled out of the visible view, they will either be recycled or will disappear entirely. Their state will either be lost—or worse, be inappropriately applied to the contents of the recycled cell.

To the user, this will seem as if the state of the cell isn't "sticky." If the user taps a row or item to set a value and display a check mark, the selection might change if the user scrolls up or down.

This applies not just to selections, but also to insertions, deletions, and reordering. Take a row deletion in a table, for example. Your user taps the `Edit` button on the navigation bar and deletes a row. The `tableView` handles revealing the edit controls, removing the deleted row, and animating the "closing of ranks" as the rows move up to fill the empty space. As far as the user is concerned, the job is done—the row has gone, never to return.

But the underlying data in the model hasn't yet been altered by any of the user interface changes. If the table is reloaded (which is likely if it's part of a `UINavigationController`, for example), the original data will be reloaded, and the deleted row will appear again. Worse still, if a new row was apparently inserted, the information that the user provided will be lost.

The bottom line is that any changes that your user—or your app—makes in the views must be reflected in the model in order for them to persist. The `tableView` or `collectionView` will handle the adding and deleting and moving of rows or items (and if you've enabled the animations, it'll do a graceful job of it), but it's up to you to reflect the changes in your model.

Cell Selection in TableViews

Unless the `tableView` is being used to display static information, at some point the user will interact with it and will need feedback. Cell selection is one part of providing that feedback.

Cell Selection Types

There are two types of cell selection that you may need to implement, depending on the app's functionality:

- *Momentary selection*, to provide feedback to the user about which row or item they're in the process of interacting with

- *Persistent selection*, where you want to show which rows in the table, or items in the collection view, are displaying items from the data model with a particular state (for example, objects that might have an "on" state)

Controlling Selection

You can control selection of rows and items in two ways: globally for the whole view or on a row or item-specific basis.

Global Selection

UITableView has an allowsSelection property, which can be set either in Interface Builder as you construct the view or programmatically at any point in the view's life cycle.

Setting the allowsSelection property to false disables row selection completely, so the view won't react to touches (other than scrolling).

There are a couple of reasons why you might want to disable selection entirely:

- Your view is only displaying data rather than allowing interaction with it.

- The table rows or items are being edited or rearranged, and selection would interfere with this process.

You can control the allowsSelection property by selecting the option in Interface Builder (see Figure 12-2).

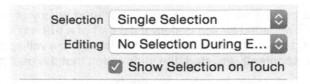

Figure 12-2. Setting the global selection property in Interface Builder

Alternatively, you can control it in code:

```
tableView.allowsSelection = false
```

Understanding How Selection Works for Tables

Managing selection in table views is the responsibility of the UITableViewDelegate object. If the table view doesn't have a delegate object set, selection events will be ignored.

There are four UITableViewDelegate functions that work together to provide selection functionality:

- tableView:willSelectRowAtIndexPath:

  This function is called after the user has touched down and lifted a finger (a TouchUpInside action, in other words), but before the tableView: didSelectRowAtIndexPath: function is called.

  By default, this function isn't implemented. Implementing this and returning nil will prevent the row selection from taking place.

  If you return an indexPath that refers to another row, that row will be selected *instead* of the row that was tapped.

■   `tableView:didSelectRowAtIndexPath:`

Assuming that the `tableView:willSelectRowAtIndexPath:` function *didn't* return `nil`, this is where you can implement your custom behavior.

The behavior could be presentational (displaying a check mark, for example) or can cause some kind of navigation action (for example, a `pushNavigationController` action).

■   `tableView:willDeselectRowAtIndexPath:`

This function is called only if an existing selection has been made. It returns the `indexPath` of the row that *should* be deselected—and so gives you the opportunity to deselect another row in place of the one that is currently selected.

Try as I might, I've never been able to conjure up a scenario where this was required, but your mileage may vary. If you return `nil` from this function, the row won't be deselected, which effectively means you can "lock" selection if required.

■   `tableView:didDeselectRowAtIndexPath:`

This function tells the delegate that the row is now deselected. It's the place where you want to reverse any custom selection traits that you created.

If you have a custom cell that shows selection by turning the `textLabel` green, for example, you would use the `tableView:didDeselectRowAtIndex Path:` function to change it back to the normal color.

Tip   If cell selection appears to lag behind the user's input, you might have inadvertently implemented `tableView:willDeselectRowAtIndexPath:` instead of `tableView:didSelect RowAtIndexPath:`. It's surprisingly easy to be tripped up by Xcode's autocompletion, and once the wrong function has been added to your code, it can be difficult to spot where the problem has been introduced.

Managing Row-Specific Selection

In addition to enabling or disabling selection at the global `tableView` level, you may also need to control it at the row level. For example, later in this chapter, you'll build a table that allows extra rows to be inserted by tapping an **Add New** row.

Depending on the requirements of your data model, you might want to disable this function.

By checking which row is being selected in the `tableView:willSelectRowAtIndexPath:` function, you can add conditional code to allow the selection of some rows and prevent the selection of others. This is shown in Listing 12-1.

Listing 12-1. Checking Row Selection in tableView:willSelectRowAtIndexPath:

```
func tableView(tableView: UITableView, willSelectRowAtIndexPath ↵
 indexPath: NSIndexPath)  -> NSIndexPath? {

    let rowNotToSelect = 3

    if indexPath.row == rowNotToSelect {
        return nil
    }

    return indexPath

}
```

This code arbitrarily prevents the selection of row 3, and returns `nil` if it's row 3 that's being checked.

You can also return an `indexPath` other than the value that was passed in if you wanted to select *another* row, rather than the one that was tapped. I haven't been able to think of any situation where you'd actually *want* to do that, but it's there if you need it.

Visualizing Selection

Visualizing the selection provides feedback to your user that their actions have been registered by the app. It can also provide a cue that something is about to happen or is taking place.

When the user taps a table row, the standard behavior turns the row's background light grey and the `textLabel` black, as shown in Figure 12-3.

Figure 12-3. The default row selection style

You may also want to disable the selection highlight completely if it will interfere with any custom selection behavior that you implement.

Somewhat counter-intuitively, setting the `selectionStyle` to None does *not* prevent cell selection, so all the selection-related functions will fire. It just doesn't provide any feedback to the user.

All styles are set by the cell's `selectionStyle` property. In most scenarios, you'd set this in the `tableView:cellForRowAtIndexPath:` function, for example:

```
cell.selectionStyle = UITableViewCellSelectionStyle.None
```

Alternatively, you can set the `Selection` property to None in Interface Builder.

Customizing Selection

You're not restricted to the standard white-on-blue or white-on-gray selection highlight styles. If you've customized the `tableView` cells, this highlighting style probably won't be appropriate anyway.

By adding custom code, you can manipulate your cells as you see fit. You could do this as cells are dequeued by using the `tableView:didSelectRowAtIndexPath:` function, or you can manage this in a `UITableViewCell` subclass.

Figure 12-4 shows an example from one of my apps.

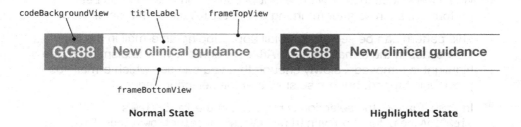

Figure 12-4. A custom cell in normal and highlighted state

The cell background and outlines are `UIViews`, so it's possible to manipulate their `backgroundColor` properties. They're set to orange in the cell's XIB file, and then switched to blue in the `tableView:didSelectRowAtIndexPath:` function:

```
// Set cell highlight
let blueColor = UIColor(colorWithRed:0.08 green:0.4 blue:0.58 alpha:1.0)
cell.codeBackgroundView.backgroundColor = blueColor;
cell.frameTopView.backgroundColor = blueColor;
cell.frameBottomView.backgroundColor = blueColor;
cell.titleLabel.textColor = blueColor;
```

> **Tip**   One of the limitations of Interface Builder is that there's no line tool (or shape tools of any description, for that matter). This makes drawing lines awkward. One option is to include line graphics as `UIImageViews`, but that's quite expensive in rendering terms.
>
> Another option is to place `UIViews` where the lines are required, and set the width (or height) to a very small value—say, 1 or 2 points. You can use the `UIView`'s `backgroundColor` property to set the color of your "line." You're restricted to solid lines of a single color, but it's often a quicker process than creating line graphics in another package and importing them as images.

Handling Deselection

If you stick with the default selection behavior, deselection is handled for you. The white-on-gray cell style will revert back to the default black-on-white.

If there's custom selection behavior in play, however, you need to handle that manually. This need can arise in two situations:

- When another cell has been selected. In this situation, you can add your deselection code to either the `tableView:willDeselectRowAtIndexPath:` or `tableView:didDeselectRowAtIndexPath:` function.

- When the selection is now irrelevant because some action has been performed, such as after returning to the `tableView` from a detail view.

- This pattern can be seen in the Mail app. Tapping an e-mail in the list view slides in the e-mail content. After the content view is dismissed, the highlight is removed—slowly enough that you can see which e-mail you previously tapped, but not so slow that the selection lingers.

- In this situation, the selection is removed in the `tableView`'s `viewDidAppear` function with `UITableView`'s `deselectRowAtIndexPath:` `animated:` function.

Visualizing Persistent Selection

Visualizing persistent selection is required for one of two reasons:

- Your user is selecting multiple rows prior to some other action, such as deleting records from the model.

- The selection reflects the underlying state of a property of the object that the row represents, such as an item in a checklist has been "checked off."

Either way, you need a means of indicating selection that's distinct from the momentary selection indicating which row has been tapped.

Apple makes an overt point in the iOS Human Interface Guidelines that selection traits associated with momentary selection shouldn't be used to indicate state.

In other words, don't use the default cell highlighting options to indicate the state of the underlying data in the model. Doing so risks confusing your users, and also may get your app rejected from the App Store.

To show persistent selection, a couple of options are available:

- Use `UITableViewCell`'s built-in `accessoryView` to show a selection mark.

- Create some other visual indication in a custom cell.

Your options in the second scenario are limited only by taste and what it's possible to get a cell to do, so I'll concentrate on the first.

Using Selection Marks to Indicate Multiple Selections

You're not limited to selecting rows one at a time, although the table has to be configured to permit it. The default is `false`, which restricts the selection of rows to one at a time. Setting the value to `true` allows a number of rows to be selected simultaneously.

This is controlled at the table level. You can set the property in Interface Builder, as shown in Figure 12-5.

Figure 12-5. *Controlling table selection traits in Interface Builder*

Or you can set the property programmatically:

```
tableView.setAllowsSelection = true
```

```
tableView.setAllowsMultipleSelection = false
```

If the `allowsSelection` property is false, the `mutipleSelection` setting is ignored.

Working with Selections

After selection has taken place, the row or rows that have been selected can be accessed through two `tableView` properties:

- `indexPathForSelectedRow`
- `indexPathsForSelectedRows`

As their names suggest, they return `indexPaths`. The results returned are different, though, so it's important not to mix the two up (the names of the properties being so similar doesn't help here).

`indexPathForSelectedRow` returns a single `indexPath`. If only one cell is selected, this will be the `indexPath` that's returned, as you would expect.

If more than one row is selected, `indexPathForSelectedRow` will return the *first* row that was selected.

`indexPathsForSelectedRows` returns an Array of `indexPaths` for *all* rows that are selected. The `indexPath` objects in the array are in the order that the rows were selected—index 0 is the first row, index 1 is the second, and so on.

If no rows are selected at all, both these properties will return nil.

Visualizing Multiple Row Selection

There are basically two options when it comes to visualizing multiple row selections: using the default cell's accessory view or customizing your cell.

Which option to use will depend first on whether your cell has an accessory view. If you've created a custom subclass of UITableViewCell, it might not. Second, the option chosen depends on whether showing an indicator at the right-hand end of the cell is visually appropriate.

Using the Cell's Accessory View to Show a Selection Mark

The default UITableViewCell (shown in Figure 12-6) has an accessory view at its right-hand end, which is often used to indicate that selecting the row will cause some kind of action, such as pushing in a detail view.

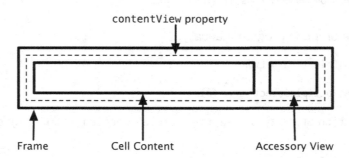

Figure 12-6. The default accessory view

The accessory view is exposed in two ways:

- As the cell's accessoryType property, which can be set to one of the four UITableViewCellAccessoryType values
- As a UIView property, which can be customized directly

Listing 12-2 shows how you could indicate selection in response to a selection.

Listing 12-2. An Example tableView:cellForRowAtIndexPath: Function

```
func tableView(tableView: UITableView, didSelectRowAtIndexPath indexPath: NSIndexPath) {

    let cell = tableView.cellForRowAtIndexPath(indexPath)
    cell?.accessoryType = UITableViewCellAccessoryType.Checkmark

}
```

For situations where you need to set the selection to match the properties of the corresponding object in the tableView's model, you need to set this up as the cell is dequeued.

Listing 12-3 is an example of a tableView:cellForRowAtIndexPath: function that displays the default tick mark when an object property is set.

Listing 12-3. An Example `tableView:cellForRowAtIndexPath:` *Function*

```
func tableView(tableView: UITableView, cellForRowAtIndexPath indexPath: NSIndexPath)↵
 -> UITableViewCell {

    let cell = tableView.dequeueReusableCellWithIdentifier("CellIdentifier",↵
      forIndexPath: indexPath)

     let theObject = tableData.objectAtIndex(indexPath.row)

    if theObject.isSelected == true {
       cell.accessoryType = UITableViewCellAccessoryCheckmark;
    } else {
       cell.accessoryType = UITableViewCellAccessoryNone;
    }

    cell.textLabel!.text = theObject.name

    return cell
}
```

Assuming that three of the `objects` have their `selected` property set to `true`, the result would appear as in Figure 12-7.

Figure 12-7. The default selection tick mark

Using the Cell's Accessory View to Show a Custom View

Because the accessory view is exposed as a `UIView` property, it can be manipulated accordingly. Listing 12-4 is a code snippet showing how you can set the `accessoryView` property to display an image.

Listing 12-4. Inserting an Image into the Accessory View

```
let accessoryImage = UIImage(name:"accessory")
let accessoryImageView = UIImageView(image:accessoryImage)
cell.accessoryView = accessoryImageView
```

Showing Selection in Other Ways

You're not restricted to using accessory views to show selection, especially if you're implementing custom cells. Virtually any combination of images, text formatting, or area highlighting can be used, depending on your inclination and the needs of the project. Whatever you decide to do, you need to implement it in either tableView:willSelectRowAtIndexPath: or tableView:didSelectRowAtIndexPath:.

Handling Deselection After Selection

If you've implemented custom selection (either by an accessory view function or by something more adventurous), you're also responsible for handling the deselection process.

Basically, this means undoing whatever selection trait you supplied when the row was selected. There are two places where this can be done: tableView:willDeselectRowAtIndex↵Path: and tableView:didDeselectRowAtIndexPath:.

In either case, the row in question is located at the indexPath provided.

Here's an example of how you might handle this to *reverse* the effect of the code in Listing 12-4:

```
func tableView(tableView: UITableView, didDeselectRowAtIndexPath ↵
  indexPath: NSIndexPath) {

    let cell = tableView.cellForRowAtIndexPath(indexPath)
    cell.accessoryView = nil

}
```

Keeping the Data Model in Sync

If you need the cell selection to persist after the cell has been scrolled off the visible area, you need to update the underlying data model that powers your table.

Obviously the detailed implementation will depend on the structure of the data that your table is modeling, but here's a very simple example to give you a structure to work with. The table's data is stored in the tableData property of the viewController, which is an Array that stores Bools:

```
var tableData = Array<Bool>()
```

In the cellForRowAtIndexPath: function in the table's dataSource you set the cell's accessory view to match the value of the selection flag in the tableData array (Listing 12-5).

Listing 12-5. The cellForRowAtIndexPath: Function

```
func tableView(tableView: UITableView, cellForRowAtIndexPath indexPath: NSIndexPath)↵
 -> UITableViewCell {

    let cell = tableView.dequeueReusableCellWithIdentifier("CellIdentifier",↵
    forIndexPath: indexPath)
```

```
    let selectionFlag = tableData[indexPath.row]

    cell.textLabel?.text = "Row \(indexPath.row)"

    switch selectionFlag {

        case true:
            cell.accessoryType = UITableViewCellAccessoryType.Checkmark

        case false:
            cell.accessoryType = UITableViewCellAccessoryType.None

    }

    return cell

}
```

Then in the tableView's delegate you handle selection (Listing 12-6).

Listing 12-6. Handling Selection

```
func tableView(tableView: UITableView, didSelectRowAtIndexPath indexPath: NSIndexPath) {

    let cell = tableView.cellForRowAtIndexPath(indexPath)

    cell!.accessoryType = UITableViewCellAccessoryType.Checkmark

    tableData[indexPath.row] = true

}
```

Here you get the cell for the selected row with the cellForRowAtIndexPath: function and set the accessoryView to show a checkmark. Then you update the tableData array to store whether the row has been selected or not.

Handling deselection is the reverse, shown in Listing 12-7.

Listing 12-7. Handling Deselection

```
func tableView(tableView: UITableView, didDeselectRowAtIndexPath indexPath:↵
NSIndexPath) {

    let cell = tableView.cellForRowAtIndexPath(indexPath)

    cell!.accessoryType = UITableViewCellAccessoryType.None

    tableData[indexPath.row] = false

}
```

Once again, you get the cell for the selected row, but this time you remove the accessory view checkmark. Then the `tableData` array is updated with the new value for the given item. The effect of these three functions is that the selection will persist as the table is scrolled around.

Optimizing Selection Performance

Although the standard pattern of cell creation and configuration tends to use the `cellForRowAtIndexPath:` function to dequeue and configure cells, there is an alternative approach that can help eke out the last gram of performance from your table views.

The `cellForRowAtIndexPath:` function is called in advance of the cell being needed for display in the table view, so the cells "hang around" for a while before they're actually displayed.

Just before the cell is drawn in the table view, the `tableView:willDisplayCellAtIndexPath:` function is called on the `tableView`'s delegate. This is the last chance you have for the cell to be updated in relation to the table view's data model, before the internal cell functions such as `layoutSubviews` take over.

If you have an expensive operation relating to the data model that you want to defer to the last possible moment, you can move it from `cellForRowAtIndexPath:` to `willDisplayCellAtIndexPath:`. Listing 12-8 shows how you could refactor the function from Listing 12-7 to use this approach.

Listing 12-8. Using the willDisplayCellAtIndexPath: Function

```
func tableView(tableView: UITableView, willDisplayCell cell: UITableViewCell,↵
 forRowAtIndexPath indexPath: NSIndexPath) {

    let selectionFlag = tableData[indexPath.row]

    switch selectionFlag {

    case true:
        cell.accessoryType = UITableViewCellAccessoryType.Checkmark

    case false:
        cell.accessoryType = UITableViewCellAccessoryType.None

    }

}
```

> **Caution**   As with life, there are few miracle cures for sluggish table views. Implementing the `will DisplayCell:forRowAtIndexPath:` *might* help to improve your table's performance, but it's not a given. You will need to look closely using tools like Instruments to be sure.

Selection Dos and Don'ts

There are a few of things to bear in mind when configuring row selection:

- **Don't** use selection to indicate the state of the row's object. Selection works at the view level of the MVC hierarchy, so it's independent of the model.

- Unless multiple selections are allowed, **always** programmatically deselect the previously selected row before a new row is selected.

- If the response to the row selection is to push a new view onto the display (for example, if you have a navigation controller that pushes on a detail view), **always** programmatically deselect the previous rows after the detail view is dismissed. This will ensure that the rows aren't still highlighted after the detail view is popped off the view stack, but provides a visual cue as to which row the detail view referred to.

Responding to Selections with More Detail

Selection of a row by the user generally requires some kind of response in return. These can be broadly categorized in one of two patterns:

- The selection results in the display of additional data, either by "drilling down" into a navigation hierarchy or displaying some form of detail view.

- The selection reflects some kind of choice on the part of the user and results in the update of a model.

A common pattern is to push in a new view of some description—a navigation view that reveals another `tableView` enabling drill-down into the information hierarchy, for example, or a detail view that contains more information about the row that was tapped.

Listing 12-9 is an example of that second process.

Listing 12-9. An Example of a `tableView:didSelectRowAtIndexPath:` Function

```
func tableView(tableView: UITableView, didSelectRowAtIndexPath indexPath: NSIndexPath) {

    let modelForDetailView = tableData[indexPath.row]

    let storyboard = UIStoryboard(name: "Main", bundle: nil)
    let detailVC = ↩
  storyboard.instantiateViewControllerWithIdentifier("DetailViewController") ↩
  as! DetailViewController

    detailVC.model = modelForDetailView

    tableView.deselectRowAtIndexPath(indexPath, animated: true)

    detailVC.modalTransitionStyle = UIModalTransitionStyle.FlipHorizontal
    self.presentViewController(detailVC, animated: true, completion: nil)

}
```

This is a `UITableViewDelegate` function that takes two parameters: a reference to the `tableView` itself and the `IndexPath` that has been selected.

The first task is to get a reference to the object in the model that corresponds to the row that's been selected. Bear in mind that it's the row that's been selected, and not the model object itself:

```
let modelForDetailView = tableData[indexPath.row]
```

In this situation, the table's data model is an `Array` of `Model` objects, so it's simply a case of getting the `model` instance that resides at the corresponding index.

After you have a reference to the selected object, the code instantiates an instance of a `DetailViewController`, having first deselected the row. It then sets the `DetailViewController`'s model property, and pushes in the new view with a modal transition.

Design Patterns and UITableViews

In addition to architectural design patterns such as MVC, there are also interaction patterns. Whereas architectural patterns help you consider how to structure and build an application, interaction patterns can help to manage what you do with it.

After you've used the MVC pattern to build the table, the question arises, "What are you going to do with the data that the table contains?" Clearly, the user will read the content of the cells, but what then? What sort of user behaviors do you need to anticipate?

A useful pattern to use when thinking about data and how to work with it is *create, read, update, delete*, or *CRUD* for short. This is most commonly used when working with records in a database, but it's also applicable when considering what might happen to a row in a `UITableView`.

Read

In database terms, *reading* is concerned with retrieving records from the database, usually with some kind of SQL `SELECT` query. In `UITableView` terms, you can think of reading as the process of getting data out of the model and into the table itself through functions such as `tableView:cellForRowAtIndexPath:`. We've covered this in detail elsewhere, so you don't need to trouble yourself much with the Read action.

Create

In addition to displaying information, table views are often used to enable the user to create and enter new information. The Contacts app is a good example of this: tapping the + button at the top of the list of names causes a modal view containing a form for a new contact to be pushed in from the bottom of the screen. The form that arrives in response to tapping + isn't part of the tableView itself, but after the new `Contact` object has been created, the `tableView` does have to react to that and insert the new row at the appropriate place.

Update

The Contacts app allows existing contact information to be updated by selecting a contact and then tapping the Edit button. Again, this isn't, strictly speaking, a `tableView` concern until the amended data is saved, at which point it may be necessary to rearrange the rows to cope with the changed data.

A more `tableView`-specific action would be the user wanting to rearrange rows or sections. The `UITableView` `dataSource` and `delegate` protocols provide a number of functions to support this, which you'll look at later in this chapter.

Delete

An equally common interaction pattern is deleting an entire record. The iPhone's Reminders app, shown in Figure 12-8, enables the deletion of notes by swiping left or right in the row to reveal a Delete control. Tapping Delete animates the removal of the row, which slides away to the left, after which the rows below are scrolled up to fill the gap.

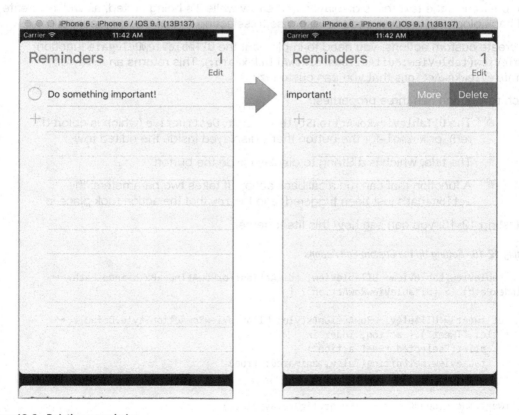

Figure 12-8. Deleting a reminder

All these functions and animations come for free through the built-in UITableViewDelegate functions. We'll start by looking at the actions that have the greatest impact on the tableView itself: inserting new rows and deleting existing ones.

> **Note** If your table view controller is a subclass of UITableViewController, you'll get a lot of insertion and deletion behavior for free courtesy of the UITableViewController superclass. That's great as far as implementing the functionality is concerned, but not that helpful if you're trying to figure out how things work so you can adapt them later. Therefore, I'm working through this section with a generic UIViewController and adding the table view functionality in manually.

Custom Row Actions

The standard row editing options can be further extended by using custom actions; you can customize the text that's displayed in the row while it's being edited, as well as create callback blocks to execute code in response to selecting one of the row actions.

To create custom actions, you need to implement the UITableViewDelegate function tableView(tableView:editActionsForRowAtIndexPath:). This returns an Array of UITableViewRowActions that you can customize.

Each row action has three properties:

- The UITableViewRowActionStyle–Default, Destructive (which is colored red), or Normal–for the button that's displayed inside the edited row
- The title, which is a String to display inside the button
- A function that can run a callback action. It takes two parameters: the action that's just been triggered, and the row that the action took place in.

In Listing 12-10, you can see how this fits together.

Listing 12-10. Setting Up the Custom Edit Actions

```
func tableView(tableView: UITableView, editActionsForRowAtIndexPath indexPath: ↵
NSIndexPath) -> [UITableViewRowAction]? {

    let tweet = UITableViewRowAction(style: UITableViewRowActionStyle.Default, ↵
    title: "Tweet") { action, index in
        print("selected tweet action")
        tableView.setEditing(false, animated: true)
    }

    tweet.backgroundColor = UIColor.lightGrayColor()
```

```
    let facebook = UITableViewRowAction(style: .Normal, title: "Facebook") ↵
    { action, index in
        print("selected facebook action")
        tableView.setEditing(false, animated: true)
    }

    facebook.backgroundColor = UIColor.blueColor()

    let email = UITableViewRowAction(style: .Normal, title: "Email")↵
    { action, index in
        print("selected email action")
        tableView.setEditing(false, animated: true)
    }

    email.backgroundColor = UIColor.purpleColor()

    return [tweet, facebook, email]

}
```

This inserts three buttons into the row when it moves into edit mode, as shown in Figure 12-9.

Figure 12-9. *Custom editing actions*

If you want deselect the row after triggering the action, you need to call the tableView.setEditing(false, animated: true) function. This will slide the action buttons back out again, to reset the row.

Inserting and Deleting Rows

As you'll probably be expecting by now, inserting and deleting rows is a multistage process that involves the tableView, the delegate, and the dataSource working in tandem with each other.

The process involves the following:

1. Putting the table into editing mode.

2. For each row, checking whether editing is allowed and displaying the editing controls if it is.

3. Responding to the user's touches on the editing controls by sending a message to the dataSource.

4. Updating the model.

5. Updating the table's rows.

The sequence of events, and the passing of messages between tableView, dataSource, and delegate, is illustrated in Figure 12-10.

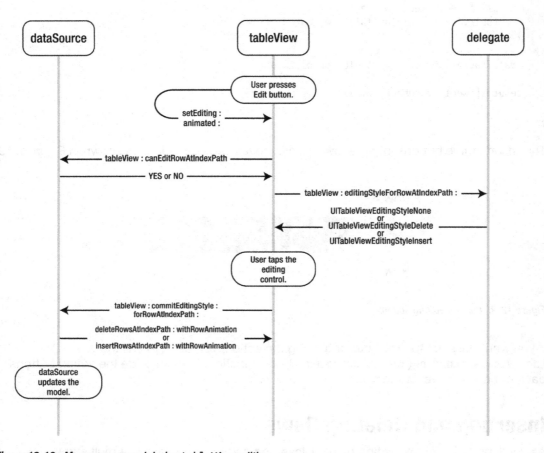

Figure 12-10. Messages passed during tableView editing

At first glance, this looks horrendously complicated. It's actually not that bad, as you'll see as you step through it.

```
                              THE SAMPLE APP
```

If you want to follow along with the upcoming examples, you will need a simple table to experiment with. I'm not going to go into detail about how to do that (hopefully you can build a table after having read this far!) but a couple of specifics are worth mentioning:

- ■ Because tables with editing functions are often found in UINavigationControllers, I've implemented the table view inside a navigation controller.

- ■ The tableView's data model is deliberately simple, so that the data doesn't overshadow the more relevant matters of editing, updating, and deleting.

CREATING A UINAVIGATIONCONTROLLER-BASED TABLE

To create the UINavigationController-based table, I've taken the standard Single View Application template provided by Xcode, and embedded the View Controller inside a Navigation Controller.

CREATING THE SAMPLE TABLE'S DATA MODEL

The data model for this app is very simple. It's just an Array of Strings, which gets created in ViewController's viewDidLoad function:

```
override func viewDidLoad() {

    super.viewDidLoad()
    // Do any additional setup after loading the view, typically from a nib.

    self.navigationItem.title = "Row insertion"
    self.navigationItem.rightBarButtonItem = self.editButtonItem()

    for index in 0...100 {
        tableData.append("Row \(index)")
    }
}
```

There are a couple of other setup-related tasks in this function. The following sets up the title of the navigation bar:

```
self.navigationItem.title = @"Row insertion";
```

This code creates an Edit button:

```
self.navigationItem.rightBarButtonItem = self.editButtonItem;
```

The overall effect is shown in Figure 12-11.

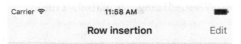

Figure 12-11. The customized navigation bar

Putting the Table into Editing Mode

The first step is to put the table into editing mode, which is invoked by calling the setEditing:animated function on the table view:

```
tableView.setEditing(true, animated:true)
```

Normally this would be done in response to a button tap. If you are using a UINavigationController, the UINavigationBar at the top of your screen comes with a handy Edit button baked in. You can set this up in the viewDidLoad function:

```
self.navigationItem.rightBarButtonItem = self.editButtonItem;
```

This gives you not only an Edit button at the top right of the navigation bar, but one that will automatically toggle between Edit (before the table goes into editing mode) and Done (while the table is in editing mode). The effect is shown in Figure 12-12.

Figure 12-12. The toggling Edit button

If you're not using a UINavigationController, you need to add a button that calls the setEditing:animated: selector, and then handles the toggling between Edit and Done modes manually.

Listing 12-11 shows an example of adding an Edit button.

Listing 12-11. Adding an Edit Button

```
let editingButton = UIButton(type: UIButtonType.RoundedRect)
editingButton.frame = CGRectMake(0, 0, 60, 40)
editingButton.setTitle("Edit", forState: UIControlState.Normal)
editingButton.addTarget(self, action: "setEditing:", forControlEvents:↵
UIControlEvents.TouchUpInside)
self.view.addSubview(editingButton)
```

If you have a "standard" button, you need to implement the setEditing:animated function in Listing 12-12.

Listing 12-12. The setEditing:animated: Function

```
override func setEditing(editing: Bool, animated: Bool) {
    tableView.setEditing(!tableView.editing, animated: true)
}
```

Controlling Whether Rows Can Be Edited

After the table is in editing mode, the table view will then ask the data source whether each row should be editable. If the `tableView:canEditRowAtIndexPath:` function is implemented, this is called for each row in turn. Listing 12-13 shows how to use this function to prevent a specific section and row from being edited.

Listing 12-13. Controlling Whether a Section or Row Can Be Edited

```
func tableView(tableView: UITableView, canEditRowAtIndexPath indexPath: NSIndexPath)↵
 -> Bool {

    if indexPath.section == 0 || indexPath.row == 3 {
        return false
    }

    return true;

}
```

If the `tableView:canEditRowAtIndexPath:` function returns `false`, the row won't be indented. Figure 12-13 shows the effect of this.

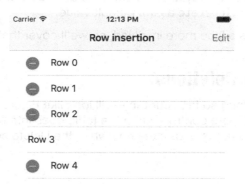

Figure 12-13. Preventing editing of an entire section

If the `tableView:canEditRowAtIndexPath:` isn't implemented, the table view assumes that each row *can* be edited. In effect, the default return value is `true`.

To temporarily disable editing of the table view as a whole, you can return `false` from the `canEditRowAtIndexPath:` regardless of the `indexPath` being passed into the function.

Controlling Each Row's Editing Style

Having established whether a row can be edited, the table view then asks the delegate which editing style each row should use:

```
func tableView(tableView: UITableView, editingStyleForRowAtIndexPath indexPath:↵
 NSIndexPath) -> UITableViewCellEditingStyle {
    return UITableViewCellEditingStyle.Delete
}
```

If the `tableView:editingStyleForRowAtIndexPath:` function is implemented, it will return one of three possible options:

- `UITableViewCellEditingStyleDelete`: This causes the deletion control to be inserted at the left end of the cell.

- `UITableViewCellEditingStyleInsert`: This causes the insertion control to be inserted at the left end of the cell.

- `UITableViewCellEditingStyleNone`: Somewhat unsurprisingly, this does not insert an editing control.

As with `tableView:canEditRowAtIndexPath:`, if the `tableView:editingStyleForRowAtIndex Path:` isn't implemented, the `tableView` will assume that all cells will be deletable and return `UITableViewCellEditingStyleDelete` as the default value.

Inserting additional rows is a little more involved, so we'll cover that later in this chapter.

Dealing with Row Deletions

If you've been following along so far, your table will look like Figure 12-14, with an Edit button, cells that display Delete controls when the table goes into editing mode, and a Delete button that appears at the end of the row when the Delete control is tapped.

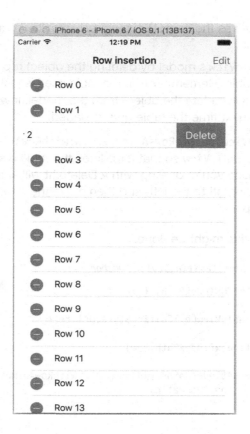

Figure 12-14. *Progress so far*

However, tapping that Delete button is something of an anticlimax. Nothing happens.

When the Delete button is tapped, the tableView sends the tableView:commitEditingStyle: forRowAtIndexPath: message to the data source. It takes three parameters:

- A reference to the tableView itself (in case the data source needs to distinguish between a number of tableViews)

- The UITableViewCellEditingStyle of the control that's just been tapped, which in this case is UITableViewCellEditingStyleDelete

- An indexPath object locating the row in question

When the data source receives the `commitEditingStyle:forRowAtIndexPath:` message, it needs to do two things:

1. Update the `tableView`'s model by deleting the object represented by the row in the table. Remember that the table itself is just a view, and unless you actually delete the object from the model, it will reappear in the table the next time the table gets reloaded.

2. Send the `tableView:deleteRowsAtIndexPath:withRowAnimation:` message to the `tableView` so that it updates the table display. In this case, because you're dealing with a Delete, it will animate the deleted cell sliding off to the left, and then move the cells below it up to close the gap.

Listing 12-14 shows how this might be done.

Listing 12-14. Implementing the `commitEditingStyle:` Function

```
forRowAtIndexPath indexPath: NSIndexPath) {

    if editingStyle == UITableViewCellEditingStyle.Delete {

        tableData.removeAtIndex(indexPath.row)

        tableView.deleteRowsAtIndexPaths([indexPath], withRowAnimation:↵
        UITableViewRowAnimation.Automatic)

    }

}
```

There's a reasonable amount going on here. First, you need to check what kind of action is required (you'll be adding the insert action shortly).

If it's a delete, you need to remove the object in question from the data model. In this simple instance, it's just a case of removing an object from an array, but in a more complex app, this might require a database deletion:

```
tableData.removeAtIndex(indexPath.row)
```

Then you can send that delete message to the `tableView`, passing in the `indexPaths` to be deleted as an Array:

```
tableView.deleteRowsAtIndexPaths([indexPath], withRowAnimation:↵
    UITableViewRowAnimation.Automatic)
```

There's a range of table cell insertion and deletion animations to choose from. These are listed in Table 12-1.

Table 12-1. The UITableViewRowAnimation Options

UITableViewRowAnimation Type	Effect
.Fade	Rows fade in and out.
.Right	Inserted rows slide in from the right; deleted rows slide out to the right.
.Left	Inserted rows slide in from the left; deleted rows slide out to the left.
.Top	Inserted rows slide down from the bottom of the row above; deleted rows slide up toward the bottom of the row above.
.Bottom	Inserted rows slide up from the top of the cell below; deleted rows appear to be covered by the row below sliding up.
.None	Inserted rows simply appear; deleted rows simply disappear.
.Middle	Cells are inserted and deleted with an accordion-style effect.
.Automatic	The tableView automatically chooses an appropriate animation style

It's worth noting that the Top, Bottom, and Middle styles can produce some bizarre effects if you try to apply them to rows at the very top or bottom of the tableView.

For that reason UITableViewRowAnimationAutomatic automatically applies the correct top, bottom, or middle style depending on which row is being animated. This saves a lot of work, so unless you have a very good reason to do otherwise, it's the way to go.

Swipe-Style Row Deletions

In addition to the "tap-Edit-and-then-tap-the-Delete-control-and-then-tap-the-Delete-button" approach to deleting rows, UITableView provides another option. Swiping from side to side in the cell will cause a Delete button to slide in from the right side. Tapping the button will then call the commitEditingStyle function as usual.

Because it's a user-initiated action, the call to tableView:commitEditingStyle:forRowAtIndexPath: is bracketed by two other calls: tableView:willBeginEditingRowAtIndexPath: and tableView:didEndEditingRowAtIndexPath:.

There are a couple of reasons why I think this is a Bad Idea, and you shouldn't implement it:

- It is hidden functionality. Until the user swipes over the row, there's no indication that this action will trigger any effect. Neither is it intuitive how to cancel the action. Tapping elsewhere in the cell will do so, but that runs the risk of accidentally tapping the Delete button by mistake.

- Using a swipe in a row to trigger the Delete action means that this action isn't available for other, potentially more useful actions, such as revealing controls "underneath" the row. (Yes, I *know* this contradicts my first point, but if you're going to use "hidden" gestures to trigger actions, at least make the actions the most useful ones!).

There's a counter-argument, of course. The swipe-to-delete approach is a standard part of iOS table views that's used extensively in apps such as Mail, so users may tend to expect it. Apple's user interface designers are very clever people, and they clearly think it's okay.

However, if I *have* managed to convince you that enabling swipe-to-delete is a Bad Thing, here's how to disable it. Swiping in the cell triggers the tableView:editingStyleForRowAt IndexPath: function. By default, this always returns UITableViewCellEditingStyle.Delete. If you want to restrict cell editing unless the table is in editing mode, you can test for this before returning the editing style. That's what Listing 12-15 does.

Listing 12-15. Disabling Swipe-to-Delete

```
func tableView(tableView: UITableView, editingStyleForRowAtIndexPath indexPath:↵
  NSIndexPath) -> UITableViewCellEditingStyle {

    if tableView.editing {
        return UITableViewCellEditingStyle.Delete
    }

    return UITableViewCellEditingStyle.None

}
```

Unless the table is in editing mode (that is, tableView.editing == true), this function will return UITableViewCellEditingStyle.None, preventing the Delete control from being shown.

Dealing with Row Insertions

If your app needs to handle row deletions, there's a fair chance it will also need to deal with row insertions. This process is not too dissimilar to dealing with deletions.

1. Put the table into editing mode.

2. Check whether the row can be edited.

3. Return the editing style for the row in question (in this case, UITableViewEditingStyle.Insert).

4. Handle whatever actions are needed to create a new object model—for example, presenting a modal data entry view.

5. Commit the editing action with tableView:commitEditingStyle:↵ forRowAtIndexPath: and then update the model.

6. Update the table by inserting a row with insertRowAtIndexPath:with Animation:.

The first two steps we've already covered with the deletion process. The third is a little more involved, so let's look at it.

A common requirement is a need to insert a new row to the end of a table or a section. There are a couple of ways that this could be approached. One option is to place an Add button onto the navigation bar in a similar way to the Edit/Done button that you saw earlier.

The downside to this approach is that you may already have an Edit button in place—or you might not have a navigation bar at all. In this case, a different approach is needed: placing the call to action into the table itself, as shown in Figure 12-15.

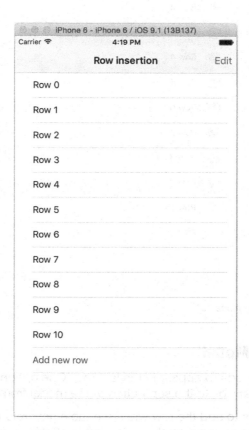

Figure 12-15. The call to action in the table

Tapping the Add New Row row when the table is not in editing mode will switch it into editing mode. Tapping any other row will result in the "normal" row selection actions.

Regardless of how the table entered editing mode, the Add New Row row will show an Insert control, while all the other rows will show a Delete control (shown in Figure 12-16).

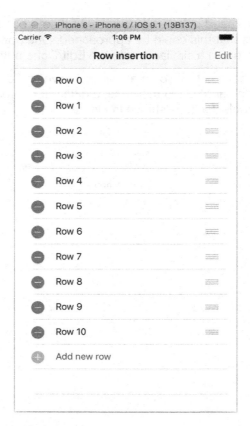

Figure 12-16. *The table in editing mode*

Amending the Data Model

The Add New Row item needs to appear in the last row. One option is to add this to the data model itself, but that would violate the separation of the model from the view.

The "cleaner" alternative is to add the row when the table gets reloaded. First, you need to tell the table to expect an extra row, as shown in Listing 12-16.

Listing 12-16. *The Updated tableView:numberOfRowsInSection: Function*

```
func tableView(tableView: UITableView, numberOfRowsInSection section: Int) -> Int {
    return tableData.count + 1
}
```

And then add the extra row in the `tableView:cellForRowAtIndexPath:` function, as shown in Listing 12-17.

Listing 12-17. The Updated tableView:cellForRowAtIndexPath: Function

```
func tableView(tableView: UITableView, cellForRowAtIndexPath indexPath: NSIndexPath) ↵
 -> UITableViewCell {

    let cell = tableView.dequeueReusableCellWithIdentifier("CellIdentifier", ↵
    forIndexPath: indexPath)

    if indexPath.row == tableData.count {
        cell.textLabel?.text = "Add new row"
        cell.textLabel?.textColor = UIColor.darkGrayColor()
    } else {
        cell.textLabel?.text = tableData[indexPath.row]
    }

    return cell

}
```

The magic happens after the cell is created. If the function is dealing with the last row (in other words, the indexPath's row value is the same as the number of items in the data model), then the cell.textLabel.text property is set to "Add New Row".

> **Note**   Bear in mind that while indexPath values start from 0, counting the number of elements in the data model starts from 1. Hence—usually—the indexPath's row value for the final item in the table will be (tableData.count - 1). If the indexPath's row value equals tableData.count, you're actually one row *beyond* the end of the array, and therefore you need to insert the Add New Row item here.

Working with the New Row

Having created the new row, you now have to handle the user interaction. When the row is tapped, you want the table to enter editing mode, which means revising the tableView:didSelectRowAtIndexPath: function in Listing 12-18.

Listing 12-18. The tableView:didSelectRowAtIndexPath: Function

```
func tableView(tableView: UITableView, didSelectRowAtIndexPath indexPath: NSIndexPath) {

    if (indexPath.row == tableData.count) {

        // put table into edit mode
        tableView.setEditing(true, animated: true)

    } else {

        // Handle "normal" selection

    }

}
```

Again, you test to see whether the selected row is the one at the end of the table. If it is, you override the default setEditing:animated: function to put the cell into editing mode, as shown in Listing 12-19.

Listing 12-19. The Custom setEditing:animated: Function

```
override func setEditing(editing: Bool, animated: Bool) {
    tableView.setEditing(!tableView.editing, animated: true)
}
```

You will need to amend the tableView:editingStyleForRowAtIndexPath: function to supply the insertion control to the last row (shown in Listing 12-20).

After the table is in editing mode, it's up to the user to either edit something with the Delete or Insert controls, or take the table out of editing mode.

If they do the latter, you don't need to worry about responding to their action. The updated setEditing:animated: function will handle that.

An editing action, on the other hand, is something you need to handle.

Listing 12-20. Handling an Editing Action

```
func tableView(tableView: UITableView, editingStyleForRowAtIndexPath indexPath: ↵
NSIndexPath) -> UITableViewCellEditingStyle {

    if tableView.editing {
        if (indexPath.row == tableData.count) {
            return UITableViewCellEditingStyle.Insert;
        } else {
            return UITableViewCellEditingStyle.Delete;
        }
    }

    return UITableViewCellEditingStyle.None

}
```

Tapping a row's control will fire the tableView:commitEditingStyle:forRowAtIndexPath: function, supplying references to the tableView itself, the row that was tapped, and the type of control.

There are two possibilities here: a UITableViewCellEditingStyle.Delete or a UITableViewCellEditingStyle.Insert. If it's a delete, then you handle it as you did previously: remove the object from the relevant index of the data model and then delete the row from the table.

An insert, on the other hand, needs the opposite approach. First, you need a new object. For demonstration purposes, create an NSString containing a date stamp:

```
let thingToInsert = "\(NSDate())"
```

Then, this new object needs to be added to the data model. It's important that this takes place *before* the table gets updated, because the table will need to determine the number of rows it now has in order to be able to insert the new row:

```
tableData.append(thingToInsert)
```

Array's append function inserts the new object at the end of the existing array, but you could, of course, insert it at a particular position with the `append(:atIndex:)` function.

Now that you have the new object safely stored in the data model, you can insert the new row into the table. You'll want this to appear in the penultimate row—above Add New Row, but below the existing rows (along the lines of Figure 12-17).

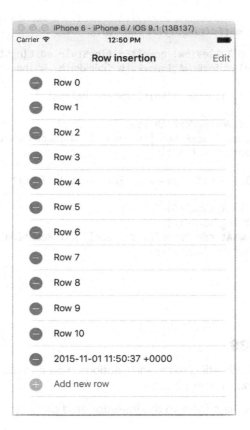

Figure 12-17. The newly inserted row

UITableView's `insertRowsAtIndexPath:withRowAnimation:` takes an `Array` of `IndexPath` objects where new rows are required and calls the `tableView`'s `cellForRowAtIndexPath:` function to fill them.

It'll automatically shift existing rows down. Your table currently has ten rows, and your `indexPath.row` value is 9 (remember, table rows are zero-indexed.) Inserting a new row at `indexPath.row` 9 will cause whatever's currently in that row to be shifted down to the new `indexPath.row` 10.

```
tableView.insertRowsAtIndexPaths([indexPath], withRowAnimation: ↵
 UITableViewRowAnimation.Automatic)
```

The `UITableViewRowAnimation.Automatic` value will force the `tableView` to take care of moving existing rows around to keep the animation seamless.

Putting that all together (with a little bit of refactoring to keep the function tidy) looks like Listing 12-21.

Listing 12-21. The Completed `commitEditingStyle:` Function

```
func tableView(tableView: UITableView, commitEditingStyle editingStyle:↵
 UITableViewCellEditingStyle, forRowAtIndexPath indexPath: NSIndexPath) {

    if (editingStyle == UITableViewCellEditingStyle.Delete) {

        tableData.removeAtIndex(indexPath.row)
        tableView.deleteRowsAtIndexPaths([indexPath], withRowAnimation:↵
        UITableViewRowAnimation.Automatic)

    } else if (editingStyle == UITableViewCellEditingStyle.Insert) {

        let thingToInsert = "\(NSDate())"
        tableData.append(thingToInsert)
        tableView.insertRowsAtIndexPaths([indexPath], withRowAnimation:↵
        UITableViewRowAnimation.Automatic)

    }

}
```

Rearranging Tables

In addition to inserting and deleting rows and sections, you can also rearrange them, both programmatically and through user actions.

The rearrangement process is similar to the insertion and deletion process, as shown in Figure 12-18.

1. The table enters editing mode.

2. The `tableView`'s delegate is consulted about the permissibility of moving the row.

3. The row gets moved.

4. The data model is updated.

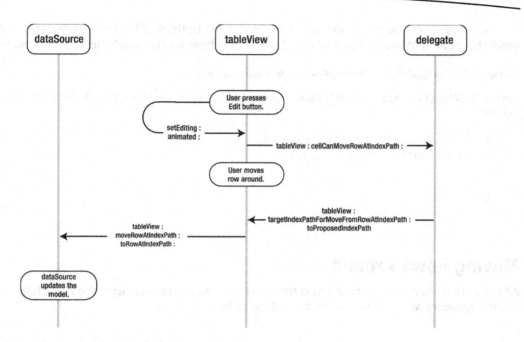

Figure 12-18. The row rearrangement process

Entering Editing Mode

In order to rearrange rows, the table needs to be in editing mode. As with deletions, there are two ways of doing this. In the case of UITableViewController subclasses, the user can tap the navigation bar's Edit button or override the tableView's setEditing:animated: function.

In order for the rearrange control to be displayed, you need to implement the tableView (moveRowAtIndexPath:toIndexPath) function, as shown in Listing 12-22.

Listing 12-22. The Custom setEditing:animated: Function

```
func tableView(tableView: UITableView, moveRowAtIndexPath sourceIndexPath:↩
  NSIndexPath, toIndexPath destinationIndexPath: NSIndexPath) {
    //
}
```

This doesn't do anything yet, but it's necessary to get the table to show the rearrangement control.

Checking Whether Rows Can Be Moved

As the tableView enters editing mode, it asks the delegate whether each visible row can be moved by calling the tableView:canMoveRowAtIndexPath: function. This returns either true or false. Returning false will enable you to "lock" particular rows into place.

For example, if you have an "Add New Row" row at the bottom of the table, it doesn't make sense to be able to move this. Listing 12-23 shows how you'd "lock" this row into place.

Listing 12-23. The tableView:canMoveRowAtIndexPath: Function

```
func tableView(tableView: UITableView, canMoveRowAtIndexPath indexPath: NSIndexPath)↵
    -> Bool {

    if (indexPath.row == tableData.count) {
        return false
    }

    return true

}
```

Moving Rows Around

After the table is in editing mode and the rows are flagged as movable, the Reordering control appears at the right end of the cell, as in Figure 12-19.

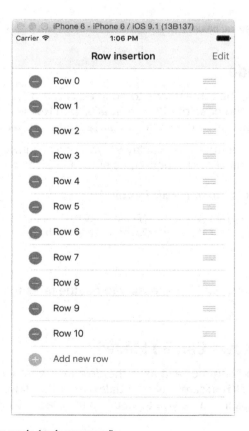

Figure 12-19. The table in editing mode (and rearranged)

Touching the Reordering control will cause the row to be animated away from the table and become draggable. As the row passes over other rows, the tableView will animate the shuffling around to make room.

Can the Row Be Moved to Here?

In addition to controlling whether rows can be moved at all, UITableView's delegate can also control whether a row can be moved to a particular location.

As the row in motion passes over the static rows in the table, the tableView will call the tableView:targetIndexPathForMoveFromRowAtIndexPath: toProposedIndexPath: function. (This is probably the function that's responsible for critics of iOS complaining about long-winded function names.)

This function takes three parameters: a reference to the tableView itself, the original indexPath of the row that's being moved, and the indexPath that has just been moved over. The tableView doesn't know yet whether the user is going to release the Reordering control and "drop" the cell into place, so this function will be called repeatedly as the row in motion moves over indexPath positions as it travels up and down the table.

If the row can be moved to this position, the function simply returns the proposedDestinationIndexPath to confirm that this move is permissible.

You can use this function to complement "freezing" the Add New Row row to the bottom of the table. In addition to not wanting to move the Add New Row row, you also want to prevent the user from moving another row to the very bottom. Figure 12-20 shows what you're trying to avoid.

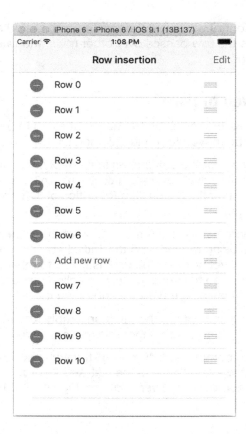

Figure 12-20. Not allowed!

You can implement this by checking whether the proposed indexPath is the end of the table. If it is, you can "send" the row back to where it came from by returning sourceIndexPath. If it isn't, the move can be allowed by returning proposedDestinationIndexPath. Listing 12-24 shows this in action.

Listing 12-24. Preventing a Move to the End of the Table

```
func tableView(tableView: UITableView, targetIndexPathForMoveFromRowAtIndexPath↩
sourceIndexPath: NSIndexPath, toProposedIndexPath proposedDestinationIndexPath:↩
NSIndexPath) -> NSIndexPath {

    if proposedDestinationIndexPath.row == tableData.count {
        return sourceIndexPath
    }

    return proposedDestinationIndexPath
}
```

Updating the Model

After completing the shuffling of rows, the user will take the table out of editing mode either by tapping the Done button on the navigation bar or by tapping whatever custom control you implemented.

At this stage, it's vital to remember that all the changes have taken place only in the view. The underlying data model has not been updated with the changes. Unless you explicitly update the model, the changes won't persist.

This could manifest itself in a couple of ways. The next time the table is reloaded, the rows will have reverted to their original ordering. Worse, if your table has more rows than can be displayed at once, as the table scrolls, you'll get some extremely weird ordering effects appearing.

If the delegate has allowed the move, the tableView will call its delegate's tableView:moveRowAtIndexPath:toIndexPath: function. This takes three parameters: the usual reference to the tableView itself; the indexPath of the source row, and the indexPath of the destination row.

How you go about rearranging the model is obviously dependent on how your model is implemented. In this simple example, you can exploit Array's insert:atIndex: and removeAtIndex: functions, as shown in Listing 12-25.

Listing 12-25. Updating the Model with Rearranged Objects

```
func tableView(tableView: UITableView, moveRowAtIndexPath sourceIndexPath: ←
  NSIndexPath, toIndexPath destinationIndexPath: NSIndexPath) {

    tableData.insert(tableData[sourceIndexPath.row], atIndex: ←
    destinationIndexPath.row)

    tableData.removeAtIndex(sourceIndexPath.row + 1)

}
```

This function first grabs the object from the donor row and inserts it at the destination. If you just left things there, you'd end up with two copies of the original object.

The insert:atIndex: function inserts a new index at the specified index, moves the other objects beyond the insertion down by one, and inserts a copy of the object from the source indexPath.

Enabling Batch Insertion and Deletion

In most user-controlled situations, rows will be affected one by one. You can, however, combine a number of insertion or deletion commands by wrapping them into a block:

```
tableView.beginUpdates()

// do lots of
// insertions and deletions here

tableView.endUpdates()
```

This takes care of a lot of heavy lifting for you. The manipulation of the `tableView` and the data model will take place in the sequence you specify, but you don't need to worry about tracking the changes as you go along.

This is quite subtle and quite powerful. If you delete row 1 of the table, then what was row 2 will move up to become row 1. So now you have to refer to row 1 to affect what was previously row 2, and so on. The update block handles this for you. If you delete row 1 and then delete row 2 within the block, *row 2* will refer to the original row 2.

You mustn't call any functions that will update the `tableView` within an update block (`reloadData` and so on). If you do, you have to handle the animations yourself.

Batch Insertion and Deletion of Sections

As well as batch insertion of rows, it's also possible to insert or delete entire sections. The animations are handled for you.

Inserting sections is performed with the `insertSections:withRowAnimation:` function. You pass an `NSIndexSet` containing the sections to insert, and the table view will call its `dataSource` to obtain the necessary data before inserting the section.

If there's already a section in the position you're attempting to insert at, the existing section will be moved down automatically.

The `rowAnimation` parameter allows you to control the type of animation that's used to insert the new section.

Deleting sections uses the `deleteSections:withRowAnimation:` function. Again, you need to provide an `NSIndexSet` of the sections to remove, and a `rowAnimation` parameter to control the animation. The table view will then handle removing the section and closing up the gap.

You need to be careful when constructing the `NSIndexSet` – if you attempt to insert or remove a section that doesn't exist in the underlying data model, you'll get a runtime crash.

Selection in UICollectionViews

One way of thinking of a `UICollectionView` is as a two-dimensional `UITableView`—that is, a control that manages cells but can scroll in x and y coordinates, rather than the up-down direction of `UITableView`.

With that mental model in mind, it shouldn't come as a surprise to learn that selection in `UICollectionViews` is managed in very similar ways to selection in `UITableViews`.

The main difference is that because collection views can be implemented in radically different ways to table views, they come with fewer built-in features such as in-cell controls. If you want to add edit, delete, or rearrangement controls into cells, you need to handle this yourself.

Cut, Copy, and Paste with Collection Views

Having said that collection views provide less out of the box, there are some neat features that they provide. Support for displaying menus in response to long-presses in cells is one.

A common requirement is support for cut, copy, and paste options for content that is displayed inside a collection view cell. The good news is that this is very simple to implement.

Figure 12-21 shows the effect of implementing cut/copy/paste, in response to a long press on cell 20.

Figure 12-21. Implementing cut/copy/paste

You need to implement three `UICollectionViewDelegate` functions:

- `collectionView(shouldShowMenuForItemAtIndexPath:) -> Bool`
- `collectionView(canPerformAction:forItemAtIndexPath:` ↵ `withSender:  -> Bool`
- `collectionView(performAction:forItemAtIndexPath:withSender:)`

The first function controls whether a menu should be displayed at all for the selected item; return `true` if it should, or `false` if not (Listing 12-26).

Listing 12-26. The shouldShowMenuForItemAtIndexPath: Function

```
override func collectionView(collectionView: UICollectionView, ↵
 shouldShowMenuForItemAtIndexPath indexPath: NSIndexPath) -> Bool {
    return true
}
```

The second controls whether a specific action can be performed for that item. This is where you could disable the cut function, for example, with the code in Listing 12-27.

Listing 12-27. Disabling the Cut Function

```
override func collectionView(collectionView: UICollectionView, canPerformAction↵
 action: Selector, forItemAtIndexPath indexPath: NSIndexPath, withSender↵
 sender: AnyObject?) -> Bool {

    if action.description == "cut:" {
        return false
    }

    return true

}
```

There are a range of actions that you can respond to. If you check the `description` property of the `action` when it's passed into the function, you can see the full list.

Figure 12-22 shows the effect of the code in Listing 12-27.

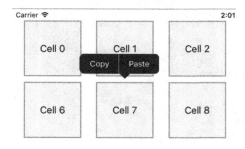

Figure 12-22. Disabling cut

The final function is where you implement the action that you want to enable (Listing 12-28).

Listing 12-28. Implementing the Action

```
override func collectionView(collectionView: UICollectionView, performAction↵
 action: Selector, forItemAtIndexPath indexPath: NSIndexPath, withSender↵
 sender: AnyObject?) {
    //

    switch action.description {

    case "copy:" :
        // Implement copy functionality

    case "paste:" :
        // Implement copy functionality

    }

}
```

Implementing Custom Menus in a Collection View

Although cut, copy, and paste are useful, you're not restricted to these. You can add custom items to the menu that is displayed in response to a long-press in the cell to implement your own functionality.

Long-pressing on the cell will display your custom menu, which will then call a function in the cell. If you need to manipulate the data model by, for example, deleting a cell, then you need to get the cell to call back to the collection view's controller. It can look something like Figure 12-23.

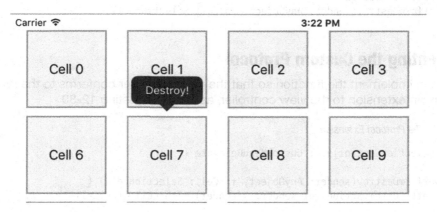

Figure 12-23. The custom menu item

The process has several steps:

- Define a menu delegate protocol, and declare a function to handle your custom action.

- Implement this custom function in your view controller, so that it conforms to the menu delegate protocol.

- Create a custom subclass of UICollectionViewCell and add a delegate property for an object that conforms to the menu delegate protocol.

- In the cell subclass, implement a function to call the delegate. The cell will handle the initial menu press, and then call through to its delegate to perform any action that's required on the data model.

- Create a menu item for the new action, and assign it to the shared menu controller.

- When dequeuing the cell, set the collection view controller as the cell delegate.

- Optionally, update the UICollectionViewDelegate functions to restrict the menu items that are displayed in the pop-over.

Defining the Custom Protocol

The protocol can be defined in the collection view's view controller. Add the declaration at the top of the file (Listing 12-29).

Listing 12-29. Declaring the Custom Menu Protocol

```
protocol CustomMenuDelegate {
    func performDestroy(sender: AnyObject, forCell:SelectionCell)
}
```

Implementing the Custom Protocol

Now you can implement the function so that the view controller conforms to the protocol. Add this as an extension to the view controller, as shown in Listing 12-30.

Listing 12-30. The Protocol Extension

```
extension SelectionController : CustomMenuDelegate {

    func performDestroy(sender: AnyObject, forCell: SelectionCell) {
        print("Custom action for sender: \(sender) with cell \(forCell)")
    }

}
```

Updating the Collection View Cell Subclass

If you don't already have a custom `UICollectionViewCell` subclass, you need to implement one. If you have one, you need to update it so that it has a delegate property and a function to implement the action that's called from the custom menu. An example is shown in Listing 12-31.

Listing 12-31. An Example Custom UICollectionViewCell

```
import UIKit

class SelectionCell: UICollectionViewCell {

    var delegate: CustomMenuDelegate?

    func performDestroy(sender: AnyObject) {
        if let delegate = delegate {
            delegate.performDestroy(sender, forCell: self)
        }
    }

}
```

Creating the Custom Menu Item

Now you can create the custom menu item. In the view controller, add the following code to the `viewDidLoad` function:

```
let menuItem = UIMenuItem(title: "Destroy!", action: "performDestroy:")
UIMenuController.sharedMenuController().menuItems = [menuItem]
```

This creates a new menu item titled `Destroy!` that will call the `performDestroy:` function when it's tapped. The function will be called on the cell, because that's the object that the menu will be attached to.

It's then added to the `sharedMenuController` so that it can be added to the cell in response to a long press.

Linking the Cell to Its Delegate

Now you need to update the `cellForItemAtIndexPath:` function so that the cell's delegate is set as it's dequeued. Add the following line to the `cellForItemAtIndexPath:` function, after the cell is dequeued but before it's returned:

```
cell.delegate = self
```

Updating the UICollectionViewDelegate Functions

The `UICollectionViewDelegate` functions that control the actions that can be performed in response to a long press need to be updated. Assuming you only want to provide the `Destroy!` menu option, update the `collectionView(canPerformAction:forItemAtIndexPath:withSender:)` function as shown in Listing 12-32.

Listing 12-32. The Updated collectionView(canPerformAction:forItemAtIndexPath:withSender:) Function

```
override func collectionView(collectionView: UICollectionView, canPerformAction↵
action: Selector, forItemAtIndexPath indexPath: NSIndexPath, withSender↵
sender: AnyObject?) -> Bool {

    if action.description == "performDestroy:" {
        return true
    }

    return false

}
```

With these updates in place, you're ready to run the app again, and try a long press action in a cell. You should see the Destroy! item pop up, as shown in Figure 12-24.

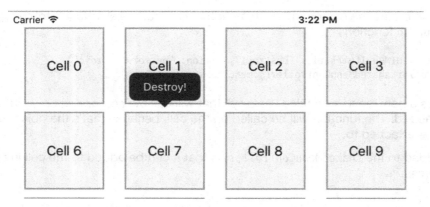

Figure 12-24. The Destroy! menu item

Removing Cells in Response to the Menu Item

To complete this process, let's implement the functionality needed to remove the cell item in response to selecting the Destroy! option. Update the `performDestroy` function so that it matches Listing 12-33.

Listing 12-33. The Updated performDestroy Function

```
func performDestroy(sender: AnyObject, forCell: SelectionCell) {

    if let indexPath = collectionView?.indexPathForCell(forCell) {
        dataArray.removeAtIndex(indexPath.row)
        collectionView?.reloadData()
    }

}
```

This uses the cell that "owns" the menu to get the indexPath from the collection view, and then deletes the object at that index. When the collection view's data is reloaded, the selected cell will have been removed, as shown in Figure 12-25.

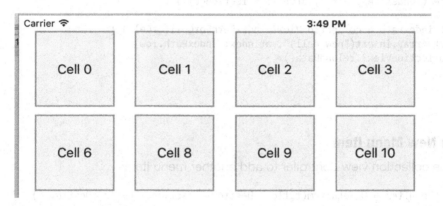

Figure 12-25. Cell 7 has been removed

Implementing an "Add Cell" Option

Implementing the functionality to add a cell, instead of remove one, is a virtually identical process.

Extending the Protocol to Add a Function to Insert a Cell

Update the protocol to add a definition for addItem(sender:atCell:):

```
protocol CustomMenuDelegate {
    func performDestroy(sender: AnyObject, forCell:SelectionCell)
    func addItem(sender: AnyObject, atCell: SelectionCell)
}
```

Adding the New Function to the Cell Subclass

Add the addItem function to the SelectionCell subclass:

```
func addItem(sender: AnyObject) {
    if let delegate = delegate {
        delegate.addItem(sender, atCell: self)
    }
}
```

Implementing the addItem Function in the Collection View Controller

Add the function to insert an item into the collection view's data model, and refresh the data:

```
func addItem(sender: AnyObject, atCell: SelectionCell) {

    if let indexPath = collectionView?.indexPathForCell(atCell) {
        dataArray.insert("new cell)", atIndex: indexPath.row)
        collectionView?.reloadData()
    }

}
```

Adding a New Menu Item

Update the collection view controller to add another menu item:

```
let destroyMenuItem = UIMenuItem(title: "Destroy!", action: "performDestroy:")
let addMenuItem = UIMenuItem(title: "Add!", action: "addItem:")
UIMenuController.sharedMenuController().menuItems = [addMenuItem, destroyMenuItem]
```

Run the project again, and you'll see a new item in the pop-up menu, as shown in Figure 12-26.

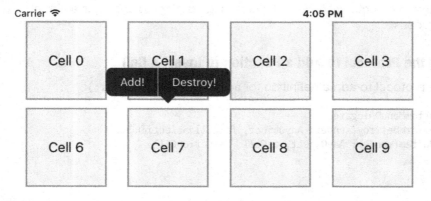

Figure 12-26. The new menu item

Tap the Add! button, and you'll see a new item appear in the collection view, as shown in Figure 12-27.

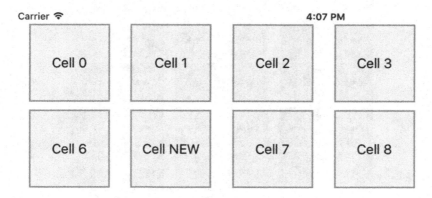

Figure 12-27. The new cell

Rearranging UICollectionViews

A collection view is a great control for presenting data for your user to sort interactively–rearranging the order of photos in an album, for example. UICollectionView makes it almost trivial to implement this kind of feature.

To demonstrate this, you'll create a very simple collection view that displays a number of cells, and then you'll implement the functionality that allows them to be sorted by dragging and dropping.

Implementing drag-and-drop reordering involves adding some UICollectionViewDelegate functions to the collection view's delegate object; the exact approach depends on whether you're using a subclass of UICollectionViewController or not. You'll look at both processes in turn.

Prerequisites

This process assumes that you've got a collection view that displays cells in a single section based on the underlying data stored in a model. The source code for this chapter includes two projects: one for the initial state to get you started, and one with the functionality fully implemented.

Assuming you're starting from the initial state, the app will look like Figure 12-28.

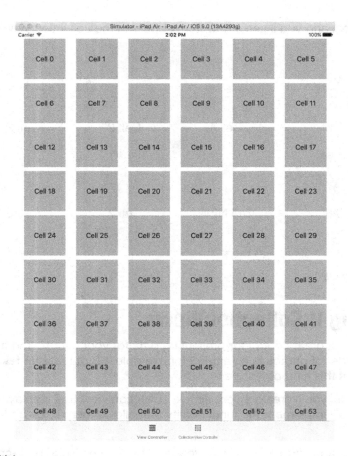

Figure 12-28. The initial app

There are two tabs, one containing a UIViewController-based collection view, and one with a UICollectionViewController subclass. Both have identical data structures: a Struct of 100 Strings, which are displayed in 100 x 100 cells under the control of a flow layout.

At the moment, the only interaction that's possible is the default vertical scrolling behavior. You're going to enhance that by implementing drag-and-drop reordering of the collection view.

The process begins with a long press on the item; once that's been detected, the delegate is asked whether the item at that index path is allowed to move. If it is, the cell will follow the pan gesture.

When the user lifts their finger and the pan gesture ends, the cell is inserted into the collection view in the space that's opened up, and a second delegate function is called to allow the data source to be updated.

Adapting the UICollectionViewController-based collection view is the simpler of the two, so you implement this first and then use it as the starting point for the same functionality in a UIViewController.

Implementing Drag-and-Drop with UICollectionViewController

The process begins with updating the `UICollectionViewController` to set the `installsStandardGestureForInteractiveMovement` property to `true`. Add this to `viewDidLoad` function:

```
self.installsStandardGestureForInteractiveMovement = true
```

Adding UICollectionViewDelegate Functions

Next, there are two optional `UICollectionViewDelegate` functions that you need to implement:

- `collectionView(_:canMoveItemAtIndexPath:)`
- `collectionView(_:moveItemAtIndexPath:toIndexPath)`

The first function simply controls whether the selected item can be moved or not, and is called *before* the interaction begins. You may have items that must remain in place, in which case you need to return `false` for those specific index paths.

In your case, you're allowing all items to move, so you simply return `true` from the function, as shown in Listing 12-34.

Listing 12-34. collectionView(_:canMoveItemAtIndexPath:)

```
override func collectionView(collectionView: UICollectionView, canMoveItemAtIndexPath ↵
indexPath: NSIndexPath) -> Bool {
    return true
}
```

The second function is called once the interaction is completed. This is the point where you can update the underlying data source to match the changes in the collection view.

> **Caution**   The action of rearranging the items in the collection view **doesn't** update the underlying data model; the changes only take place in the view. If you don't update the data model to reflect how the items have been moved, then the changes will disappear the next time the collection view updates.

This function takes three parameters: the `collectionView` itself, the `indexPath` that the item came from, and the `indexPath` that it's going to. Armed with this data, you can update the data according, as shown in Listing 12-35.

Listing 12-35. Updating the Data Model

```
override func collectionView(collectionView: UICollectionView, moveItemAtIndexPath
sourceIndexPath: NSIndexPath, toIndexPath destinationIndexPath: NSIndexPath) {

    // Find object to move
    let thingToMove = dataArray[sourceIndexPath.row]

    // Remove old object
    dataArray.removeAtIndex(sourceIndexPath.row)

    // insert new copy of thing to move
    dataArray.insert(thingToMove, atIndex: destinationIndexPath.row)

    // Reload the data
    collectionView.reloadData()

}
```

The final reloadData() call isn't strictly necessary to update the view, but it means that the collectionView and its underlying data are back in sync once the interaction is completed.

With those three changes implemented, you can now drag and drop cells around the collection view with impunity!

Highlighting the Move

As things stand, it can be a little difficult to see what's going on as you're moving a cell around, because the cell in motion looks the same as all the others. To make it stand out a little more, you can tap into the two delegate functions you've just implemented to highlight the cell while it's in motion.

To begin with, let's change the background color of the cell when the pan gesture starts.

Add a property to the class to hold a reference to the cell that's in motion:

```
private var selectedCell: UICollectionViewCell?
```

Next, update the collectionView(_:cellForItemAtIndexPath:) function to set the cell's border when it's dequeued, by adding these two lines after the label has been updated:

```
cell.contentView.layer.borderColor = UIColor.lightGrayColor().CGColor
cell.contentView.layer.borderWidth = 2.0
```

Now update the collectionView(_:canMoveAtIndexPath:) function so that it looks like Listing 12-36.

Listing 12-36. The Updated collectionView(_:canMoveAtIndexPath:) Function

```
override func collectionView(collectionView: UICollectionView, canMoveItemAtIndexPath ↵
indexPath: NSIndexPath) -> Bool {

    selectedCell = collectionView.cellForItemAtIndexPath(indexPath)
    selectedCell?.contentView.layer.borderColor = UIColor.redColor().CGColor

    return true
}
```

This gets a reference to the cell that's been selected, and changes the color of the border to red as the interaction begins.

To set the border color back to its original value when the interaction ends, update the `coll ectionView(_:moveItemAtIndexPath:toIndexPath:)` function by adding this line just before the `reloadData()` call:

```
selectedCell?.contentView.layer.borderColor = UIColor.lightGrayColor().CGColor
```

Using Drag-and-Drop Interaction

With these updates in place, you can drag and drop cells to rearrange, as shown in Figure 12-29.

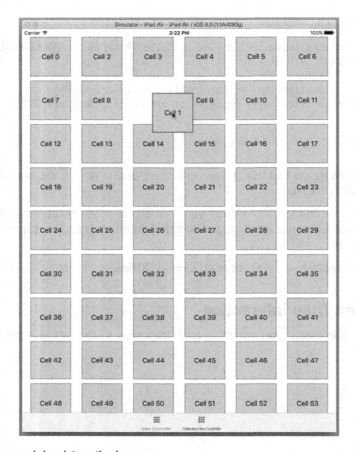

Figure 12-29. The drag-and-drop interaction in progress

Implementing Drag-and-Drop with UIViewController

If your collection view is managed by a UIViewController subclass rather than a UICollectionViewController, there is slightly more involved in implementing drag-and-drop interaction. The end result is exactly the same, however.

To begin with, follow the UICollectionViewController process shown above to add the UICollectionViewDelegate functions and highlight the moving cell.

Adding Properties

Next, you need to add three properties to the view controller:

```
var longPressGesture: UILongPressGestureRecognizer!
var panGesture: UIPanGestureRecognizer!
var selectedIndexPath: NSIndexPath!
```

The longPressGesture property holds a reference to the gesture recognizer that controls the start of the drag-and-drop process. panGesture holds a reference to the gesture recognizer that handles the tracking of the cell underneath the touch point; and selectedIndexPath is a reference to the cell that's being manipulated.

Adding the Gesture Recognizers

Now you need to add the gesture recognizers to the collection view. This is done in viewDidLoad, as shown in Listing 12-37.

Listing 12-37. The Updated viewDidLoad Function

```
override func viewDidLoad() {
    super.viewDidLoad()

    panGesture = UIPanGestureRecognizer(target: self, action: "handlePanGesture:")
    self.collectionView.addGestureRecognizer(panGesture)
    panGesture.delegate = self

    longPressGesture = UILongPressGestureRecognizer(target: self, ←
  action: "handleLongGesture:")
    self.collectionView.addGestureRecognizer(longPressGesture)
    longPressGesture.delegate = self

}
```

A new function is needed to handle the longGesture; add this as shown in Listing 12-38.

Listing 12-38. The handleLongGesture(_:) Function

```
func handleLongGesture(gesture: UILongPressGestureRecognizer) {

    switch(gesture.state) {

    case UIGestureRecognizerState.Began:
        selectedIndexPath = self.collectionView.indexPathForItemAtPoint←
        (gesture.locationInView(self.collectionView))

    case UIGestureRecognizerState.Changed:
        break

    default:
        selectedIndexPath = nil

    }

}
```

This updates the selectedIndexPath in response to the UILongPressGesture starting; and resets it when the gesture finishes.

The handlePanGesture(_:) function is responsible for passing the movement to the collection view, so add the code shown in Listing 12-39.

Listing 12-39. The handlePanGesture(_:) Function

```
func handlePanGesture(gesture: UIPanGestureRecognizer) {

    switch(gesture.state) {

    case UIGestureRecognizerState.Began:
        collectionView.beginInteractiveMovementForItemAtIndexPath(selectedIndexPath!)

    case UIGestureRecognizerState.Changed:
        collectionView.updateInteractiveMovementTargetPosition ↵
        (gesture.locationInView(gesture.view!))

    case UIGestureRecognizerState.Ended:
        collectionView.endInteractiveMovement()

    default:
        collectionView.cancelInteractiveMovement()

    }

}
```

There are three possible states of a pan gesture recognizer:

- Began is where you tell the collection view to begin moving the item at the selected index path.

- Changed occurs as the touch point moves, so the collection view is told to move the target to match the touch point.

- Finally, Ended occurs after the touch-up event, at which point the collection view is told to cancel the movement. This causes the moving element to "snap" into its new position.

Adding UIGestureRecognizerDelegate Functions

As you'll have noticed in the updated viewDidLoad function, the two gesture recognizers have delegates. These have both been set to the view controller. You need to add two delegate functions. The easiest way to do this is to add an extension to the view controller, as shown in Listing 12-40.

Listing 12-40. The View Controller's UIGestureRecognizerDelegate Extension

```
extension ViewController: UIGestureRecognizerDelegate {

    func gestureRecognizer(gestureRecognizer: UIGestureRecognizer, ⏎
    shouldRecognizeSimultaneouslyWithGestureRecognizer otherGestureRecognizer: ⏎
    UIGestureRecognizer) -> Bool {

            if gestureRecognizer == longPressGesture {
                return panGesture == otherGestureRecognizer
            }

            if gestureRecognizer == panGesture {
                return longPressGesture == otherGestureRecognizer
            }

            return true
    }

    func gestureRecognizerShouldBegin(gestureRecognizer: UIGestureRecognizer) -> Bool {

        guard gestureRecognizer == self.panGesture else {
            return true
        }

        return selectedIndexPath != nil
    }

}
```

Finishing Up

With the extension functions in place, you're now ready to run the app, and see the drag-and-drop interaction implemented in the view controller tab, as shown in Figure 12-30.

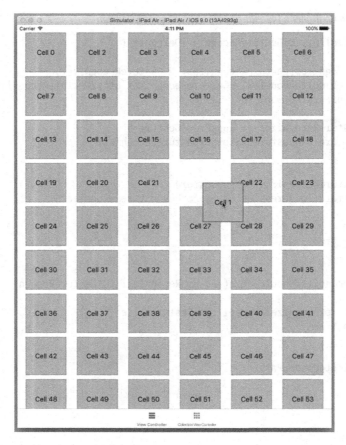

Figure 12-30. The drag-and-drop interaction in progress

Summary

In this chapter, you looked at how tables and collection views can be extended from being presenters of static, unreactive data to handle user input through selection traits. You saw how they can be used to rearrange data and to facilitate the updating of the underlying data model.

Finally, you took things to their logical conclusion and extended them still further to allow users to add, amend, and delete information from the data model—taking tables and collection views from being a read-only views to a fully interactive components.

Chapter 13

Static Tables

Many table views are built dynamically, populating instances of prototype cells on demand as the data is displayed. But that's not the only way of building them; static table views can also be useful components of a user interface.

With a static table, you define the cells and their contents up front. This is useful in situations where you know the content to be displayed won't change, such as when displaying a list of settings. Many parts of the built-in iOS Settings app are based on a static table view, as shown in Figure 13-1.

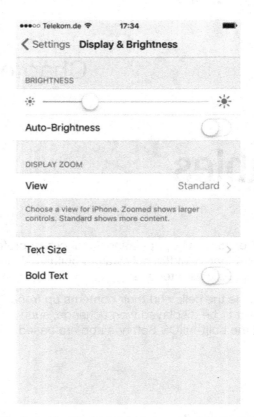

Figure 13-1. A static table used to display the Display & Brightness controls in the Settings app

Static tables can also be used to take advantage of the layout flexibility that a table view offers, even for static content, and even if the interface looks nothing like a table at first glance.

In this chapter, you'll look at the process of building static tables, and some of the uses for such tables.

How to Build Static Tables

When you add a table view object, either as a child of an existing view, or as the root object of a table view controller scene, it appears with an area for prototype content, as shown in Figure 13-2.

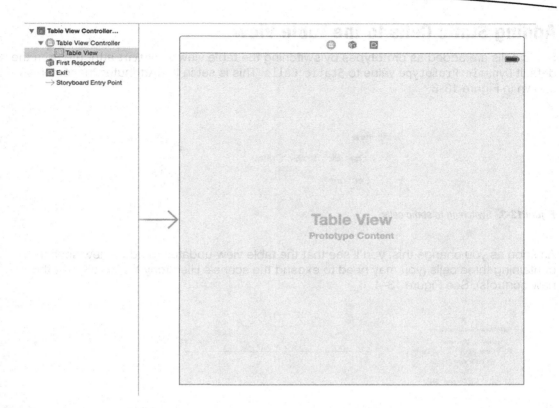

Figure 13-2. *The prototype content area*

In Chapter 7, you looked at how to add prototype cells that could then be used by the table view's dataSource as "templates" for cells that are created at runtime.

The table view controller control in a Storyboard or XIB can also be used to create static cells; these are created and laid out up front, so they aren't created dynamically at runtime.

> **Tip**   Static table view cells can only be created in a Storyboard when you are using a UITableViewController. If you try to create static cells in a UITableView, Xcode will complain.

Adding Static Cells to the Table View

Static cells are added as prototypes by switching the table view's Content attribute from the default Dynamic Prototype value to Static Cells. This is set in the Attributes Inspector, as shown in Figure 13-3.

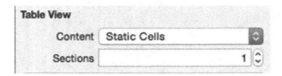

Figure 13-3. *Switching to static cells*

As soon as you change this, you'll see that the table view updates to add a new section containing three cells (you may need to expand the scene's Hierarchy tree to expose the new controls). See Figure 13-4.

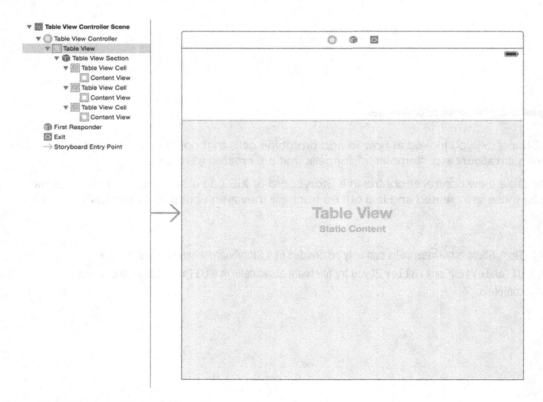

Figure 13-4. *The new section and static cells*

The new cells are the standard 44 points high with a transparent separator so it's not immediately apparent whether anything is there, but you can change this by playing around with the attributes of the table, section, and cell in the Attributes Inspector.

Figure 13-5 shows an updated table that now includes some header and footer text, together with a light gray cell separator. The three cells have been changed from Custom to Default, and the title fields have been updated.

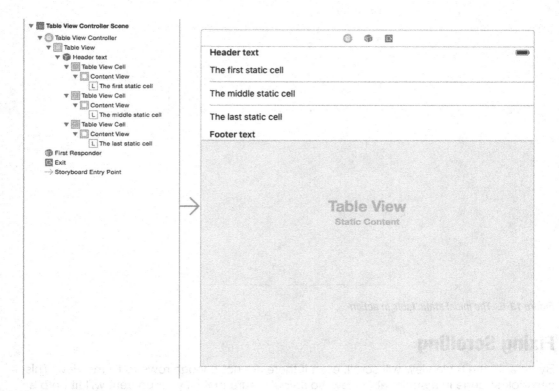

Figure 13-5. The updated cells

If you run the app now (shown in Figure 13-6), you'll see that the table view appears with the three cells, all without the need to implement any UITableViewDataSource methods!

Figure 13-6. The initial static table in action

Fixing Scrolling

By default, the table view will scroll, even if there are not enough rows to fill the view. This can look strange in a static table view, so if you're sure that all your content will fit onto a single screen even on smaller devices (and where appropriate, in landscape orientations) then you may want to prevent the table from scrolling.

To prevent scrolling, select the TableView in the view hierarchy, and uncheck the Scrolling Enabled setting in the Attributes Inspector (Figure 13-7).

Figure 13-7. Preventing the table from scrolling

Adding Controls to the Static Cells

With the static cells in place, you're now ready to start customizing them. If you change the cell types back to Custom, you can treat the content view of each cell as if it was an empty UIView–placing other controls inside and positioning them with AutoLayout constraints.

Adjusting the Cell Heights

Before placing other controls in the cell, you'll probably need to adjust the height. By default, the empty custom cells have a height of 44 points. To change this, select the row in the object hierarchy, then adjust the row height in the Size Inspector, as shown in Figure 13-8.

Figure 13-8. Adjusting the row height

Adding Interactive Controls

Linking controls to methods in a static table view is done in the standard way: the control event is linked to an IBAction method in a controller, which is triggered by user interaction.

But you've added a UITableViewController scene without an associated UIViewController subclass, so the question that arises is, link to an IBAction method *where*?

The answer is "In some controller class that *does* exist." In this case, you could link the buttons in the static table view to IBAction methods in a UIViewController subclass that you either added previously, or create to handle this UITableViewController scene.

In order to connect this static table's scene up to a view controller, you need to add a reference to the view controller. To do this, select an object from the Object browser, and drag this into the table view controller's scene, as shown in Figure 13-9.

Figure 13-9. Adding the object to the scene

This also now shows up as a placeholder in the scene's header, as shown in Figure 13-10.

Figure 13-10. The object in the scene's header

With the Object placeholder selected, switch to the Identity Inspector and update the Custom Class value to the class that this will represent (in this case, add the didTapStaticTableButton IBAction method to the ViewController class), as shown in Figure 13-11.

Figure 13-11. Setting the custom class

With the class set, you can now Ctrl-drag from the control to the placeholder, where the available IBAction methods will show up in the HUD, as shown in Figure 13-12.

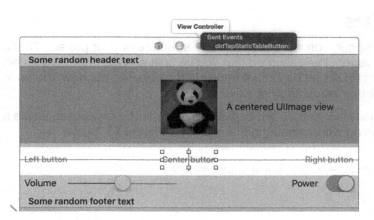

Figure 13-12. Connecting controls to actions

Using Static Tables Inside Container Views

Up to now, you've been creating static table layouts inside UITableViewController scenes placed in the Storyboard. That's fine, but the UITableViewController scene makes assumptions about how it's going to be used, chiefly that it will be displayed full-screen.

So what can you do if you want to include a static table view inside another view controller (if it doesn't fill the full interface, for example)?

You could try adding a standard UITableView object into the view controller's view as if you were building a dynamic table view. Interface Builder will let you change the table view from dynamic prototypes and static cells, and lay out the static cells, as you did earlier in this chapter.

When you come to build the project, though, the compiler will refuse, with the error shown in Figure 13-13.

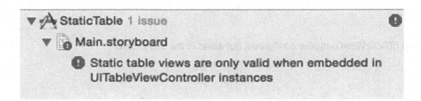

Figure 13-13. The error that occurs if you try to build static cells in a standard UITableView

That's annoying, to say the least. So what's the work-around?

The answer is to use a UITableViewController to create the static table layout as you have done previously, and then embed this into a container inside the UIViewController.

Prerequisites

As the exact configuration will depend on the structure of your project, I'll show a hypothetical situation. I've assumed that you've built a static table layout using a UITableViewController as described earlier in the chapter; but now you've realized that you need to present this *inside* another view.

I've also assumed that your UITableViewController is the only scene inside a Storyboard, so you'll be starting with something that looks like Figure 13-14.

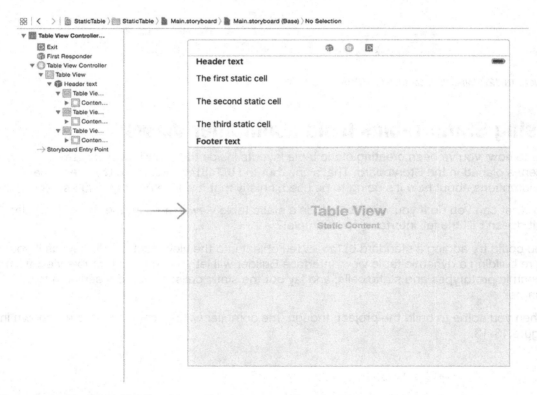

Figure 13-14. The UITableViewController configured, but alone in the Storyboard

Adding a UIViewController Scene

The first step is to drag in a UIViewController object from the Object browser, so you now have two scenes in the Storyboard, as shown in Figure 13-15.

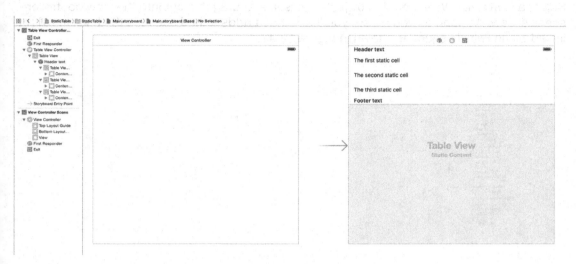

Figure 13-15. *Adding a UIViewController scene to the Storyboard*

At the moment, the UITableViewController is the Storyboard's entry point, shown by the grey entry point arrow pointing to the scene. You need to change this so that it's the view controller that's loaded first, so select the View Controller Scene in the Stack, and select the Is Initial View Controller checkbox in the Attributes Inspector, as shown in Figure 13-16.

Figure 13-16. *Setting the UITableViewController as the initial view*

As soon as you do this, the entry point arrow switches to point to the UIViewController scene.

Adding a Container View to the UIViewController

Now you need to add a container view into the UIViewController so that you can embed the static table view inside.

Select a Container View from the Object browser, and drag this out into the view controller scene's view. As soon as you do so, you'll see that it adds a third scene, a UIViewController linked by an Embed segue, as shown in Figure 13-17.

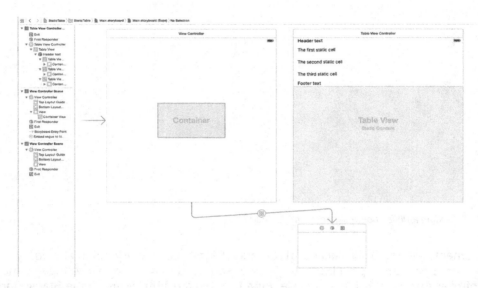

Figure 13-17. The container view added to the first UIViewController scene

Since you want the static table to be shown full-screen, you need to add some AutoLayout constraints to the Container view so that it fills the full view.

Select the Container view, then add top, bottom, leading, and trailing constraints as shown in Figure 13-18.

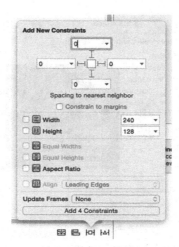

Figure 13-18. Adding AutoLayout constraints to the container view

With constraints added and the container view full-screen, you need to get rid of the spare UIViewController scene that the Container object arrived with. Select the entire scene in the object hierarchy on the left of the canvas and press delete. The scene and the segue will disappear.

Embedding the Static Table View into the View Controller

Embedding the static table view into the view controller is the final step. Ctrl-click the Container view in the object hierarchy, and drag the blue connection line to the table view controller object in the table view controller scene. When you release the mouse button, a HUD menu will appear next to the table view controller, as shown in Figure 13-19.

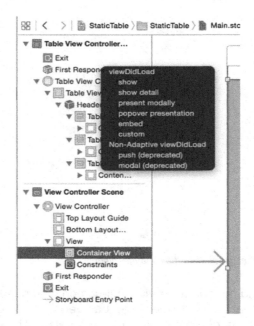

Figure 13-19. *Adding the embed segue*

Select the Embed item, and a new Embed segue will be created to link the table view controller scene with the Container, as shown in Figure 13-20.

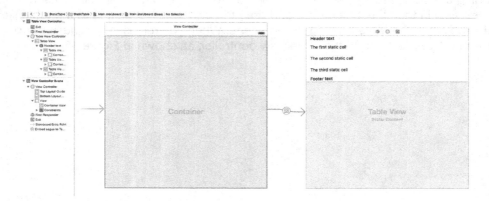

Figure 13-20. *The static table view embedded in the UIViewController*

Running the app now will show the static table inside the view controller. From a user experience point of view, not a lot has changed, but by adjusting the constraints of the container view, you now have the ability to control the placement of the static table as you wish.

Other Uses for Static Tables

The "canonical" use of a static `UITableView` is the Settings app, but it has uses beyond this type of situation.

By taking advantage of `UITableView`'s vertical layout capabilities, you can use static tables whenever you have a layout that looks like a stack of elements one on top of each other, and need a greater level of control and flexibility than `UIStackView`.

Forms are basically a series of headings and text fields. By placing headings and textfields into alternating rows, you can use the static table view to build the form and let the table view handle the vertical scrolling.

Summary

In this chapter, you looked at the process of creating static table views, for use in situations where the data to be displayed isn't dynamic. It's a simple process that can be used to build views for features like preferences and settings, or for displaying static information in a table-style layout.

Chapter 14

Tables in WatchKit

In this chapter, you're going to look at how to create, configure, and use the table control that forms part of WatchKit.

WatchKit is designed for the small, low-powered Apple Watch, so the `WKInterfaceTable` control is much less powerful than `UITableView`, but nonetheless it can be used to present table-based information and act as a navigation interface.

You'll look at the following:

- The anatomy of the WatchKit table and the `WKInterfaceTable` class
- How to create and configure table rows in Storyboards
- How to create and configure row controller classes
- How to configure tables with data at runtime
- How to respond to user interaction with the WatchKit table
- How to use WatchKit tables as a navigation interface.

About WatchKit

While the power and complexity that's been squeezed into the confines of the Apple Watch is an impressive feat of engineering, there's no getting away from the fact that the device is a lot less powerful than an iPhone.

To get the best out of WatchKit tables, there are a number of caveats and limitations that you need to bear in mind:

- Apple Watch effectively acts as the view of the WatchKit extension within the app on the paired iPhone, so all communication has to go across the Bluetooth link. This can be slow, so it's important to keep interface updates as small as possible.

- The WKInterfaceTable control doesn't use an on-demand caching mechanism, unlike UITableView. All the rows that will be displayed in the table have to be created and sent to the Watch before they can be displayed. For this reason, it's usually best to limit the number of rows in a table to 20 or so.

- The Watch interface is small and is designed for quick glances. When designing your table interface, it's important to keep the information density low and the controls large enough to be easily accessible.

- The WatchKit interface must be laid out in a Storyboard; there's no option to build it in code, or amend it at runtime other than changing the content or visibility of controls.

- WatchKit interfaces don't support AutoLayout.

The Anatomy of a WatchKit App

WatchKit apps have two parts: a WatchKit extension that runs on the paired iPhone, and user interfaces that are installed on the Watch itself.

The WatchKit extension runs in the background to send updates to the user interface, and react to user interaction with the Watch.

WatchKit apps have three kinds of interfaces: the full app user interface, which is where WKInterfaceTables live; Glances, which provide quick access to read-only information; and notifications.

Interface updates and user interactions are communicated between the iPhone and the paired Watch over a Bluetooth connection.

What Are WatchKit Tables?

The WatchKit SDK includes WKInterfaceTable, a class that supports single column tables. A table can consist of multiple types of rows. Each row type has its own row controller, which is backed by a custom class that you need to create. The row controller contain the outlets to connect to the interface elements, and (where needed) functions to handle interactions with the controls.

The relationship between table, rows and row controllers is shown in Figure 14-1.

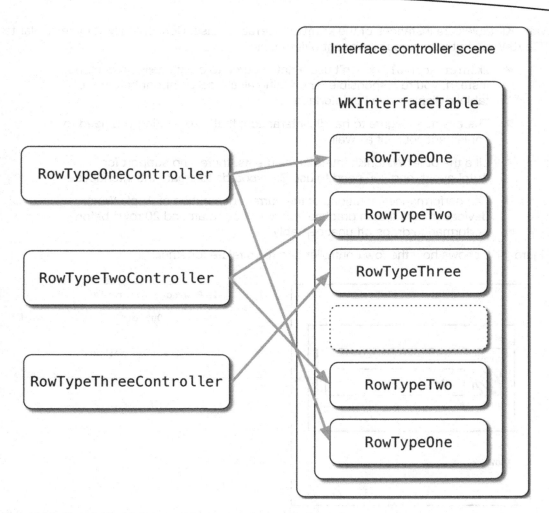

Figure 14-1. *The relationship between table, rows and row controllers*

The process of creating a table-based WatchKit app has four steps.

1. Creating a table object in the Storyboard and laying out controls in the rows.

2. Creating NSObject subclasses to act as controllers for each type of row that will be displayed, with outlets to the controls in the Storyboard.

3. Creating instances of the row controller classes and providing them to the table at runtime.

4. Responding to user interaction with the rows.

WatchKit tables are instances of the `WKInterfaceTable` class. Conceptually, they're similar to `UITableView`, but with some significant differences:

- `WKInterfaceTable` doesn't use a data source to create cells on demand. Instead, you're responsible for creating all the cells upfront before the table is displayed in the interface.

- There is no delegate to handle interaction; that's something you need to implement yourself as well.

- Like the other WatchKit interface elements, there's no support for AutoLayout, and you need to use Storyboards to create the interfaces.

- The performance limitations of the current generation of Apple Watch devices means that in practice you're limited to around 20 rows before performance drops off unacceptably.

Figure 14-2 shows how the row controller and rows relate together.

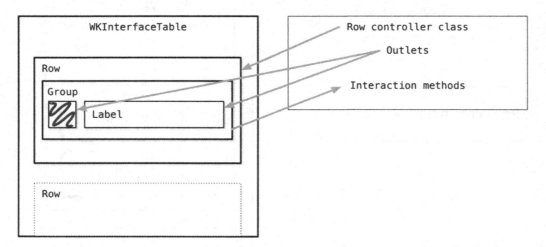

Figure 14-2. How WKInterfaceTable objects fit together

At runtime, you're responsible for telling the table the type, number, and order of the rows, and then creating instances of the row controllers before configuring their outlets. You have two options here:

- If your table will only have one type of cell, you can use the `setNumberOfCells:withRowType` function:

  ```
  table.setNumberOfRows(5, withRowType: "ContactRow")
  ```

- If your table will have more than one type of cell, you need to pass an array of cell identifier strings into the `setRowTypes:` function. For example, if you have one header, two data and one footer row, you pass in the array `["HeaderCell", "DataCell", "DataCell", "FooterCell"]`:

  ```
  table.setRowTypes(["HeaderCell", "DataCell", "DataCell", "FooterCell"])
  ```

Once you've told the table which row has which type of cell, you then need to get the row controller for each row in turn with the rowControllerAtIndex: function. Now you're able to configure the outlets that you previously defined in the row controller class. An example of this process is shown in Listing 14-1.

Listing 14-1. Configuring and Updating a Watch Table

```
func updateTable() {

    // Create array to hold the row types
    var rowsArray = [String]()

    // Add header row as the row 0
    rowsArray.append("HeaderRow")

    // Add a contact row for each object in the dataArray
    for index in 1...self.dataArray.count {
        rowsArray.append("ContactRow")
    }

    // Add a footer row as the last row
    rowsArray.append("FooterRow")

    // Configure the table to display the rows as defined in the rowsArray
    self.watchTable.setRowTypes(rowsArray)

    // Retrieve each contact row and set the contents from the dataArray
    // Start at row 1, because row 0 is the header row
    for index in 1...self.dataArray.count {

        var contactRow: ContactRowController = ↩
        self.watchTable.rowControllerAtIndex(index) as! ContactRowController

        var rowContent = self.dataArray[index]

        contactRow.nameLabel!.setText(rowContent)

    }

    // Get the last row, and configure it as the footer

    let contactCount = self.dataArray.count

    var footerRow: FooterRowController = ↩
    self.watchTable.rowControllerAtIndex(contactCount + 1) as! FooterRowController

    footerRow.footerLabel.setText("\(contactCount) messages")

}
```

The Storyboard presents the table as one or more rows. Inside each row there's a group, which is where you add your custom controls, shown in Figure 14-3.

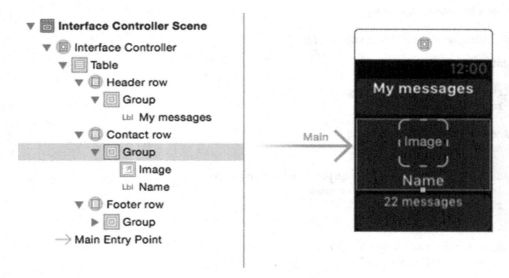

Figure 14-3. The groups inside each row

Controls in the group are connected to outlets in the same way as a normal Storyboard or Xib file.

Creating a Basic Table

In this section, you'll go through the process of creating a demonstration WatchKit table. It won't be a fully-featured app with a dynamic data source, because that's beyond the scope of creating a table interface, but it will show you how to wire up a table that you can extend further.

There are four steps involved, assuming you're creating a new project from scratch:

- Create a new iPhone project to act as the host for the extension.

- Create a WatchKit app as a new target, to create the app that will run on the watch and the extension that will configure the table.

- Lay out the table in the Storyboard.

- Create the functions to populate the table at runtime.

Creating the Project

To begin, you'll need a new iPhone project. Create a new project in Xcode with File ➤ New ➤ Project and select the Single View Application template. Give the project a name (I'm calling mine WatchTable), and save the project somewhere appropriate.

Adding the WatchKit Target

As you saw above, there are three components to a WatchKit app:

- The **iPhone app**, which handles the heavy lifting of things like communicating with APIs, etc.

- The **WatchKit app**, which runs on the watch itself. This is where you'll lay out the table's visual appearance in the Storyboard.

- The **Watchkit extension**, which runs on the iPhone and contains the code for managing the content and interaction of the table.

All three components are bundled together into the app, and if a paired watch is present as the app is installed, the user will be asked whether they want to install the WatchKit app onto the watch itself.

To begin extending an iPhone app with watch functionality, you first need to create a new target that adds the WatchKit app and extension.

From the File ➤ New ➤ Target menu, select the WatchKit App template, as shown in Figure 14-4.

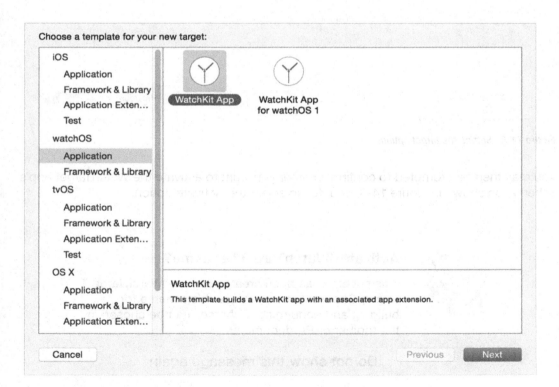

Figure 14-4. Adding the WatchKit target

You'll then be prompted to set the options for the new target. Most of these are read-only, but you can select the language and whether you want to add Notification and Glance scenes to the target. You don't, so change the options so they match those shown in Figure 14-5, and select Finish.

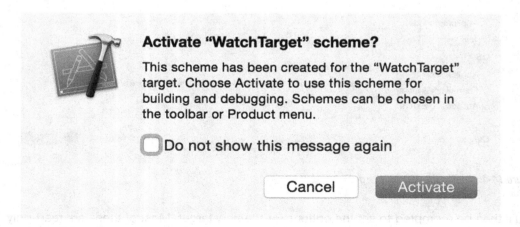

Choose options for your new target:

Product Name:	WatchTarget
Organization Name:	Tim Duckett
Organization Identifier:	de.duckett.WatchTable
Bundle Identifier:	de.duckett.WatchTable.WatchTarget
Language:	Swift
	◯ Include Notification Scene
	◯ Include Glance Scene
	◯ Include Complication
Project:	WatchTable
Embed in Companion Application:	WatchTable

Cancel   Previous   Finish

Figure 14-5. Setting the target options

You may then be prompted to confirm whether you want to activate the WatchTarget app's scheme, as shown in Figure 14-6. You do, so select the Activate option.

Activate "WatchTarget" scheme?

This scheme has been created for the "WatchTarget" target. Choose Activate to use this scheme for building and debugging. Schemes can be chosen in the toolbar or Product menu.

◯ Do not show this message again

Cancel   Activate

Figure 14-6. Activating the WatchTarget scheme

You should now see that you've got two new folders in the Navigator, and two new Targets in the Projects and Targets list, as shown in Figure 14-7.

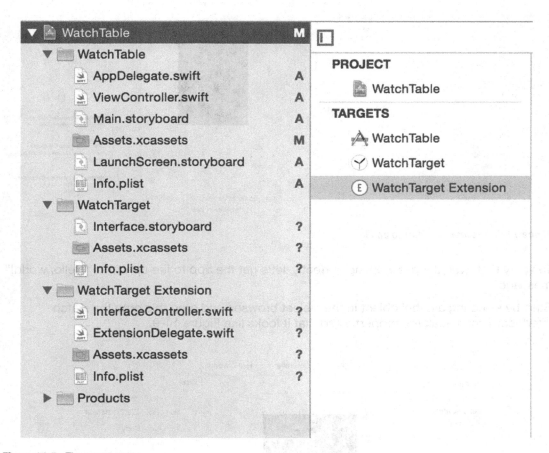

Figure 14-7. The new targets

Building the Table Interface

You're going to begin by building the table interface, so select the Interface.storyboard file in the WatchTarget App folder so that it's shown in the main pane, as shown in Figure 14-8.

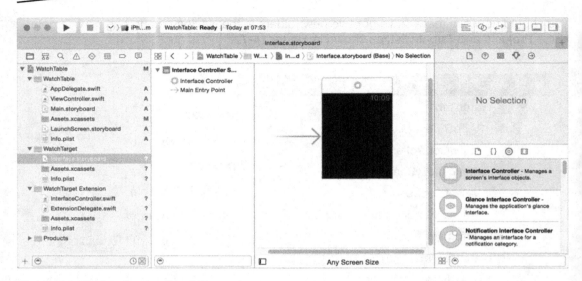

Figure 14-8. *The Interface.storyboard file*

To verify that everything is working correctly, let's get the app to fire up with a "Hello, world!" message.

Start by selecting a Label object in the Object browser, and drag this onto the watch interface. Then tweak the properties so that it looks like Figure 14-9.

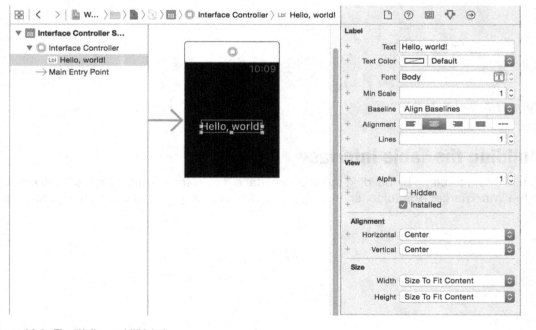

Figure 14-9. *The "Hello, world!" label*

You'll notice that the options are much more limited than you would see with a `UILabel`. The Apple Watch doesn't support AutoLayout, so there are only a few layout options available.

If you now select the WatchTarget app from the Schemes drop-down (shown in Figure 14-10) and run the app, the iPhone and Watch simulators will start.

Figure 14-10. *Selecting the WatchTarget to run the app in the Apple Watch Simulator*

You'll see the results as shown in Figure 14-11. This verifies that everything is running correctly, and that the WatchKit app has been correctly installed.

Figure 14-11. *The "Hello, world!" app running on the Apple Watch*

> **Tip**   The default Apple Watch simulator doesn't really give you much of a feel for how the app will look when it's running on an actual device. To get a better impression, I'm using an app called Bezel (http://infinitapps.com/bezel), which displays the Simulator output inside a mocked-up watch bezel. You can select the bezel type to use, so it's definitely the cheapest option for testing on an 18-karat Rose Gold Watch with a Link bracelet.

Having confirmed that the WatchKit app runs, you can start the process of building the table.

Creating the Table

Switch back to the WatchKit app's Interface.storyboard, delete the label that you created a moment ago, and replace it with a table dragged from the Objects list. This will auto-size in the frame to create a table with a single row (shown in Figure 14-12).

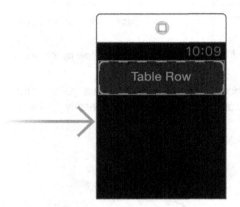

Figure 14-12. The table placed in the Watch interface

As well as rows containing actual data, you're also going to add header and footer rows to the table. Each type of row (header, data, and footer) will have its own row controller, which will be an instance of a custom class that you'll create in a moment.

Setting this up takes four steps:

- Increase the number of rows in the table so that there is a row for each type of cell that will appear.

- Create the layout for each cell type in the Storyboard by adding controls.

- Create a custom class for each row type with outlets to connect to the controls in the cell, and (if required) functions to handle user interaction with those controls.

- Associate each row type with its custom class.

Remember that unlike `UITableView`, the cell layout takes place in the Storyboard.

Creating the Rows

To create the new rows, highlight the table in the Interface Controller scene, and switch to the Attributes Inspector if it's not already visible, as shown in Figure 14-13.

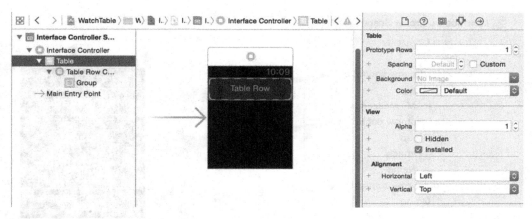

Figure 14-13. Setting the number of rows in the table

Increase the number of rows by updating the field in the Attributes Inspector. This will add another row type in the Storyboard, and add another Interface Controller object in the object hierarchy.

Your layout will need three row types; one for the header, one for data rows, and one for the footer. Update the number of rows to 3, so that the object hierarchy looks like that in Figure 14-14.

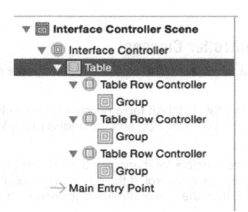

Figure 14-14. The three rows

Laying Out the Rows

With the three rows in place, you can now lay out the controls in each one. Figure 14-15 shows what my cells look like; you can play around with the layouts as you want (it's good practice!) but make sure that you've got a WKInterfaceImage and a WKInterfaceLabel in the contact row, and a WKInterfaceLabel in the footer.

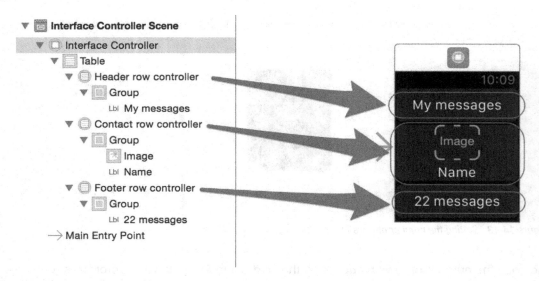

Figure 14-15. Laying out the interface

> **Tip**   The limitations of the WatchKit UI can make laying out interfaces tricky. To achieve the contact row layout, select its `Group`, then change the layout to `Vertical` in the Attributes Inspector.

Creating the Row Controller Classes

With the three rows laid out, now you can create the row controller classes that will handle each row.

Each different type of row in your WatchKit table needs a custom class to act as its controller; these are subclasses of NSObject, and are added to the WatchKit Extension (*not* the WatchKit app).

The row controller class is responsible for managing the content of the controls in its row, so it needs an outlet for every dynamic control. If the controls respond to user interaction, such as a tap on a button control, then the row controller class needs to implement functions to handle this.

The simplest type of row has only static controls and doesn't respond to any user interaction. That describes your header row, so you'll create it first.

Select the WatchTarget Extension folder in the Navigator pane, and then add a new class with File ➤ New ➤ File. In the list of templates, select the Source group, and the Cocoa Touch Class. Click the Next button, and then name your class HeaderRowController. Make sure that the subclass is set to NSObject, and check that you're creating the class using the correct language.

Click Next, and double-check that the new class will be created in the WatchKit Extension Group and Target (see Figure 14-16). Then click Create to add the new class file(s).

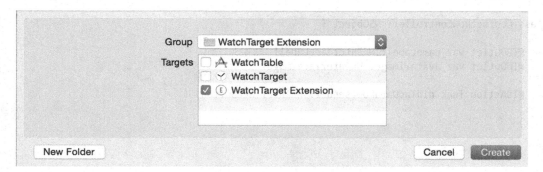

Figure 14-16. Selecting the group and target for the new class

For the header row, that's all you need to do. It doesn't have any items that will be updated at runtime, and it doesn't react to any user interaction, so the class can remain as an empty NSObject subclass.

The footer is slightly more sophisticated, in that it has one item that's dynamically updated, so you'll create this next. Go through the same process as above to create an NSObject subclass called FooterRowController.

This needs one outlet, an IBOutlet property for a WKInterfaceLabel called footerLabel. Add this to the class as shown in Listing 14-2.

Listing 14-2. The FooterRowController Class

```
import UIKit
import WatchKit

class FooterRowController: NSObject {

    @IBOutlet var footerLabel: WKInterfaceLabel!

}
```

Note that you'll need to import the WatchKit framework so that you can add the outlet to the WKInterfaceLabel.

Finally, you can add the class for the ContactRowController. This has two outlets, one for the image and one for the label, and one interaction function to handle taps on the cell.

Add a new NSObject subclass as before, and update it as show in Listing 14-3.

Listing 14-3. The ContactRowController Class

```
import UIKit
import WatchKit

class ContactRowController: NSObject {

    @IBOutlet var nameLabel: WKInterfaceLabel!
    @IBOutlet var avatarImage: WKInterfaceImage!

    @IBAction func didTapDataRow(sender: WKInterfaceButton) {

    }

}
```

Connecting the Classes to the Rows

With the custom classes created, it's time to link these to the controls in the Storyboard. Switch back to the Storyboard in the WatchTarget, and expand the tree of controls so that you can see all three rows. Then select the header row, and open the Identity Inspector in the Utilities panel if it's not visible. The top section allows you to define the custom class that controls the row (see Figure 14-17).

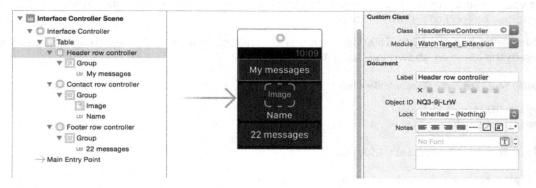

Figure 14-17. Connecting the custom class with the row

Update this so that it shows `HeaderRowController`, and then select the Attributes Inspector. Here, you need to provide an identifier for the row that will be used as the rows are populated at runtime (it's analogous to the `rowIdentifier` property used by `UITableView`).

This can be an arbitrary string, but to keep things neat, my approach is to use the name of the custom class (in this case, `HeaderRowController`). It's shown in Figure 14-18.

Row Controller

Identifier HeaderRow

☐ Selectable

Figure 14-18. The row identifier

As this row is simply a text header, you don't want it to be selectable, so uncheck the Selectable box.

Now repeat the same process for the contact row; the custom class is ContactRowController, and the identifier is ContactRow. This row *will* be selectable.

Finally, complete the process with the footer row. The custom class for this row is FooterRowController, and the identifier is FooterRow. As with the header, this row shouldn't be selectable.

Connecting Outlets

With the rows connected to their custom classes, it's possible to connect up the controls. This is done in the usual Interface Builder way: Ctrl-clicking on the row in the object tree will pop up a HUD window showing the outlets defined in the custom class, which you can then connect by clicking and dragging over to the control.

You need to complete this process for the Contact and Footer rows. There are no outlets defined in the Header, so there's nothing connected. When it's complete, the outlets for the Contact row will look like Figure 14-19.

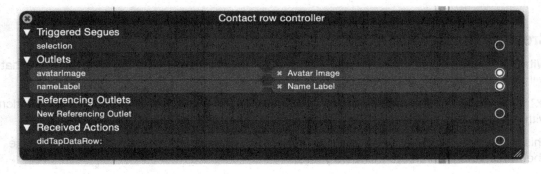

Figure 14-19. The connections to the Contact row

The Footer row should look like Figure 14-20.

Figure 14-20. *The connection to the Footer row*

While you're in the process of connecting outlets, you also need to add one for the table itself. In the `InterfaceController.swift` file, add an `IBOutlet` property for the table:

`@IBOutlet var watchTable: WKInterfaceTable!`

Then switch to the Storyboard and connect this outlet to the table, as shown in Figure 14-21:

Figure 14-21. *Connecting the table*

Creating the Rows in Code

With the interface connections made and data set up, it's time to start creating the code that will populate the table with cells and data at runtime.

`WKInterfaceTable` differs significantly from `UITableView` in that it doesn't operate in conjunction with a datasource. All the rows have to be created upfront when the table is configured.

This means you'll have to figure out how many rows of each type there will be, tell the table about this, and then create the rows yourself.

If you have a simple table consisting of only one row type, then you can use the `setNumberOfRows:withRowType:` function to tell the table how many rows of what type it will be displaying. An example that you could use to display a table consisting only of `ContactRows` is shown below:

`self.watchTable.setNumberOfRows(self.dataArray.count, withRowType: "ContactRow")`

In your case, things are more complex. You've got three row types, so there's a bit more to do.

First, you need some dummy data. In this example, it's an Array of four Strings, corresponding to the name of some avatar images – add the function in Listing 14-4 to the bottom of the InterfaceController:

Listing 14-4. The setupData() Function

```
func setupData() {
    dataArray.append("Bob")
    dataArray.append("Felix")
    dataArray.append("Jim")
    dataArray.append("Fred")
}
```

You can find the four sample images in this chapter's code, or of course you're free to add your own.

Having added some dummy data, you're now in a position to feed that data to the table. Add the code in Listing 14-5 to the bottom of the InterfaceController class.

Listing 14-5. The updateTable() Function

```
private func updateTable() {

    // Create array to hold the row types
    var rowsTypes = [String]()

    // Add header row as the row 0
    rowsTypes.append("HeaderRow")

    // Add a contact row for each object in the dataArray
    for _ in dataArray {
        rowsTypes.append("ContactRow")
    }

    // Add a footer row as the last row
    rowsTypes.append("FooterRow")

    // Configure the table to display the rows as defined in the rowsArray
    watchTable.setRowTypes(rowsTypes)

    // Retrieve each contact row and set the contents from the dataArray
    // Start at row 1, because row 0 is the header row
    for index in 0..< dataArray.count {

        var contactRow = watchTable.rowControllerAtIndex(index+1) ↵
      as! ContactRowController

        var rowContent = dataArray[index]

        contactRow.nameLabel!.setText(rowContent)
```

```
        if let image = UIImage(named: rowContent) {
            contactRow.avatarImage.setImage(image)
        }

    }

    // Get the last row, and configure it as the footer

    let contactCount = dataArray.count

    let footerRow = watchTable.rowControllerAtIndex(contactCount + 1) ↵
    as! FooterRowController

    footerRow.footerLabel.setText("\(contactCount) messages")

}
```

Walking through this code, you're going to have three distinct types of row, so you can't use the one-shot `setNumberOfCells:withRowType` function. Instead, you create an array of the cell types: first a header cell, then the same number of contact rows as you have elements in the data array, and finally a footer cell. This array is used to tell the table what rows types it will have to display.

The row types are created when the `setRowTypes` function is called, according to what identifier has been provided in the row types array. If there are outlets in the row that you need to update dynamically, it's your responsibility to iterate over each row in turn and make the necessary changes.

Each row can be accessed by asking the table, using the `rowControllerAtIndex` function, and casting the type if necessary. Once you've got a reference to the cell, you can update it with the corresponding data from the model.

In the case of contact rows, it's the relevant element from the `dataArray`. In the case of the footer, it's done with a calculation based on the total number of elements in the `dataArray`.

Finishing up

To finish the process, you need to call the two new functions when the interface is loaded. Update the `awakeWithContext(:_)` function to match Listing 14-6 – this is called when the interface is loaded, equivalent to the `viewDidLoad` function in `UIViewController`.

Listing 14-6. The updated awakeWithContext() function

```
override func awakeWithContext(context: AnyObject?) {
    super.awakeWithContext(context)

    // Configure interface objects here.
    setupData()
    updateTable()

}
```

If you run the app in the Simulator, you'll see the table being loaded and populated with data, as shown in Figure 14-22.

Figure 14-22. The app running in the Apple Watch Simulator

Adding Interactivity

Just like a UITableView, rows in a WatchKit table can respond to user interaction. It's limited to simple taps in the current WatchKit SDK, but this may change in the future.

Unlike UITableView, a WKInterfaceTable doesn't have a delegate object. Instead, if the row has selection enabled, then the table will call the interface controller's table:didSelectRowAtIndex: function if that is implemented.

Listing 14-7 shows an example of a function that logs the index of the row that's been selected and then changes the color of the text in the row.

Listing 14-7. Handling Selection in WatchKit Tables with Swift

```
override func table(table: WKInterfaceTable, didSelectRowAtIndex rowIndex: Int) {

    print("Row \(rowIndex) selected")

    for index in 0..< dataArray.count {

        let contactRow: ContactRowController = ↩
        self.watchTable.rowControllerAtIndex(index+1) as! ContactRowController
```

```
        contactRow.nameLabel!.setTextColor(UIColor.whiteColor())

    }

    let selectedRow: ContactRowController = ↵
    self.watchTable.rowControllerAtIndex(rowIndex) as! ContactRowController

    selectedRow.nameLabel.setTextColor(UIColor.redColor())

}
```

> **Caution**   The interface controller code is executed on the iPhone, and updates to the interface
> are passed to the Apple Watch via Bluetooth. This can introduce a noticeable lag between taps and
> interface updates.

Navigation with WatchKit Tables

UITableViews are often used as a navigation mechanism for "drilling down" into a hierarchy of data. WKInterfaceTable can also be exploited for this purpose, albeit within the constraints of a much smaller interface.

There are two ways of navigating between screens of content with WatchKit: page-based, which is designed for moving between independent screens; and hierarchical, where new screens are pushed into view together with an on-screen control for moving back through the "tree."

Although you can use other controls to control movement between screens in a hierarchical-based app, doing so with a WKInterfaceTable is a very common interface pattern.

The transitions between screens are either segues, which you set up in Interface Builder, or are triggered by calling the pushControllerWithName:context: function, which can be called from the didSelectRowAtIndex: function in response to a tap on a row.

To pass information between screens, such as the object that's displayed in the selected row, so that the detail interface can show data about it, you pass a context object between the two controllers. In your case, this would be the object from the dataArray at the index corresponding to the selected row.

Extending the example app from the previous section to add hierarchical navigation isn't difficult. It takes three steps:

- Add a new interface controller class to manage the new screen.
- Add a new interface controller to the Storyboard, and lay out the controls.
- Implement the navigation, either by adding a push seque or extending the didSelectRowAtIndex: function to push the new screen in response to selection of the row.

Adding a New Interface Controller

The first step is to add a new class to act as the interface controller. To do this, add a new file (File ➤ New ➤ File) and select the Cocoa Touch template. Create a subclass of WKInterfaceController and call it DetailInterfaceController, as shown in Figure 14-23.

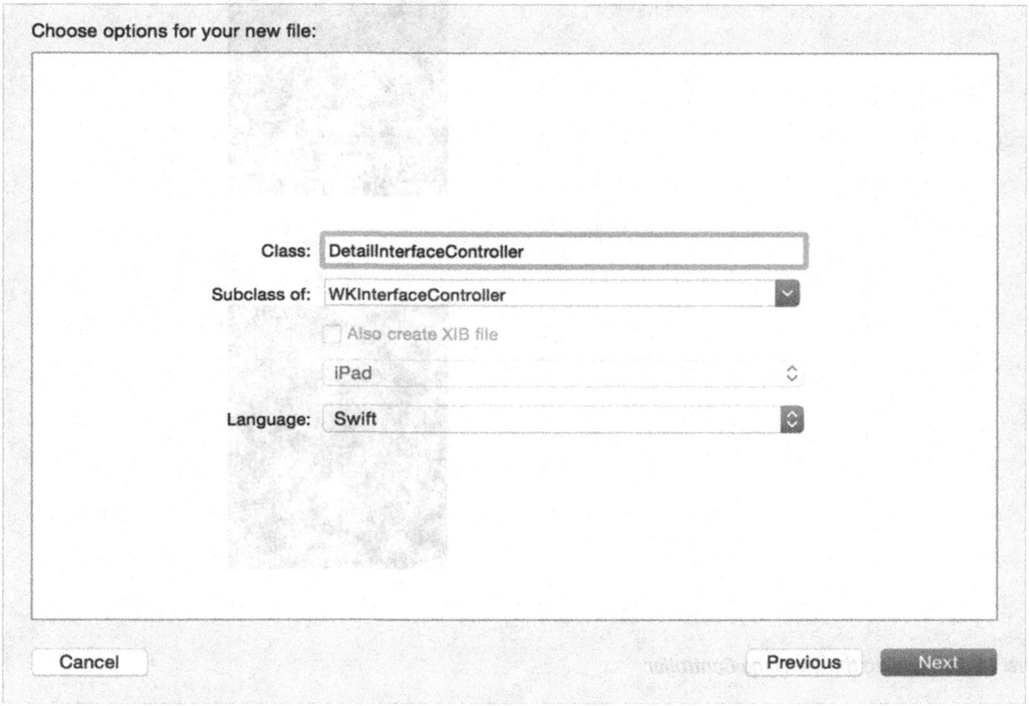

Figure 14-23. *Creating the DetailInterfaceController*

Make sure that the new file is created in the WatchTarget Extension, *not* the main or WatchTable apps.

Adding a New Screen to the Storyboard

To add a new screen to the existing Storyboard, select the Interface Controller in the Object browser and drag it out into the Storyboard, as shown in Figure 14-24.

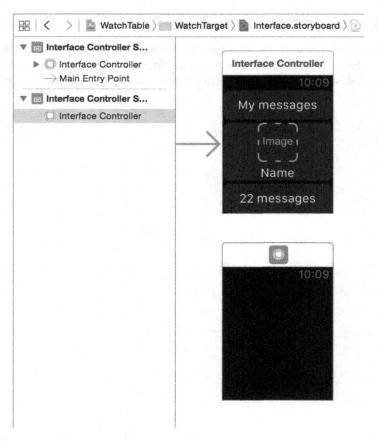

Figure 14-24. Adding the Interface Controller

With the new Interface Controller in the Storyboard and selected, open the Identity Inspector and update the class name. If you already created the DetailInterfaceController class, the Class field will autofill after typing a couple of characters, as shown in Figure 14-25.

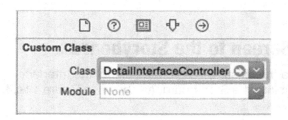

Figure 14-25. Updating the class of the new Interface Controller in the Storyboard

Implementing the Navigation

There are two ways of implementing the push navigation between the two controllers:

- Adding a push segue in Interface Builder
- Extending the didSelectRowAtIndex: function in the interface controller class

The two approaches are identical in terms of end results, but have different implementations.

Adding a Push Segue

Adding a push seque has two steps:

- Adding the seque itself
- Optionally, implementing the contextForSegueWithIdentifier:inTable: rowIndex: function in order to pass a data object to the next screen. In most cases, you'll want to do this in order to pass the object to be displayed on the next screen.

> **Tip**   If you set up navigation using a push segue, the didSelectRowAtIndex function won't be called; you need to use the prepareForSegue function instead.

Adding a segue is simplicity itself. In the Storyboard, select the row that will trigger the navigation and Ctrl-drag down to the Detail Interface scene, as shown in Figure 14-26.

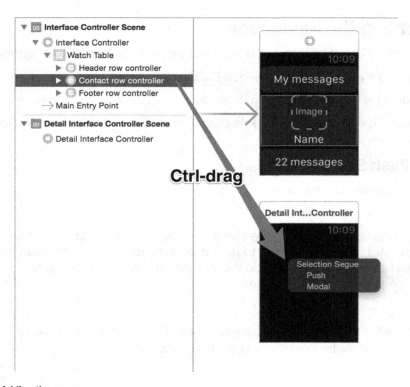

Figure 14-26. *Adding the seque*

When you release the mouse button, the Selection Segue HUD will pop up: select the Push option from the HUD, and the segue will be added, as shown in Figure 14-27.

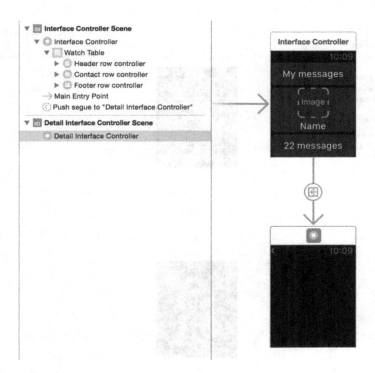

Figure 14-27. The added segue

Finally, you need to add an identifier to the segue so that it can be identified in the
contextForSegueWithIdentifier function. Highlight the segue in Interface Builder, switch
to the Attributes Inspector, and add the segue identifier string in the field, as shown in
Figure 14-28.

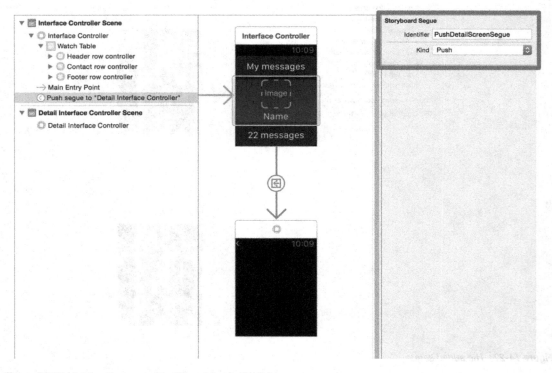

Figure 14-28. Adding the segue identifier string in the field

If you run the app now, you'll see that the detail screen is pushed in when you tap on a row, and popped back if you tap on the back chevron at the top left of the screen (shown in Figure 14-29).

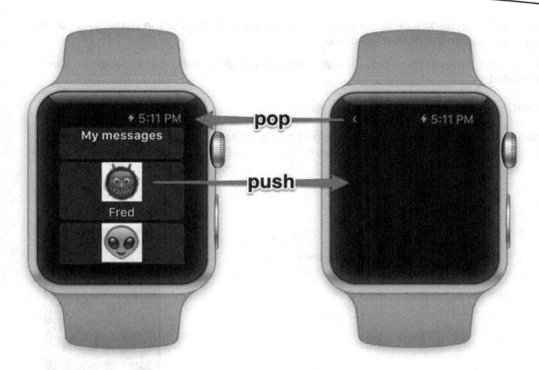

Figure 14-29. Pushing and popping between screens

Now add the contextForSegueWithIdentifier:table:rowIndex: function to the
InterfaceController class. This is shown in Listing 14-8.

Listing 14-8. The contextForSegueWithIdentifier:table:rowIndex: Function

```
override func contextForSegueWithIdentifier(segueIdentifier: String,↵
   inTable table: WKInterfaceTable, rowIndex: Int) -> AnyObject? {

   if segueIdentifier == "PushDetailScreenSegue" {
      return dataArray[rowIndex - 1]
   }

   return nil

}
```

This will return the name from the data array at the index corresponding to the selected row,
and pass it to the DetailInterfaceController in the context. Note that you're subtracting 1
from the rowIndex that's passed into the function, to compensate for the fact that the first
row of the table is actually the header row.

The context can be any object that will be used by the detail interface controller so will have
a type of AnyObject.

Here, you're creating a dictionary containing the name of the person at the selected row. Now let's update the controller to use this.

In the DetailInterfaceController class, add an outlet for a WKInterfaceLabel called nameLabel:

```
@IBOutlet var nameLabel: WKInterfaceLabel!
```

Then switch back to Interface Builder, and add a WKInterfaceLabel object to the DetailInterfaceController, as shown in Figure 14-30.

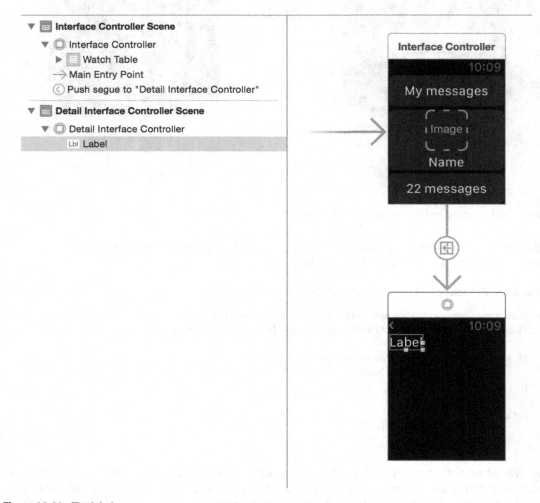

Figure 14-30. The label

Set the label's Lines property to 0 so that it will automatically wrap the content. Finally, connect the outlet to the control by dragging and dropping in Interface Builder.

With the control connected, you can update the DetailInterfaceController class to use the context object that will be passed to it from the InterfaceController.

When the detail interface is loaded, it will call the awakeWithContext: function. The context object is passed in as a parameter, so it's here that you can use the contents of the dictionary that you created earlier.

Listing 14-9 shows the awakeWithContext: function.

Listing 14-9. The awakeWithContext Function

```
override func awakeWithContext(context: AnyObject?) {
    super.awakeWithContext(context)

    if let selectedName = context as? String {
        nameLabel.setText("You selected the row for \(selectedName)")
    }

}
```

If you run the app now and tap on a row, you'll see the detail interface pushed in and updated with the name of the person in the row that you tapped, as shown in Figure 14-31.

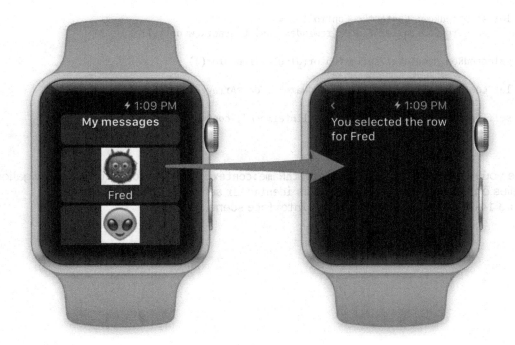

Figure 14-31. The detail view

This is a very simplistic implementation, but the context object allows you to pass information between controllers to build up a drill-down style navigation journey.

Adding Navigation in Code

In the previous section, you saw how to implement a navigation flow using Storyboards and segues. You can also create the same end results by using code instead.

Instead of linking the two Storyboard scenes with a segue, you can rely on the didSelectRowAtIndex function, and trigger the push of the detail controller with the pushControllerWithName:context: function.

Listing 14-10 shows the updated didSelectRowAtIndex: function.

Listing 14-10. Pushing the Detail Controller in Code

```
override func table(table: WKInterfaceTable, didSelectRowAtIndex rowIndex: Int) {

    for index in 0..<dataArray.count {

        var contactRow: ContactRowController = ↩
    watchTable.rowControllerAtIndex(index+1) as! ContactRowController

        contactRow.nameLabel!.setTextColor(UIColor.whiteColor())

    }

    let selectedRow: ContactRowController = ↩
    watchTable.rowControllerAtIndex(rowIndex) as! ContactRowController

    selectedRow.nameLabel.setTextColor(UIColor.redColor())

    let contextDictionary = ["selectedName" : dataArray[rowIndex - 1]]

    self.pushControllerWithName("DetailInterface", context: contextDictionary)

}
```

Here you're using the pushControllerWithName:context: function to perform the navigation. It relies on the detail controller having its identifier set in the Attributes Inspector. Figure 14-32 shows this for the DetailInterface scene.

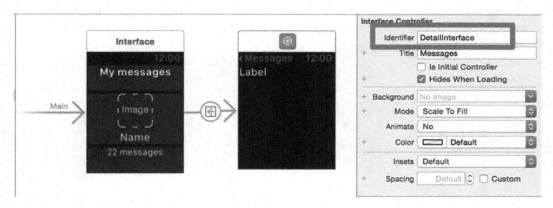

Figure 14-32. Setting the Interface controller's identifier

Summary

In this chapter, you learned how to create, configure, and use the table control that forms part of WatchKit.

WatchKit is designed for the small, low-powered Apple Watch, so the `WKInterfaceTable` control is much less powerful than `UITableView`, but nonetheless, it can be used to present table-based information and act as a navigation interface.

Chapter 15

Collection View Flow Layouts

In this chapter, you'll look at one of the most useful components of the `UICollectionView` family, the flow layout. The flow layout allows you to build collection views containing rows or columns of items with very little effort, but also provides some fine-grained control over various attributes to allow you to fine tune its appearance.

The sample application code for this chapter implements a flow-based layout to illustrate many of its features and to provide a template that you can adapt for your own purposes.

About Flow Layouts

A layout consisting of rows or columns of items is a very common user interface design. It's a staple of apps ranging from galleries to bookshelves. Some examples are shown in Figures 15-1 through 15-3.

Figure 15-1. A flow layout in action on an iPhone 6

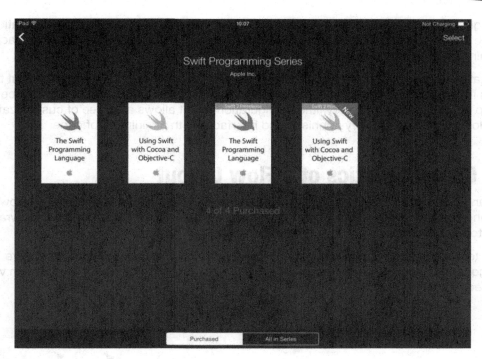

Figure 15-2. A simple flow layout in action in iBooks

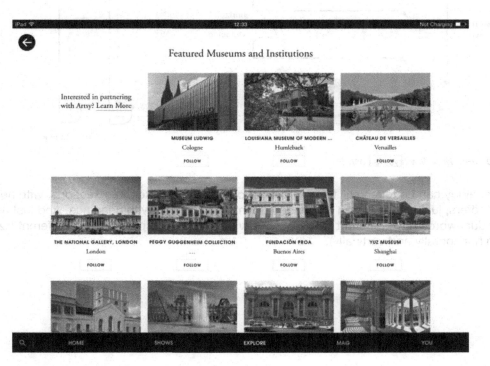

Figure 15-3. A highly customized flow layout in the Artsy app

Although grid-style layouts can appear visually simple, when you consider the calculations that are involved in figuring out aspects such as spacing of items, or where to wrap each line, things get complex very quickly.

Fortunately, Apple recognized this and ships UICollectionView with a "canned" layout that makes it very easy to create line-based interfaces. UICollectionViewFlowLayout can be used to whip up grid layouts with very little configuration, but it allows a degree of customization that allows you to create very sophisticated interfaces with a minimum of code.

The Characteristics of a Flow Layout

You can think of a flow layout as being like a sentence where words are arranged in rows from one side to the other, and when the row reaches the side of the page, the line "wraps" down to the next one.

In iOS terms, the page corresponds to the collection view's bounds, and the words are analogous to the collection view items. Each line of words corresponds to a collection view row. See Figure 15-4.

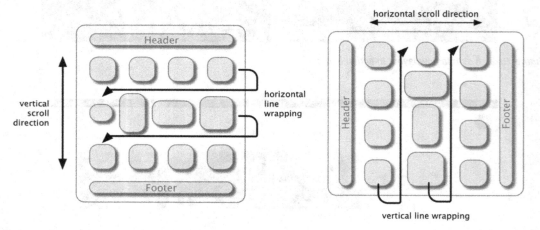

Figure 15-4. How flow layouts operate

The analogy can be taken still further: flow layouts can be broken into sections, with headers and footers, just as pages can be divided up into paragraphs with headings. And just as individual words have different lengths, so flow layouts can display items of different sizes (both horizontally and vertically).

UICollectionViewFlowLayout

A UICollectionViewFlowLayout is a concrete subclass of UICollectionViewLayout that adds a number of attributes to control the flow of items. It handles most of the calculations involved in figuring out item and line spacing, together with line wrapping.

Attributes that you can control are the following:

- The scroll direction (vertically or horizontally relative to the collection view)
- Line and item spacing
- Item sizing
- Header and footer sizing
- Section insets

Once you've provided those values, the flow layout handles all the calculations involved in figuring out how to position and space items, and when to break lines in order to fit all the items neatly into the space available.

The size and spacing attributes of UICollectionViewFlowLayout apply globally to all items, headers, footers, and sections, which is useful if the collection view's items will be constant sizes. If you need to display items with varying sizes, you need to implement an optional delegate object that conforms to the UICollectionViewDelegateFlowLayout protocol.

The flow layout's delegate object provides fine-grain control over the size of items, section spacing, and the sizing of headers and footers. This is useful if your items will vary in size, such as if you're building a gallery that will display thumbnail images of different heights or widths.

The functions of the delegate protocol are all optional, so you do not need to implement them unless you need to control the attribute in question.

Creating and Configuring Flow Layouts

You can create UICollectionViewFlowLayouts in code or in Interface Builder. Regardless of which approach you take, there are six steps involved.

- Create an instance of UICollectionViewFlowLayout.
- Assign the flow layout to the collection view that will use it.
- Provide values for the height and width of the cells if the cells will all be the same size. If your layout will have different sizes, you'll need to implement the collection view delegate's collectionView(_:layout:size ForItemAtIndexPath:) function.
- If required, set values for the item and line spacing (or implement the delegate functions if they will vary).

- Optionally, specify sizes for the section headers and footers (again implementing the delegate functions for sizes that will vary).

- Set the layout's direction of scrolling (either vertically or horizontally relative to the collection view itself).

Instantiating a Flow Layout

To instantiate a flow layout, you have two options:

- Create and configure the flow layout in code.
- Configure the flow layout in Interface Builder.

Creating and Configuring a Flow Layout in Code

Creating a flow layout in code has two basic steps:

- Instantiating a flow layout object
- Setting this as the collection view's layout

Once the flow layout is created and attached to the collection view, you have two options:

- Set the flow layout's properties directly if all configurable values will be static for the lifetime of the collection view, *or*

- Implement the relevant UICollectionViewDelegateFlowLayout functions to dynamically configure the flow layout's properties.

Creating the Flow Layout

Creating a flow layout object isn't difficult. If the values will be static, then you don't need to create a property for it:

```
let flowLayout = UICollectionViewFlowLayout()
```

If the values will be set by UICollectionViewDelegateFlowLayout functions, you need to declare a property before instantiating it, so that the delegate functions will have a reference available:

```
let flowLayout = UICollectionViewFlowLayout()
```

Setting the Collection View's Layout

Once there's an instantiated flow layout, the next step is to set this as the collection view's layout. Assuming that you have a collection view called myCollectionView and a flow layout called flowLayout, you would do this with

```
myCollectionView.collectionViewLayout = flowLayout
```

It's possible to change a collection view's layout at runtime, although this will cause the items to be reloaded.

Configuring Static Flow Layout Values

If the items in your collection view will all have the same size, then you can set the flow layout attributes globally. For example,

```
flowLayout.scrollDirection =.Vertical
flowLayout.itemSize = CGSizeMake(200, 100)
flowLayout.minimumInteritemSpacing = 10.0
flowLayout.minimumLineSpacing = 10.0
flowLayout.sectionInset = UIEdgeInsetsMake(25.0, 25.0, 25.0, 25.0)
```

Details of the various flow layout attributes that you can control are shown in the following sections.

Configuring Flow Layout Values Dynamically

If elements such as items, headers, or footers will be updated dynamically in response to the data model, then you can't set attributes relating to dynamic item properties directly. Instead, you'll need to create an object to act as the flow layout's delegate, and implement the relevant UICollectionViewDelegateFlowLayout function(s). This is covered in detail in the next section.

Configuring a Flow Layout in Interface Builder

When you drag a collection view or collection view controller out into a Storyboard or XIB, it comes with a UICollectionViewFlowLayout attached, as shown in Figure 15-5.

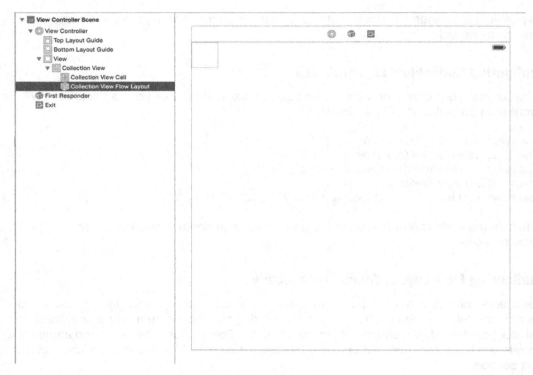

Figure 15-5. The flow layout attached to the collection view

Selecting this allows you to set the following basic properties statically for all items in the collection view:

- The scroll direction, which is found in the Attributes inspector, as shown in Figure 15-6.

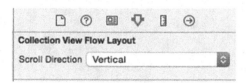

Figure 15-6. Setting the scroll direction

■ Cell size and spacing, and header and footer sizes. These are found in the Size inspector, shown in Figure 15-7.

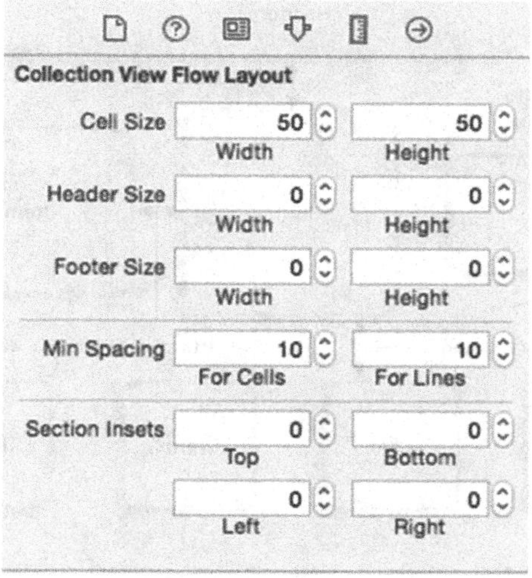

Figure 15-7. Setting sizes

If you need to set these values dynamically, you need connect the flow layout to an outlet in your controller and manage the values in code.

To do this, first create an outlet for the flow layout:

```
@IBOutlet var flowLayout: UICollectionViewFlowLayout!
```

Then connect the outlet with the flow layout object in Interface Builder.

Once connected, you can set the values from within the controller, like so:

```
flowLayout.itemSize = CGSizeMake(100, 100)
flowLayout.scrollDirection = .Vertical
```

Customizing Flow Layouts

Despite implementing all the heavy lifting of figuring out where line breaks should occur, `UICollectionViewFlowLayout` still allows for a high degree of customization within the constraints of a line-based layout.

The attributes of `UICollectionViewFlowLayout` that you can customize are shown in Figure 15-8.

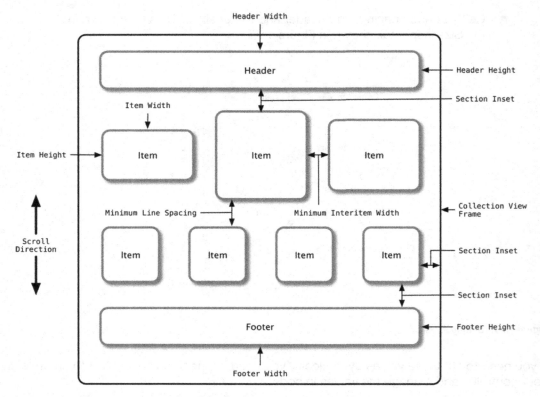

Figure 15-8. The UICollectionViewFlowLayout attributes

The attributes can be customised though a mix of directly setting the property of the `UICollectionViewFlowLayout` object or by implementing the appropriate `UICollectionViewDelegateFlowLayout` function.

Customizing with Attributes

The following attributes can be customized by directly setting the properties of the `UICollectionViewFlowLayout` object, such as

```
collectionView.scrollingDirection = .Vertical
```

Scrolling Direction

Scrolling direction determines whether collection view scrolls vertically or horizontally. The lines of items are laid out perpendicularly to the direction of scrolling, as shown in Figure 15-9.

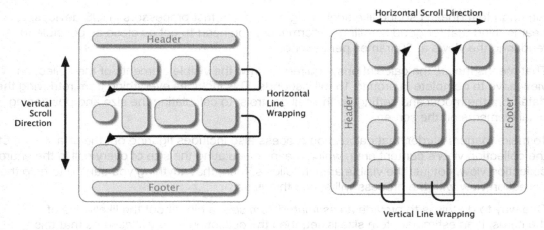

Figure 15-9. Scroll direction

Property	Value	Effect
scrollDirection	UICollectionViewScrollDirection.Vertical	Forces the collection view to scroll vertically and arrange lines of items horizontally
	UICollectionViewScrollDirection.Horizontal	Forces the collection view to scroll horizontally and arrange lines of items vertically

Item Size

Item size determines the width and height of each collection view cell, regardless of the intrinsic size of the cell contents. If left unset, it will default to (50.0, 50.0).

If the UICollectionViewDelegateFlowLayout collectionView:layout:sizeForItemAtIndexP ath: function is implemented, this will override any item size value that is set directly on the flow layout object.

Property	Value	Effect
itemSize	CGSize	Sets the size and width of each collection view item

Estimated Item Size

If you implement per-item sizing, this imposes an additional processing load on the `UICollectionViewDataSource` object. It is now responsible for calculating the size of every item on demand.

Although that doesn't sound like such a big deal for the fast processors in iOS devices, bear in mind that for good scrolling performance, you need to get as close as possible to rendering the views at 60 frames per second.

That means that *all* the calculations required to draw the visible elements of the collection view have to complete in around 15 milliseconds. This includes everything from retrieving the data from the model and setting up the cell controls, to calculating the size and positioning of all elements on the screen.

To make matters harder, that calculation process also includes figuring out the total height of the collection view's content area, which means calculating the size of every cell in the entire collection view, not just the visible area. It follows, then, that anything you can do to help the collection view with the process will speed things up.

One way to do this is to provide an *estimated item size*, a hint about the likely size of the items. If an estimated item size is set, then the collection view will assume that this is the size of all cells that are not currently visible and not bother to calculate their sizes individually. This can have a dramatic effect on collection view performance.

Property	Value	Effect
estimatedItemSize	CGSize	Sets an estimated item size, which will be used for calculations involving cells that are not currently visible

Item Spacing

When laying out the collection view's items, the flow layout uses the width of the collection view's bounds and the width of the collection view items to calculate the spacing between each item.

The `minimumInteritemSpacing` property sets the lower limit on the spacing between items. The collection view will not fit additional items onto a line if it would mean the spacing between each item falls below this value. Left undefined, this value defaults to 10.0 points (see Figure 15-10).

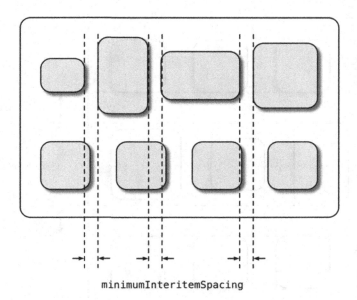

minimumInteritemSpacing

Figure 15-10. Minimum interitem spacing

This spacing is applied perpendicularly to the collection view's scroll direction. In other words, if the collection view scrolls vertically, the minimum interitem spacing attribute controls the horizontal space between items, and vice versa for a horizontally-scrolling collection view.

If the UICollectionViewDelegateFlowLayout collectionView:layout:minimumInteritem SpacingForSectionAtIndex: function is implemented, this will override any interitem spacing value that is set directly on the flow layout object.

Property	Value	Effect
minimumInteritemSpacing	CGFloat	Sets the minimum spacing allowed between each item in the section.

Line Spacing

The flow layout uses its lineSpacing attribute to control the minimum amount of space between the bottom of the item in an upper line and the top of an item in the line below.

The actual value will depend on the height of the tallest item on each line, but is guaranteed not to fall below the value you set for this attribute (see Figure 15-11).

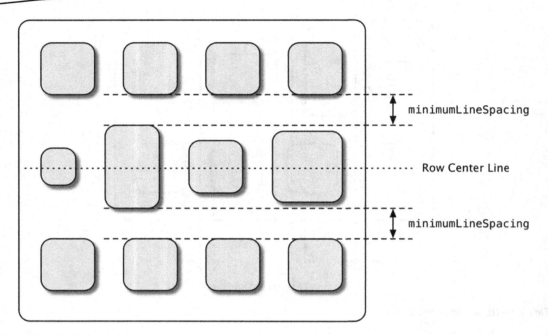

Figure 15-11. Minimum line spacing

Note that the default behavior of UICollectionViewFlowLayout is to vertically center all items in the row; if you want to change this behavior, you need to create a subclass of UICollectionViewFlowLayout and override it.

If the collection view's scroll direction is vertical, this attribute controls the vertical spacing between lines. If the scroll direction is horizontal, this attribute controls the horizontal spacing.

Note that this doesn't affect the spacing between the bottom of the header and the top of the first row in the section, or the spacing between the bottom of the last row and the top of the footer. These values are controlled by the sectionInset property.

Property	Value	Effect
minimumLineSpacing	CGFloat	Sets the minimum spacing allowed between each line in the section.

Section Insets

Section insets control the amount of horizontal space between the frame of the collection view and the items, as shown in Figure 15-12.

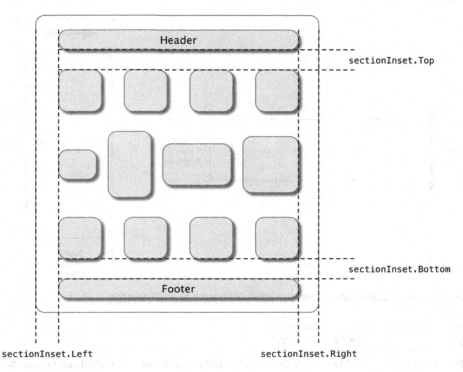

Figure 15-12. Section insets

It also controls the spacing between the header and footer views (if present) and the items between the bottom of the header view and the top of the first row, and the bottom of the last row and the top of the footer view.

Property	Value	Effect
sectionInset	UIEdgeInset	Sets the spacing between items and collection view frame, and between header/footer and rows

Supplementary View Sizes

The two supplementary view size attributes control the size of the section's header and footer views. Setting these values fixes the header and footer sizes for all sections; if the headers and footers need to vary in size per section, you have to implement the collection View:layout:referenceSizeForHeaderInSection: function.

One important caveat to note is that the collection view will only apply the attribute that applies in the scroll direction, as shown in Figure 15-13.

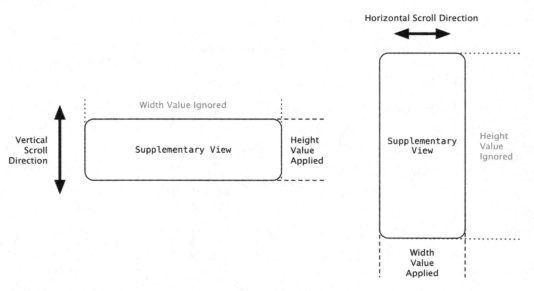

Figure 15-13. Applying supplementary view size attributes relative to scroll direction

Property	Value	Effect
headerReferenceSize	CGSize	Sets the size of the header view; the attribute perpendicular to the scroll direction is ignored.
footerReferenceSize	CGSize	Sets the size of the footer view; the attribute perpendicular to the scroll direction is ignored.

Customizing with UICollectionViewDelegateFlowLayout

Setting the attributes of UICollectionViewFlowLayout directly has a "global" effect. If you set the item size to 100 points wide by 200 points high, for example, then all cells will be displayed with this size.

The same process also applies to insets, line spacing, headers, and footers for each section. Set these values globally at the flow layout level, and all sections will use the same values.

If you want to vary these values (per-item for cells, and per-section for the other attributes), then you can provide the UICollectionViewFlowLayout with a delegate object that handles these calculations on its behalf. The UICollectionViewDelegateFlowLayout is the protocol that defines the optional functions required to calculate these values on-demand.

There are six optional functions declared by UICollectionViewDelegateFlowLayout, and each one takes a parameter for the UICollectionView and UICollectionViewFlowLayout. This means you can implement a single delegate object that can work with multiple collection views and/or flow layouts.

Controlling Item Size

Item size is controlled by the collectionView(_:layout:sizeForItemAtIndexPath:) function.

Parameters

It takes three parameters for the collection view and layout objects, and the index path.

Parameter	Type	Purpose
collectionView	UICollectionView	A reference to the collection view that the delegate is dealing with. This enables a single delegate object to support multiple collection views.
Layout	UICollectionViewFlowLayout	A reference to the collection view flow layout that the delegate is dealing with. This enables a single delegate object to support multiple flow layouts.
indexPath	NSIndexPath	Identifies the section and item for which the calculation should be performed.

Return Values

It returns the item size:

Return value	Type	Purpose
Item size	CGSize	The calculated size of the item at the specified index path

Example

Listing 15-1 shows an example implementation of the collectionView(_:layout:sizeForItemAtIndexPath:) function.

Listing 15-1. An Example sizeForItemAtIndexPath: Function

```
func collectionView(collectionView: UICollectionView, layout ↵
    collectionViewLayout: UICollectionViewLayout, sizeForItemAtIndexPath↵
    indexPath: NSIndexPath) -> CGSize {

        // Get the dictionary for this suit
        let suitDictionary = suitsArray[indexPath.section]

        // Get the array of cards in this suit
        let cardsArray = suitDictionary["cards"]

        // Get the dictionary for this card
        let cardDictionary: NSDictionary = cardsArray[indexPath.row] as! Dictionary
```

```
        // Get the name of the card's image
        let cardImageName = cardDictionary["cardImage"] as! String

        // Load the image for this card
        let cardImage: UIImage? = UIImage(named: cardImageName)

        if let unwrappedCardImage = cardImage {
            // If the image was loaded successfully, return its size
            return unwrappedCardImage.size
        }

        // There was a problem finding the image, so return a zero size
        return CGSizeZero

    }
```

Managing Section Spacing

The UICollectionViewDelegateFlowLayout protocol defines three optional functions for controlling section spacing:

collectionView(_:layout:insetForSectionAtIndex:)

This function takes parameters for the collection view and flow layout, and the index of the section for which the insets should be calculated.

Parameter	Type	Purpose
collectionView	UICollectionView	A reference to the collection view that the delegate is dealing with. This enables a single delegate object to support multiple collection views.
Layout	UICollectionViewFlowLayout	A reference to the collection view flow layout that the delegate is dealing with. This enables a single delegate object to support multiple flow layouts.
Index	Int	Identifies the section for which the calculation should be performed.

It returns a UIEdgeInsets struct:

Return value	Type	Purpose
Insets	UIEdgeInsets	CGFloat values for top, left, bottom, and left insets. Positive values inset the items relative to the collection view's frame; negative values outset the items.

collectionView(_:layout:minimumLineSpacingForSectionAtIndex:)

This function takes parameters for the collection view and flow layout, and the index of the section for which the minimum line spacing should be calculated.

Parameter	Type	Purpose
collectionView	UICollectionView	A reference to the collection view that the delegate is dealing with. This enables a single delegate object to support multiple collection views.
Layout	UICollectionViewFlowLayout	A reference to the collection view flow layout that the delegate is dealing with. This enables a single delegate object to support multiple flow layouts.
Index	Int	Identifies the section for which the calculation should be performed.

It returns a CGFloat:

Return value	Type	Purpose
Minimum line spacing	CGFloat	A CGFloat value for the minimum line spacing of rows of items. Items will never positioned closer together than this value, although they can be further apart depending on their vertical (or horizontal) alignment.

collectionView(_:layout:minimumInteritemSpacingForSectionAtIndex:)

This function takes parameters for the collection view and flow layout, and the index of the section for which the minimum interitem spacing should be calculated.

Parameter	Type	Purpose
collectionView	UICollectionView	A reference to the collection view that the delegate is dealing with. This enables a single delegate object to support multiple collection views.
layout	UICollectionViewFlowLayout	A reference to the collection view flow layout that the delegate is dealing with. This enables a single delegate object to support multiple flow layouts.
index	Int	Identifies the section for which the calculation should be performed.

It returns a CGFLoat:

Return value	Type	Purpose
Minimum interitem spacing	CGFloat	A CGFloat values for the minimum interitem spacing of items in rows. Items will never be positioned closer together than this value, although they can be further apart depending on their vertical (or horizontal) alignment.

Managing Header and Footer Sizes

The UICollectionViewDelegateFlowLayout protocol defines two optional functions for controlling header and footer sizes:

collectionView(_:layout:referenceSizeForHeaderInSection:)

This function takes parameters for the collection view and flow layout, and the index of the section for which the header size should be calculated.

Parameter	Type	Purpose
collectionView	UICollectionView	A reference to the collection view that the delegate is dealing with. This enables a single delegate object to support multiple collection views.
layout	UICollectionViewFlowLayout	A reference to the collection view flow layout that the delegate is dealing with. This enables a single delegate object to support multiple flow layouts.
index	Int	Identifies the section for which the calculation should be performed.

It returns a CGSize struct:

Return value	Type	Purpose
Header size	CGSize	The size of the header for this section.

collectionView(_:layout:referenceSizeForFooterInSection:)

This function takes parameters for the collection view and flow layout, and the index of the section for which the footer size should be calculated.

Parameter	Type	Purpose
collectionView	UICollectionView	A reference to the collection view that the delegate is dealing with. This enables a single delegate object to support multiple collection views.
layout	UICollectionViewFlowLayout	A reference to the collection view flow layout that the delegate is dealing with. This enables a single delegate object to support multiple flow layouts.
index	Int	Identifies the section for which the calculation should be performed.

It returns a CGSize struct:

Return value	Type	Purpose
Footer size	CGSize	The size of the footer for this section.

Subclassing UICollectionViewFlowLayout

Used in conjunction with a UICollectionViewDelegateFlowLayout delegate, you can apply fine-grained control to a line-based collection view without needing to implement the heavy lifting involved in calculating line layouts.

Sometimes, though, you need to be able to customize the layout still further. In these situations, you can still benefit from the behind-the-scenes calculations of the flow layout, but implement further customizations, by creating a custom subclass of UICollectionViewFlowLayout.

There are several scenarios where you might want to do this:

- You want to control layout attributes for items.
- You want to add custom layout attributes to items.
- You want to add new supplementary and/or decoration views.
- You want greater control over item insertion or deletion animations.

The process for subclassing UICollectionViewFlowLayout is identical to that for creating custom layouts; this is covered in detail in Chapter 16.

Controlling Item Layout Attributes

Controlling layout attributes allows you to update values such as the item's frame, bounds, position, transform, z-index, and alpha properties.

You need to implement the flow layout's layoutAttributesForElementsInRect: function to override the desired attributes. Bear in mind that UICollectionViewFlowLayout normally figures out the positioning of items for you, so updating these may result in unexpected results!

Adding Additional Custom Layout Attributes to Items

UICollectionView doesn't restrict you to just the "standard" item layout attributes. If needed, you can define your own. This involves creating custom subclasses of UICollectionViewLayoutAttributes (you'll look at this in Chapter 16).

Once you have a custom layout attributes class, you need to override UICollectionViewLayout's layoutAttributesClass function to return your custom attributes class instead of the default.

Then, using layoutAttributesForElementsInRect:, you can apply the custom attributes to items as required.

Adding New Supplementary Views

By default, UICollectionViewFlowLayout doesn't support decoration views. If you want to add additional supplementary and decoration views, you need to implement four functions:

- ▣   layoutAttributesForElementsInRect:
- ▣   layoutAttributesForItemAtIndexPath:
- ▣   layoutAttributesForSupplementaryViewOfKind:atIndexPath:
- ▣   layoutAttributesForDecorationViewOfKind:atIndexPath:

Controlling Insertion and Deletion Animations

The default insertion and deletion animation is a simple fade, but you can change these if you want.

Creating new insertion effects is achieved by tweaking the item attributes when appearing using one of these functions:

- ▣   initialLayoutAttributesForAppearingItemAtIndexPath:
- ▣   initialLayoutAttributesForAppearingSupplementaryElementOfKind:↩
    atIndexPath:
- ▣   initialLayoutAttributesForAppearingDecorationElementOfKind:↩
    atIndexPath:

New deletion effects are obtainable using the corresponding removal functions:

- `finalLayoutAttributesForDisappearingItemAtIndexPath:`
- `finalLayoutAttributesForDisappearingSupplementaryElementOf↵`
  `Kind:atIndexPath:`
- `finalLayoutAttributesForDisappearingDecorationElementOf↵`
  `Kind:atIndexPath:`

Summary

In this chapter, you looked at one of the most useful parts of the `UICollectionView` family, and you saw how it can allow you to rapidly create line-breaking layouts with a minimum of configuration or code.

It's also possible to get fine-grained control over many attributes of the layout by implementing the `UICollectionViewDelegateFlowLayout` delegate functions, or go further by subclassing to customize even more.

In the next chapter, you'll take things further by implementing completely custom layouts, many aspects of which are also relevant to creating fully-customized `UICollectionViewFlow` layouts.

Chapter 16

Collection View Custom Layouts

Custom UICollectionView layouts allow you to take complete control over every aspect of the look and feel of the collection view, and produce spectacular effects with visual appearance and transitions. The downside to this is that you're responsible for calculating every aspect, so custom layouts are more complex to implement than flow layouts.

Don't let that put you off, however. Custom layouts aren't *that* complex to implement, and the results are often worth the extra effort!

This chapter covers the process of creating custom layouts for UICollectionView. In the first part of the chapter, I'll introduce the processes that are involved in calculating the various layout attributes that are required. Next, you'll look in detail at the functions necessary to create a completely custom layout.

In the next chapter, you'll look at custom layouts in even more detail, using supplementary and decoration views, animating simple layout changes, and creating complex custom layout transitions.

The kind of custom layout you need to create is of course entirely dependent on the nature of your projects, so it's impossible to cover every combination in a book of a finite length. To put what you'll learn in the first section into practice, therefore, in the second part you'll work through a layout that is completely different in look and feel to anything you've seen before. Instead of a grid of regular items, you'll create a working collection view-based analogue clock.

About Custom Layouts

Collection view layouts have the potential to get complex quickly, so Apple thoughtfully provided a "canned" layout in the shape of UICollectionViewFlowLayout. This is based around lines or columns of items, and takes care of the calculations involved in positioning "line breaks" and spacing items for you. With a bit of judicious subclassing here and there, you can go a long way without needing to create a layout of your own from scratch.

Eventually, though, you'll come across a situation where your collection view looks nothing like a line or a grid, or you want to a fine degree of control over customizing attributes. In this kind of situation, the line-breaking nature of UICollectionViewFlowLayout might not work, so it becomes time to take complete control and implement a custom layout.

Figure 16-1 shows some possibilities: both apps are collection views, and both apps are based on exactly the same source data.

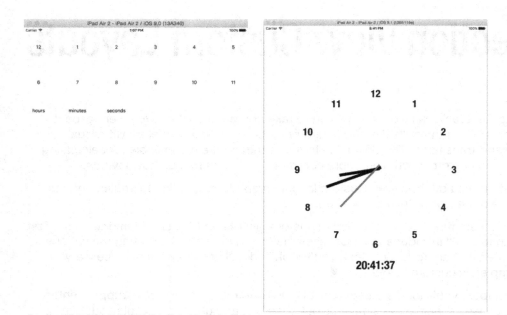

Figure 16-1. *Before and after*

With a custom layout, you're responsible for all the heavy lifting of figuring out where each item and view should be placed. As an exercise, reimplementing UICollectionViewFlowLayout yourself will quickly give you a newfound respect for the amount of work that went into creating it!

Actually, though, this makes the task of creating custom layouts sound harder than it really is. There's a very clearly defined process that you'll work through to perform these calculations, so with a bit of practice you'll find that you can create sophisticated-looking layouts very quickly.

The process of creating a custom layout has six steps, two of which are optional:

▪ Create a custom subclass of UICollectionViewLayout.

▪ Decide whether your layout needs to compute the attributes of each item on the fly, or whether it can do this en masse.

▪ Implement the four core functions to calculate the placement of each item in the collection view.

- Optionally, implement custom subclasses of
  UICollectionViewLayoutAttributes to customize additional attributes of
  cells and views.

- Optionally, implement the supporting functions for things like
  supplementary and decoration views, and animated insertion and
  deletion of items.

- Create a new instance of your custom UICollectionViewLayout subclass
  and set it as the collection view's collectionViewLayout property.

With those steps in place, the collection view will interact with your custom collection view layout in exactly the same way as it would with a UICollectionViewFlowLayout, with the difference that you have complete control over the placement of all elements.

When to Create a Custom Collection View Layout

The question of when to create a custom collection view layout instead of relying on a flow layout is a tricky one. There's a trade-off between the convenience of UICollectionViewFlowLayout's calculations and the amount of work involved in getting it to provide the effect that you're after.

As a rule of thumb, if your intended layout doesn't have a recognizable row-and-column feel to it, then a custom layout is probably going to be easier to implement in the long run.

Creating a Custom Layout Subclass

Your collection view expects a layout that is a subclass of UICollectionViewLayout. This is an abstract class that can't be implemented as-is in the way that you could, say, a UICollectionView itself. Instead, you have to create a subclass and implement the functions.

You can do this on the fly in your view controller, but it's more common to create a separate UICollectionViewLayout subclass.

Deciding When to Calculate Attributes

The collection view itself doesn't care when the layout attributes are calculated; all that matters is that they can be returned by the layout on demand when the collection asks for them. Because the collection view will call layoutAttributesForItemsInRect: and layoutAttributesForItemAtIndexPath:, you could calculate the attributes on the fly. However, this might not be necessary.

If your layout is highly dynamic (it can scroll, or perhaps there are many items that will change presence, size, or location), then you will most likely have to calculate layout attributes when the collection view calls for them.

If, on the other hand, you've got a layout that's largely static, another option might be to calculate the layout attributes up front in the prepareLayout function, and then simply return the pre-calculated values in response to layoutAttributesForItemsInRect:.

Which approach to take is a balance between the effort involved in the calculations and the frequency of updates. There's no obviously right answer, unfortunately, other than to bear in mind the saying "premature optimization is the root of all evil."

What the Custom Layout Does

The custom layout has three main tasks that it carries out on behalf of the collection view. These are

- **Calculating the size of the collection view's content area**, that is, how large the scrolling content area will be, based on the size and position attributes for each item that the collection view will display.

- **Calculating the layout attributes for the item at each index path**.

- **Returning an array of layout attributes** for the items in a given area of the collection view's content area.

What Are Layout Attributes?

With all this talk of layout attributes, what exactly are they?

The UICollectionViewLayoutAttributes class defines a series of layout-related attributes that can be applied to a collection view item (or supplementary or decoration view) to customize the way in which it is displayed.

The class defines a number of "standard" attributes, but if these aren't sufficient you can create a subclass of UICollectionViewLayoutAttributes and create your own as required.

The standard attributes provided are

- **frame**, which determines where the item will be displayed within the collection view. Changing this attribute also sets the item's center and size properties.

- **bounds**, which determines the bounds rectangle of the item relative to its own coordinate system. Changing this attribute will also change the size property.

- **center**, which locates the center of the item relative to the collection view. Changing this attribute will also update the frame property.

- **size**, which determines the size of the item. Changing this attribute will also cause the frame and bounds properties to be updated.

- **transform3D**, which allows the item to be transformed in the x, y, and z planes to create 3D effects. Changing this attribute will also update the transform property.

- **transform**, which allows the item to be transformed in the x and/or y planes to get scale or skew effects. Changing this attribute will also update the transform3D property.

- **alpha**, which controls the transparency of the item. By default, the item is totally non-transparent with an alpha value of 1. Setting the alpha value to 0 will make the item appear to vanish; setting it somewhere between 1 and 0 will provide varying degrees of transparency. Note that this isn't the same as setting the hidden property to YES, as items with an alpha property of 0 will always be created by the collection view.

- **zIndex**, which determines whether the item is displayed "above" or "below" other items in the collection view. By manipulating the zIndex for each item, you can get the appearance of items "stacking" or overlapping. The higher the number, the closer to the "front" or "top" the item will be.

- **hidden**, which controls the overall appearance of the item. If this is set to YES or true, the item won't be displayed. Note that this isn't the same as setting the alpha attribute to 0, because the collection view may self-optimize and choose not to create items with hidden set to YES.

Custom Layout Attributes

If the standard set of layout attributes doesn't give you the level of control that you need, you can create your own custom attributes. These can control any other aspect of the item's visual appearance (text color, font, or orientation, for example), although the possibilities are more or less limitless.

You can extend the standard attributes by subclassing UICollectionViewLayoutAttributes and adding your own properties as required. If you do this, there are three additional steps that you need to implement:

- A custom UICollectionViewLayoutAttributes subclass must conform to the NSCopying protocol, so that the collection view can copy them as and when it needs to.

- A custom UICollectionViewLayouAttributes subclass must override the inherited isEqual: function so that any custom properties are checked. The collection view won't apply attributes to an item unless they've changed, so if you've implemented your own custom attributes, the collection view needs a way of determining whether they are the same or not.

- Any items that have custom attributes applied to them (cells, supplementary view, or decoration views) must implement the applyLayoutAttributes: function. This function is where you take the attribute (say text color, for example) and apply it (in this case, to a UILabel in the item).

The Four Key Functions to Implement

There are four key functions that you need to implement in your custom
UICollectionViewLayout in order to provide the collection view with the layout attributes
it needs:

- func prepareLayout()

- func collectionViewContentSize() -> CGSize

- func layoutAttributesForElementsInRect(_ rect: CGRect) -> ↵

  [UICollectionViewLayoutAttributes]?

- func layoutAttributesForItemAtIndexPath(_ indexPath: ↵

  NSIndexPath) -> UICollectionViewLayoutAttributes?

Let's look at each one in turn.

prepareLayout

This function is called when the collection view first asks its layout object for attributes, and
again at any point where the layout is invalidated in response to a bounds change or an
explicit request.

Depending on the specific details of your custom layout, there may be values that it makes
most sense to calculate "globally" for the layout as a whole.

For example, the individual items might get placed relative to the center of the collection
view's bounds. This center point won't change unless the bounds of the collection view
change, so prepareLayout is a good place to calculate this and place it in a class property.

If you've got a relatively static layout, you could use prepareLayout to calculate all the
attributes for all the items and then store them in a property. If your layout is more dynamic,
however, this might not make sense.

By default, UICollectionViewLayout doesn't implement prepareLayout, so if there aren't any
preparations that need to occur, you can simply omit the function completely.

collectionViewContentSize

In order to figure out its scrolling behaviour, the collection view needs to know how big the
content size is going to be; remember that UICollectionView is a subclass of UIScrollView,
and the content view can be larger than the visible area within the collection view's bounds.

It's called early in the layout process as the collection view is drawn for the first time, and
then subsequently if the bounds of the collection view change or the invalidateLayout
function is called.

This function is mandatory, so you need to implement code that calculates the maximum size of
the content view for all the items that the collection view will display, and returns it as a CGSize.

Sometimes all the items will fit within the bounds of the collection view; for example, the circular example you'll see later in the chapter places all the items inside the visible area. In this situation, the content size and the visible area are the same.

However, you always need to bear in mind that `collectionViewContentSize` is the size required to display *all* the items in the collection view, not just the ones that are visible within the collection view's bounds.

The reason this value is calculated by the collection view layout rather than the collection view's view controller is that it's the layout that controls the size of the items, and therefore the size of the content view that's going to be required.

You also need to be prepared to repeat the process if the bounds of the collection view change, for example during device rotation.

layoutAttributesForElementsInRect

Once the collection view knows the content size, it can then start asking its layout object for the attributes that it needs to display the items within a given rectangle.

Sometimes this rectangle will be the same as the collection view's frame (which is the case in the circular example later in the chapter).

In other situations, it may be different. A collection view that scrolls is likely to ask its layout for attributes for items that aren't actually being displayed yet, but may be scrolled into the visible area depending on the user's interaction. By asking for attributes items that aren't yet visible, the collection view can attempt to maximize scrolling performance.

In either situation, it's your layout's responsibility to do three things:

- Figure out which items appear within the rect that's provided.
- For each of those items, create a `UICollectionViewLayoutAttributes` object and set the attributes so that the item will be correctly placed in the rectangle that the collection view asked for.
- Return those objects as an `NSArray`.

The detailed implementation of this is hidden from the collection view. All it is concerned about is receiving the `NSArray` containing the `UICollectionViewAttributes`.

layoutAttributesForItemAtIndexPath

The role of the `layoutAttributesForItemAtIndexPath:` function is to return the individual layout attributes for the item at the index path provided as an instance of `UICollectionViewLayoutAttributes`. The index path acts as the "key" to link a specific instance of `UICollectionViewLayoutAttributes` with a specific cell or view.

This function may or may not get called by the collection view, but it has to be implemented. `layoutAttributesForElementsInRect:` is the main function that will be called by the collection view, but it may need layout attributes on a per-item basis at certain times, for example during insertion or deletion of items.

Note that you shouldn't use this function to calculate the attributes; this should already have been done in either `prepareLayout` or `layoutAttributesForElementsInRect`. There's no way of knowing when the collection view will call this function on its datasource, so it's possible that recalculating attributes here may result in their values changing before the collection view is ready to deal with this. While this probably won't cause crashes, it has the potential to create very hard-to-debug layout errors.

If you've stored the layout attributes in a property of the layout subclass, for example, you need to retrieve the attribute with the matching `indexPath` value and return it.

Supplementary and Decoration View Attributes

Just as the collection view needs to know how to lay out items, so it will also need attributes to figure out how to lay out supplementary and decoration views.

Whether you need to go through this process will depend on whether your custom layout utilizes supplementary and decoration views. Clearly, if you're not using decoration views, for example, there's no need to calculate attributes for them. All the supplementary and decoration view functions are optional.

The process for calculating and returning supplementary and decoration view attributes is almost identical to that for items, and has three steps:

- Figure out if supplementary and/or decoration views will be found within the rect supplied to the `layoutAttributesForElementsInRect:` function.

- If required, calculate their attributes.

- Return their attributes from one of two functions available for the purpose: `layoutAttributesForSupplementaryViewsOfKind:AtIndexPath:` and/or `layoutAttributesForDecorationViewOfKind:atIndexPath:`.

Checking if Supplementary or Decoration Views Are Required

Supplementary or decoration views may not necessarily appear in the rect for which the collection is requesting layout attributes; this will depend on the design of your layout, and the size of the rect requested.

For example, if the rect in question only covers the middle area of a section, the headers and footers might not appear within the visible area. Similarly, decoration views may or may not appear.

Calculating Supplementary and Decoration View Attributes

If supplementary and/or decoration views will appear in the rect, your custom layout is responsible for calculating the necessary attributes.

As with attributes for items, you have the option of calculating these up front in `prepareLayout`, or on demand during `layoutAttributesForElementsInRect:` The choice is a balance between expense of calculation and frequency of need.

Supplementary and decoration views can also be demanded by the collection view at any time, so you need to implement the two functions available for this:

- `layoutAttributesForSupplementaryViewsOfKind:AtIndexPath:`
- `layoutAttributesForDecorationViewOfKind:atIndexPath:`

Both functions take two parameters: the kind of view that's being requested (for example, `UICollectionElementKindHeader` or `UICollectionElementKindFooter`) and the associated index path. Just as with items, you shouldn't use these functions to change the attributes.

The `kind` and `indexPath` values enable you to determine which supplementary or decoration view you're dealing with.

`kind` is a string that acts in the same way as a cell identifier. For this reason, you should define them as constants because they'll be referred to in the collection view's controller and `dataSource` as well as the layout subclass.

As with cells, `indexPath` is the means of relating a given instance of `UICollectionViewLayoutAttributes` to a supplementary or decoration view at a specific index path.

Once you've retrieved the attributes, you need to return them as instances of `UICollectionViewLayoutAttributes`.

This Chapter's Project

In the rest of this chapter, you will implement a collection view with a custom layout. This first example will be relatively static, in that the collection view's frame encompasses the whole of the content area.

SwiftClock: The "Static" Example

The "static" example is a working analogue clock that displays the current device time, complete with ticking second hand. It uses a combination of supplementary and decoration views to display the face and numerals, and cells for hour, minute, and second hands.

Having built a basic layout, you'll then extend it to add the ability to swap between different styles of clock faces, and change between time zones. All the changes will be smoothly animated.

The project is iPad-based, with a single view controller containing a `UICollectionView` that fills the whole screen, shown in Figure 16-2.

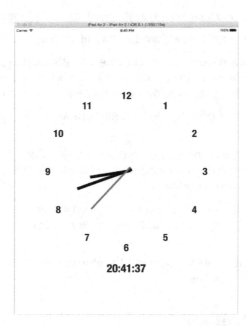

Figure 16-2. The UICollectionView clock

Getting Started

To speed things up, I've created a project to act as a starting point. It implements the data model and displays the twelve numerals in a grid with a basic flow layout. It also includes the images assets that you'll use later.

You'll adapt this to use a custom circular layout by removing the flow layout and implementing your own custom layout.

There are two reasons for taking this approach. First, it will speed things up by providing all the collection view "plumbing" for you; and second, it reinforces the point that layouts are independent of the data that feeds the collection view. You won't change the initial data–just the way it's displayed.

The Initial Project

The initial project can be downloaded from the Apress website as part of this book's source code or directly from GitHub (this is more likely to be up-to-date; the latest version will be on the `master` branch).

The initial project is available at

https://github.com/timd/InitialSwiftClock

The final version of the project is available at

https://github.com/timd/SwiftClock

Setup

The initial project is a straightforward collection view running full screen on an iPad. It has a single view controller, ClockViewController, and a Storyboard that contains a full-screen UICollectionView object.

To separate the elements controlling the collection view, the ClockViewController has two extensions: one that implements the UICollectionViewDelegate and UICollectionViewDataSource functions; and one for custom functions that support the collection view.

The Data Model

The data model for the collection view lives in a property of the support class, and is an array that contains two elements:

var dataArray: Array<Array<String>>!

The first element is an array that contains elements for each of the hands, and the second is an array that contains elements for each of the hours. Figure 16-3 shows how the data model is arranged as Arrays containing Strings.

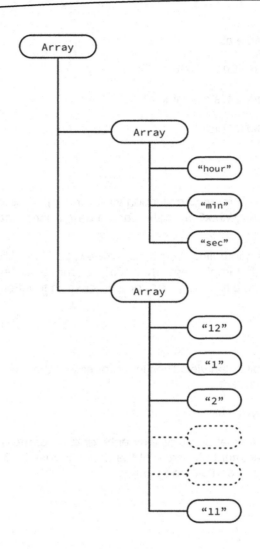

Figure 16-3. The data model

The data model is set up in the setupData() function, which is shown in Listing 16-1.

Listing 16-1. The setupData Function

```
func setupData() {

    let hoursArray = ["12", "1", "2", "3", "4", "5", "6", "7", "8", "9", "10", "11"]
    let handsArray = ["hours", "minutes", "seconds"]

    dataArray = [handsArray, hoursArray]
}
```

> **Note**   The numbering of the hours array starts from 12. That's because 12 is the first label that is
> displayed at the top of the clock.

The cell that will contain the clock's numerals is laid out in a nib file, ClockCell, and
contains a single label that displays the content of the data model for the relevant index
path (shown in Figure 16-4). The label has a tag of 1000 so that it can be accessed by the
UICollectionViewDatasource.

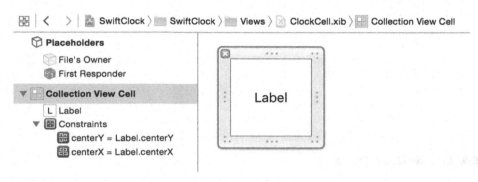

Figure 16-4. The hour label cell

At the moment, the collection view is set up to use a simple UICollectionViewFlowLayout
that displays all the elements of the data model in a line, as shown in Figure 16-5. It's not
pretty, but that doesn't matter at this stage; the purpose of the initial project is to get things
wired up, ready to adapt to the custom layout.

Figure 16-5. The initial state of the project

Updating the Project

You're going to update the project so that the layout is transformed from the hideous flow layout to a sleek analogue clock. The end result will look like Figure 16-6.

Figure 16-6. The finished clock

That's going to involve three stages:

- Creating a custom layout class to replace the existing flow layout
- Creating new cells to display the clock's hands
- Switching the collection view over to using the new custom class

The bulk of the work is contained in creating the new custom layout, so let's get started with that.

Adding the Custom Layout Class

A custom layout is a subclass of UICollectionViewLayout. Add a new file (File ➤ New ➤ File) and give the class a name (I've called mine ClockLayout). Make it a subclass of UICollectionViewLayout, as shown in Figure 16-7.

Choose options for your new file:

Class:	ClockLayout
Subclass of:	UICollectionViewLayout
	☐ Also create XIB file
	iPhone
Language:	Swift

Cancel   Previous   Next

Figure 16-7. Creating a custom class for the layout

Setting Up Properties

The position of the hands of the clock will obviously depend on the time, so you need a way of passing that data around the layout. Create an NSDate property called let clockTime: NSDate!

There are several other properties that will be needed at various points, so you might as well add them to the class while you're setting it up. This is shown in Listing 16-2.

Listing 16-2. The Properties of the Class

```
private var clockTime: NSDate!
private let dateFormatter = NSDateFormatter()

private var timeHours: Int!
private var timeMinutes: Int!
private var timeSeconds: Int!

var minuteHandSize: CGSize!
var secondHandSize: CGSize!
var hourHandSize: CGSize!

private var hourLabelCellSize: CGSize!

private var clockFaceRadius: CGFloat!
private var cvCenter: CGPoint!

var attributesArray = [UICollectionViewLayoutAttributes]()
```

Working through these,

- The time that the clock displays is stored in the clockTime property.

- An NSDateFormatter is needed to calculate the time in the appropriate format. Since these are expensive to create, you'll create one as a class property and change the date format each time you need to calculate hours, minutes, or seconds.

- To move the individual hands, you need to calculate the separate hours, minutes, and seconds.

- The cells will be created outside of the layout, so you need to be able to pass the size of them into the layout class through the four size properties.

- The clock face radius is derived from the size of the collection view; as this is set up externally to the layout, you need to pass this value in.

- The center point of the layout is needed to fix the position of the hands and the hour labels.

- The calculated attributes are stored in an Array of UICollectionViewLayoutAttributes.

How the Custom Layout Will Operate

The custom layout is going to need to be able to calculate layout attributes for four elements:

- The numbers of the clock face, which will be arranged in a circle around the center.

- The rotation of the cell containing the hour hand, which will be dependent on the time being displayed. You also need to make an adjustment to take into account of the number of minutes past the hour, so that the hour hand moves smoothly during the course of the hour.

- The rotation of the cell containing the minutes hand, which is also dependent on the time being displayed. This will also be adjusted as the number of seconds increases.

- The rotation of the second hand.

Let's break these calculations down into four stages:

- A "master" function called `calculateAllAttributes` that iterates across the entire data model and calls the appropriate function to calculate the attributes for each date item in turn.

- A function called `calculateAttributesForItemAtIndexPath` that takes the indexPath for a data item, and calls the appropriate calculation function depending on the type of item (hour, minute, or second hand) or hour label.

- A function to calculate the position of the three hand cells:`calculate AttributesForHandCellAtIndexPath:`

- A function to calculate the position of the hour labels: `calculateAttributesForHourLabelWithIndexPath:`

The overall process will follow the flow shown in Figure 16-8.

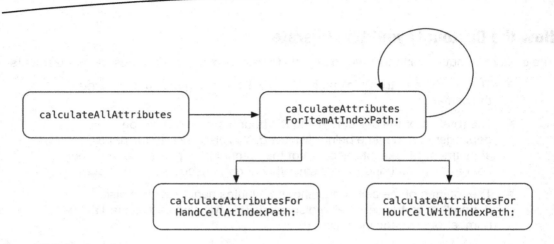

Figure 16-8. The layout process

The rationale for separating out each stage of the calculation is two-fold:

- By breaking down the calculations into individual actions, the functions become smaller, easier to read, and (if you're using a test-driven approach) easier to test.

- Later, you'll be able to adapt the existing functions to extend the custom layout to handle different display styles.

Implementing the Layout Functions

As well as the custom functions needed to calculate the placement of the numerals and hands, there are a number of UICollectionViewLayout functions that you will need to implement.

Let's start the process of building the custom layout by implementing the following:

- prepareLayout
- collectionViewContentSize
- layoutAttributesForElementsInRect:
- layoutAttributesForItemAtIndexPath:

The prepareLayout Function

As you saw earlier, the prepareLayout function is called when the layout is initialized for the first time, and then subsequently as the layout is invalidated, either because you've called it explicitly, or when the bounds of the collection view change.

It's a good place to perform "global" calculations that affect the collection view as a whole. In this project, it will be called every time you need to update the position of the hands, so you can use this to calculate the hours, minutes, and seconds that will be displayed.

Listing 16-3 shows the prepareLayout function.

Listing 16-3. The prepareLayout Function

```
override func prepareLayout() {

    cvCenter = CGPointMake(collectionView!.frame.size.width/2, ↩
    collectionView!.frame.size.height/2)

    clockTime = NSDate()

    dateFormatter.dateFormat = "HH"
    let hourString = dateFormatter.stringFromDate(clockTime)
    timeHours = Int(hourString)!

    dateFormatter.dateFormat = "mm"
    let minString = dateFormatter.stringFromDate(clockTime)
    timeMinutes = Int(minString)!

    dateFormatter.dateFormat = "ss"
    let secString = dateFormatter.stringFromDate(clockTime)
    timeSeconds = Int(secString)!

    clockFaceRadius = min(cvCenter.x, cvCenter.y)

    calculateAllAttributes()

}
```

First, you calculate the center of the collection view and store that in the cvCenter property. Then you take the current time and extract the hours, minutes, and seconds values by passing the time property through an NSDateFormatter.

Next, you calculate the radius of the clock face (which is the smaller value of either the cvCenter's x or y coordinate) and then finally call the calculateAllAttributes function, which you'll create in a moment.

collectionViewContentSize

Because all the elements of the clock are going to be displayed within the visible bounds of the collection view, the collectionView's contentSize is going to be the same as the bounds. This makes the collectionViewContentSize function very easy to implement, as shown in Listing 16-4.

Listing 16-4. The collectionViewContentSize Function

```
override func collectionViewContentSize() -> CGSize {
    return collectionView!.frame.size
}
```

layoutAttributesForElementsInRect:

The layoutAttributesForElementsInRect: function has to return an array of attributes for *all* the elements that will appear either fully or partially within the given rect.

With a complex layout, you're responsible for determining whether each element lies within the rect, so you need to implement something like this for each item:

```
if CGRectIntersectsRect(item.frame, rect) {
    /*
        the item at least partially appears within the rect,
        so add its attributes to the array that will be returned
    */
}
```

The clock layout is simpler, though. Because all the elements lie within the collection view's bounds, you can return all the attributes that are stored in the attributesArray property. This is shown in Listing 16-5.

Listing 16-5. The layoutAttributesForElementsInRect: Function

```
override func layoutAttributesForElementsInRect(rect: CGRect) ->
  [UICollectionViewLayoutAttributes]? {
    return attributesArray
}
```

layoutAttributesForElementAtIndexPath:

The layoutAttributeForElementAtIndexPath: function can be called by the collection view at any time, and it's expected to return a UICollectionViewLayoutAttributes object for the item at the index path provided.

Often this function will be called during the insertion and deletion process. Because you can't guarantee the state that the collection view will be in at the time, it's important that this function doesn't alter the attributes for the item. Instead, it should just return the attributes that were calculated previously.

To do this, you find the UICollectionViewLayoutAttributes in the attributes array that has an indexPath property that matches the indexPath supplied by the collection view, and return it. This is shown in Listing 16-6.

Listing 16-6. The layoutAttributesForElementAtIndexPath: Function

```
override func layoutAttributesForItemAtIndexPath(indexPath: NSIndexPath) -> ↵
UICollectionViewLayoutAttributes? {

    // return the item from attributesArray with the matching indexPath

    return attributesArray.filter({ (theAttribute) -> Bool in
        theAttribute.indexPath == indexPath
    }).first

}
```

Other UICollectionViewLayout Functions

There are three other UICollectionViewLayout functions that form part of the layout process, but you don't need to implement them. Two of them are related to supplementary and decoration views, which you're not using in this layout.

- layoutAttributesForSupplementaryViewOfKind(_:atIndexPath:)

- layoutAttributesForDecorationViewOfKind(_:atIndexPath:)

The third function controls if the layout should change in response to a bounds change of the collection view, for example after a rotation event:

- shouldInvalidateLayoutForBoundsChange(_:)

If this function isn't implemented, the layout will assume that the attributes *won't* change. This is fine for you, so you don't need to explicitly implement it.

Implementing the Custom Layout Functions

Now that you've implemented the main layout functions, you can turn your attention to the custom functions that will handle the heavy lifting of calculating the attributes for your custom layout.

It's worth noting at this point that you're striking out on your own here. The way in which the attributes are calculated isn't defined by any of the UICollectionView protocols. How you go about this is entirely dependent on the needs of your specific layout, so will vary greatly from project to project.

As you saw earlier, you're going to do this in four stages:

- Iterate across the entire data model to call the calculateAttributesForItemAtIndexPath: function for each item in the data model with calculateAllAttributes.

- Call the appropriate calculation function depending on the index path that's passed in with calculateAttributesForItemAtIndexPath:.

- Calculate the position of the hour labels with calculateAttributesForHourLabelWithIndexPath:.

- Calculate the position of the three hand cells with calculateAttributesForHandCellAtIndexPath:.

The position of the hands will depend on the time and their sizes.

You've exposed properties for the sizes of the hand and label cells. Although you don't need to make these dynamic right now because you're building a single style of clock face, by exposing the properties you'd be able to reuse this layout class for other face styles.

They need to be declared as properties of the layout:

```
var minuteHandSize: CGSize!
var secondHandSize: CGSize!
var hourHandSize: CGSize!
var hourLabelCellSize: CGSize!
```

The calculateAllAttributes Function

This function exists so that you can quickly iterate across the whole of the collection view's data model and calculate the attributes for each item.

Recall that items and their attributes are connected by an indexPath property, so it follows that if you iterate across all indexPaths, you'll have calculated attributes for each element.

The function to do this is shown in Listing 16-7.

Listing 16-7. The calculateAllAttributes Function

```
func calculateAllAttributes() {

    for section in 0..<collectionView!.numberOfSections() {

        for item in 0..<collectionView!.numberOfItemsInSection(section) {

            // Create index path for this item
            let indexPath = NSIndexPath(forItem: item, inSection: section)

            // Calculate the attributes
            let attributes = calculateAttributesForItemAt(indexPath)

            // Update or insert the newAttributes into the attributesArray
            if let matchingAttributeIndex = attributesArray.indexOf( { (attributes: ↵
            UICollectionViewLayoutAttributes ) -> Bool in
                attributes.indexPath.compare(indexPath) == ↵
            NSComparisonResult.OrderedSame
            }) {

                // Attribute already existed, therefore replace it
                attributesArray[matchingAttributeIndex] = attributes

            } else {

                // New set of attributes required
                attributesArray.append(attributes)

            }

        }

    }

}
```

As you can see, there's not a huge amount to this.

In this example, the collection view's data model has two inner arrays inside an outer array. You iterate across each element of the outer array in turn, and then iterate across the inner array.

You're not restricted to using arrays for the data model, of course – any model structure that allows the section and rows to be determined can be utilized.

For each element of the inner array, you call the calculateAttributesForItemAtIndexPath: function, which you'll look at next. This returns an instance of UICollectionViewLayoutAttributes for the item at this index path.

You then need to check if there are any pre-existing attributes for this indexPath that need to be updated. If there are, the new attributes replace the old ones in the attributesArray; if not, the new attributes are appended to those that are already stored.

The calculateAttributesForItemAtIndexPath: Function

The calculateAttributesForItemAtIndexPath: function is called by the calculateAllAttributes function for each item in turn.

Because you've got four different types of items in your collection view (three types of hands and the hour labels), this function uses the indexPath to decide which kind of item it is.

If it's a hand cell, it will call calculateAttributesForHandCell(:_), and if it's an hour label, it will call calculateAttributesForHourLabelWith(:_). Both functions return a set of UICollectionViewLayoutAttributes that will get returned. See Listing 16-8.

Listing 16-8. The calculateAttributesForItemAtIndexPath: Function

```
func calculateAttributesForItemAt(itemPath: NSIndexPath) -> UICollectionViewLayoutAttributes
{

    var newAttributes = UICollectionViewLayoutAttributes(forCellWithIndexPath: itemPath)

    if itemPath.section == 0 {
        newAttributes = calculateAttributesForHandCellAt(itemPath)
    }

    if itemPath.section == 1 {
        newAttributes = calculateAttributesForHourLabelWith(itemPath)
    }

    return newAttributes

}
```

Calculating the Position of the Hour Labels

In your calculateAttributesForIndexPath: function you're calling a function called calculateAttributesForHourLabelWithIndexPath:. This is going to lay out the hour labels around the center of the collection view, one for each element in the data model's first section.

The full function is shown in Listing 16-9. It takes an NSIndexPath as the hourPath parameter, and returns an instance of UICollectionViewLayoutAttributes.

Listing 16-9. The calculateAttributesForHourLabelWithIndexPath: Function

```
func calculateAttributesForHourLabelWith(hourPath: NSIndexPath) -> ↩
UICollectionViewLayoutAttributes {

    let attributes = UICollectionViewLayoutAttributes(forCellWithIndexPath: hourPath)

    attributes.size = CGSizeMake(hourLabelCellSize.width, hourLabelCellSize.height)

    let angularDisplacement: Double = (2 * M_PI) / 12

    let theta = angularDisplacement * Double(hourPath.row)

    let xDisplacement = sin(theta) * Double(clockFaceRadius - ↩
    (attributes.size.width / 2))

    let yDisplacement = cos(theta) * Double(clockFaceRadius - ↩
    (attributes.size.height / 2))

    let xPosition = cvCenter.x + CGFloat(xDisplacement)

    let yPosition = cvCenter.y - CGFloat(yDisplacement)

    let center: CGPoint = CGPointMake(xPosition, yPosition)

    attributes.center = center

    return attributes

}
```

The attributes that you need to calculate for each hour label are the size and center.

Size isn't a problem; this is passed into the layout's hourLabelCellSize parameter, so you can use that:

```
attributes.size = hourLabelCellSizeSize
```

Calculating the center of the label is a bit more involved, and is going to require some trigonometry. Fear not if that's a distant high school memory; I'll explain it as we go.

The first thing you need to do is calculate how far around the clock face the label needs to be placed, assuming that it's a traditional clock with 12 at the top.

If there are 12 numerals, then the angle between each one is (360° ÷ 12) = 30°. iOS measures angles in radians rather than degrees, so the calculation is actually

`let angularDisplacement: Double = (2 * M_PI) / 12`

The labels for the numerals are stored in the data model: row 0 holds "12", row 1 holds "1", row 2 holds "2" and so on. By multiplying the angularDisplacement by the label's index, you can calculate how far around the clock face the label needs to be placed:

`let theta = angularDisplacement * Double(hourPath.row)`

Figure 16-9 shows how this calculation would work for 2 o'clock:

```
angularDisplacement = 360 ÷ 12 = 30
theta = 30 * 2 = 60°
```

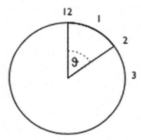

Figure 16-9. Calculating theta

Once you know the value of theta for a given label, you can then calculate the position of its center, as shown in Figure 16-10.

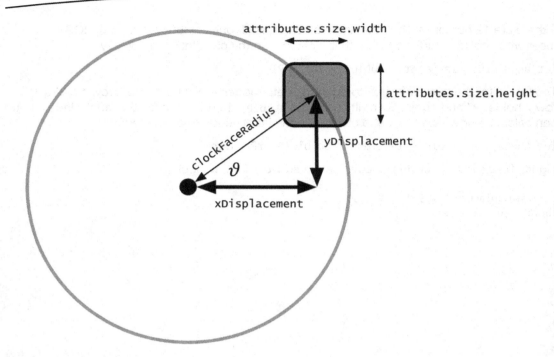

Figure 16-10. *Calculating the label's center*

This involves the high school trigonometry I mentioned earlier:

```
let xDisplacement = sin(theta) * Double(clockFaceRadius - (attributes.size.width / 2))
let yDisplacement = cos(theta) * Double(clockFaceRadius - (attributes.size.height / 2))
```

clockFaceRadius is a property on the layout that is passed in when the layout is instantiated, which is derived from the size of the collection view. Let's assume that the collection view is 500 points wide, so that means you're dealing with a radius of 250 points.

To calculate the x displacement from the center, you use `sin(theta) * clockFaceRadius` and then adjust that to account for the width of the hour label (remember that you're calculating the center point of the label).

Calculating the y displacement is exactly the same, but uses `cos(theta)`, and adjusts for the height of the label.

Once you've made those calculations, you can set the x and y position of the label through its center attribute:

```
let xPosition = cvCenter.x + CGFloat(xDisplacement)

let yPosition = cvCenter.y - CGFloat(yDisplacement)

let center: CGPoint = CGPointMake(xPosition, yPosition)

attributes.center = center
```

Note that the xDisplacement is positive as it moves to the right, and the yDisplacement is negative as it moves towards the top. This holds for all positions because the results of sin(theta) and cos(theta) will change from positive to negative as the calculations move round the circle.

Finally, having calculated all the attributes you need, they can be returned to the calling function:

```
return attributes;
```

Calculating the Position of the Hands

The final task in creating the custom layout is to calculate the position of the hands. These are cells that have been set up in the ClockViewController, but there are some layout-related things you need to set up, such as rotating the hands around the center of the collection view to indicate the time.

The function that handles this is calculateAttributesForHandCellAtIndexPath: It's not dissimilar to the previous function you just built: it takes an indexPath parameter, and returns a UILayoutViewAttributes object.

The full function is show in Listing 16-10.

Listing 16-10. The calculateAttributesForHandCell Function

```
func calculateAttributesForHandCellAt(handPath: NSIndexPath) -> ↵
UICollectionViewLayoutAttributes {

    let attributes = UICollectionViewLayoutAttributes(forCellWithIndexPath: handPath)

    let rotationPerHour: Double = (2 * M_PI) / 12

    let rotationPerMinute: Double = (2 * M_PI) / 60.0

    switch handPath.row {

    case 0: // handle hour hands

        attributes.size = hourHandSize
        attributes.center = cvCenter

        let intraHourRotationPerMinute: Double = rotationPerHour / 60

        let currentIntraHourRotation: Double = intraHourRotationPerMinute * ↵
        Double(timeMinutes)

        let angularDisplacement = (rotationPerHour * Double(timeHours)) + ↵
        currentIntraHourRotation

        attributes.transform = ↵
        CGAffineTransformMakeRotation(CGFloat(angularDisplacement))
```

```
    case 1: // handle minute hands

        attributes.size = minuteHandSize
        attributes.center = cvCenter

        let intraMinuteRotationPerSecond: Double = rotationPerMinute / 60

        let currentIntraMinuteRotation: Double = intraMinuteRotationPerSecond * ↵
        Double(timeSeconds)

        let angularDisplacement = (rotationPerMinute * Double(timeMinutes)) + ↵
        currentIntraMinuteRotation

        attributes.transform = ↵
        CGAffineTransformMakeRotation(CGFloat(angularDisplacement))

    case 2: // handle second hands

        attributes.size = secondHandSize
        attributes.center = cvCenter

        let angularDisplacement = rotationPerMinute * Double(timeSeconds)

        attributes.transform = ↵
        CGAffineTransformMakeRotation(CGFloat(angularDisplacement))

    default:
        break

    }

    return attributes

}
```

The first step is to create an instance of UICollectionViewLayoutAttributes:

```
let attributes = UICollectionViewLayoutAttributes(forCellWithIndexPath: handPath)
```

Next, you calculate the rotation per hour (360° ÷ 12 for hours, 360° ÷ 60 for minutes):

```
let rotationPerHour: Double = (2 * M_PI) / 12
let rotationPerMinute: Double = (2 * M_PI) / 60.0
```

Then there are three cases you need to handle here, for hours, minutes, and seconds. They are in rows 0, 1, and 2, respectively, of the handPath, so you can use a switch statement to handle each one:

```
switch handPath.row {
    ...
}
```

Each case is very similar. First, set the size and center attributes:

```
attributes.size = hourHandSize;
attributes.center = cvCenter;
```

The size of the hands is passed into the layout as a property, so that it's independent of the image being used. You can change this at will without needing to update the layout class.

Then you calculate the rotation required for the current hour:

```
let intraHourRotationPerMinute: Double = rotationPerHour / 60
```

Because the hour hand starts at the one hour label, and gradually moves to the next one during the course of the hour, you need to calculate how much adjustment is needed based on the current minute:

```
let currentIntraHourRotation: Double = intraHourRotationPerMinute * ↩
    Double(timeMinutes)
```

With both of these values, you can calculate the actual movement:

```
let angularDisplacement = (rotationPerHour * Double(timeHours)) + ↩
    currentIntraHourRotation
```

Finally, the hands view can be rotated by setting its transform property:

```
attributes.transform = CGAffineTransformMakeRotation(CGFloat(angularDisplacement))
```

Next Steps

That completes all the steps for creating the custom layout. Now all that's left is to build the views for the clock's hands, and wire the collection view up to use the custom class.

First, declare the clockLayout property:

```
var clockLayout: ClockLayout!
```

Before you start with the hands and numerals, update the ClockViewController's configureCollectionView() function to instantiate and set the ClockLayout:

```
clockLayout = ClockLayout()
collectionView.setCollectionViewLayout(clockLayout, animated: false)
```

Displaying the Numerals and Hands

The clock's numerals and hands are displayed in instances of UICollectionViewCells. You create a custom UICollectionViewCell subclass for the hands, and use a XIB file for the numerals.

Creating a XIB File for the Hour Labels

To create a XIB file for the hour labels, select File ➤ New ➤ File, and select the User Interface section in the sidebar. Then highlight the Empty item in the main section, as shown in Figure 16-11.

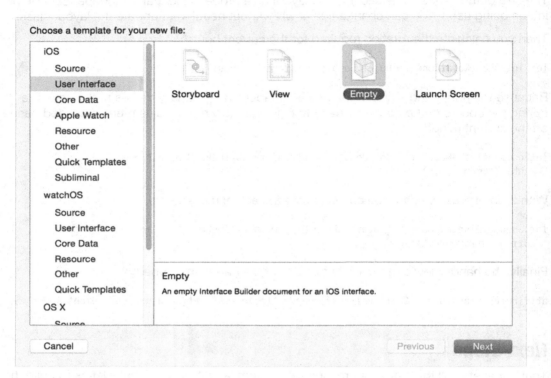

Figure 16-11. Creating a XIB file

Name the file HandCell and click Create.

Now open the new XIB file in the Interface Builder, and drag out a Collection View Cell object out into the main pane, as shown in Figure 16-12.

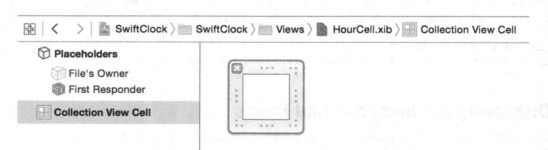

Figure 16-12. Adding a Collection View Cell object

Adjust the size so that the cell is 100 points wide by 100 points tall, and set its reuse identifier to HourCellView.

Now drag a Label out into the cell, center it with AutoLayout constraints, and update the font according to your preferences. The finished result will look something like Figure 16-13.

Figure 16-13. The updated label

Finally, update the label's tag property in the Attributes Inspector to 1000 so that it can be accessed from within the view controller, as shown in Figure 16-14.

View	
Mode	Left
Semantic	Unspecified
Tag	1000

Figure 16-14. Setting the label's tag property

Now that you have your XIB file created, it's time to switch back to the ClockViewController and register this for use. In the configureCollectionView() function, add the following lines:

```
collectionView.registerNib(UINib(nibName: "HourCell", bundle: nil), ↵
  forCellWithReuseIdentifier: HourCellView)

    clockLayout.hourLabelCellSize = CGSizeMake(100.0, 100.0)
```

Creating a UICollectionView Subclass for the Clock Hands

Instead of creating the hands in nib files, you'll take a different approach and create a custom subclass of UICollectionViewCell. Both techniques are equivalent, but using a custom subclass gives you the opportunity to configure various aspects of the cell in code.

The first step is to create a new UICollectionViewCell subclass as a new file. Select File ➤ New ➤ File. Call the class HandCell, and change the Subclass Of field to choose UICollectionViewCell. Selecting OK will create a new class files.

Now you need to register the class with the collection view as you did with the nib file. This needs to be done three times, one each for the three types of hands, First, add the reuse identifier declarations at the top of the class:

```
let HourCellView = "HourCellView"
let HourHandCell = "HourHandCell"
let MinsHandCell = "MinsHandCell"
let SecsHandCell = "SecsHandCell"
```

Next add the following code to the configureCollectionView function:

```
collectionView.registerClass(HandCell.self, forCellWithReuseIdentifier: HourHandCell)
collectionView.registerClass(HandCell.self, forCellWithReuseIdentifier: MinsHandCell)
collectionView.registerClass(HandCell.self, forCellWithReuseIdentifier: SecsHandCell)
```

You also need to set the sizes of the hand cells:

```
clockLayout.hourHandSize = CGSizeMake(10.0, 140.0)
clockLayout.minuteHandSize = CGSizeMake(10.0, 200.0)
clockLayout.secondHandSize = CGSizeMake(6.0, 200.0)
```

The rest of the process will be dealt with as you update the collection view's view controller in the next step.

Using the Custom Layout

With the layout in place, you now need to update the cellForItemAtIndexPath: function in the collection view's datasource object, as shown in Listing 16-11.

Listing 16-11. The updates collectionView:cellForItemAtIndexPath: Function

```
func collectionView(collectionView: UICollectionView, cellForItemAtIndexPath ↩
  indexPath: NSIndexPath) -> UICollectionViewCell {

    var cell: UICollectionViewCell!

    // Handle time labels
    switch (indexPath.section) {

    case 0:
```

```
// Handle hands

switch (indexPath.row) {

case 0:

    // Handle hour hands
    cell = collectionView.dequeueReusableCellWithReuseIdentifier↵
    (HourHandCell,  forIndexPath: indexPath) as! HandCell
    let hourHandView = UIView(frame: CGRectMake(0, 0, ↵
    clockLayout.hourHandSize.width, clockLayout.hourHandSize.height))
    hourHandView.backgroundColor = UIColor.blackColor()
    cell.contentView.addSubview(hourHandView)
    cell.layer.anchorPoint = CGPointMake(0.5, 0.9)

case 1:

    // handle minute hands
    cell = collectionView.dequeueReusableCellWithReuseIdentifier↵
    (MinsHandCell, forIndexPath: indexPath) as! HandCell
    let minuteHandView = UIView(frame: CGRectMake(0, 0, ↵
    clockLayout.minuteHandSize.width, clockLayout.minuteHandSize.height))
    minuteHandView.backgroundColor = UIColor.blackColor()
    cell.contentView.addSubview(minuteHandView)
    cell.layer.anchorPoint = CGPointMake(0.5, 0.9)

default:

    // handle second hands
    cell = collectionView.dequeueReusableCellWithReuseIdentifier↵
    (SecsHandCell, forIndexPath: indexPath)
    let secondHandView = UIView(frame: CGRectMake(0, 0, ↵
    clockLayout.secondHandSize.width, clockLayout.secondHandSize.height))
    secondHandView.backgroundColor = UIColor.redColor()
    cell.contentView.addSubview(secondHandView)
    cell.layer.anchorPoint = CGPointMake(0.5, 0.9)

}

default:

// Handle hours labels
cell = collectionView.dequeueReusableCellWithReuseIdentifier↵
(HourCellView, forIndexPath: indexPath) as UICollectionViewCell

let hourLabelsArray = dataArray[1]
let hoursText = hourLabelsArray[indexPath.row]

if let cellLabel: UILabel = cell.viewWithTag(1000) as? UILabel {
    cellLabel.text = hoursText
}
```

```
    }

    return cell

}
```

There are two parts to this: handling the hour labels, and dealing with the hands.

The first thing you do here is create an optional to hold the cell that will be returned:

```
var cell: UICollectionViewCell!
```

Now if you think back to how the data model is configured, elements in the first section of the array contain placeholders for the hands, and the second section holds the numeral values.

By checking the `indexPath` parameter that's passed into the function, you can take the appropriate action with a `switch` statement:

```
switch (indexPath.section) {
    case 0: // handle hands
    ...

    default: // handle hour labels
    ...
}
```

An `indexPath` section of 1 means you need to dequeue and configure an hour cell:

```
default: // Handle hours labels

    cell = collectionView.dequeueReusableCellWithReuseIdentifier↩
    (HourCellView, forIndexPath: indexPath) as UICollectionViewCell

    let hourLabelsArray = dataArray[1]
    let hoursText = hourLabelsArray[indexPath.row]

    if let cellLabel: UILabel = cell.viewWithTag(1000) as? UILabel {
        cellLabel.text = hoursText
    }
```

Once the cell's dequeued, you can access the label through its tag property and set the text so that it shows the hour numeral.

An `indexPath` section of 0 means you're dealing with hand cells. Again, the process is similar:

```
case 0: // Handle hands

    switch (indexPath.row) {

    case 0: // Handle hour hands
```

```
    cell = collectionView.dequeueReusableCellWithReuseIdentifier↵
    (HourHandCell, forIndexPath: indexPath) as! HandCell
    let hourHandView = UIView(frame: CGRectMake(0, 0, ↵
    clockLayout.hourHandSize.width, clockLayout.hourHandSize.height))
    hourHandView.backgroundColor = UIColor.blackColor()
    cell.contentView.addSubview(hourHandView)
    cell.layer.anchorPoint = CGPointMake(0.5, 0.9)

case 1: // handle minute hands

    cell = collectionView.dequeueReusableCellWithReuseIdentifier↵
    (MinsHandCell, forIndexPath: indexPath) as! HandCell
    let minuteHandView = UIView(frame: CGRectMake(0, 0, ↵
    clockLayout.minuteHandSize.width, clockLayout.minuteHandSize.height))
    minuteHandView.backgroundColor = UIColor.blackColor()
    cell.contentView.addSubview(minuteHandView)
    cell.layer.anchorPoint = CGPointMake(0.5, 0.9)

default: // handle second hands

    cell = collectionView.dequeueReusableCellWithReuseIdentifier↵
    (SecsHandCell, forIndexPath: indexPath)
    let secondHandView = UIView(frame: CGRectMake(0, 0, ↵
    clockLayout.secondHandSize.width, clockLayout.secondHandSize.height))
    secondHandView.backgroundColor = UIColor.redColor()
    cell.contentView.addSubview(secondHandView)
    cell.layer.anchorPoint = CGPointMake(0.5, 0.9)

}
```

There are three possible scenarios here. You're dealing with an hour, a minute, or a second hand, corresponding to rows 0, 1, or 2 in the index path.

Each process is virtually the same:

- First, you dequeue a cell with the appropriate reuseIdentifier.
- Next, you create a UIView for the hand, set the size, and color the background black.
- Then you add the UIView into the cell.
- Finally, you adjust the cell's anchorPoint property.

The last line of each section moves the anchor point for the rotation that the layout applies. By default, a CALayer's rotation point is at its center (or (0.5, 0.5) in coordinate terms), shown in Figure 16-15.

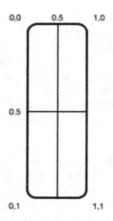

Figure 16-15. The default rotation point

What you actually want to do is rotate around the bottom of the hand image, as shown in Figure 16-16.

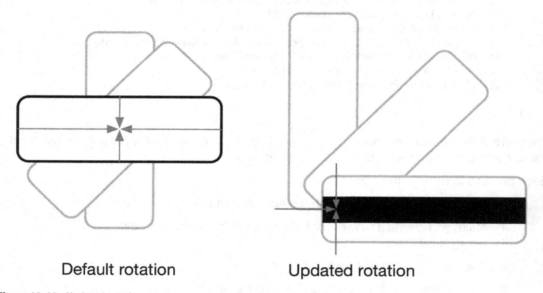

Default rotation   Updated rotation

Figure 16-16. Updated rotation

Since the rotation point is slightly "inside" the image, the offset is adjusted accordingly to give the impression that the hands are rotating around fixed points.

With the cells configured, finally the function returns it to the collection view:

```
return cell
```

Getting the Clock to "Tick"

That's all you need to do to display the hands and the hours, but the clock isn't yet ready to run. The last task is to get it to "tick."

This involves invalidating the collection view's layout to force it to recalculate the attributes for each element. Because you set the time in the layout, every time the layout is invalidated, it will calculate attributes for a new time; invalidate the layout once a second, and the clock will appear to tick.

You can do this by adding an updateClock() function to the view controller, as shown in Listing 16-12.

Listing 16-12. The updateClock() Function

```
func updateClock() {

    collectionView.collectionViewLayout.invalidateLayout()

}
```

With this function in place, you can now set up a timer to call it once per second. First, add a property to the view controller:

```
var tickTimer: NSTimer!
```

Then update the viewDidLoad() function so that it looks like Listing 16-13.

Listing 16-13. The updated viewDidLoad() Function

```
override func viewDidLoad() {

    super.viewDidLoad()

    setupData()

    configureCollectionView()

    tickTimer = NSTimer.scheduledTimerWithTimeInterval(1.0, target: self,  ↵
    selector: "updateClock", userInfo: nil, repeats: true)

    NSRunLoop.currentRunLoop().addTimer(tickTimer, forMode: NSRunLoopCommonModes)

}
```

This creates an instance of NSTimer that fires once per second and calls the updateClock() function. The timer is then added to the main run loop to create the illusion that time is passing.

Finally, it's a good idea to clean up the NSTimer once the view is dismissed, so add the viewWillDisappear() function to the view controller, as shown in Listing 16-14.

Listing 16-14. The viewWillDisappear() Function

```
override func viewWillDisappear(animated: Bool) {
    super.viewWillDisappear(animated)

    tickTimer.invalidate()

}
```

If you run the project now you'll see a ticking clock like Figure 16-17, built entirely from a
UICollectionView with a custom layout.

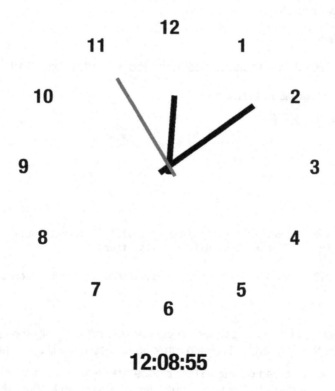

Figure 16-17. The finished UICollectionView clock

Summary

In this chapter, you looked at the process of going beyond the constraints of flow layout to something that's completely customized. You learned how to create custom `UICollectionViewFlowLayout` classes and calculate the layout attributes needed to place views according to your design.

Using combinations of all of these techniques, you can now create custom layouts. In the next chapter, you're going to take things a few stages further.

Chapter 17

Animated and Interactive Collection Views

Combine the flexibility of the collection view with the tactile user interface of iOS devices, and you've got a world of interface possibilities to explore. One of the most satisfying approaches from a user interaction perspective is combining collection views with gesture recognizers to build truly interactive interfaces.

So far, you've mainly looked at collection views with fairly static layouts, albeit with some scrolling. But UICollectionView is capable of doing much more. It has sophisticated support for reacting to user interaction through gesture; and by using custom layouts, you can bring your collection views to life with animations.

In this chapter, you'll look first at controlling collection views with gestures. By implementing gesture recognizers that update layout attributes, you can make your collection views react to user interaction in naturalistic ways.

You'll also look at enhancing the user experience by animating collection view transitions such as insertion and deletion. In conjunction with the powerful iOS animation APIs, you can create fluid and engaging interfaces with ease.

Controlling Collection Views with Gestures

iOS devices are inherently interactive and tactile. The touch screens allow apps to create interfaces that offer interaction possibilities much more flexible than anything that's achievable with a keyboard and mouse.

The family of UIGestureRecognizer classes provide easy but powerful ways to allow your users to control apps with interactive gestures such as taps, pans, swipes, and pinches. You can very easily combine UICollectionViewLayouts with gesture recognizers to build immersive interfaces.

In Chapter 12, you saw how to build collection views that allowed interactive ordering and rearrangements. In this chapter, we'll look at using gestures to directly control layout attributes.

Connecting Gestures with Layouts

You can very easily connect gesture recognizers to collection views. By receiving the gesture events and using the values obtained to update layout attributes, you can make your layouts interactive.

You'll build two separate effects that use a pinch gesture to control a flow layout. In the first, you'll update the item spacing; in the second, you'll control item sizing.

The basic approach is very simple:

- Create a `UIGestureRecognizer` to handle the type of interaction you need, in this case a `UIPinchGestureRecognizer`.

- Install this gesture recognizer on the collection view controller.

- Implement the callback functions to receive the data relating to the gestures.

- Use these values to update the attributes of the collection view's layout.

To speed things up, you can use the base project from the Chapter 17 source code in the book's GitHub repo. This creates a `UITabBarController`-based project with two tabs, each containing a collection view. Both display 20 items with a standard `UICollectionViewFlowLayout`, as shown in Figure 17-1.

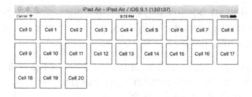

Figure 17-1. The base project with a flow layout

Adding the Gesture Recognizer

The gesture recognizer needs to be added to the collection view controller so that it can intercept the gesture and then pass the data onto the collection view's view controller class.

Add the following lines to the setupCollectionView function in the SpaceViewController class:

```
let pinchRecognizer = UIPinchGestureRecognizer(target: self, action: ↩
  "didGetPinchGesture:")
collectionView.addGestureRecognizer(pinchRecognizer)
```

This creates an instance of a UIPinchGestureRecognizer and sets the target property to the didGetPinchGesture: function. Then it adds the newly-created gesture recognizer to the collection view.

Handling Gestures

You don't yet have the function to handle the gestures when the gesture recognizer intercepts them, so add the function in Listing 17-1 to the SpaceViewController.

Listing 17-1. The didGetPinchGesture: Function

```
func didGetPinchGesture(sender: UIPinchGestureRecognizer) {

    guard sender.numberOfTouches() == 2 else {
        return
    }

    let pointOne = sender.locationOfTouch(0, inView: collectionView)
    let pointTwo = sender.locationOfTouch(1, inView: collectionView)

    let dX = pointOne.x - pointTwo.x
    let dY = pointTwo.y - pointTwo.y

    let distance = sqrt(dX * dX + dY * dY)

    let layout = collectionView.collectionViewLayout as! UICollectionViewFlowLayout
    layout.minimumLineSpacing = distance / 5
    layout.minimumInteritemSpacing = distance / 5

    layout.invalidateLayout()

}
```

The first thing you need to do is make sure that you're reacting to the right gesture. UIGestureRecognizers has a numberOfTouches property that contains the number of contact points that the gesture recognizer has detected. For a tap with a single finger, this would be 1. If five fingers were on screen, the numberOfTouches would be 5.

In this case, you're only interested in two-fingered pinch gestures, so you can reject any gesture that doesn't have a `numberOfTouches` property of 2:

```
guard sender.numberOfTouches() == 2 else {
    return
}
```

Assuming that you do only have two touches, you can now start to use them to control the collection view layout.

First, get the coordinates of the two touches relative to the `collectionView`:

```
let pointOne = sender.locationOfTouch(0, inView: collectionView)
let pointTwo = sender.locationOfTouch(1, inView: collectionView)
```

> **Tip**   The touch number refers to the order in which the touch was detected by the gesture recognizer, not which finger is doing the touching!

Each touch point has an x and y coordinate, so you can use this to calculate the difference between the two touches. This needs some trigonometry, as shown in Figure 17-2.

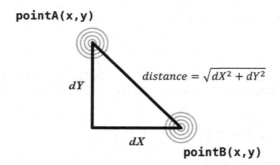

Figure 17-2. *Calculating the distance between the touches*

In code, this is expressed as

```
let distance = sqrt((dX * dX) + (dY * dY))
```

With the calculation out of the way, get a reference to the flow layout:

```
let layout = collectionView.collectionViewLayout as! UICollectionViewFlowLayout
```

And update the spacing-related attributes with the distance value:

```
layout.minimumLineSpacing = distance / 5
layout.minimumInteritemSpacing = distance / 5
```

Since the touch distance is relative to the collection view size, you need to scale it down a bit so that the spacings don't become too big.

Finally, you can force the layout to update itself:

```
layout.invalidateLayout()
```

The effect isn't easy to reproduce on paper, but as the spacing between the touch points increases, the spacing between the cells will increase as shown in Figure 17-3.

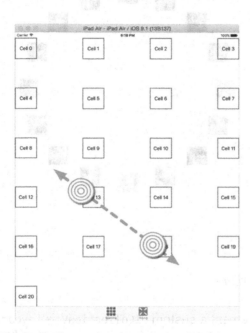

Figure 17-3. Increasing cell spacing

Collection Views and Animations

So far, the collection view layouts that you've built have relied on the in-built classes to handle placement when inserting and deleting items. This saves a lot of time and effort, and it's fine if you're happy with the basic effects. But if you need more control over the way items are added and removed, you can exploit custom `UICollectionViewLayouts` to give you complete control.

To illustrate this, you're going to build a collection view that

- Arranges the items in a completely non-linear way; which means you will be responsible for calculating their placements

- Inserts and removes items with animated transitions that you determine

The end result will look like Figure 17-4. Cells are arranged in an even-spaced circle; they're inserted by flying out from the center to their place in the ring (while the existing cells shuffle up to make space). They'll be removed in the opposite direction: flying into the center, while the remaining cells space themselves out.

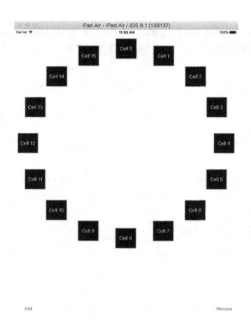

Figure 17-4. *The custom layout in action*

To achieve this, you'll implement a custom `UICollectionViewLayout`. This isn't the first time you've done this, but in this example, you'll take things one step further by calculating both the initial and final layout attributes for an item. The collection view will then handle smoothly animating the change between the initial and final positions.

The Process

In order to have the collection view animate the insertion and deletion of items, you need to provide three sets of attributes for each item:

- The initial layout attributes, which the collection view uses to place the item in the collection view when it first appears. In your example, this will be the center of the circle.

- The layout attributes that determine the "final" home for the item. In this example, each item will be at a point on a circle, with the spacing between each item determined by the number of items in total.

- The final layout attributes, which the collection view uses as the final place for the item before it's removed. In this example, items will appear to fly back to the center of the circle, fading and getting smaller as they go.

The other processes involved in setting up the custom layout are the same as you've seen before, but you'll work through them in detail.

Prerequisites

To begin with, you're going to need a collection view, so to save some setup time, I've created a stub project. It contains a single view controller that acts as the data source and delegate for the collection view. The Storyboard contains a full-screen collection view and two buttons to add and remove items.

The collection view's data source is an Array of Strings, and the cells are very basic 75pt x 75pt UICollectionViewCells that display the String from the relevant row. Finally, there's a basic UICollectionFlowLayout that results in an app that looks like Figure 17-5.

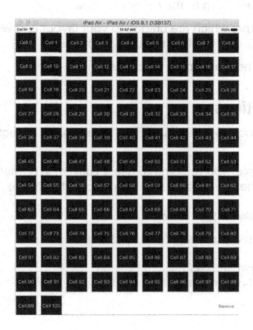

Figure 17-5. The initial app

As you can see, it's going to need a bit of work.

Creating the Custom Layout

The first thing you need is a custom layout. This will be a subclass of UICollectionViewLayout, so create a new one with File ➤ New ➤ File, selecting the Cocoa Touch item from the Source section, and then creating a subclass of UICollectionViewLayout called BounceLayout.

This creates a depressingly empty class, shown in Listing 17-2.

Listing 17-2. The Initial BounceLayout

```
import UIKit

class BounceLayout: UICollectionViewLayout {

}
```

There are three sets of functions you need to implement:

■ Housekeeping functions that that handle preparing the layout

■ Attributes functions, responsible for creating and vending the layout attributes for each item to the collection view

■ Custom functions, which are unique to your layout and will handle the calculations required by the attributes functions

You'll start with the basic housekeeping functions.

Housekeeping Functions

The first housekeeping function that you need is to return the collection view's contentSize to the collection view.

In this case, it's quite simple. You're going to use a contentSize that's the same as the collection view itself, so there will be no scrolling involved. Add the function in Listing 17-3.

Listing 17-3. The collectionViewContentSize Function

```
override func collectionViewContentSize() -> CGSize {

    super.collectionViewContentSize()
    return collectionView!.frame.size

}
```

This is very straightforward. After calling the superclass function, you return the size of the collectionView's frame.

Next, you need prepareLayout(). This is called at the start of each layout pass, and is an opportunity to carry out any "bulk" operations that affect all items. There are several things you need to do:

■ Add some properties to the layout class to hold the calculated attributes, and some values for dimensions.

■ Remove all the existing layout attributes (adding or removing an item will cause all the other items to move, so all existing attributes will become invalid).

- Do some up-front calculations about the overall dimensions of the layout.

- Calculate the attributes for each item in turn..

First, add the properties shown in Listing 17-4.

Listing 17-4. The BounceLayout's Properties

```
var layoutAttributes = [UICollectionViewLayoutAttributes]()
var cvCenterPoint: CGPoint!
var itemSize: CGSize!
var sidePadding: CGFloat!
```

The layout attributes will be stored in an `Array` of `UICollectionViewLayoutAttributes`. There are some dimension-related properties that you'll need: the center point of the collection view, the size of each item, the padding between the edges of the item, and the edge of the collection view.

Next, you need the `prepareLayout()` function. This is called at the start of the layout process, after the layout has been invalidated. It's both an opportunity to configure layout-wide values, and the point where you can trigger the calculation of all the attributes required.

Add the function shown in Listing 17-5.

Listing 17-5. The prepareLayout() Function

```
override func prepareLayout() {

    super.prepareLayout()

    layoutAttributes.removeAll()

    // Figure out where the centre of the collection view is
    cvCenterPoint = CGPointMake(collectionView!.frame.size.width / 2, ↩
    collectionView!.frame.size.height / 2);

    // Figure out the number of items that we're dealing with
    // Here, we assume that there is only one section in the collection view
    let numberOfItems = collectionView!.numberOfItemsInSection(0)

    calculateAllAttributes(numberOfItems)

}
```

Walking through this, you first call the superclass function. Then you remove all the existing layout attributes; inserting or removing an item will cause all the other items to move, so all attributes become invalid.

The center point of the circle will be important, as it's both the origin of the calculation for the position attributes for each item, and also the starting point of the insertion calculation.

```
cvCenterPoint = calculateCenterForFirstItem()
```

This will be needed in several places later, so to reduce code duplication, add the function in Listing 17-6.

Listing 17-6. Calculating the Center Point of the Collection View

```
func calculateCenterForFirstItem() -> CGPoint {
    return CGPointMake(collectionView!.frame.size.width / 2, ↩
  collectionView!.frame.size.height / 2);
}
```

You also need the number of items that you're dealing with to calculate the spacing.

```
let numberOfItems = collectionView!.numberOfItemsInSection(0)
```

Finally, you call the as-yet unimplemented calculateAllAttributes(:_) function for the given number of items.

Calculating Attributes

This is where the real work starts. Add the function shown in Listing 17-7.

Listing 17-7. The calculateAllAttributes Function

```
func calculateAllAttributes(numberOfItems: Int) {

    // Create the attributes for each item in turn
    for index in 0..<numberOfItems {

        // Construct the index path for the item we're dealing with
        let itemIndexPath = NSIndexPath(forItem: index, inSection: 0)

        // Create a UICollectionViewLayoutAttributes item for this indexPath
        let attributes = UICollectionViewLayoutAttributes(forCellWithIndexPath: ↩
      itemIndexPath)

        // Calculate where the centre of the item should be
        let center = calculateCenterForItemAtIndexPath(itemIndexPath)
        attributes.center = center

        // Set the item's size
        attributes.size = itemSize

        // Set the Z-index so they "stack" on top of each other
        attributes.zIndex = index + 1

        // Add our new set of attributes into the array
        layoutAttributes.append(attributes)

    }

}
```

This takes one Int parameter, the number of items in the collection view. It then repeats, in order to calculate the attributes for each item.

First, you create an NSIndexPath for the item:

```
let itemIndexPath = NSIndexPath(forItem: index, inSection: 0)
```

Next, you use this indexPath to create an instance of UICollectionViewLayoutAttributes:

```
 let attributes = UICollectionViewLayoutAttributes(forCellWithIndexPath: itemIndexPath)
```

For this item, you now calculate where the center point should be, with the aid of a helper function that you'll implement in a moment:

```
let center = calculateCenterForItemAtIndexPath(itemIndexPath)
attributes.center = center
```

You set the item size. This is the same for all items.

```
attributes.size = itemSize
```

The Z-index of each item increases so that when they overlap, they'll appear to stack:

```
attributes.zIndex = index + 1
```

With all the necessary attributes calculated, you can add them to the array:

```
layoutAttributes.append(attributes)
```

Now let's add the function to calculate the center point of the item.

Calculating the Center Point

Calculating the center point of the item is the function that involves the most math, but it's not as intimidating as it looks. Add the function shown in Listing 17-8.

Listing 17-8. Calculating the Center for an Item

```
func calculateCenterForItemAtIndexPath(indexPath: NSIndexPath) -> CGPoint {

    // If there's only one item, then it should be centered
    if (collectionView!.numberOfItemsInSection(0) == 1) {
        return calculateCenterForFirstItem()
    }

    // Get angular displacement for this item
    let angularDisplacement: CGFloat = calculateRotationPerItem()

    // Calculate rotation required for this item
    let theta = (angularDisplacement * CGFloat(indexPath.row))
```

```
// Trig to calculate the x and y shifts required to
// get the moved around a circle of diameter spoke radius
let xDisplacement = CGFloat(sinf(Float(theta))) * calculateSpokeRadius()
let yDisplacement = CGFloat(cosf(Float(theta))) * calculateSpokeRadius()

// Make the centre point of the hour label block
let xPosition = (collectionView!.bounds.size.width/2) + xDisplacement
let yPosition = (collectionView!.bounds.size.width/2) - yDisplacement

return CGPointMake(xPosition, yPosition)

}
```

First, you need to deal with a special case of only one item in the collection view. In this situation, you want the item to be placed in the center of the collection view:

```
if (collectionView!.numberOfItemsInSection(0) == 1) {
    return CGPointMake(collectionView!.bounds.size.width / 2, ↵
    collectionView!.bounds.size.height/2)
}
```

Now you can calculate the rotation around the center of the collection view for this item. Figure 17-6 shows how the rotation is calculated.

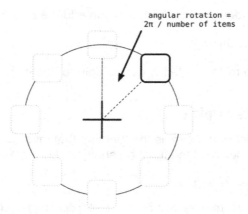

Figure 17-6. Calculating angular rotation

This is implemented as a separate function, shown in Listing 17-9.

Listing 17-9. Calculating the Rotation Per Item

```
func calculateRotationPerItem() -> CGFloat {

    // Shouldn't rotate if there's only one item

    if (collectionView!.numberOfItemsInSection(0) == 1) {
        return 0.0;
    }

    // Otherwise, the rotation is given by 360 / number of items
    // (or 2Pi / number of items as we're dealing with radians here)

    return ( CGFloat(2 * M_PI) / CGFloat(collectionView!.numberOfItemsInSection(0)))

}
```

Again, the situation with only one item in the collection view is a special case; there's no rotation involved.

Assuming there's more than one item, then the rotation per item is 2π divided by the number of items (2π is the number of radians in a full circle; iOS uses radians for trigonometric calculations).

Looking back to the calculateCenterForItemAtIndexPath: function, you'll see that there's another helper function you need to implement. It is to calculate the radius of the circle: the smaller of the height or the width of the collection view.

Add the function in Listing 17-10.

Listing 17-10. Calculating the Circle Radius

```
func calculateSpokeRadius() -> CGFloat {

    // Calculates the radius of the 'spoke' connecting the item's center and the
    // center of the collectionView

    // Find out which is the shorter side, in case
    // the collectionView's not square
    let shorterSide = min(collectionView!.bounds.size.width, 
    collectionView!.bounds.size.height)

    let collectionViewAllowance = shorterSide / 2
    let itemWidthAllowance = itemSize.width / 2

    // Adjust for side padding (if any)
    return (collectionViewAllowance - (itemWidthAllowance + sidePadding))

}
```

Here, you get the length of the shorter side of the collection view, and then you adjust for the width of the item and any padding between the item and the collection view frame.

The value returned by the `calculateSpokeRadius` function is used by `calculateCenterForItemAtIndexPath:` to calculate the horizontal and vertical distance between the center of the collection view and the center of the item:

```
let xDisplacement = CGFloat(sinf(Float(theta))) * calculateSpokeRadius()
let yDisplacement = CGFloat(cosf(Float(theta))) * calculateSpokeRadius()
```

This requires a bit of high school math, and uses the `sinf` and `cosf` trigonometry functions. The angles involved form a right-angled triangle. This is the same technique you used in Chapter 16, so check back there if you need a refresher.

With the distances calculated, you're now in a position to calculate the center coordinates for the item:

```
let xPosition = (collectionView!.bounds.size.width/2) + xDisplacement
let yPosition = (collectionView!.bounds.size.width/2) - yDisplacement
```

Now return the entire set of attributes back to the calling function:

```
return CGPointMake(xPosition, yPosition)
```

With all this in place, you can calculate the attributes for any item within the collection view. Now you need to implement the functions to return them to the collection view when they're required.

Supplying Attributes to the Collection View

The process of supplying attributes for items to the collection view can take place in one of four phases:

- En masse, where the collection view will ask for **all** attributes for items in a given CGRect. Since your collection view will always be completely visible, you're effectively being asked for attributes for all the items.

- Individually, where the collection view supplies an NSIndexPath and expects the attributes for the relevant item.

- During insertion of items, when the collection view will ask for **initial** attributes for items that are appearing. The collection view will handle interpolating between the initial attributes and those that the item will use for the duration of its stay in the collection view.

- During removal of items, when the collection view will ask for final attributes for items that are being removed. As with initial attributes, the collection view will handle interpolating from the current state of the item to its final values.

Let's tackle these one by one.

Supplying Attributes En Masse

The layout needs to implement the `layoutAttributesForElementInRect:` function, which is passed a `CGRect` parameter and is responsible for figuring out which elements fit within the rect and returning their attributes. These get returned as an `Array` of `UICollectionViewLayoutAttributes`.

There are a couple of things to note about this function. Firstly, it's your responsibility to determine which elements appear in the supplied `CGRect`. The collection view doesn't know about this, and in any case it may ask the layout for this information repeatedly as it scrolls.

Secondly, *elements* refers to cells, supplementary views, *and* decoration views. If your collection view uses these items, you need to figure out which are visible in the `CGRect` and return their attributes.

In this case, things are a little simpler. You only have cells, and the collection view won't scroll. Therefore you can simply return all the attributes you have, as shown in Listing 17-11.

Listing 17-11. The layoutAttributesForElementsInRect: Function

```
override func layoutAttributesForElementsInRect(rect: CGRect) ↵
  -> [UICollectionViewLayoutAttributes]? {

    // As all elements will be shown, return all of them
    return layoutAttributes

}
```

Supplying Individual Item Attributes

The contrasting function to `layoutAttributesForElementsInRect` is `layoutAttributesForItemAtIndexPath`. It receives an `NSIndexPath` as a parameter. The calling code will expect an optional `UICollectionViewLayoutAttributes` instance.

There are two ways to implement this function: either by calculating the attributes on the fly when they're requested, or calculating them upfront while preparing the layout, storing them, and returning the pre-calculated values in response to `layoutAttributesForItemAtIndexPath`.

Which approach is the right one will depend on the situation. If your layout is very dynamic and the calculation isn't too expensive, there may be no reason to prematurely optimize. The flip side to this if the calculations require heavyweight calculations, or are simply not going to change very often.

Bear in mind that this function is called by the `collectionView` while it's drawing the items, so a slow response could result in choppy scrolling. If you are having problems with scrolling performance, you might want to take a closer look at this function.

You're using the prepare-everything-upfront approach, so your function is simple and is shown in Listing 17-12.

Listing 17-12. The layoutAttributesForItemAtIndexPath

```
override func layoutAttributesForItemAtIndexPath(indexPath: NSIndexPath) -> ↵
  UICollectionViewLayoutAttributes? {
    // Return the layout attributes for the specific item
    return layoutAttributes[indexPath.row]
}
```

Supplying Initial Layout Attributes

Up to now, you've been implementing required functions to return UILayoutAttributes to the collection view. If you don't supply initial attributes, then the collection view will use what it's given from the previous two functions to place the item. If the item is newly added, it will appear in the correct place immediately.

If you want the initial attributes to differ–in your case, to have items appear at the center of the collection view and be animated into position–then you need to supply a set of initial attributes by implementing the initialLayoutAttributesForAppearingItemAtIndexPath function.

If you don't implement this function, the collection view won't get any initial attributes and will go on to ask for attributes by calling the layoutAttributesForItemAtIndexPath function.

Any UICollectionViewLayoutAttribute, built-in or custom, can be included in the initial set. In your case, you're going to supply the center and alpha attributes, so that the item appears in the center and appears to fade in as it animates out towards the circle.

Before the collection view asks for initial attributes, it will call the prepareForCollectionViewUpdates function, supplying an Array of UICollectionViewLayoutUpdateItems. Any item that will be affected by the update will have a corresponding UICollectionViewLayoutUpdateItems, which has three properties:

- indexPathBeforeUpdate: This is an NSIndexPath that contains the index path of the item at the **start** of the update.

  In the case of an item being inserted, this will be empty. If the item is being removed, it will contain the current index path.

- indexPathAfterUpdate: This is an NSIndexPath that contains the index path of the item at the **end** of the update.

  In the case of an item being removed, this will be empty. If the item is being added, it will contain the target index path where the item will end up.

- updateAction: This contains a UICollectionUpdateAction constant indicating the action that's being performed on the item: Insert, Delete, Reload, Move, or None.

You need to check what's going on with the item being inserted or removed, so add a property to store the details:

```
var indexPathsBeingUpdated = [UICollectionViewUpdateItem]()
```

Now add the function shown in Listing 17-13.

Listing 17-13. The prepareForCollectionViewUpdates Function

```
override func prepareForCollectionViewUpdates(updateItems: ↵
[UICollectionViewUpdateItem]) {
    indexPathsBeingUpdated = updateItems
}
```

This simply copies the array and stores it in the indexPathsBeingUpdated property.

Now you're ready to implement the initialLayoutAttributesForAppearingItemAtIndexPath, as shown in Listing 17-14.

Listing 17-14. The initialLayoutAttributesForAppearingItemAtIndexPath Function

```
override func initialLayoutAttributesForAppearingItemAtIndexPath(itemIndexPath: ↵
  NSIndexPath) -> UICollectionViewLayoutAttributes? {

    // Check to see if this indexPath is in the BeingUpdated list
    // if it isn't, we can just bail out
    let indexFound = indexPathsBeingUpdated.indexOf { (element) -> Bool in
        element.indexPathAfterUpdate == itemIndexPath
    }

    if indexFound == nil {
        return layoutAttributes[itemIndexPath.row]
    }

    let attributes = UICollectionViewLayoutAttributes(forCellWithIndexPath: ↵
    itemIndexPath)

    // Test to see if we're dealing with a situation where we're removing
    // the second item - there will now only be 1 item, and the indexPath.row that we're
    // dealing with will be 0.
    //
    // In this situation the first item needs to start where it originated, at the top
    if (collectionView!.numberOfItemsInSection(0) == 1) && (itemIndexPath.row == 0) {
        attributes.center = calculateCenterForFirstItem()
        attributes.size = itemSize
        return attributes
    }

    // This is a brand new item, so we need to set its alpha, size, z-index and center
    attributes.center = CGPointMake(collectionView!.bounds.size.width / 2, ↵
    collectionView!.bounds.size.height / 2)
    attributes.alpha = 0.0
    attributes.size = itemSize
    attributes.zIndex = 0

    return attributes;

}
```

You begin by checking if the indexPath you've been passed is included in the indexPathsBeingUpdated array:

```
let indexFound = indexPathsBeingUpdated.indexOf { (element) -> Bool in
    element.indexPathAfterUpdate == itemIndexPath
}
```

If it isn't, then it's an item that's already present in the collection view. The initial attributes for this will be the same as the calculated attributes, so you can return them:

```
if indexFound == nil {
    return layoutAttributes[itemIndexPath.row]
}
```

Assuming that the item **is** one you need to handle, you need a UICollectionViewLayoutAttributes instance to configure:

```
let attributes = UICollectionViewLayoutAttributes(forCellWithIndexPath: itemIndexPath)
```

You need to handle the removal of the second item as a special case:

```
if (collectionView!.numberOfItemsInSection(0) == 1) && (itemIndexPath.row == 0) {
    attributes.center = calculateCenterForFirstItem()
    attributes.size = itemSize
    return attributes
}
```

Otherwise you're dealing with a new item, so you need to set the attributes accordingly:

- The center at the middle of the collection view
- An alpha value of 0, so that the item will appear to fade in
- The correct size
- A zIndex of 0, so that the newest item is always on the top of the "pile"

```
attributes.center = CGPointMake(collectionView!.bounds.size.width / 2, ↵
collectionView!.bounds.size.height / 2)
attributes.alpha = 0.0
attributes.size = itemSize
attributes.zIndex = 0
```

Having set the attributes, you can return them:

```
return attributes;
```

Supplying Final Layout Attributes

Final layout attributes allow you to control how items are removed from the collection view. In this situation, you want the item to move to the center of the collection view, fading as it goes.

These attributes are returned to the collection view by the finalLayoutAttributesForDisppearingItemAtIndexPath function. This is very similar to initialLayoutAttributesForAppearingItemAtIndexPath, but it returns the attributes for the end of the removal process.

Add the function shown in Listing 17-15.

Listing 17-15. The finalLayoutAttributesForDisppearingItemAtIndexPath Function

```
override func finalLayoutAttributesForDisappearingItemAtIndexPath(itemIndexPath: ⤦
  NSIndexPath) -> UICollectionViewLayoutAttributes? {

    let attributes = UICollectionViewLayoutAttributes(forCellWithIndexPath: ⤦
    itemIndexPath)

    // Check to see if this indexPath is in the BeingUpdated list
    // if it isn't, we can just bail out
    let indexFound = indexPathsBeingUpdated.indexOf { (element) -> Bool in
        element.indexPathBeforeUpdate == itemIndexPath
    }

    if indexFound == nil {
        return super.finalLayoutAttributesForDisappearingItemAtIndexPath(itemIndexPath)
    }

    // Test to see if we're handling the removal of the first item as it moves to make
    // way for the second one.  In this case, there will be 2 items, and the handling
    // indexPath.row of the item we're dealing with will be 0
    //
    // In this scenario, the item needs to end up back at the top center as the
    // only one

    if ( (collectionView?.numberOfItemsInSection(0) == 2) && ⤦
    (itemIndexPath.row == 0)  ) {
        attributes.center = calculateCenterForFirstItem()
        attributes.size = itemSize
        attributes.zIndex = 0
        return attributes;
    }

    // This is a disappearing item, so we need to set its alpha,
    // size, z-index and center so that it zooms into towards the centre

    attributes.center = calculateCenterForFirstItem()
    attributes.alpha = 0
    attributes.size = itemSize
    attributes.zIndex = 0
    return attributes;
}
```

The difference here is that the center value is the middle of the collection view and the alpha is 0.

That completes the implementation of your custom UICollectionViewLayout. Now it's time to finish wiring up the collection view.

Wiring Up the Collection View

Currently, the collection view is using a standard flow layout to arrange the items, as shown in Figure 17-7.

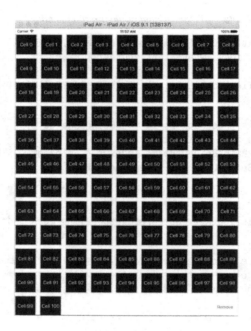

Figure 17-7. The flow layout

You need to update the ViewController to create and apply the custom layout to the collection view.

Update the setupCollectionView() function as shown in Listing 17-16.

Listing 17-16. The setupCollectionView() Function

```
func setupCollectionView() {

    let layout = BounceLayout()
    layout.itemSize = CGSizeMake(75,75)
    layout.sidePadding = 10
    collectionView.setCollectionViewLayout(layout, animated: false)

    collectionView.collectionViewLayout = layout

}
```

This isn't especially complicated. You create an instance of the BounceLayout class and set the item size and padding properties. Then it is assigned to the collection view as the layout.

If you run the project now, you'll see that you've got a circular layout, as shown in Figure 17-8.

Figure 17-8. The newly-applied BounceLayout

Adding New Items

That's good, but not quite what you were after. First, let's reduce the number of items that you start with to 1:

```
func setupData() {
    cvData.append("0")
}
```

Now let's add functions to connect to the buttons. First, add the didTapAdd function, as shown in Listing 17-17.

Listing 17-17. The didTapAdd Function

```
@IBAction func didTapAdd(sender: AnyObject) {

    // Get index of last item
    let index = cvData.count

    cvData.append("\(index)")
```

```
// Create an NSIndexPath object for the new item
let newItemIndexPath = NSIndexPath(forItem: index, inSection: 0)

// Now update the collection view
collectionView.insertItemsAtIndexPaths([newItemIndexPath])
}
```

This isn't too complex. You get the number of items that are currently in the data array:

```
let index = cvData.count
```

And use this to add a new entry:

```
cvData.append("\(index)")
```

Now you need an NSIndexPath object for the new item:

```
let newItemIndexPath = NSIndexPath(forItem: index, inSection: 0)
```

And you can tell the collection view to insert the new item:

```
collectionView.insertItemsAtIndexPaths([newItemIndexPath])
```

Removing Items

The didTapRemoveItem function is shown in Listing 17-17, and it's very similar to the didTapAdd function.

Listing 17-18. The didTapRemoveItemFunction

```
@IBAction func didTapRemoveItem(sender: AnyObject) {

    let itemIndex = cvData.count - 1

    removeItemAtIndexPath(NSIndexPath(forItem: itemIndex, inSection: 0))
}
```

It uses a helper function to remove the item from collection view, shown in Listing 17-19.

Listing 17-19. The removeItemAtIndexPath Function

```
func removeItemAtIndexPath(indexPath: NSIndexPath) {

    // Don't attempt to remove the last item!
    if cvData.count == 0 {
        return
    }
```

```
    // Remove it from the data array
    cvData.removeAtIndex(indexPath.row)

    // Now update the collection view
    collectionView.deleteItemsAtIndexPaths([indexPath])

}
```

Firstly, this prevents you from removing the last item. Assuming there is more than one item left, you remove the corresponding entry from the dataArray, and then pass the indexPath to be removed to the collection view's deleteItemsAtIndexPaths function.

The final touch is to implement the UICollectionViewDelegate's didSelectItemAtIndexPath function so that you can tap items to delete them. Add this in an extension to the viewController, as shown in Listing 17-20.

Listing 17-20. The didSelectItemAtIndexPath Function

```
extension ViewController: UICollectionViewDelegate {

    func collectionView(collectionView: UICollectionView, didSelectItemAtIndexPath ↵
    indexPath: NSIndexPath) {

        switch indexPath.row {

        case 0:
            didTapAdd(indexPath)

        default:
            removeItemAtIndexPath(indexPath)
        }

    }

}
```

Selecting the item will trigger the removeItemAtIndexPath: function, and the item will fly out of the collection view.

Connect the UIButtons in the Storyboard to their respective IBAction functions, run the project again, and you'll be able to tap the Add button to insert new items and tap either the Remove button or on an item to remove it.

Controlling Insertion and Removal Animations

Currently, the insertion and removal animations are controlled by the collection view itself. It uses standard timing and easings. This might be fine for some projects, but it would be nice to add a bit more control over them.

The key to this is to wrap the `insertItemsAtIndexPaths` and `removeItemsAtIndexPaths` function inside a `UIView` animation block.

Listing 17-21 shows an example of the kind of effect that you can achieve.

Listing 17-21. Custom Insertion Animations

```
UIView.animateWithDuration(1.0, ↩
    delay: 0.0, ↩
    usingSpringWithDamping: 0.6, ↩
    initialSpringVelocity: 0.0, ↩
    options: UIViewAnimationOptions.CurveEaseIn, ↩
    animations: { () -> Void in

            // Insert items into collection view
            self.collectionView.insertItemsAtIndexPaths([newItemIndexPath])

}) { (finished) -> Void in

    // block to run when animations complete

}
```

The syntax could perhaps be a little clearer, but what you're doing here is

- Setting an animation duration of 1 second:
  `animateWithDuration(1.0`

- Providing no delay before starting the animation:
  `delay: 0.0`

- Using the spring capabilities of `UIKitDynamics` to add some bounce:
  `usingSpringWithDamping: 0.6,`
  `initialSpringVelocity: 0.0`

- Using a `CurveEaseInOut` easing curve to start the animation slowly, speed it up, and then slow down again before it completes:
  `options: UIViewAnimationOptions.CurveEaseIn`

It's difficult to show the effect of animations on the printed page or static screen, but if you run the project now, you'll see that the items appear with a smooth animation and a very satisfying bounce effect.

Beware—it's possible to spend hours tweaking animations to get that perfect bounce!

Summary

Gestures and animations can be used to bring your collection views to life, both deepening the interactions available and enhancing the user experienced with animations.

By creating gesture recognizers that capture user input, it's possible to interactively update collection views by manipulating layout attributes. This provides the possibility for interfaces that allow users to interact directly with data and controls.

By adding animation effects to insertion and deletions, the user experience delivered by your collection views can be enhanced. This can also be used as a tool to emphasize information and interaction possibilities. The powerful iOS animation APIs allow you to create fluid and engaging interfaces with ease.

Index

■ X, Y, Z

Get the eBook for only $5!

Why limit yourself?

Now you can take the weightless companion with you wherever you go and access your content on your PC, phone, tablet, or reader.

Since you've purchased this print book, we're happy to offer you the eBook in all 3 formats for just $5.

Convenient and fully searchable, the PDF version enables you to easily find and copy code—or perform examples by quickly toggling between instructions and applications. The MOBI format is ideal for your Kindle, while the ePUB can be utilized on a variety of mobile devices.

To learn more, go to www.apress.com/companion or contact support@apress.com.

Printed in the United States
By Bookmasters